Equal Educational Opportunity for Blacks

Equal Educational Opportunity for Blacks in U.S. Higher Education

An Assessment

**Institute for the Study of Educational Policy
Howard University** , *Washington, D.C.*

**Published for ISEP by
Howard University Press
Washington, D.C.
1976**

This report was made possible by a grant from the Ford Foundation.

Library of Congress Catalog Card   Number 75-43488
International Standard Book   Number 0-88258-072-8

CONTENTS

LIST OF TABLES   *ix*

LIST OF FIGURES   *xxv*

FOREWORD   *xxix*

PREFACE   *xxxi*

OVERVIEW   *1*

Chapter 1   **Problems of the Data on Blacks in College**

Introduction   *9*
Methodological Considerations   *9*
Errors of Usage   *12*
Incompatibility of the Data on Blacks in College   *13*
Missing Data   *16*
Summary   *18*

Chapter 2   **Access, Distribution, and Persistence of Blacks in College**

Introduction   *19*
The 1973-74 Academic Year   *19*
Access of Blacks to Undergraduate,
   Graduate, and Professional Schools   *22*
    Black enrollment in Undergraduate School,
     Fall 1973   *24*
    Black enrollment in Graduate and
     Professional Schools   *38*
    Summary   *46*
Distribution of Black Students in Schools and Programs   *47*
    College Distribution   *47*
    Program Distribution   *61*
    Summary   *65*

Persistence of Black Students in College   *66*
    Dropout Rates   *66*
    Degrees Earned   *70*
    Summary   *83*

Chapter 3   **Barriers to Equal Educational Opportunity for Blacks**

Introduction   *85*
Categorical Barriers   *87*
    Aspiration   *90*
    Family income   *96*
    Summary   *104*
Educational Barriers   *106*
    Admissions tests   *106*
    Family income   *112*
    College costs   *123*
    Financial aid practices and policies   *128*
    Educational preparation and
       academic failure   *145*
    Transfer policies   *152*
    Counseling practices   *154*
    Recruitment   *154*
    Extracurricular activities and
       student employment   *156*
    Summary   *158*
Psychosocial Barriers   *159*
    White students/Black campuses   *159*
    Black students/white campuses   *160*
    Psychosocial barriers and program
       distribution   *162*
    Psychosocial barriers and persistence   *164*
    Summary   *164*

Chapter 4   **Impact of Higher Education on Black Income**

Introduction   *167*
Education and Income   *174*
Lifetime Influence of Education   *181*
Black and Total Population Income Comparisons   *185*
Unequal Educational Opportunity and Income Loss   *190*
Education and Occupation   *200*

Chapter 5   **Federal Policies Related to Equal Educational Opportunity**

Introduction   *207*
Federal Facilitators of Equal Educational
    Opportunities for Blacks in Higher Education   *211*

Categorical, Educational, and Psychosocial Facilitators	211
Federal Programs	212
A Limited Assessment of the Federal Role in Equal Educational Opportunity for Blacks in Higher Education	215
Civil Rights Act of 1964	216
Education Amendments of 1972	220
BEOGs	221
SEOGs, CW-S, NDSL	225
Guaranteed Student Loan Program	228
Federal Responsibility in Graduate and Professional Education of Minorities	237
Summary	240

Appendix A   **Federal Higher Education Legislation**   243

Appendix B   **Survey of National Data Collectors**   265

Appendix C   **Enrollment in Selected Institutions**   269

Appendix D   **Graduate and Professional School Enrollment**   279

Appendix E   **College Costs**   305

Appendix F   **Income Redistribution**   323

Appendix G   **References**   325

List of Tables

Table 1-1   Total and percent Black enrollment in Fall 1970 and Fall 1972 as reported by U.S. Office for Civil Rights (DHEW) and U.S. Census.   15

Table 1-2   Availability of racial data on Fall 1973 enrollment and degrees earned by 53 state commissions of higher education.   18

Table 2-1   Percentages of all post-secondary students in higher education and other post-secondary institutions by race and sex, October 1973.   23

Table 2-2   Total college enrollment of Blacks in all public and private institutions, 1970 through 1974.   24

Table 2-3   Estimated college enrollment of students 16 to 34 years old by year in school, full-time enrollment, and race, October 1973.   25

Table 2-4   Percent of age group between 16 and 34 years old, enrolled full and part-time in college by race and sex, October 1973.   26

Table 2-5   Years of school completed by race and sex of persons 25 years and older as of March 1973.   28

Table 2-6   Proportion of non-high school graduates (not enrolled in school) ages 16 to 21, by race and sex, October 1973.   29

Table 2-7   Percent of high school dropouts by race, age, and place of residence as of October 1973.   29

Table 2-8   Blacks as percent of undergraduate availability pool by age, March 1973.   31

Table 2-9   Percent Blacks in high school graduate availability pool by age, March 1973.   31

Table 2-10 Percent of high school seniors who expressed need for special college assistance by race, 1973. 33

Table 2-11 Mean annual estimated parental contribution toward college education by race, 1973. 33

Table 2-12 Degree aspirations of minority high school students by gross family income, Spring 1973. 34

Table 2-13 Blacks enrolled in first four years of college needed to achieve parity, assuming constant enrollment, October 1973. 35

Table 2-14 Percent of high school graduates age 16 to 34 enrolled in college by race, October 1973. 35

Table 2-15 Percent distribution of post-secondary plans of Black and white high school seniors, October 1972. 36

Table 2-16 Percent of high school graduates who attended college in the same year, 1970 to 1973 by race. 36

Table 2-17 Percent distribution of first-year college students by year of high school graduation, 1973. 38

Table 2-18 Full-time enrollment in graduate and professional schools receiving federal assistance by race, Fall 1972. 39

Table 2-19 Minimum needed financial support and current work hours of the Black graduate availability pool, Spring 1974. 42

Table 2-20 Blacks as percent of graduate/professional availability pool by age, March 1973. 43

Table 2-21 Needed Black graduate enrollment in 154 Ph.D-granting institutions and in 5th year and beyond to achieve parity with graduate availability pool, age 20 to 34 assuming constant total enrollment, Fall 1973. 46

Table 2-22 Total enrollment in college and percent Blacks enrolled by control and type of institution, October 1973. 49

Table 2-23 Combined undergraduate and graduate availability pool and percent Black, age 18 to 34, Fall 1973. 49

Table 2-24   Estimated enrollment of Black college students by age and type of institution, October 1973.   50

Table 2-25   Estimated enrollment of white college students by age and type of institution, October 1973.   51

Table 2-26   College enrollment of students 16 years and older by race, sex, and type of institution, October 1973.   52

Table 2-27   Percent male and female enrolled in college by race and type of institution, October 1973.   52

Table 2-28   Percent college distribution of Black and white college students by sex and type and control of the institution, October 1973.   53

Table 2-29   Black undergraduate enrollment in land-grant colleges, Fall 1972.   54

Table 2-30   Enrollment at historically Black colleges and universities and first-time freshmen enrollment by control and sex, Fall 1966, 1969, 1971, and 1973.   55

Table 2-31   Public and private enrollment patterns of graduate students in Ph.D.-granting institutions by race, Fall 1973.   59

Table 2-32   Graduate enrollment of graduate students in Ph.D.-granting institutions by size of the student body and race, Fall 1973.   59

Table 2-33   Black enrollment needed for parity in combined undergraduate/graduate availability pool by type of institution, Fall 1973.   60

Table 2-34   Black graduate enrollment needed for parity in 154 Ph.D.-granting institutions, by size of institution, Fall 1973.   61

Table 2-35   Distribution of Blacks in graduate programs of 154 Ph.D.-granting institutions, Fall 1973.   62

Table 2-36   Enrollment in graduate programs in 154 Ph.D.-granting institutions, by type of control, race, and field of study, 1973.   62

Table 2-37   Program distribution of Black and white graduate students in 154 Ph.D.-granting institutions, Fall 1973.   63

Table 2-38 Black enrollments in selected professional fields, Fall 1971. 65

Table 2-39 National persistence rates for 1966 Black and other freshmen, Spring 1970 (weighted population estimates). 67

Table 2-40 Proportion of college returns age 14 to 24, by race and years of college completed, October 1973. 68

Table 2-41 Estimated baccalaureate degrees awarded by race and ethnic group, Spring 1974. 70

Table 2-42 Percentage of bachelor degrees awarded by selected fields in historically Black colleges and nationally. 72

Table 2-43 Number and percent of masters, doctorates, and professional degrees awarded by historically Black public and private institutions, 1972-73 academic year. 74

Table 2-44 Professional degrees awarded by historically Black colleges in selected fields, 1972-73. 74

Table 2-45 Doctorates awarded by historically Black colleges, 1972-1973 academic year. 75

Table 2-46 Doctorates awarded by race and citizenship, June 1973. 77

Table 2-47 Institutions awarding doctorates to native-born and naturalized U.S. citizens by race, Spring 1973. 78

Table 2-48 Proportion of doctorates awarded to men and women, by citizenship, status, race and ethnic group, Spring 1973. 79

Table 2-49 Doctorates awarded, by field and race, U.S. native-born citizens, 1972-73 academic year (75% of all awarded). 82

Table 2-50 Number of years between baccalaureate and doctoral degrees by race, Spring 1973. 83

Table 3-1 Percent distribution of years of school completed by race and age, March 1973. 90

Table 3-2 Immediate degree aspirations of Black college students by sex, October 1973. 91

Table 3-3 Immediate degree aspirations of white college students by sex, October 1973. 91

Table 3-4   Plans of college seniors by race, 1972.   93

Table 3-5   Percentage of college seniors engaged in planned activity one year later by race, Spring 1972.   94

Table 3-6   Highest degrees held and planned by 1961 and 1966 freshmen by race, 1972.   95

Table 3-7   Primary families with dependent members 18 to 24 years old and percent with members enrolled full-time in college by family income, October 1967 to October 1973.   96

Table 3-8   Students 18 to 24 years old enrolled in college who are dependent (members of households) by race and sex, October 1973.   98

Table 3-9   Percent of Blacks and all family members age 18 to 24 in college availability pool and with college experience by family income, October 1973.   99

Table 3-10   Enrollment of bright (high school GPA of B+ or better) full-time freshmen from low-income ($4,000 or less) families by race and type of institution, Fall 1973.   103

Table 3-11   Enrollment of bright (high school GPA of B+ or better) full-time freshmen from low-income ($4,000 to $5,999) families by race and type of institution, Fall 1973.   103

Table 3-12   Enrollment of bright (high school GPA of B+ or better) full-time freshmen from moderate-income families ($6,000 to $7,999) by race and type of institution, Fall 1973.   104

Table 3-13   Enrollment of bright (high school GPA of B+ or better) full-time freshmen from lower middle-income families ($8,000 to $9,999) by race and type of institution, Fall 1973.   104

Table 3-14   Special attention to minority/disadvantaged graduate student applications in the admissions process, 1972.   109

Table 3-15   Special attention given by departments to minority/disadvantaged graduate school applications in the admissions process, 1972.   110

Table 3-16   Enrollment of dependent college students age 18 to 24 by race and family income, October 1973.   114

Table 3-17   College enrollment of students 34 years old and younger by sex of head of household and race, October 1973.   116

Table 3-18   Percent distribution of Black and white full-time freshmen in public and private institutions by family income, October 1973.   118

Table 3-19   Percentage distribution of doctorates earned, by native-born Blacks and whites, by educational level of fathers and mothers, Spring 1973.   121

Table 3-20   Percent of college seniors engaged in planned activity one year later by family income and father's education, 1972.   122

Table 3-21   Average college costs as percent of family income by race and type of institution, Fall 1973.   124

Table 3-22   Estimated parental contribution toward college education of high school seniors by race, 1973-74 academic year.   125

Table 3-23   Percent distribution of Blacks and all students enrolled by type of institution, October 1973.   126

Table 3-24   The importance of financial aid in college choice of freshmen attending public and private four-year colleges and universities by race, Fall 1973.   127

Table 3-25   Amount needed for graduate school by 1971 graduates not enrolled, by race, Spring 1972.   129

Table 3-26   Estimated median educational costs of financially dependent and independent full-time students by race and type of institution, October 1973.   131

Table 3-27   Estimated differences in the average amount of tuition aid received by Black and white independent and dependent college students by type of institution, Fall 1973.   131

Table 3-28   Special funds allocated solely for financial aid to minority/disadvantaged graduate students by type of institution, 1972.   143

Table 3-29   Approximate percentage from different sources of special funds for minority graduate student aid, 1972.   144

Table 3-30   Financial characteristics of students in advanced study by race, 1972.   145

Table 3-31	Sources of financial support of doctoral recipients by race, Spring 1973.	146
Table 3-32	Persistence of 1966 freshmen attending four-year colleges and universities by race, Spring 1970.	148
Table 3-33	Relation between participation in CLEO program and enrollment status, 1969 minority entrants to 98 law schools.	151
Table 3-34	Relation between kind and amount of financial aid and enrollment status, 1969 minority entrants to 98 law schools.	151
Table 3-35	Immediate degree aspirations of Black students attending two-year colleges by sex, October 1973.	152
Table 3-36	Number of years in school of two-year college Black students aspiring for baccalaureate degrees or higher, by sex, October 1973.	153
Table 3-37	Employment status in 1971-72 academic year of doctoral recipients by race, Spring 1973.	157
Table 3-38	Type of school attended by persons 35 years old and over by race, October 1972.	158
Table 3-39	Differences in perceptions of graduate school by Black and white students, 1972.	165
Table 4-1	Mean income for 1969 of Blacks by year of school completed, sex, and regions.	175
Table 4-2	Gains in mean incomes for 1969 by level of school completed, by region and sex of Blacks 18 years and older.	176
Table 4-3	Percentage gains in mean incomes for 1969 by level of school completed, region and sex of Blacks 18 years and older.	176
Table 4-4	Total average lifetime earnings in 1969 and incremental differences in average lifetime earnings by years of school completed, race, and sex.	177
Table 4-5	Discounted present value of average lifetime earnings and incremental differences in discounted present value of average lifetime earnings in 1969 by year of school completed, race and sex.	178

Table 4-6   Percentage of Black male 1969 income received by Black females by region of the country and educational level.   180

Table 4-7   Mean income in 1969 of Black males 18 years and over by years of school completed and age.   182

Table 4-8   Mean income in 1969 of Black females 18 years and over by years of school completed and age.   182

Table 4-9   Difference in mean 1969 incomes between Blacks with four years of college and Black high school graduates by age and sex.   183

Table 4-10   Difference in mean 1969 incomes between Blacks with five or more years of college and Blacks with four years of college, by age and sex.   184

Table 4-11   Absolute gains in mean 1969 earnings by level of school completed, region, and sex, for total population 18 years and older.   185

Table 4-12   Percentage gains in mean 1969 incomes by level of school completed, region, and sex, for total population 18 years and older.   186

Table 4-13   Index of Black to total mean 1969 incomes by sex, years of school completed, and region.   187

Table 4-14   Ratio of mean incomes in 1969 of Black males to all males 18 years and older by years of school completed and age.   188

Table 4-15   Ratio of mean income in 1969 of Black females to all females 18 years and older by years of school completed and age.   189

Table 4-16   Total and proportion of Black individuals with at least one year of college by sex and age group for the total U.S., 1970.   191

Table 4-17   Distribution of total males above high school by age group, 1970.   192

Table 4-18   Distribution of Black males above high school by age group, 1970.   192

Table 4-19   Distribution of Black females above high school by age group, 1970.   193

Table 4-20 Distribution of total females above high school by age group, 1970. 193

Table 4-21 Mean 1969 incomes and aggregate incomes by race, educational level and sex, and ratio of Black to total U.S. income. 194

Table 4-22 Mean 1969 incomes of Blacks with college persistence equal to persistence of total population by sex. 196

Table 4-23 Estimated 1969 mean incomes of Blacks with college access equal to access of total population and persistence held constant, by sex. 197

Table 4-24 Estimated mean 1969 incomes of Blacks with college access and persistence equal to access and persistence of total population, by sex. 198

Table 4-25 Estimated mean 1969 income of Black males with income distribution equal to distribution of total population. 199

Table 4-26 Estimated 1969 incomes of Blacks with college access, persistence, and income distribution equal to that of total population, by sex. 200

Table 4-27 Occupational distribution of Black males age 25 to 64 by highest level of school completed. 201

Table 4-28 Occupational distribution of males age 25 to 64 who have completed one or more years of college, by race, 1970. 202

Table 4-29 Percentage distribution of males age 25 to 64 by broad occupational groups, years of college completed and race, 1970. 203

Table 4-30 Mean earnings in 1969 of male workers age 25 to 64 selected by broad occupational groups, race, and years of college completed, 1970. 205

Table 5-1 Estimated average amount awarded by type of institution and assistance program, 1973-74 academic year. 214

Table 5-2 Distribution of undergraduate institutions receiving federal assistance by percent Blacks enrolled, Fall 1970 and 1972. 217

Table 5-3   Full-time undergraduate Black enrollment by region of the country, Fall 1968, 1970 and 1972.   219

Table 5-4   BEOGs applicants as percent of all first-year full-time college students and all high school graduates by race, Fall 1973.   223

Table 5-5   Number of Black college students who had heard of BEOGs by age and type of institution attended, Fall 1973.   223

Table 5-6   Number of white college students who had heard of BEOG's by age and type of institution attended, Fall 1973.   224

Table 5-7   Proportion of college students 16 to 21 years old who applied for BEOGs by type of institution and race, Fall 1973.   224

Table 5-8   How college students heard about BEOGs by type of institution attended, October 1973.   225

Table 5-9   Participation in SEOGs, College Work-Study and NDSL by race, Fiscal Years 1968 through 1970.   226

Table 5-10   Financial assistance to Black students by type of program, Fiscal Years 1968 through 1970.   227

Table 5-11   Financial assistance to white students by type of program, Fiscal Years 1968 through 1970.   227

Table 5-12   Awards in College Work-Study, SEOG and NDSL by race of recipient, Fiscal Years 1968, 1969, 1970, 1972 and 1973.   229

Table 5-13   Average student loan amounts for Blacks and whites for Fiscal Years 1968 through 1973 in the federally insured student loan program.   231

Table 5-14   Average student loan amounts for Blacks and whites in Fiscal Years 1967 through 1973 in the state guarantee agency programs.   231

Table 5-15   Estimated total and average amounts borrowed in federal loans (NDSL and GSLP) by full-time freshmen attending four-year colleges and universities, by control of institution, family income, and race, Fall 1973.   234

Table 5-16   Total annual loans under the Guaranteed Student Loan Program, Fiscal Years 1966 through 1974.   236

Table 5-17   Claims paid summary for the Guaranteed Student Loan
Program as of May 1974.   236

Table 5-18   Claims paid as of May 1974 as a percent of the volume ($) of
guaranteed student loans in Fiscal Year 1974.   237

Table A-1   Summary of federal higher education laws affecting the
1973-74 school year, in chronological order.   243

Table A-2   Authorized appropriations for higher educational programs
administered by USOE, Fiscal Years 1973 and 1974.   247

Table A-3   Summary of domestic assistance programs affecting higher
education, 1973-74 academic year by department in alphabetical order.   248

Table A-4   Authorized appropriations by agency programs, research
and training grants to colleges, Fiscal Years 1973 and 1974.   252

Table A-5   Supplemental Educational Opportunity Grants in rank order
of federal funds allocated by state, Fiscal Year 1974.   254

Table A-6   National Direct Student Loans in rank order of federal funds
available by state, Fiscal Year 1974.   255

Table A-7   College Work-Study Programs in rank order of federal funds
allocated by state, Fiscal Year 1974.   256

Table A-8   State scholarship programs by state and type of program for
the 1972 and 1973 academic years.   258

Table A-9   Numbers of increases and decreases in state student assistance programs between 1972-73 academic year and the
1973-74 academic year.   262

Table A-10   Rank order of states by number of awards, total dollars
awarded, and average award for 1973-74 academic year.   262

Table A-11   OCR regional categories of the states used in Table 2-2.   263

Table A-12   Students receiving financial assistance by type of federal
campus-based programs and race, Fiscal Years 1968 through
1970.   263

Table B-1   Do you collect racial statistics on enrollment?   266

Table B-2	From which institutions do you collect racial statistics?	266
Table B-3	How are your racial statistics collected?	267
Table B-4	What were the usable response rates for enrollment statistics?	267
Table B-5	What percent of the total entering fall enrollment in 1972 was Black?	268
Table C-1	Land-grant colleges and universities.	269
Table C-2	List of predominantly Black colleges, based on Fall 1972 undergraduate enrollment.	272
Table C-3	State institutions in NASUL-G with highest and lowest charges for tuition and required fees, Fall 1972.	273
Table C-4	Title III, Higher Education Act of 1965, Strengthening Developing Institutions, Basic Institutional Development Program.	274
Table C-5	Title III, Higher Education Act of 1965, Strengthening Developing Institutions, Advanced Institutional Development Program.	275
Table C-6	Rank order of top ten states by public two-year college enrollments, Fall 1973.	276
Table C-7	Rank order of top ten states by private two-year college enrollments, Fall 1973.	276
Table C-8	Private college enrollment ranked by state, Fall 1973.	276
Table C-9	Enrollment in 185 two-year colleges by sex and type of institution, Fall 1973.	278
Table C-10	Percent enrolled in career education and transfer programs in 158 two-year colleges by sex and type of institution, Fall 1973.	278
Table D-1	Proposed graduate majors of Black graduate availability pool, Spring 1974.	279
Table D-2	Undergraduate majors of Black graduate availability pool, Spring 1974.	280

Table D-3 Characteristics of the ETS Black graduate availability pool, Spring 1974. 280

Table D-4 Doctorates earned, by field of study and race, Spring 1973. 282

Table D-5 Doctorates awarded within fields of study to native-born U.S. citizens, by race (equals 85% of the doctorates awarded), Spring 1973. 283

Table D-6 Enrollment in Ph.D.-granting institutions in 1973, by race and control. 284

Table D-7 Field of study of college students 14 to 34 years old by race and sex, October 1972 (in thousands). 285

Table D-8 Percent distribution of field of study of college students 14 to 34 years old by sex and race, October 1972 (in thousands). 286

Table D-9 Field of study of college students 14 to 34 years old by region of residence, type of college, whether attending full- or part-time, and race, October 1972 (in thousands). 287

Table D-10 Enrollments in health professions by race and field of study, Fall 1971 or 1972. 291

Table D-11 Distribution of health aspirants, by health study and by race, for 1972 (in percentage). 291

Table D-12 Enrollment in U.S. dental schools by race and year in training, Fall 1973. 292

Table D-13 Total dental auxiliary enrollment, by race and type of program, Fall 1972. 293

Table D-14 Enrollment in U.S. medical schools by race for first-year classes and total, Fall 1973. 294

Table D-15 First-year U.S. and foreign student enrollments in U.S. medical schools by race, 1968 through 1972. 295

Table D-16 Percent minority enrollment in U.S. medical schools by region, 1969-1970 and 1972-73. 296

Table D-17 AACP undergraduate enrollment in Pharmacy by class and race for final three years of training, Fall 1973. 297

Table D-18   AACP graduate enrollment in Pharmacy by degree level, Fall 1973.   299

Table D-19   Black Engineering college enrollments by year in school, 1969 to 1973.   299

Table D-20   Total minority enrollments in law schools, by race and ethnic group, 1971-72 to 1973-74.   300

Table D-21   Percent distribution of Black enrollment in 148 ABA-approved law schools by year in school, 1973.   300

Table D-22   Undergraduate Black enrollment in 47 schools of business by field of study, 1972.   301

Table D-23   Graduate students in Business currently enrolled in doctoral programs, by race (based on responses from 47 graduate schools of business), Fall 1973.   301

Table D-24   Black enrollment in schools of business, masters programs, Fall 1972 (52 institutions represented).   302

Table D-25   Percent Black enrollments in Business by degree level, Fall 1972.   303

Table D-26   Black enrollment in doctors of Religion by field of study, 1973.   303

Table D-27   Minority enrollment in graduate programs in Public Affairs and Public Administration at NASPAA institutions, Fall 1972.   304

Table E-1   Itemized costs of health training by type of institution, 1973.   305

Table E-2   Average annual expenses of students in medical schools, 1968.   305

Table E-3   Costs of attending college in health fields, 1973.   306

Table E-4   Estimated minimum expenses for first-year students at U.S. medical schools (1975-76).   307

Table E-5   Admissions policies and practices of public and private colleges and universities, Spring 1973.   308

Table E-6   Graduate and professional schools requiring one or more entrance exams by field, 1973-74 academic year.   310

Table E-7   Financial assistance pattern of Black full-time freshmen attending public four-year colleges and universities by family income, Fall 1973 (unweighted).   312

Table E-8   Financial assistance pattern of white full-time freshmen attending public four-year colleges and universities by family income, Fall 1973 (unweighted).   314

Table E-9   Financial assistance pattern of Black full-time freshmen attending private four-year colleges and universities by family income, Fall 1973 (unweighted).   316

Table E-10   Financial assistance pattern of white full-time freshmen attending private four-year colleges and universities by family income, Fall 1973 (unweighted).   318

Table E-11   Total number of awards by sources of income for Black and all post-secondary students 16 years old and over, Fall 1973.   320

Table E-12   Distribution of federal loans to low-income students ($5,999 or less) in public and private four-year colleges and universities by race, Fall 1973.   320

Table E-13   Distribution of federal loans to moderate income students ($6,000 to $9,999) in public and private four-year colleges and universities by race, Fall 1973.   321

Table E-14   Distribution of federal loans to middle-income students ($10,000 to $14,999) in public and private four-year colleges and universities by race, Fall 1973.   322

Table E-15   Distribution of federal loans to upper-income students ($15,000 and above) in public and private four-year colleges and universities by race, Fall 1973.   322

Table F-1   Income redistribution of Blacks with college experience to equal incomes of whites with college experience, Fall 1973.   323

Table F-2   Income redistribution of Blacks in availability pool to equal white distribution by income level, Fall 1973.   324

List of Figures

Figure 2-1   Percent change in total college enrollment by race, Fall 1970 through 1974.   21

Figure 2-2   Percent of age groups enrolled in college by race, October 1973.   27

Figure 2-3   Comparison of high school dropout rates, ages 25 and older with 21 years and under, by race and sex, 1973.   30

Figure 2-4   College aspirations and college enrollment of high school seniors, by race, October 1973.   37

Figure 2-5   Percent of Blacks enrolled full-time in undergraduate, graduate, and professional schools receiving federal assistance, Fall 1972.   40

Figure 2-6   Undergraduate and proposed graduate majors of Black males in the ETS graduate availability pool, Spring 1974.   44

Figure 2-7   Undergraduate and proposed graduate majors of Black females in the ETS graduate availability pool, Spring 1974.   45

Figure 2-8   College enrollment of students 14 years and older by race and sex, October 1973.   48

Figure 2-9   Percent change in first-time freshmen enrollment, Fall 1972 to Fall 1973 by type of institution.   57

Figure 2-10   Proportion of college students age 14 to 24 enrolled in October 1972 who did not return in October 1973, by race and sex.   69

Figure 2-11   Proportion of full-time Black freshmen, 1968-1974.   71

Figure 2-12   Doctorates awarded by race and citizenship, Spring 1973.   76

Figure 2-13   Black (U.S. native) doctorates in Education by baccalaureate fields of study, Spring 1973.   81

Figure 3-1   Percent of male high school graduates 20 and 21 years old who completed one year of college or more by race, 1940 to 1974.   88

Figure 3-2   Percent of female high school graduates 20 and 21 years old who completed one year of college or more by race, 1940 to 1974.   89

Figure 3-3   Percent of spring high school graduates who attend college the following fall by race, 1970 through 1973.   92

Figure 3-4   Percent of family members 18 to 24 years old enrolled in college full-time, by family income, 1967 to 1973.   97

Figure 3-5   Percent of college availability pool with college experience, age 18 to 24, by race and family income, October 1973.   100

Figure 3-6   Proportion of Black to white college participation and hypothetical proportion if Black/white incomes in the availability pool were equalized, October 1973.   101

Figure 3-7   Percent of bright students by income and race enrolled in public and private universities, Fall 1973.   1ᑎ2

Figure 3-8   Percent of bright freshmen enrolled in public two-year colleges by family income and race, Fall 1973.   105

Figure 3-9   Mean parental annual income by SAT score ranges for high school seniors, 1973-74 academic year.   107

Figure 3-10   Percent of public and private predominantly white universities with undergraduate special admissions programs by academic year, 1970 through 1973.   111

Figure 3-11   College enrollment of Black and white students 34 years old and younger by sex of head of household, October 1973.   115

Figure 3-12   Income distribution of Black and white freshmen enrolled full-time in college, October 1973.   117

Figure 3-13   Percent of full-time freshmen from families with incomes $5,999 or less receiving aid by race and control of four-year college or university attended, Fall 1973.   133

Figure 3-14 Percent of full-time freshmen from families with incomes
$6,000 to $9,999 receiving aid by race and control of four-
year college or university attended, Fall 1973.   135

Figure 3-15 Percent of full-time freshmen from families with incomes
$10,000 to $14,999 receiving aid by race and control of
four-year college or university attended, Fall 1973.   137

Figure 3-16 Percent of full-time freshmen from families with incomes
$15,000 and above receiving aid by race and control of
four-year college and university attended, Fall 1973.   139

Figure 3-17 Average amount of aid received by low-income ($5,999 or
less) Black and white full-time freshmen attending public
four-year colleges and universities, Fall 1973.   141

Figure 3-18 Percent of 1966 full-time freshmen not enrolled (without
degrees) by race and high school grade point averages,
Spring 1970.   149

Figure 5-1 Percent of college students (16 years and older) who have
heard of BEOGs by race, October 1973.   222

Figure 5-2 Percent of college students (16 years and older) who applied
for BEOGs by race, October 1973.   222

Figure 5-3 Percent of awards to Black college students in SEOGs,
College Work-Study, and NDSL in Fiscal Years 1968,
1969, 1970, 1972, 1973.   230

Figure 5-4 Participation in SEOGs, CW-S, and NDSL in Fiscal Year
1973 in comparison to low-income (under $7,500) depen-
dent college enrollment in Fall 1972 by race.   232

Figure 5-5 Distribution of entering full-time freshmen in public and
private four-year colleges and universities with no loans by
family income and race, Fall 1973.   235

Appendix Figure

Figure D-1 Black enrollment in U.S. medical schools that are predominantly white or Black, Fall 1973.   302

Foreword

The Institute for the Study of Educational Policy (ISEP) developed out of the need both for a national clearinghouse and for a research center on the issues affecting equal educational opportunities in higher education. As a national clearinghouse, ISEP aims to serve policy makers and interested researchers by keeping abreast of developments in higher education, within the public and private sectors. In addition, ISEP assumes responsibility for reporting such information to its constituents.

As a research and policy center, ISEP has three program objectives:

● To prepare a periodic critical assessment of the dynamic status and needs of Blacks in higher education.

● To assess the impact of law and social science research on the status of Blacks in higher education.

● To use old models creatively and to develop new models and theories of higher education for Blacks with implications for elementary and secondary education.

Through its annual reports and monographs, through its seminars and workshops, and through its announcements and public testimony, the Institute for the Study of Educational Policy attempts to fill a vacuum in the organized body of knowledge about higher educational opportunities of Blacks and other minorities. In doing so, ISEP attempts to make a significant contribution to the formulation and evaluation of contemporary educational policy.

The first annual report on the status and needs of Blacks in higher education, *Equal Educational Opportunity for Blacks in U.S. Higher Education: An Assessment*, is designed to function as a single-year study, describing the status of Blacks in the 1973-74 academic year, and as a general reference work, summarizing the best available data on Blacks in higher education.

A massive undertaking such as this report is the result of the time and talents of many people. We wish to acknowledge their contributions in helping the Institute fulfill a crucial part of its mission. The data in the report were available to the Institute through the cooperation and assistance of many people. We especially thank the staffs of the American Council on Education, the U.S. Census Bureau, the Educational Testing Service, the College Entrance Examination Board, the ERIC Higher Education Clearinghouse, the Institute for Services to Education, the National Scholarship Service and Fund for Negro Students, the U.S. Office of Education, the National

Board on Graduate Education, and the Office for Civil Rights (DHEW), and also the many professional associations that so willingly provided data for this report.

We would like to thank the following people whose painstaking and thoughtful review of earlier drafts of the report enhanced the quality of the final product: Sharon Bush, David Nolan, Donna Wilson, Langley Spurlock, Mary Lepper and Patsy Fleming.

Within the Institute this report was the result of teamwork, cooperation, and dedication. To the secretaries, research assistants, and senior fellows we extend our sincere thanks. We wish to acknowledge the special contributions of the following Institute secretaries and research assistants: Carla Mahdi, Elene Makonnen, Edith McRae, Mattie McFadden, Margaret Nealy, Vicki Turner, Geneva Sanders, Julian Smith, and Karen Yvonne Wilson. We also thank Julius Hobson, Jr., editorial assistant, for his many contributions to the development of this report.

The thoughtful development of the discussions and the analyses in this report reflect the creativity and sensitivity of the Institute senior fellows and special advisors. To the senior fellows Faustine Jones, John Fleming, and Sam Wong, we extend our sincere appreciation. To David Swinton, who provided the economic analyses in this report and who was the principal writer of Chapter 4, the "Impact of Higher Education on Black Income," we extend our thanks for his excellent contributions. We would also like to thank Michael Abramowitz, who assisted in the conceptualization of this report and in the writing of Chapter 5, "Federal Policies Related to Equal Educational Opportunity."

The massive editorial work reflected in the quality of this report is the result of the time-consuming and painstaking efforts of Jane Midgley, principal editor for this report. Ms. Midgley's contributions led not only to the smooth production of this report, but also to its attractive and readable appearance.

Finally, to senior fellow Elizabeth Abramowitz, who, as principal investigator, organized and wrote this report, we extend our congratulations for a job well done and our appreciation for the success of so large an undertaking.

The Institute also wishes to thank the Ford Foundation, and especially Benjamin Payton and Peter de Janosi, for their timely assistance and their support of the Institute and of this report. Through its support, the Ford Foundation has demonstrated its commitment to the mission of the Institute and the need for it.

Kenneth S. Tollett, Director ISEP
and Chairman ISEP National Advisory Board

Preface

Equal Educational Opportunity for Blacks in U.S. Higher Education: An Assessment brings together, for the first time, a wide range of information on Blacks in higher education in the 1973-74 academic year. The Institute for the Study of Educational Policy presents this report as the first in a series of annual reports on current educational opportunities for Blacks in higher education. Each report in the series will focus on a specific school year and will include follow-up documents recommending state and federal action. The first report covers the 1973-74 academic year, the most recent full academic year for which data were available.

In the midst of so much apparent progress for Blacks in their push for full participation in American institutions, especially education, it is important to take a careful measure of that progress and to point the way to improvements in policies, programs, and attitudes. In this report, the equality of educational opportunity is assessed as one social indication of the improved, but still unequal, status of Blacks in American society. Blacks have made significant gains in U.S. higher education in the last decade. But even with the help of supportive legislation, court decisions, affirmative action programs, and increased financial aid, the achievement has been irregular and inadequate. This report provides an exhaustive review of the recent status of Blacks in higher education, the economic returns of education for Blacks, the continuing barriers to equal educational opportunity, and the problems of the racial data by which public policies sometimes are determined.

What is equal educational opportunity? It is a societal goal that aims to provide the opportunity for all students to fulfill their promise and ambitions, and to rise to whatever heights their ability, interest, and determination can reach through education. To achieve this goal, opportunity cannot be limited by the color of one's skin or sex, by the nature of one's religious beliefs, or by family income and private circumstance. Equal educational opportunity in college is, therefore, the opportunity to enter not just some colleges, but all colleges; not just some fields, but all fields; and to earn not just certain degrees, but all degrees, unencumbered by barriers related to race, institutional practices, and personal attitudes.

Equal educational opportunity depends upon certain dynamic conditions. In this report, the necessary conditions are defined by three concepts: access, distribution, and persistence. Access to college, though essential to equal educational opportunity, is only the first step. In addition, qualified students must be able to choose and distribute themselves throughout a wide variety of institutions, programs, and fields of study, and must be provided the opportunity to stay in college and earn advanced degrees.

The ideal yardstick by which to measure equal educational opportunity is the extent to which all students, regardless of race and circumstance, are able to fulfill their educational aspirations. But, because we do not know educational aspirations in all instances, the available data on college enrollment and attainment do not easily lend themselves to such an assessment. Therefore, the concept of parity is used to measure equal educational opportunity in this report.

The distinction is made between parity with the availability pool, which this report uses, and population parity. Population parity refers to the proportional representation of all members of a group in college, regardless of whether all members are eligible for college. As a long range goal, population parity is desirable and necessary; however, as an immediate measure of equal educational opportunity it does not take into account eligibility for college.

Parity with the availability pool refers to the proportional representation of eligible students in college. Where the proportional representation of a group in the availability pool is greater than their representation in college, the group is underrepresented in college. Where the proportional representation in the availability pool is smaller than their proportion of college students, the group is overrepresented in college. And, where the two proportions are equal, equal educational opportunity in access, distribution, or persistence is approximated.

Because of conflicts and inconsistencies in racial statistics, the data in this report are treated as estimated. (For technical discussion see Chapter 1.) The problems of obtaining accurate statistics, and of formulating realistic policies without them, need attention if the true position of Blacks in higher education is to be understood and improved. Included in this report, then, is an analysis of the differences in statistics reported by data collectors, the limitations in interpretation of these statistics, and the policy questions for which data on Blacks are needed but not available.

Equal Educational Opportunity for Blacks in U.S. Higher Education: An Assessment is designed to serve not only as a discussion of the status of Blacks for a given academic year, but also as a reference document on Blacks in higher education. In order to fulfill the latter purpose, detailed tables are included throughout this report and in the appendices. The inadequacies and weaknesses in the data are stressed so that the limitations of the tables for reference and research purposes are known.

National Advisory Board

Elias Blake, Jr.
President
Institute for Services to
    Education, Inc.
2001 S Street, N.W.
Washington, D.C. 20009

James Perkins
Chairman
International Council
    for Educational Development
680 Fifth Avenue
New York, New York 10019

Overview

Chapter 1: Problems of the Data on Blacks in College

The problems of the data on Blacks in higher education necessarily limit the assessment of the status and needs of Blacks that follows in Chapters 2 through 5. The problems of the data are fourfold. First, there are methodological differences in identifying race and in weighting procedures which result in inflated or deflated estimates of Black college enrollment. Second, errors in usage due to inappropriate statistical techniques and to the use of unrepresentative samples of Black students and colleges as the sole sources of data on which conclusions about Blacks in college can be made create often-ignored data problems. The third problem is the incompatibility of the data from different sources which so limits the accuracy of the data that both the total student and the Black student absolute enrollments reported by different researchers may disagree significantly. Fourth, missing data limit any assessment of the status of Blacks in higher education. The missing data that can be regarded as basic include: associate arts, baccalaureate, masters, and professional degrees earned by race and type of institution. These data are not available from either public or private national collectors, nor at the state level.

By revising the federally funded annual Higher Education General Information Surveys to include racial items on the enrollment and degrees questionnaires, needed data could be collected routinely. In addition, by coordinating state and federal racial data-collection activities in higher education, both the burden and the costs of such data collection could be shared by the federal and state governments.

Chapter 2: Access, Distribution, and Persistence of Blacks in College

Three distinct but related concepts are used to measure different aspects of equal educational opportunity; these are access—the opportunity to enroll in college; distribution—the type of institution attended and the field of study; and persistence—the opportunity to remain in college and complete training in a timely fashion. The 1973-74 academic year was a year in which absolute total and Black college student enrollment dropped to levels below the previous year's enrollment. Black college student enrollment in Fall 1973 was only 4,000 students higher than the Black enrollment in Fall 1971.

Although the total number of Blacks with a college education has increased in the last twenty years, especially since 1968, Blacks continue to be underrepresented in

1

college. A major factor contributing to this is the high rate of high school dropouts among young Blacks. An estimated 12.1% of the 24 million high school age students age 14 to 19 years old were dropouts in Fall 1973. Of these 2.9 million dropouts, 23% were Black. In Fall 1972, of the 2 million dropouts, 17.4% were Black.

In Fall 1973, there were an estimated 684,000 Black students enrolled in college. Black students equalled 8.3% of the total 8,179,000 estimated enrollment of students under 35 years old. When the college enrollment of Blacks was compared with their proportion of the college availability pool, it was found that, assuming constant rate of enrollment, an additional 130,930 Black students would have to have been enrolled in college in Fall 1973 in order for there to have been access parity with their availability (20% more Blacks should have been in undergraduate schools and 13.5% more in graduate and professional schools).

While access to some form of higher education may have occurred for many Black high school graduates, distribution by type of institution had not. Blacks in higher education were increasingly concentrated in the lower cost, less selective institutions, without major graduate or research programs. Blacks were most likely to be enrolled in public two-year colleges and predominantly Black four-year colleges in the 1973-74 academic year. Indeed, 40% of all Blacks in college in Fall 1973 were in two-year institutions. Blacks were underrepresented in public universities and in private four-year colleges. Thus, Blacks were distributed unevenly throughout the hierarchy of higher educational institutions in 1973.

The tendency for Blacks to enter Education rather than other fields of study increased between the baccalaureate and doctoral levels. Blacks were most likely to leave technical and scientific fields as they moved into advanced training, and most likely to enter or remain in Education or professional fields. Law and Medicine continued to enroll the largest proportion of Blacks in professional schools in 1973. In these fields, however, as in all other graduate and professional fields, the proportional Black enrollment was very small.

Persistence is defined as staying in college and earning a degree. It is measured by dropout rates and degrees earned. Persistence data on minorities in higher education were more scarce than either access or distribution data. Indeed, what is unknown about the persistence of Blacks and other minorities in higher education outweighs what is known. With the exception of doctoral degrees awarded, there is no regular national collection of data on any degrees earned by minorities in the United States. In addition, there is no regular national collection of data on dropout or transfer rates of minorities in U.S. higher education.

Based on the limited data available, it appears that the one year dropout rates of Blacks and whites in 1973 were about equal. The proportion of the college students under 25 years old enrolled the previous year who returned in 1973 was equal for Blacks and whites. About 73% of the Black and white students enrolled in 1972 returned to college in 1973. Thus, over a one year period, recent information suggests equal persistence.

The type of institution attended and high school grade-point average may affect dropout rates. Students in four-year colleges are less likely to drop out than are their counterparts in two-year colleges. Compared to whites attending the same type of institution, the dropout rates of Blacks, some studies indicate, are slightly higher. As

2

might be expected, the higher the high school grade-point average, the lower the college dropout rate. Thus, when high school grade-point averages are taken into consideration, racial differences in the dropout rates of Black and white college students disappear.

Preliminary data from a special survey suggest that in Spring 1974, an estimated 5% of the baccalaureates awarded went to Black students. Of these awards to Black students, approximately one-half were awarded by historically Black colleges. In the previous academic year, Spring 1973, historically Black colleges awarded 6,231 graduate and professional degrees. The professional degrees were primarily in Law and Medicine. The masters degrees were primarily in Education, and the doctoral degrees in Physical and Natural Sciences.

Nationally, Black students received an estimated 2% of the doctorates awarded in Spring 1973. For all races, the doctorates were overwhelmingly awarded to males. The largest proportion of female doctorates within a racial group, however, were earned by Black women, who received 26% of the doctorates awarded to native-born Blacks in Spring 1973. At Black colleges, where the majority of the graduate degrees went to Black students, more than one-half (58%) of the doctorates awarded in Spring 1973 were in scientific fields. Nationally, 60% of the doctorates awarded to native-born Blacks were in Education. In contrast, only 23% of the doctorates awarded to native-born whites were in Education. The number of Blacks earning doctorates in Education reflected a shift in field of study away from the sciences and into Education as Blacks moved from undergraduate to graduate schools, especially in predominantly white institutions. Thus, as persistence in college increased, Blacks narrowed their distribution across fields of study. A factor possibly contributing to this shift was the perceived greater employment opportunities for Blacks in Education.

In general, once Black students have gained access to four-year colleges and universities, they are likely to persist. Blacks and whites of the same age cohort differed not in whether they would complete training once admitted, but in the number of calendar years it would take. It took Blacks, on the average, longer than whites to complete college, because Blacks were more likely to switch from full-to part-time status, and because Blacks were more likely to have intermittent college attendance. In Education, for example, it took Blacks, on the average, 15.27 calendar years and whites 12.51 years to go from the baccalaureate to the doctorate. In all other fields, it took Blacks, on the average 10.10 calendar years and whites 7.61 years to go from the baccalaureate to the doctorate. However, both Black and white doctoral recipients were registered on campus for about 6 years, on the average. Thus, native-born Blacks in graduate programs, especially at the doctoral level, are likely to be slightly older than their native-born white classmates when they complete training. Why Blacks are likely to spread their college education over a longer period of time is discussed in Chapter 3.

Chapter 3: Barriers to Equal Educational Opportunity for Blacks

Barriers to equal educational opportunity are defined as categorical, educational, and psychosocial: categorical barriers arise from racial discrimination, educational barriers from neutral institutional policies and practices that have adverse racial impacts, and psychosocial barriers from the lifestyles and values of students and faculty.

Two factors often cited as explanations of the differences in educational attainment and college enrollment of whites and Blacks are aspirations and family income. It was found that Black students—high school and college—tended to have equal or higher educational aspirations than white students. Yet, Black students tended to have educational attainment below their aspirations and below those of their white counterparts. It was also found that when income was held constant, Blacks had proportionately fewer high school graduates enrolled or with college experience than did whites from the same income group. At the higher income levels, the gap between white and Black rate of college participation was even larger than at lower income levels. When Blacks in the availability pool were given the income of whites, they were still unequal in college participation, although the difference was reduced by three-fifths. The remaining difference in the rate of college participation of whites and Blacks was not due to family income, but rather was the result of categorical and other educational and psychosocial barriers.

The educational barriers to equal educational opportunity were identified as the following: admissions testing, college costs, financial aid, family income, educational preparation and academic failure, transfer policies, counseling practices, recruitment, and extracurricular activities and student employment. In terms of impact on equal educational opportunity for Blacks, the financial barriers—college costs, financial aid, and family income—were the most important.

The relationship of financial barriers to access and distribution of college students was such that Black and white students from more financially advantaged homes were more likely to be enrolled in private institutions and universities. Students from low-income families were likely to be enrolled in public institutions and two-year colleges. Regardless of talent, as measured by high school grade-point average, the income of the parent was related to the type of institution attended. In addition, the expected family contributions of Black families were such that without financial assistance few Black students would have been able to afford more than the tuition at public institutions and two-year colleges.

The lack of money from either public or private sources also meant that few Black students would continue their education at the graduate or professional level. While in 1973 Blacks equaled approximately 8% of the total enrollment in undergraduate school, the proportional enrollment of Blacks in graduate and professional school was only 4 to 5%.

Of the remaining educational barriers, admissions testing has received the greatest amount of attention. Researchers have concluded that achievement and aptitude tests were better than other measures in predicting first-year college grades. However, the test scores are directly related to family income in such a way that the social class consequences of testing in admissions leave two options: to eliminate or to de-emphasize the use of standardized tests in college admissions.

Finally, psychosocial barriers influenced the stereotypic thinking of students and faculty in selecting not only the type of institution to attend but also the major subject, and advanced training. It was found that Black students tended to feel more alienated on white than on Black campuses. Yet they would remain on the white campuses and

4

graduate if they had the academic ability and resiliency to resist what they regarded as a hostile environment. Black students, however, were likely to be reluctant and sometimes discouraged from entering fields of study in which there were few Blacks, such as scientific and technical fields. Fear of failure on the part of the student and lack of acceptance on the part of the faculty, together formed psychosocial barriers to program distribution. Thus, in spite of dramatic gains in college enrollment and attainment, barriers to equal educational opportunity, some unique to Blacks and others shared by other minority and disadvantaged groups, persisted in the 1973-74 academic year.

Chapter 4: Impact of Higher Education on Black Income

While for the population in general the rate of return on an investment in education has in fact decreased within the last few years, the return for Blacks has not. Completing four or more years of college education produced significant gains in average Black income and lifetime earnings. Using 1969 income, it was found that there were significant income differences between the college-educated and non college-educated Black males and females. The gains in income were largest for Black males with five or more years of college, but were small for Black males with fewer years of college. Indeed, with less than five years of college, the relative standing of Black males to all males in annual income was lower, and Black gains in income from experience were small. For Black females, completing four years of college produced the largest gains in income. A college education at all levels produced higher relative average income for Black females than was true of the all female population.

In the relation of income to access, persistence, and employment discrimination, it was found that for college-educated Black males, mean incomes and aggregate Black male incomes increased modestly from improvements in persistence, while Black female incomes barely changed. Achieving equality of access to college, however, produced significant income gains for both Black males and females. And, improving both persistence and access simultaneously increased Black male income still further, but had only a modest effect on Black female incomes. The most dramatic effect on Black male income, however, was caused by reducing the income differentials of Blacks and whites with the same amount of college education (i.e., reducing employment discrimination). For Black females, this resulted in a slight deterioration of their position, because of their greater labor force participation than all women in the same educational cohort. Ending employment discrimination and providing equal access and persistence simultaneously would increase the aggregate Black male income by 26.5%, while increasing the aggregate Black female income by 7.8%. In other words, the effect of unequal educational and employment opportunities was an annual income loss at the 1969 income level of $8.507 billion a year to Blacks.

Chapter 5: Federal Policies Related to Equal Educational Opportunity

The status of Blacks in higher education in 1973, as in all other years, was a result of the combined actions of federal, state, and local governments, in addition to the actions of higher educational institutions and the private sector. The major federal response to equal educational opportunity has been the Education Amendments of 1972, especially the student assistance programs which attempted to remove financial barriers to access and distribution, as well as the Civil Rights Act of 1964 (Title VI) which attempted to remove categorical barriers to equal educational opportunity based on race.

The number of Black students participating in BEOGs, SEOGs, NDSLs, and College Work-Study programs was greater than their proportion of the college student enrollment. The number of awards to Blacks in the programs was such that the programs could not have assisted all of the Black college students from families with incomes less than $7,500. The programs may have assisted more than half of these low-income Black students enrolled in college, however, by meeting some of their financial need. In the federal student aid programs, it was found that Blacks were most likely to receive awards in College Work-Study and the Supplemental Educational Opportunity Grant Programs from 1968 to 1973. Whites during this same period tended to receive National Direct Student Loans. In the federally insured loan programs (NDSL and GSLP), Black freshmen borrowed more often than white freshmen attending the same type of institution. For individual borrowers, however, the average federal loans to white freshmen were larger, as were loans to higher-income freshmen of both races.

In 1973, Black students received 18% of the 105,000 BEOGs grants. Black BEOGs recipients equaled 12% of all Black full-time first year college students in 1972. Of all Blacks in college who applied for BEOGs for Fall 1973, 20.6% received them. The first year implementation of the Basic Educational Opportunity Grant program in 1973 was impeded by the short time in which to apply for the BEOGs (6 weeks) and the use of different applications for each federal student assistance program. In addition, the advertising of BEOGs was such that students most likely to know about it were between the ages of 16 and 21 and were enrolled in universities or were high school seniors. Two-year and four-year college students and past high school graduates were the least likely to know about BEOGs. This undoubtedly contributed to the underutilization of the new grants program by entering full-time freshmen in its first year.

Another critical problem in implementation which affected several student aid programs was the definition of dependence. It was found that personal college costs of dependent and independent Black and white students attending the same type of institution differed. The most likely explanation is the difference in the amount of financial aid the students received from public and private sources. Thus, independent whites followed by dependent Black students, who were largely females, were the most likely recipients of student aid in 1973. Conversely, the least likely students to receive aid were independent Black students, who were largely male, and dependent white students.

Enforcement of the Civil Rights Act of 1964 (Title VI) undoubtedly contributed to the increased access of Blacks to previously all-white institutions. Within states and across regions of the country, however, access of Blacks to college remained unequal, a point underscored in *Adams* v. *Richardson*. Because current enforcement

6

of Title VI does not require the routine analysis of data on educational practices and policies to determine if they adversely affect access, distribution, or persistence of Blacks and other minorities, the enforcement of Title VI has been extremely limited. Where enforcement of Title VI has been active, Black access has been facilitated.

Finally, the need for federal responsibility to facilitate access, distribution, and persistence of talented and able minorities in graduate and professional schools by removing financial barriers is in the public interest. Minorities are needed among the ranks of highly trained professionals as leaders, because of the unique understanding and sensitivity they can bring to solving this society's critical internal problems. Federal responsibility is also needed to help meet the nation's commitment to equal educational opportunity. A combination of need-based grants with a maximum of $5,000 and average $3,000, research and teaching fellowships, and cost-of-education allowance for institutions are the essential elements of such a federal effort.

Appendices

The appendices of the report include detailed tables that supplement those found in the body of the report. *Appendix A* reviews federal policies and programs affecting higher education. It also includes federal appropriations in Fiscal Year 1973 and 1974 for higher education programs, the distribution of federal student aid money to the states, and funding of state-operated student aid programs. Appendix A also includes the number of Black, white, and other students participating in the federal campus-based student aid programs in the Fiscal Years 1968 through 1970. Finally, in Appendix A the states in each U.S. Office of Education region are listed.

In *Appendix B* a survey of national data collectors is summarized. This survey studied the size and causes of discrepancies in enrollment data collected by public and private collectors. The survey found that the degree of compatibility of data from different sources was influenced by whether racial data were expressed as percents, whether identifying race was required, and whether the data were collected in the Fall or Spring semester.

In *Appendix C* data on land-grant colleges are included along with a discussion of Title III (HEA-1965) programs to aid developing institutions. Appendix C also includes the Fall 1973 enrollment in public and private two-year colleges, the number of such institutions by state, and male/female enrollment in transfer and terminal programs at two-year colleges.

Appendix D includes supplemental data on Black students in the Black graduate availability pool, and doctorates earned in Spring 1973 by race and field of study. It also includes racial data on Fall 1973 enrollment at public and private Ph.D.-granting institutions, and major fields of Black and white college students in Fall 1972. Appendix D also includes Black enrollment in selected professional and academic fields.

Appendix E includes data on health training costs and on admissions policies and practices at colleges and universities. It also reports the number of graduate and

7

professional schools requiring one or more admissions tests by graduate and professional fields. Appendix E also includes detailed tables on the patterns of financial assistance by which Black students met their college costs in Fall 1973.

Appendix F reports the supporting data used in the discussion of categorical barriers. These data are the income redistribution figures for all Blacks in the availability pool to equal the income distribution of whites in the availability pool.

Appendix G lists the major publications used and cited in this report.

CHAPTER 1

Problems of the Data On Blacks in College

INTRODUCTION

The scope and accuracy of the following analysis of the status and needs of Blacks in higher education are limited by the availability and quality of the data. This chapter presents the types of data problems that methodological differences generate, the impact of these differences on actual racial enrollment statistics, the consequences of these differences in interpreting the status of Blacks, and the immediate data needs. This discussion on the data problems precedes rather than follows the description of the status and needs of Blacks in order to caution and advise the reader adequately.

The data problems on Blacks in college are fourfold: first, the accuracy of the data, which revolves around methodological consideration; second, the errors in usage, which include delineation of the sample and selection of appropriate statistics; third, the incompatibility of current data; and fourth, the missing data.

METHODOLOGICAL CONSIDERATIONS

Any quantitative assessment of social phenomena is predicated on the assumption of reliable data. Only to the extent that the reported statistics are reliable and valid can conclusions based upon them be used to assess and revise public policy. Yet numerical estimates of what constitutes a straightforward analysis do vary. And nowhere is this problem more acute than in the area of racial statistics.

Discussions and arguments about the differences in data bases used to answer research and policy questions can in many instances be reduced to basic methodological differences in how and when the data were originally collected. It goes without saying that the methodological differences that have confused and exasperated social science researchers have been inherited by those studying the status and needs of minorities in higher education. To state that it is not a new problem, however, does nothing to diminish its disastrous consequences for public policy formulation and evaluation.

How individuals respond to items about race is influenced by their perceptions of the legal and social implications of the questions. Providing accurate counts on the number of Black students at a given institution is not simply the objective task of enumeration. It means stating unequivocally the racial mix at the institution, and being prepared, if necessary, to defend it. Institutions, therefore, like individual students, are reluctant to associate themselves with racial statistics out of concern about how the data will be used to hurt them.

The two methodological differences important in racial statistics are (1) weighting procedures; and (2) identifying race by self-report and visual examination methods.

Identifying Race

In the collection of racial enrollment data, self-reports and visual examinations of students or their photographs are often used. In self-reports, the student completes a questionnaire on a voluntary or compulsory basis, identifying his race. Depending on the timing of the questionnaire (at the end or beginning of a testing session), its appearance, and the way the question is phrased, students may or may not answer truthfully. Different national data collectors report completion rates that range from 50% to 90% on race identification items. Since racial questions on a survey are by their very nature often emotion-laden, student racial data based on self-identification are most likely to be incomplete and thus to undercount minorities. The wording of a question requesting racial self-definition and its location in a series of items on a questionnaire influence how respondents will behave. The wording of the question in such a way as to neutralize its emotional potential is one-half of the problem in racial identification items. The wording used by the College Entrance Examination Board, the American Council on Education, and other private data sources used in this report is—"How do you describe yourself?" Students may respond: Black or Negro, White or Caucasian, American Indian or Native American, and Spanish surname, Spanish-speaking, Puerto-Rican, or Mexican-American. The completion and error rates for race identification items are worse than for other items on these surveys, with the exception of family income. Moreover, it is not uncommon for students either hostile or playful to identify themselves as "Other" or "American Indian." In sum, two weaknesses inherent in racial data based on self-identification are, first, that not all students will volunteer race and, second, there is no way of knowing whether the students responded truthfully to the race item without independent verification.

The other frequently used method of collecting racial information is visual examination, by which others report racial identities using either actual inspection or photographs, student last names, and racial stereotypes. This method is used primarily by public collectors, such as the Office for Civil Rights (DHEW) surveys and the U.S. Census Bureau household surveys. The size of the error depends on the ability of the collectors to classify correctly students who do not have ethnic last names, as Spanish surname heritage people often do not, and students who do not fit the stereotypic physiognomy, as Blacks often do not. Error also depends on the decision rule being used, such as, if in doubt, classify as minority, or, if in doubt classify as white. The decision rule being used can inflate the minority figures, such as Civil Rights Law enforcement (OCR) data. The opportunity for systematic bias on the part of the persons collecting the racial data is greater in visual examination methods than in self-reports.

Weighting Procedures

For U.S. Census data, the major source of error may not be in how race is identified, but rather in how raw data are treated in weighting. Weighting is the process by which raw data from samples, such as the 50,000 households in the U.S. Census surveys and the member institutions in the American Council on Education surveys, are multiplied by a constant in order to approximate the total universe. The problem in weighting in racial statistics is the validation of the assumptions about Blacks underlying the weighting procedure. The primary assumptions are as follows:

(a) that stratification cells are based on the significant variables,

(b) that all cases within a given stratification cell are alike, and

(c) that the raw data are valid.

If the weight is too large, the resulting numbers are inflated. If the weight is too small, the numbers are deflated. In both cases, if the assumptions underlying the weighting are wrong, the weights produce erroneous results and incorrect conclusions.

The weighting procedures used by the U.S. Census, based on raw data collected from households, are adjusted by demographic stratification cells and may result in inflated college enrollment data on Blacks. Either the raw data or the stratification design or both were erroneous, producing Black enrollment figures higher than any other source. For some American Council on Education data, the question is the validity of using the type and control of institution in stratification cell design to determine Black college enrollment and degrees earned. Factors other than the type and control of the institution may be more appropriate in approximating total Black enrollment (or any other data on Blacks in higher education) from sample raw data. Institution-based stratification may also inflate Black enrollment, especially at private institutions and universities where fewer Blacks are likely to be included in the raw data.

Region, racial policy, costs, and other factors discussed throughout this report as barriers to equal educational opportunity determine Black enrollment patterns. Weighting procedures based on households or type and control of institutions are both likely to err on the side of overestimating Black figures. In addition, weighting, like all inferential statistical techniques, includes measurement error. Because the total number of Blacks in the college universe is small, samples drawn from this universe increase the probability of significant measurement error. The larger the weights, when applied to small raw data on Blacks, whether based on households or institutional data, the larger the resultant measurement error.

More research is obviously needed on the sources and solutions of errors and inconsistencies in Black enrollment data. Extensive work is especially needed on alternative stratification designs based on known patterns of Black enrollment. Sucn studies would be able to produce more appropriate weighting procedures that could be applied to sampling data on Blacks in higher education.

ERRORS OF USAGE

Even when accurate data are provided by public or private sources, conflicts and inconsistencies arise out of the way in which the data are used. Two sources of such conflicts that are noted in this report are delineation of the cohort and the choice of the statistics.

The Sample

The sample or specific cohort is often poorly described in studies about Blacks in general; higher education is no exception. In selecting Black students for studies it is far too common to find that the description of the students is missing. Such simple data as sex, age, and family income are generally not reported. Yet these factors do tend to have a significant relationship to equal educational opportunity questions. As a consequence, studies on the same topic report different findings because they may be in reality studying completely different age or sex cohorts of Black college students.

Even when the student samples are fully described and the appropriate control variable introduced, a problem may remain. This time, however, the problem is one of describing the institution in the population of interest. A definition of what is an institution of higher learning is still unresolved. The boundaries separating higher educational institutions from other post-secondary training institutions are blurred. The U.S. Office of Education's *Higher Education Directory* is rapidly becoming the definition of the universe. If an institution is listed here, it is in the higher education universe. But another office within the U.S. Office of Education publishes the *Directory of Post-Secondary Schools with Occupational Programs.* As might be expected, some institutions are listed in both directories. How such schools should be treated in national studies on higher education depends on who completes the survey and the purpose of the study. The result of this confusion is that one survey may define higher education very broadly and thus include more students and institutions, while another study may define it more narrowly and include fewer students and institutions.

The American College Testing Program (1974) survey of two-year colleges found that within junior and community colleges, all students are not in higher educational programs. At least one-half of the students in two-year colleges were in terminal vocational training rather than transfer academic programs. Yet in enrollment statistics on two-year colleges, this fact is usually obliterated. All students enrolled in two-year colleges are treated as if they were higher education students. Neither OCR nor U.S. Census surveys, for example, separate transfer from vocational students when reporting two-year college enrollment statistics. This is another possible source of inflated numbers on Black enrollment, since about one-half of all Black college students are enrolled in two-year colleges.

The broader cohort problem is the questionable external validity, as defined by Campbell and Stanley (1969), which refers to the generalizability of the findings. Unfortunately, the question of the representativeness of the sample is not raised often enough when reporting research on Blacks in higher education. This tends to be true regardless of whether the sample includes only Black students in Black colleges, Black students in public universities, or all full-time Black students. The seemingly irresistible tendency is to over-generalize from the actual data for all institutions and programs. The equally irresistible tendency seems to be to accept the over-generalizations as if they were in fact supported by the data.

Selecting Appropriate Statistics

How the status of Blacks in higher education is assessed is a direct function of the statistical yardstick used. Confusion over which denominator to use to calculate even a simple percent is a recurring problem even if the question seems clear. If one asks—What is the percent of Black students age 18 to 34 enrolled full-time in college in 1970?—the denominator could be (a) *all Blacks* age 18 to 34 in the United States, or (b) *all full-time* college students age 18 to 34. Although the answer is (a), both percents are obviously mathematically correct, but conceptually different.

Another problem in statistical techniques is the abuse of sampling statistics. All sampling statistics contain standard sampling and random errors which together explain variances in repeated measures of the same event. In sample research on Blacks in higher education, as in all sample research, there is a standard error embedded in the obtained statistics. The size of the standard error varies as a function of the number of cases in the sample compared with the size of the universe.

Because Blacks in higher education constitute a relatively small universe from which to sample, especially if a stratification design is used, there will be higher error than in similar samples of the vastly more numerous white students. In reporting findings based on samples of Black students, the standard errors are often omitted. The standard errors, however, are critical to the interpretation of such findings because they indicate the amount of reliance that can be placed on the findings. This is a problem especially for data derived from the U.S. Census survey of 50,000 households. The standard error increases and the data become less reliable with each refinement. Consequently, October 1973 Census data on Black student college enrollment by year in school are less reliable than total Black enrollment. And, Black student college enrollment by sex *and* year is less reliable than Black student enrollment by year in school *only*.

INCOMPATIBILITY OF THE DATA ON BLACKS IN COLLEGE

The various sources of information on higher education enrollment and attainment used in this report present differing statistics on Blacks which are not necessarily inconsistent but are rarely compatible. The Office for Civil Rights (OCR) of the Department of Health, Education, and Welfare and the U.S. Census Bureau are the primary public national data collectors of racial statistics on college enrollment used in this report. These two sources differ not only in the statistics they report, but also in their methods of collecting and presenting data. As a result, the data from different collectors reported at different points within this report are not always comparable or consistent. The reader must pay careful attention to variances in the details of the data in this report; these include the age range, full-time vs. part-time vs. total enrollment, year in school, and type of institution.

The incompatibility and inconsistencies in the data are obviously not limited to public sources. Private sources used in this report, such as the American Council on Education, the College Entrance Examination Board, Educational Testing Service, the National Scholarship Service and Fund for Negro Students, the American College Testing Program, and professional associations, also give inconsistent and often incompatible figures because the private collectors often use only member institutions or other samples of convenience in their surveys. These private sources generally do not collect as extensively or as regularly as the public collectors, with the notable exception of the freshmen surveys of the American Council on Education.

An example of the size of the discrepancies in even seemingly simple racial enrollment statistics is given in Table 1-1, using 1970 and 1972 enrollment data provided by the Office for Civil Rights (DHEW) and the U.S. Census Bureau. The OCR data are from institutions receiving federal assistance who completed and returned their survey instruments as requested. Two different U.S. Census surveys reported: U.S. Census survey (1) reported college enrollment based on a 15% sample of all people age 16 to 49 in 1970; U.S. Census survey (2) reported college enrollment based on a 15% sample of people age 34 years old and younger in the 1970 census and 50,000 household members in this age range in 1972.

In 1970, OCR, which did not include all colleges or part-time students, reported that there were 365,929 Black students enrolled full-time in undergraduate, graduate, and professional schools receiving federal assistance. In 1970, U.S. Census survey (1) reported that there were 457,426 Black students (full-time and part-time) in college between the ages of 16 and 49. U.S. Census survey (2) reported that in 1970, there were 430,747 Black students (full-time and part-time) in college age 34 years old and younger.

In 1972, OCR reported an increase of 128,731 Black students (or 494,000). In 1972, U.S. Census survey (2) reported 727,000 Black students age 34 and younger in college, an increase of 296,253 over the same age group in 1970. (U.S. Census survey (1) did not report Black student college enrollment.)

In absolute numbers, the differences in Black enrollment between OCR and U.S. Census (1) and (2) data in 1970 were 91,497 and 64,818 respectively. The difference in Black enrollment between OCR and the only Census survey in 1972 was 232,340 Black students. The consequence of these differences in assessing the status of Blacks is that if OCR data are used, there has been a moderate increase in Black college enrollment between 1970 and 1972. But, if Census data are used, Black enrollment

TABLE 1-1 Total and percent Black Enrollment in Fall 1970 and Fall 1972 as Reported by U.S. Office for Civil Rights (DHEW) and U.S. Census.

Source	Year 1970	Year 1972	Increase in Enrollment
BLACK STUDENT ENROLLMENT			
Office for Civil Rights	365,929	494,660	128,731
U.S. Census[1]	457,626	—	—
U.S. Census[2]	430,747	727,000	296,253
BLACK PERCENT OF TOTAL ENROLLMENT			
Office for Civil Rights	6.7%	8.1%	—
U.S. Census[1]	6.2½	—	—
U.S. Census[2]	6.2%	8.7%	—
TOTAL STUDENT ENROLLMENT			
Office for Civil Rights	5,477,772	6,128,746	650,974
U.S. Census[1]	7,325.778	9,096,000	1,770,222
U.S. Census[2]	6,966,033	8,313,000	1,346,967

SOURCES: U.S. Office for Civil Rights, *Racial and Ethnic Enrollment Data From Institutions of Higher Education, Fall 1970*, p. 205 and U.S. Census, *School Enrollment*, Tables 3 and 10. U.S. Office for Civil Rights, *Racial and Ethnic Enrollment Data From Institutions of Higher Education, Fall 1972*, p. 125, and U.S. Census, *Social and Economic Characteristics of Students. October 1972*, Tables 2 and 16.

[1] Reports college enrollment of people age 16 to 49 based on 15% sample in 1970.

[2] Reports college enrollment of people age 34 and younger based on 15% sample in 1970, and 50,000 households in 1972.

has increased by over one-quarter of a million (296,253) Black college students between 1970 and 1972.

In the appendix of this report the results of a special study by the Institute for the Study of Educational Policy (Abramowitz, 1975) on discrepancies in enrollment statistics are reported. What was found in that study is also found in Table 1-1 above. When Black enrollment is expressed as a percent of the total enrollment, regardless of methodological differences, the discrepancies are reduced. For example, OCR reported that in 1970 Blacks were 6.7% of the students enrolled, while both Census surveys found Blacks to be 6.2% of the enrollment. In 1972, OCR reported Blacks as 8.1% of the students enrolled, and Census reported them to be 8.7%. The factors that contribute to the discrepancies in Black enrollment, therefore, also operate on total college enrollment. Thus, expressing Blacks as a percent of that total enrollment reduces but does not eliminate the difference in the enrollment statistics from different sources.

The U.S. Census and the Office for Civil Rights differ not only in the enrollment figures they report and data collection methods, but also in survey purpose. Respondents to the Office for Civil Rights surveys are college administrators who must be prepared to defend their minority enrollment successfully or risk the possible loss of federal funds. For them, the process of reporting minority enrollment is not innocuous. OCR survey data are most likely to err on the side of inflating Black enrollment out of the desire for institutions to report the highest possible number of minorities on campus.

Respondents in the U.S. Census surveys of 50,000 households are volunteers for whom participating in the survey does not have significant direct consequences. These surveys are most likely to inflate Black enrollment through weighting assumptions, errors in racial classification, and through the desire of household members, especially low-income families, to exaggerate their educational attainment in order to impress favorably the interviewer questioning them.

The point to be stressed here is that inconsistencies and incompatibilities of the current data place severe limitations on our assessment of the status of Blacks in higher education. Data from different sources cannot be compared with each other or used interchangeably. Data from sources such as the U.S. Census give the most optimistic picture possible of the status of Blacks, while data from private sources tend to give an incomplete picture of Blacks in higher education. Because of these data limitations there is the need to augment available data with more complete information on Blacks and other minorities in higher education.

MISSING DATA

Since national racial statistics on higher education are scarce, the impact of proposed higher education policies on the access, distribution, and persistence of Blacks cannot be accurately measured as part of the policy formulation process. Higher education policy and administrative decisions are often made without the benefit of needed quantitative data. The unfortunate outcome of this lack of statistics is that policies designed to facilitate equal opportunity may not be able to do so because of miscalculations of the status and needs of the minority students.

The minimal general racial information needed from all higher education institutions is not available. These data include (a) part-time and full-time enrollment by subject field and grade levels, and (b) associate, baccalaureate, masters, and professional degrees conferred by subject field and citizenship. (Doctorates earned by race, sex, and citizenship are collected annually by the National Research Council, beginning in Spring 1973.)

At present, the Higher Education General Information Survey (HEGIS) of the National Center for Education Statistics (USOE) does collect from higher educational institutions a wide range of annual information including fall enrollment and degrees earned by sex and subject field, but not by race. These data provide basic general information on the status of males and females in higher education, but no information on minority groups. Some racial enrollment data are collected by the Office for Civil Rights (DHEW) biannually as part of its enforcement of Title VI of the Civil Rights Act of 1964, and by the U.S. Census Bureau through the 50,000 household sample surveys.

These data are useful, but as we have seen, they are also incompatible and incomplete. We do know how many Black students were enrolled in either federally assisted institutions or at certain age ranges. We do not know from these national data sources the degrees earned by Blacks, or undergraduate, graduate, and professional school enrollment of Blacks in all colleges and universities. We also do not know Black persistence, that is, the college dropout rates of Black students or transfers of Blacks from institution to institution or department to department.

These missing data are not collected at the state level either. The Institute for the Study of Educational Policy in 1974 conducted a survey of state commissions of higher education. The purpose of the survey was to determine the amount of information state commissions collected from public and private institutions on racial enrollment within the state. Using Fall 1973 enrollment, the state commissions were asked to report Fall enrollment by racial group and degrees earned. Whether or not a state could provide racial statistics was important, because it indicated the existence of a management information system that included racial enrollment. As can be seen in Table 1-2, only a small number of the state commissions were able to provide either enrollment or degrees earned data on public and private undergraduate, graduate, and professional institutions within their states. Over one-half of the states were able to provide such data for public colleges only. However, only four states were able to provide enrollment data at all public and private institutions within their states—Arkansas, North Dakota, Illinois, and Louisiana. Only South Dakota was also able to indicate the number of degrees awarded by race in Spring 1974 in the whole state. The other states had either not yet compiled such information or did not plan to do so.

State commissions unable to provide the racial statistics did not conduct independent data collection of all higher educational institutions within the state. A common reason given by state commissions for not being able to provide racial statistics on Fall 1973 enrollment was that the state commissions relied upon the Office for Civil Rights surveys. And, since the OCR survey was not administered in 1973, they did not have access to racial enrollment data. (All state commissions responding to the questionnaire could, however, provide total enrollment and enrollment by sex, undoubtedly using copies of the HEGIS survey filed with them.)

Thus, few state commissions carried on independent data collection. They were more likely to rely on data collected by federal surveys. The effectiveness of the state role in access, distribution, and persistence of Blacks and other minorities in higher education depends in part on the availability of annual statewide information on racial enrollment, dropouts, and degrees conferred by public and private institutions. But as the data in Table 1-2 indicate, few states are able to effectively assume this role based on their current access to and reporting of racial statistics in higher education.

Data on student characteristics are important for policy formulation and evaluation. These data are the bases for selection criteria for federal financial aid programs to facilitate equal educational opportunity. Financial aid policies are tied to such student characteristics as the family's expected contribution to college education of its members, the type and cost of institution the individual students attend, and marital status and major subject area of students. In addition, the racial impact of proposed changes in financial aid policies are not now possible because a national data base does not exist. At present, policy makers and researchers must rely upon a variety of data bases generated from different public and private sources for different purposes and producing often incompatible data, in order to answer pressing policy questions.

TABLE 1-2. Availability of Racial Data on Fall 1973 Enrollment
and Degrees Earned by 53 State Commissions of Higher Education.[1]

Number of States				
Data Requested	Total	Provided Full Data	Not Provided Full Data	No Response
Entering fall enrollment in 1973	53	4	35	14
Degrees earned in Spring 1974	53	1	38	14

SOURCE: Institute for the Study of Educational Policy Staff, Howard University (1975).

[1]Includes Guam, Virgin Islands, and District of Columbia.

SUMMARY

The problems of data on Blacks in higher education are large. The sources of the problems are fourfold: methodological differences, usage errors, incompatibility of data, and missing data. In this report the available data have been pulled together and fit into the picture of Blacks in college. But because of the data problems discussed in this chapter, the picture is incomplete and possibly distorted.

Access, Distribution, and Persistence of Blacks in College

INTRODUCTION

Equal educational opportunity embodies three concepts—access, distribution, and persistence. In this chapter and the one that follows, these distinct but related concepts are used to assess the status and needs of Blacks in higher education in the 1973-74 academic year. Each concept is a measure of equal educational opportunity, but from a different perspective. All three concepts can be applied to other groups of students as well.

Access means that Black students have the opportunity to enroll in undergraduate, graduate, or professional schools. Distribution refers to choice, the opportunity for Black students to enter different types of institutions and fields of study. And persistence refers to the opportunity to remain in college and complete their training in a timely fashion. In order to have equal educational opportunity, a Black student must not just have the opportunity to enroll in college, but a choice of institutions and programs, and a chance to complete the training once begun.

THE 1973-74 ACADEMIC YEAR

Since the late 1940's, as the number of high school graduates and the number of people with a college education has risen, the median educational attainment of Blacks and whites has also risen. In absolute numbers there have been gains in equal educational opportunities for Blacks, especially following the death of Dr. Martin Luther King in 1968, when affirmative action programs in many colleges were accelerated.

Although there is still a disparity between the educational attainment of Blacks and whites, the recent history of Black educational status reflects progress. The number of

Blacks with one or more years of college has risen from an estimated 414,000 (non-whites) in 1950 to an estimated 779,000 (non-whites) in 1960, to an estimated 1,655,983 in 1970, to an estimated 1,684,000 in 1974 (U.S. Census). The greatest gains in Black college attainment were made between 1960 and 1970, a period which combined an increase in federal civil rights and higher education legislation with an increase in Black student protest activities.

The focal point of this analysis of the status of Blacks in higher education is the 1973-74 academic year. In Fall 1973, unlike previous years, there was a sharp decline in the college enrollment of Blacks. Based on U.S. Census estimates, which tend to be higher than all other estimates of college enrollment, there were 522,000 Blacks age 16 to 34 enrolled in college in 1970. This figure increased to 680,000 in 1971, 727,000 in 1972, and dropped to 684,000 in 1973. In Fall 1974, however, Black enrollment, age 18 to 34, increased to 814,000, which, according to the U.S. Census estimates, was 19% over Fall 1973. In Figure 2-1 below, the annual percent changes in Black and total college enrollment based on these U.S. Census data are illustrated. In all academic years except 1973, the percent increase in Black enrollment over the previous year was greater than that of the total college enrollment.

In Fall 1973, both total and Black enrollment dropped; in fact, the estimated Black enrollment in Fall 1973 was only 4,000 students higher than the Black 1971 level. This decline in the total and Black college enrollment in the 1973-74 academic year was in part determined by the general economic and political events of the period and the specific events directly related to higher education. This was the first full academic year following the end of American military involvement in Southeast Asia. Twenty percent of all those killed in Southeast Asia were Blacks, and this reduced the Black college age population by approximately 11,000 men (ETS, 1974). It was the period of a severe domestic crisis, when the integrity of both the elected President and Vice President was questioned. And it was a time of economic crises and confrontations that resulted in an annual inflation rate in 1974 of 14.4%, an overall annual unemployment of Blacks in the labor force of over 10% and almost 6% for whites. The annual unemployment rate for Black youths age 16 to 19 years was 31.4% in 1973, in comparison to a rate of 12.6% for white youths (U.S. Census, 1974).

These political and economic events drew national attention away from civil rights and higher education issues, reduced the financial resources available to Black and low-income families for higher education expenses, and raised doubts about the economic benefits of a college education, in general, and a liberal arts education, in particular.

For Blacks, the 1973-74 academic year was a time of reduced campus protests and activities for equal educational opportunity in higher education. As student civil rights activity declined, the opposition to affirmative action in faculty hiring and preferential admissions policies for disadvantaged students increased. Competition for the same faculty and student positions by Black and all other students, including white females, exacerbated the difficulties in achieving racial integration on college campuses.

This was also the first academic year in which accredited trade and proprietary institutions became eligible for federal student aid programs. The positive result of

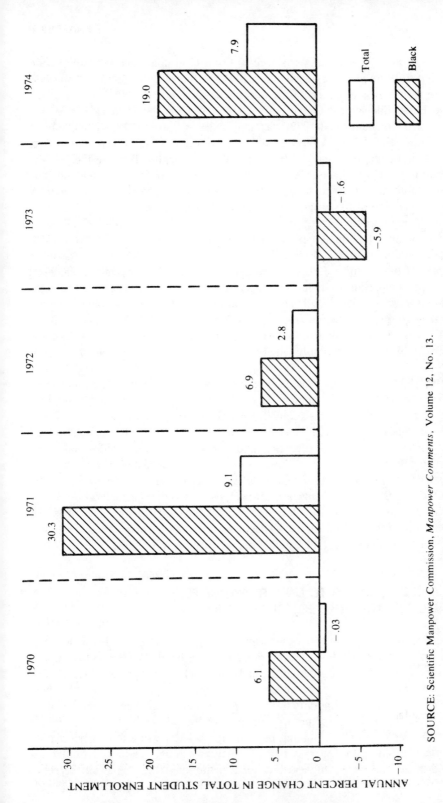

SOURCE: Scientific Manpower Commission, *Manpower Comments*, Volume 12, No. 13.

FIGURE 2-1. Percent Change in Total College Enrollment by Race, Fall 1970 Through 1974.

this was to provide financial assistance to students in non-higher-education post-secondary institutions. The negative result was to increase the number of students eligible for funds without increasing the funds available.

The Basic Educational Opportunity Grants (BEOGs), enacted as part of the Educational Amendments tf 1972, was first funded in Spring 1973, when Congress finally appropriated Fiscal Year (FY) 1973 funds for higher education programs. The 1973-74 academic year was the first year of this program. Because the BEOGs program in the 1973-74 school year was limited to full-time entering students, and because of uncertainty of funding and the abbreviated application period (about six weeks), operation of the program in its first year was hampered.

Federal appropriations for student assistance programs totaled $847.6 million in FY 1973 or 66% of all funds appropriated for higher education that year. In FY 1974, $1,266.24 million or 71% of all higher education funds went to student assistance programs. Congressional debate on appropriations for the Basic and Supplemental Educational Opportunity Grants programs brought into focus a struggle between the institution-based SEOGs program and student-based BEOGs program approaches to federal aid programs (Cheit, 1973). The largest increase in FY 1974 appropriations over FY 1973 was in the student-based BEOGs, reversing the previous year's funding pattern in which the institution-based SEOGs program received the greater appropriation.

In the 1973-74 academic year, the coordination of federal and state aid programs for higher education was important, not only to improve the financial stability of colleges, but also to insure the survival of certain programs and services. According to the studies of Cheit (1971 and 1973) and Wynn (1974), higher educational institutions in the early 1970's had begun to sacrifice educational quality considerations to the need for financial stability. Institutions in financial difficulty modified or abandoned previously held preferences for smaller class sizes, multiple program and course offerings, tenure systems, and off-campus models of higher education. While institutions with financial difficulties had stabilized in the 1973-74 academic year, a consequence of their action has been a decrease in the number and scope of programs designed to facilitate equal educational opportunity for minorities.

ACCESS OF BLACKS TO UNDERGRADUATE, GRADUATE, AND PROFESSIONAL SCHOOLS

Relative to whites and to their own aspirations, Blacks have clearly not achieved full access. White high school students remained more likely than Blacks to complete high school, enroll in college, graduate, and enter graduate and professional schools. This section on access reports undergraduate, graduate, and professional school enrollment statistics on Blacks in the 1973-74 academic year. The size of the Black undergraduate, graduate and professional availability pools are also discussed.

The former refers to all training beyond high school, while the latter refers to collegiate training. In October 1973, the overwhelming majority of all post-secondary students were in higher educational institutions rather than in other types of training, such as trade and technical schools, according to the U.S. Census. (See Table 2-1). As age increased, the proportion of Black and white students in trade schools also increased, with the exception of Blacks in their early thirties. However, among young Blacks (age 16 to 19), there was a greater tendency to enter trade and technical schools while their white counterparts entered colleges and universities.

TABLE 2-1 Percentages of All Post-Secondary Students in Higher Education and Other Post-Secondary Institutions by Race and Sex, October 1973.

	Black		White	
	Male	*Female*	*Male*	*Female*
Total All Ages	391,000	397,000	4,821,000	3,839,000
Higher Education	80.9	79.1	84.2	85.4
Other Post-secondary	19.1	20.9	15.8	14.6
Total	100.0	100.0	100.0	100.0
16-17 Year Olds				
Higher Education	82.7	83.3	90.2	85.0
Other Post-secondary	17.3	16.7	9.8	15.0
Total	100.0	100.0	100.0	100.0
18-19 Year Olds				
Higher Education	89.7	79.1	89.4	84.7
Other Post-secondary	10.3	20.9	10.6	15.3
Total	100.0	100.0	100.0	100.0
20-21 Year Olds				
Higher Education	97.4	88.7	92.1	91.0
Other Post-secondary	2.6	11.3	7.9	9.0
Total	100.0	100.0	100.0	100.0
22-24 Year Olds				
Higher Education	70.3	77.3	85.6	86.9
Other Post-secondary	29.7	22.7	14.4	13.1
Total	100.0	100.0	100.0	100.0
25-29 Year Olds				
Higher Education	59.4	76.6	81.5	85.1
Other Post-secondary	40.6	23.4	18.5	14.9
Total	100.0	100.0	100.0	100.0
30-34 Year Olds				
Higher Education	93.8	78.6	78.2	81.2
Other Post-secondary	6.2	21.4	21.8	18.8
Total	100.0	100.0	100.0	100.0
35+ Year Olds				
Higher Education	74.4	73.9	63.0	77.0
Other Post-secondary	25.6	26.1	37.0	23.0
Total	100.0	100.0	100.0	100.0

SOURCE: U.S. Census, (1975), unpublished data.

This report addresses itself to the status of Blacks in higher education, but the distinction must be made between post-secondary education and higher education.

Black Enrollment in Undergraduate School: Fall 1973

The U.S. Census is the primary source of data used here because these data are the most complete for Fall 1973 enrollment. Because of the methods of collection and analysis used, the U.S. Census data give the most optimistic picture of Black enrollment. (See discussion in Chapter 1.) The Census data, then, should be treated as high estimates.

In 1973, as in 1972, the proportional Black college enrollment was approximately 8.0%. According to U.S. Census data reported by the Scientific Manpower Commission, even with the decline in total and Black enrollment, the racial composition of the college student body remained about 8% Black, 90% white, and 2% other. (See Table 2-2.)

A limitation of U.S. Census data on college enrollment is that we cannot separate undergraduate from graduate and professional school enrollment. That is, some students in the fifth and sixth years of college are in undergraduate school. The year in school simply refers to the number of academic years of training, not class standing. However, according to Census data for the 1973-74 academic year, 83% of the Blacks enrolled were in their first four years of college. The remaining Black students (17%) were either in their fifth or sixth year of undergraduate school, or in graduate or professional schools. The U.S. Census includes two-year college enrollments of

TABLE 2-2. Total college enrollment of Blacks in all public and private institutions, 1970 through 1974.

Black Students	(in thousands)				
	1970	1971	1972	1973	1974
At public institutions	422	532	582	537	659
At private institutions	100	148	145	147	155
Men	253	363	384	358	422
Women	269	317	343	326	392
Total	522	680	727	684	814
12-month change	+6.1%	+30.3%	+6.9%	-5.9%	+19.0%
All Races					
At public institutions	5,699	6,271	6,337	6,224	6,905
At private institutions	1,714	1,816	1,976	1,955	1,922
Men	4,401	4,850	4,853	4,677	4,926
Women	3,013	3,236	3,460	3,502	3,901
Full-time	5,763	6,199	6,309	6,083	6,345
Percent Full-time	77.7%	76.7%	75.9%	74.4%	71.9%
Part-time	1,650	1,883	1,999	2,090	2,476
Total	7,413	8,087	8,313	8,179	8,827
12-month change	-0.3%	+9.1%	+2.8%	-1.6%	+7.9%

SOURCE: Scientific Manpower Commission, *Manpower Comments*, Vol. 12, No. 3, p. 17.

students in degree programs. As is discussed below, however, some non-degree students may also have been counted in these figures.

Table 2-3 reports the total, Black, white, and other student enrollment (age 16 to 34) by year in college. According to the U.S. Census, of the 6,789,000 college students enrolled in the first four years of college, 9% were Black, 89% white, and 2% other ethnic groups. Of the 1,376,000 students in the fifth year and beyond, 7% were Black, 95% were white and 4% other. Regardless of race, about three-fourths of

TABLE 2-3. Estimated college enrollment of students 16 to 34 years old by year in school, full-time enrollment, and race, October 1973.

Year in School	*(in thousands)*			
	Total	*Black*	*White*	*Other*
All Years	8,173	684	7,317	172
First Year	2,276	206	2,025	45
Second Year	1,807	168	1,606	33
Third Year	1,476	142	1,306	28
Fourth Year	1,230	108	1,090	32
Fifth Year	694	30	650	14
Sixth Year and Beyond	691	31	640	20
	Percent Enrolled			
All Years	100.0	8.4	89.5	2.1
First Year	100.0	9.1	89.0	1.9
Second Year	100.0	9.3	88.9	1.8
Third Year	100.0	9.6	88.5	1.9
Fourth Year	100.0	8.8	88.6	2.6
Fifth Year	100.0	4.3	93.7	2.0
Sixth Year and Beyond	100.0	4.5	92.6	2.9
	Percent Within Race			
All Years	100.0	100.0	100.0	100.0
First Year	27.8	30.1	27.7	26.2
Second Year	22.1	24.6	21.9	19.2
Third Year	18.1	20.8	17.8	16.3
Fourth Year	15.0	15.8	14.9	18.6
Fifth Year	8.5	4.4	8.9	8.1
Sixth Year and Beyond	8.5	4.5	8.7	11.6
	Percent Enrolled Full-Time Within Race			
All Years	74.4	78.3	73.8	*
First Year	76.8	75.7	76.6	*
Second Year	79.7	82.8	79.2	*
Third Year	83.8	81.3	83.7	*
Fourth Year	83.7	80.9	84.3	*
Fifth Year	41.5	*	38.8	*
Sixth Year and Beyond	49.6	*	49.2	*

SOURCE: U.S. Census, *Social and Economic Characteristics of Students, October 1973*, Table 5.

* Base less than 75,000.

all college students were enrolled full-time. The percent of Black and white college students enrolled full-time, however, was lower for first-year than subsequent year students, with the exception of those enrolled in the fifth or sixth year of college.

Between the ages of 16 and 34, there were an estimated 5,346,400 whites in the non-institutional population and an estimated 717,200 Blacks. As can be seen from Table 2-4 and Figure 2-2, a smaller proportion of Blacks than whites in each age group enrolled in Fall 1973, with the exception of students between the ages of 30 and 34. In the traditional college entry age range of 18 to 19 years old, 34.8% of all whites, but only 19.4% of all Blacks, were enrolled in college in October 1973. For both whites and Blacks, males were more likely than females to be enrolled in college that year. Differences in college attendance between males and females of the same race were significantly smaller than the differences between Blacks and whites.

Since all people in an age group were not eligible for college because of high school non-completion, the assessment of Black access to undergraduate school is done in terms of the undergraduate availability pool. The undergraduate availability pool refers to the U.S. citizens eligible for consideration for admission into two-year public and private colleges and universities in the United States. The principle criterion of eligibility was high school graduation or its equivalent. Because a substantially larger proportion of Black than of white males and females, regardless of age, did not complete high school (and were consequently not eligible for consideration for college), the undergraduate availability pool of Blacks was much more limited than that of whites. Labeling all those without high school diplomas who were not enrolled in school in October 1973 as dropouts may be a misnomer because some may eventually complete high school. But they were not considered part of the undergraduate availability pool in the 1973-74 school year.

TABLE 2-4. Percent of age group between 16 and 34 years old, enrolled full- and part-time in college by race and sex, October 1973.

	Whites Enrolled			Blacks Enrolled		
Age	Male	Female	Total	Male	Female	Total
	(2,613,400)	(2,733,000)	(5,346,400)	(329,800)	(385,400)	(715,200)
16 to 17	3.1	3.9	3.5	1.2	5.4	3.3
18 to 19	36.7	32.9	34.8	20.6	18.4	19.4
20 to 21	34.8	26.3	30.4	24.1	15.2	19.2
22 to 24	19.1	9.7	14.3	13.2	9.3	11.1
25 to 29	11.9	5.3	8.5	6.9	4.6	5.6
30 to 34	5.2	3.4	4.3	6.1	3.2	4.4

SOURCE: U.S. Census, (1974), *Social and Economic Characteristics of Students, October 1973,* Table 1.

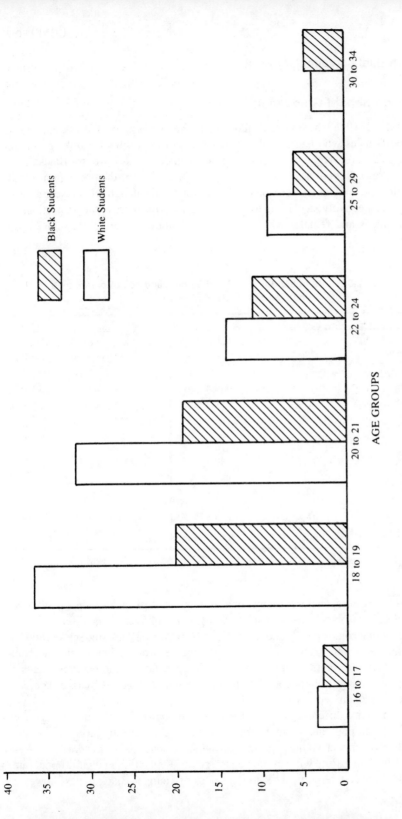

SOURCE: U.S. Census, *Social and Economic Characteristics of Students, October 1973*, Table 1.

FIGURE 2-2. Percent of Age Groups Enrolled in College by Race, October 1973.

Undergraduate Availability Pool

Black High School Graduation

As of March 1973, there were differences in the proportions of Black and white males and females who had completed four years of high school. Looking only at people age 25 or older, the rate of high school completion was lower for Blacks than for whites, regardless of sex. As can be seen from Table 2-5, the proportions of all white males and females who completed at least four years of high school were 32.8% and 40.7% respectively, according to the U.S. Census. In contrast, the proportions of all Black males and females with high school diplomas were 25.1% and 26.3% respectively.

TABLE 2-5. Years of school completed by race and sex of persons 25 years and older as of March 1973.

	Percent			
	White		Black	
Years Completed:	Male	Female	Male	Female
Elementary School				
0-4 years	3.9	3.4	14.9	10.7
5-7 years	7.5	6.9	15.3	14.5
8 years	11.7	11.5	10.8	9.6
High School				
1-3 years	14.8	16.5	20.9	25.2
4 years	32.8	40.7	25.2	26.3
College				
1-3 years	12.5	11.1	7.1	7.8
4 years or more	16.8	9.9	5.9	6.0
Total	100.0%	100.0%	100.0%	100.0%

SOURCE: U.S. Census, *Statistical Abstracts of the United States, 1974*, Table 187.

Some of the discrepancies in educational attainment of Black and white adults over the age of 25 years may have been due to past patterns of overt racial discrimination, and to economic conditions. Indeed, in 1973, 51.7% of the Black students enrolled in college full-time were from families in which the head of the household had completed less than four years of high school. In order to isolate the more current status of Black and white high school completion rates, recent graduations by race, age, and sex were also examined. (See Table 2-6.)

Although racial differences in high school completion increased with age, the differences in dropout rates of younger whites and Blacks were still large. (See Figure 2-3.) When older and younger groups of the same race and sex were compared, younger Black and white women showed the greatest reduction in their dropout rates over their older counterparts. The dropout rates of younger Black males, however,

TABLE 2-6. Proportion of non-high school graduates (not enrolled in school), ages 16 to 21, by race and sex, October 1973.

| | *Percent Not Completing High School* | | | | | |
| | White | | | Black | | |
Age Group	*Male*	*Female*	*Total*	*Male*	*Female*	*Total*
16 to 17 years old	8.7	9.2	9.0	10.6	10.0	10.3
18 to 19 years old	14.1	15.2	14.7	27.7	23.0	25.2
20 to 21 years old	14.2	13.2	13.7	27.1	33.1	30.4
All Groups	12.1	12.5	12.3	20.8	21.4	21.1

SOURCE: U.S. Census, *Social and Economic Characteristics of Students, October 1973*, Table 1.

showed the least resistance to change. High school completion rates varied with place of residence—whether students resided in urban, suburban, or rural communities. Table 2-7 summarizes the Black and white high school dropout rates in urban, suburban, and rural communities.

The Black undergraduate availability pool was short not only of older students (i.e., over 19 years old) but also of inner city students of all ages. The chances of being a high school dropout were twice as great or better, for Blacks as for whites. At all age levels, Black females, followed by Black males, were the most likely candidates to be high school dropouts.

The total undergraduate availability pool included all high school graduates without a baccalaureate. The relevant question was the proportion of this pool that was Black in 1973. While data on such an extensive pool were not available, it was possible to determine the size of the pool that includes high school graduates without

TABLE 2-7. Percent of High School Dropouts by Race, Age, and Place of Residence as of October 1973.

| | *(Percent of Age and Race Groups)* | | |
	White	*Black*	*Difference (White-Black)*
Inner City:			
16-17 years olds	10.7	10.1	0.6
18-19 year olds	17.1	27.1	−10.0
20-21 year olds	14.9	27.9	−13.0
Suburban:			
16-17 year olds	6.6	8.8	−2.2
18-19 year olds	12.0	20.6	−8.6
20-21 year olds	10.8	29.8	−19.0
Rural:			
16-17 year olds	10.8	11.8	−1.0
18-19 year olds	16.2	24.5	−8.3
20-21 year olds	16.4	37.6	−21.2

SOURCE: U.S. Census, *Social and Economic Characteristics of Students, October 1973*, Table 2.

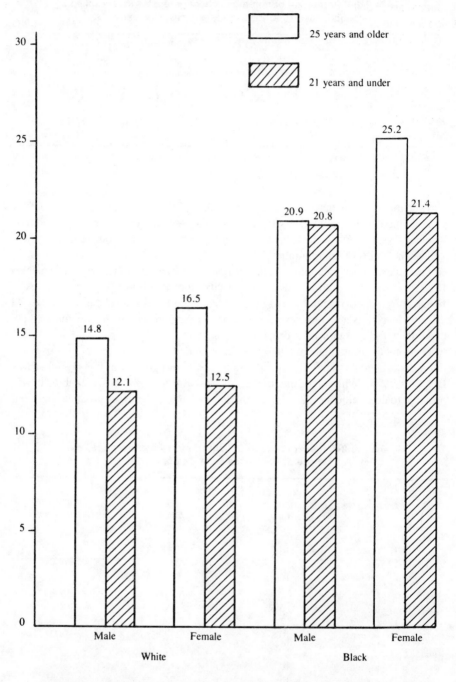

FIGURE 2-3. Comparison of High School Dropout Rates, Ages 25 and Older with 21 Years and Under, by Race and Sex, 1973.

four years of college between the ages of 16 and 34. As can be seen in Table 2-8, this pool included 34,452,000 people, of which an estimated 10.0% were Black. (A word of caution here: because of the undercounting of young Black males in census data, their representation in the pool is in all probability underestimated.) The entering freshmen pool includes all high school graduates age 16 to 34 without any college education. Blacks equalled 11.0% of this group in March 1973. (See Table 2-9.)

While at first glance this availability pool seems large and unselective, it does offer an initial referent with which to assess the status of Blacks in higher education. All people within the pool were potentially undergraduates who should be given the opportunity to attempt access to college in the 1973-74 academic year.

TABLE 2-8. Blacks as percent of undergraduate availability pool by age, March 1973.

Age	Total (In Thousands)	Percent Black
16 and 17	181	10.0
18 and 19	4,714	10.0
20 and 21	5,871	10.1
22 to 24	7,038	11.1
25 to 29	9,320	9.3
30 to 34	7,328	9.0
16 to 34	34,452	10.0

SOURCE: U.S. Census, *Educational Attainment in the United States: March 1973 and 1974*, Table 1.

TABLE 2-9. Percent Blacks in High School Graduate Availability Pool By Age, March 1973.

Age	Total (In Thousands)	Percent Black
16 and 17	164	10.4
18 and 19	3,734	11.0
20 and 21	3,160	12.4
22 to 24	4,519	12.0
25 to 29	6,675	9.4
30 to 34	5,519	9.3
16 to 34	23,771	11.0

SOURCE: U.S. Census, *Educational Attainment in the United States: March 1973 and 1974*, Table 1.

Blacks Within the Undergraduate Availability Pool

A complete description of the Black undergraduate availability pool would include the career goals, degree aspirations, ability, and financial needs of all Black high school graduates without four years of college. While such a complete description is not possible here, a more limited discussion of a self-selected proportion of the pool provides some information on a small group of Black students who wanted to go to college in 1973. (Whites and Blacks in the availability pool are contrasted with each other when comparable data are available.)

The two self-selected groups used to describe entering freshmen in the undergraduate availability pool were (a) College Entrance Examination Board Scholastic Aptitude Test applicants who voluntarily identified race on a biographical questionnaire that accompanied the SAT; and (b) Negro Scholarship Service and Fund for Negro Student (NSSFNS) survey, which was completed by minority students who went to NSSFNS for aid in securing student assistance funds or general information about college. Both sources of data are limited to recent high school graduates who voluntarily went to CEEB or NSSFNS. Therefore, general conclusions about all recent Black high school graduates or all Blacks in the undergraduate availability pool would be inappropriate based on these data.

By April, 1974, 858,111 high school students, representing 82.0% of those taking the Scholastic Aptitude Test (SAT), completed the Student Descriptive Questionnaire (SDQ) accompanying the SAT (CEEB, 1974). The SDQ was a biographical survey that was sent with SAT scores to the college designated by the students. The SDQ included an ethnic background item, which in 1974, was completed by 824,601 high school seniors, or 78.8% of those taking the SAT. While these data provided by the College Entrance Examination Board describe students interested in institutions requiring SAT scores, they obviously do not describe all Blacks in the availability pool, especially recent high school graduates planning to attend two-year colleges and non-College Board four-year institutions.

All students in the SAT pool wanted special assistance, but a greater proportion of Black than white students felt the need for it. Both Black and white high school seniors in the SAT pool expressed the need for special assistance if they enrolled in college. But a greater proportion of Black than white students felt the need for it. Blacks felt a greater need for financial assistance, while whites ranked academic assistance as their greatest need. (See Table 2-10.) The greatest need for Black students in the availability pool was for special assistance in securing part-time work.

The annual estimated parental contribution for students from white families was greater than that of students from Black families. The annual estimated average parental contributions of Black and white families in the SAT pool were $713 and $2,237 respectively. (See Table 2-11.) In addition, approximately 68% of all Black seniors in the SAT pool, compared to 21% of the white students, came from homes in which the annual expected parental contribution was under $625.

According to the Negro Scholarship Service and Fund for Negro Students (NSSFNS), of the 35,262 students who registered with them in the Spring of 1973, all but approximately 3% were Black. The distribution of minorities in NSSFNS reflected Black economic status. Almost half of the minority males who sought help

TABLE 2-10. Percent of High School Seniors Who Expressed Need For Special College Assistance By Race, 1973.

	Percent		
Types of Assistance	*Black*	*White*	*Difference (Black – White)*
Part-time work	55.5	44.4	11.1
Educ.-Voc. Counseling	34.2	46.9	−12.7
Mathematical Skills	33.6	22.5	11.1
Study Skills	30.6	26.9	3.7
Reading Skills	19.8	19.3	0.5
Writing Skills	18.9	19.7	−0.8
Personal Counseling	8.4	7.8	0.6
No. Seeking Assistance	91.9	80.9	11.0

SOURCE: College Entrance Examination Board, *College-Bound Seniors 1973-74*, Table 11; and Table 3-13 above.

TABLE 2-11. Mean Annual Estimated Parental Contribution Toward College Education By Race, 1973.

Race	*Estimated Parental Contribution*	
Black	$ 713	(n=54,567)
White	$ 2,237	(n=568,846)
Difference	$ 1,524	

SOURCE: College Entrance Examination Board, *College Bound Seniors 1973-74*, Table 20.

through NSSFNS that year were from families with gross income under $6,000 per year.

The NSSFNS data also showed a relationship between family income and aspirations of minority students. As family wealth increased, so did the desire to obtain higher college degrees and enter fields with low minority participation. Minority students in the NSSFNS pool from poorer families most often aspired to Technical Certificates, Associate Degrees, or Bachelor of Divinity or "other" degrees. The more affluent students in the pool most often aspired to advanced degrees. (See Table 2-12.)

Combining U.S. Census, CEEB, and NSSFNS data, we see that the Black proportion of the undergraduate availability pool fell at a rate from one-quarter to one-third of its potential through high school non-completion alone in 1973. The Blacks remaining in the pool included recent high school graduates with financial need larger than their white counterparts. It also included high school graduates for whom degree aspirations and choice of fields were related to family income.

TABLE 2-12. Degree Aspirations of Minority High School Students By Gross Family Income, Spring 1973.

	GROSS FAMILY INCOME					
Degree Aspirations	Under 3,000	$3,000 to 5,999	$6,000 to 7,999	$8,000 to 10,000	Above $10,000	Total*
	In Percents					
Technical Certificate	32	33	14	13	8	100% (2,095)
Associate Degree	26	36	16	12	11	100% (2,498)
Bachelors Degree	19	33	17	14	17	100% (12,801)
Masters Degree	16	29	17	15	23	100% (9,942)
Doctorate	15	27	16	15	27	100% (3,222)
M.D., D.D.S. or D.V.M.	11	25	15	16	33	100% (2,478)
LL.B. or J.D.	10	24	16	16	33	100% (1,075)
B.D. or other	30	30	14	13	13	100% (1,166)
ALL STUDENTS	19	30	16	15	20	100% (35,262)

SOURCE: NSSFNS, *Minority Youth: The Classes of 1972 and 1973*, p. 21.
*May not equal 100% due to rounding.

Access Status in Undergraduate Schools

An immediate access goal for equal educational opportunity for Blacks is parity with the undergraduate availability pool. That is, the proportion of Blacks within the availability pool should equal their proportion of the total undergraduate enrollment. As a long-range access goal, however, parity with the age group, regardless of high school completion, is desired. For the purposes of assessing access in the 1973-74 academic year, parity within the availability pool was used.

It will be recalled that the estimated Black proportion of the undergraduate availability pool, age 16 to 34, as of March 1973 was 11%. The estimated Black proportion of all entering freshmen was 10%. In October 1973, of the estimated 6,788,000 students enrolled in the first four years of college, 9.2% were Black, according to the U.S. Census. The Black proportion of first-year undergraduates enrolled in October 1973 was 9.1% of 2,276,000 college students.

Assuming a constant rate of enrollment in the first four years of college, to have achieved parity of 11% Black enrollment, the number of Blacks the first four years of college would have to be increased by 122,680 Blacks (20% more than were actually enrolled in October 1973). Assuming a constant rate of total first-year enrollment, for parity of 10% in freshmen enrollment, Blacks in the first year of college would have to be increased by 21,600 Blacks students (or 11%). (See Table 2-13.)

Comparing availability to actual college enrollment at each age level, it is clear that Black high school graduates had not achieved parity in access. Black high school graduates were underrepresented in all undergraduate schools as well as in the first year of college. Table 2-14 shows the percent of high school graduates, age 16 to 34, enrolled in college by race, October 1973, according to the U.S. Census. Between the

TABLE 2-13. Blacks Enrolled in First Four Years of College Needed To Achieve Parity, Assuming Constant Enrollment, October 1973.

First Four Years	*Number*
Black enrollment for parity (11%)	746,680
Actual Black enrollment (9.2%)	624,000
Needed for parity	122,680
First-Year Students Only	
Black enrollment for parity (10%)	227,600
Actual Black first-year enrollment (9.1%)	206,000
Needed for parity	21,600

SOURCE: U.S. Census, *Educational Attainment in the United States: March 1973 and 1974*, Table 1 and Table 2-3 preceeding.

TABLE 2-14. Percent of high school graduates age 16 to 34 enrolled in college by race, October 1973.

	In Percents		
Age	*White*	*Black*	*Difference (White-Black)*
16 to 17	57.0	63.0	–12.0
18 to 19	45.1	34.5	10.6
20 to 21	36.0	28.1	7.9
16 to 21	39.4	32.8	6.6
22 to 24	17.0	15.0	2.0
25 to 29	10.2	8.2	2.0
30 to 34	6.0	7.2	–1.2
16 years and over	19.1	17.0	2.1

SOURCE: U.S. Census, *Social and Economic Characteristics of Students, October 1973*, Table 1.

ages of 18 and 21, white high school graduates were more likely than Black high school graduates to be enrolled in college in October 1973.

Of all high school seniors under 34 in October 1972, 76.7% of the Black students and 71.5% of the white students thought they might attend college the coming academic year. Of the remaining students, approximately half of the whites and Blacks planned to enter another form of post-secondary training. (See Table 2-15.) While hopes for college attendance were shared in similar quantity by Black and white high school seniors, they were not realized in such equal proportions. Fewer Black than white high school seniors were able to fulfill their desire to enroll in college. In 1973, less than one-half of the Black high school seniors aspiring to college actually enrolled the following Fall. In contrast, two-thirds of the white high school seniors aspiring to college were able to enroll. (See Figure 2-4.)

TABLE 2-15. Percent Distribution Of Post-Secondary Plans Of Black And White High School Seniors, October 1972.

	Black	White	Difference (White-Black)
*TOTAL	100.0	100.0	—
College-Bound	76.7	71.5	5.2
Plan to attend college	43.8	45.6	−1.8
May attend college	32.9	25.9	7.0
Non-College Bound	22.1	26.7	−4.6
No school plans	10.9	14.9	−4.0
Other post-secondary training	11.2	11.8	−0.6

SOURCE: U.S. Census, *College Plans of High School Seniors, October 1972*, Table A.
*May not equal 100% due to rounding.

TABLE 2-16. Percent Of High School Graduates Who Attended College In The Same Year, 1970 to 1973 by Race.

	PERCENTS		
	Black	White	Difference (White-Black)
1973:			
Percent Enrolled	35.0	48.0	−13.0
Not Enrolled	65.0	52.0	
TOTAL	100.0	100.0	
1972:			
Percent Enrolled	44.3	49.1	−4.8
Not Enrolled	55.7	50.9	
TOTAL	100.0	100.0	
1971:			
Percent Enrolled	41.9	53.9	−12.0
Not Enrolled	58.1	46.1	
TOTAL	100.0	100.0	
1970:			
Percent Enrolled	43.7	51.7	−8.0
Not Enrolled	56.3	48.3	
TOTAL	100.0	100.0	

SOURCE: U.S. Census, *College Plans of High School Seniors, October 1972*, Table E.

Since 1970, according to the U.S. Census, the proportion of Black high school seniors who entered college in the Fall following graduation remained about 40% until 1973, when it declined to 35%. (See Table 2-16.) In contrast, the white proportion remained about 50% without a significant decline through 1973.

In addition, of all white first-year students enrolled in college in 1973, 63.5% had graduated from high school that year, but of the Black first-year students, only 50.4%

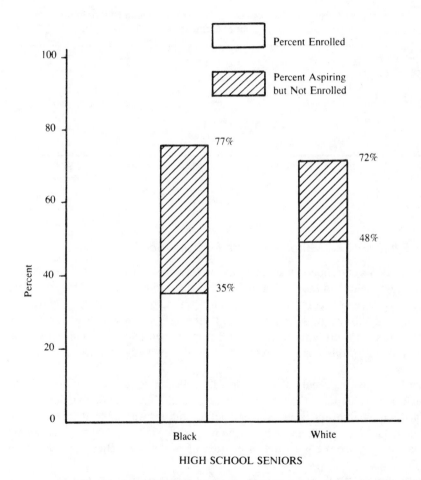

FIGURE 2-4. College Aspirations and College Enrollment of High School Seniors, by Race, October 1973.

(a difference of 13.1%) had just completed high school that year. (See Table 2-17.) One-half of all Black first-year students in 1973 had graduated from high school one or more years earlier. In fact, over one-quarter (26.6%) of all Black first-year students had graduated from high school in 1968 or earlier. Because Blacks were more likely than whites to enter undergraduate school more than one year after high school graduation, they were also more likely than whites to enroll in graduate and professional schools at older ages.

TABLE 2-17. Percent Distribution of First-Year College Students by Year of High School Graduation, 1973.

Year Graduated from High School	White	Black	Difference (Black-White)
1973	63.5	50.4	13.1
1970 to 1972	17.9	19.9	–2.0
1969	2.5	2.4	0.1
1968 or earlier	15.9	26.6	–10.7
TOTAL	100.0	100.0	

SOURCE: U.S. Census, *Social and Economic Characteristics of Students: October 1973*, Table 7.

Black Enrollment In Graduate and Professional Schools

Data on Black enrollment in graduate and professional schools in 1973 were scarce and less complete than the data on undergraduate enrollment. Data from different sources were often not comparable. The causes for the data incomparability include the following: (a) use of selective, but not necessarily representative, samples as sources of data, (b) differences in reporting part-time enrollment, (c) differences in the definition of professional degrees, (d) the different uses to which the data were put.

There was no single public or private data collector on Black enrollment in all graduate and professional schools. Therefore, a single figure estimating the number of Blacks enrolled in advanced training in all institutions was not available. (As will be seen in the following section on distribution, private professional and educational associations provide a significant proportion of the data on Black enrollment in specific fields.)

The figures on Black enrollment reported here rely primarily on data provided by the Office for Civil Rights (DHEW) and the Higher Education Panel (HEP) of the American Council on Education (ACE). OCR data were estimates of full-time Black enrollment in graduate and professional schools receiving federal assistance. HEP data were the result of a special enrollment survey of Ph.D- granting institutions that were members of ACE. Although the data on minority enrollment in graduate school from different sources included in this section were not strictly comparable, for the most part they did agree on the proportion of minorities in the total enrollment.

Status Before Fall 1973

Between the end of World War II and 1973, the number of Blacks entering graduate and professional schools increased. Between 1970 and 1973, total Black enrollment in graduate and professional schools increased from 4% to 5% in institutions receiving federal assistance, according to data provided by the Office for Civil Rights. Compared to the proportional enrollment of Blacks in undergraduate schools receiving federal assistance, the graduate and professional school enrollment of Blacks was about half. (See Figure 2-5.) Although whites were 87.6% of the full-time undergraduates in 1972, they equaled 90.8% of the total graduate and 92.2% of the total professional school enrollment in 1972. A greater percent of whites made up the graduate and professional enrollments than had made up the undergraduate enrollment. Finally, Blacks were 5.2% of the full-time students in graduate schools reporting to OCR in 1972, and 4.7% of the professional school students in institutions receiving federal assistance. (See Table 2-18.)

Fall 1973

Two data sources are used to describe the status of Blacks in advanced training in Fall 1973; these are the U.S. Census and the Higher Education Panel of the American Council on Education. The limitation of the U.S. Census data is that they report enrollment by year of school completed. And, completion of five years of college is not synonymous with graduate school, since some students take more than four years

TABLE 2-18. Full-time Enrollment in Graduate and Professional Schools Receiving Federal Assistance, by Race, Fall 1972.

	Total Enrolled			
Schools	*Black*	*White*	*Other*	*Total*
Graduate	21,371	368,812	15,910	406,093
Professional	8,555	165,459	5,435	179,449
Total	29,926	534,271	21,345	585,542
	Percent Distribution			
Graduate	5.2%	90.8%	4.0%	100.0%
Professional	4.7%	92.2%	3.1%	100.0%
Total	5.1%	91.2%	3.6%	100.0%

SOURCE: Office for Civil Rights (DHEW), *Racial and Ethnic Enrollment Data From Institutions of Higher Education, Fall 1972*, Section 4.

to earn a baccalaureate. The limitation of the HEP survey is that it reports graduate (not professional) enrollment of 154 Ph.D.-granting institutions. Thus, the HEP survey does not represent all Ph.D.-level or any M.A.-only-level graduate schools in the U.S.

Table 2-3 summarizes the Fall 1973 enrollment in the fifth year and beyond. According to the U.S. Census there were 1,385,000 students age 16 to 34 in the fifth or sixth year and beyond, in Fall 1973, of which 61,000 were Black, 1,290,000 were white, and 34,000 "other" ethnic groups. Black students were 4.3% of all students age 16 to 34 in the fifth year of college, and 4.5% of all students age 16 to 34 in the sixth year and beyond.

In 1973, the Higher Educational Panel (HEP) of the American Council on Education surveyed 154 Ph.D.-granting institutions, which equaled 53.4% of all 288 Ph.D.-granting institutions, in the United States, to determine their minority graduate

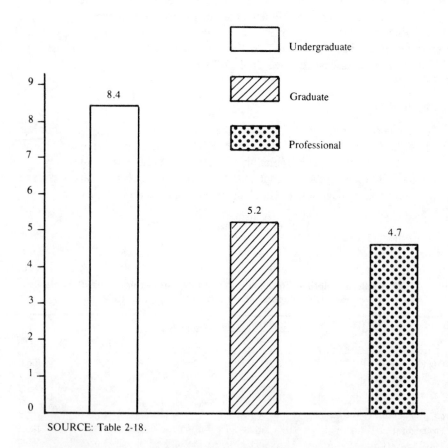

SOURCE: Table 2-18.

FIGURE 2-5. Percent of Blacks Enrolled Full-Time in Undergraduate, Graduate, and Professional Schools, Receiving Federal Assistance, Fall 1972.

enrollment. These institutions included 60% of all graduate school Fall 1973 enrollment (estimated to be 631,697 by the Council of Graduate Schools).

According to the HEP survey, Blacks equaled 4.4% of the 372,964 students enrolled in graduate schools (professional schools were omitted), while all minorities equaled 7.2%. White students accounted for 92.8% of those enrolled in HEP survey institutions. Of the approximately 16,338 Blacks enrolled in the 154 graduate Ph.D.-granting institutions, 78.1% were in public institutions, and 21.8% in private institutions.

Most Blacks in graduate schools were in masters programs. A rough estimate, using 1973 Census data, was that graduate Blacks were about 4% of the masters-level students, and 2% to 3% of the doctoral-level students in 1973. The Census data also suggested that the sex differences generally found in graduate enrollment were less pronounced among Blacks than whites. Although all women were likely to be in masters programs, Black women were better represented than other women in doctoral programs.

Blacks were only a minuscule part of the graduate (and professional) school enrollment in 1973 regardless of the degree being sought. Blacks equaled 4.5% of the total graduate student body in public Ph.D.-granting institutions, and 4.0% of the graduate students in private institutions. As the length of training increased (i.e., doctoral programs), Black enrollments dropped sharply.

HEP data reported Black enrollment in graduate programs only in Ph.D.-granting institutions. Thus, masters and doctoral-level students were combined in graduate school statistics reported, just as entering and advanced students were combined in professional school statistics reported by OCR. The data reported by these surveys were neither comparable nor complete, and obviously could not alone describe the status of Blacks in graduate and professional schools.

Graduate and Professional Availability Pool

The graduate and professional availability pool includes all holders of baccalaureate degrees. Since the size of this pool and the Black proportion within it were unknown, a complete description of the pool was not possible. However, a description of some Blacks within the pool was possible.

Blacks Within the Graduate Availability Pool

The data from the Minority Graduate Student Locator Service of the Educational Testing Service (ETS) offered a unique opportunity to describe characteristics of some Blacks in the graduate availability pool. The ETS pool was a self-selected group of Black students interested in graduate training. They were given the opportunity to complete a survey instrument that placed them on a national roster to be used by subscribing institutions. The description of the Black graduate availability pool included only those students who elected to be in the ETS files for possible recruitment by subscribing institutions in the Spring of 1974. Other Black students who were not as highly motivated, or not as well informed about the ETS Minority Student

Locator Service, were obviously not included. Consequently, the ETS data could not, and did not purport to, provide national data on the Black graduate availability pool. The data do identify characteristics of minorities that could affect the likelihood of access to graduate school.

The majority of students in the ETS pool were single and between the ages of 21 end 23. It included 991 Black males and 1,281 Black females. Most of the Blacks in the ETS pool were from either the mid-Atlantic region or the South, areas with the largest Black undergraduate enrollments. But when asked where they would like to go to graduate school, the Black students were most likely to indicate that they had no preference. Only a small fraction (10.4%) of Blacks were veterans. In addition, at the time that the students expressed an interest in graduate school, approximately three-fourths were in their senior year of college. The remainder had for the most part completed undergraduate school.

A potential barrier to access to graduate school was educational preparation of all students in the availability pool. Of the 2,258 Black students in the ETS pool, over two-thirds reported grade-point averages of B or A. In their college major and in their last two years of college, 86.1% had earned grade-point averages of B or A. (The extent to which recent GPAs reflect the recent phenomenon of grade inflation is not known. Such a phenomenon to the extent that it exists, however, would in all probability affect all students, not just Black students.)

When Black students in the ETS pool were asked their immediate objective, over two-thirds (68%) reported that they wanted a masters degree. But, when asked their long-range objectives less than three-fourths (72.4%) wanted to earn doctorate degrees. This difference in immediate and long-range objectives can be partially

TABLE 2-19. Minimum Needed Financial Support And Current Work Hours
Of The Black Graduate Availability Pool, Spring 1974.

Minimum Needed Financial Support	Male		Female		Total	
	Number	Percent	Number	Percent	Number	Percent
None	37	3.7	25	1.9	62	2.7
Loan Only	52	5.2	52	4.0	104	4.5
Tuition	211	21.3	292	22.8	503	22.1
Living Expenses	30	3.0	18	1.4	48	2.1
Tuition and Living Expenses	660	66.6	891	69.7	1,551	68.3
TOTAL	990	100.0	1,278	100.0	2,268	100.0
Current Work Hours Per Week						
None	135	13.6	183	14.3	318	14.0
1 to 5	43	4.3	69	5.4	112	4.9
6 to 10	136	13.7	251	19.6	387	17.0
11 to 20	370	37.4	526	41.2	896	39.5
Over 20	304	30.7	247	19.3	551	24.3
TOTAL	988	100.0	1,276	100.0	2,264	100.0

SOURCE: Educational Testing Service, (1975), Minority Graduate Student Locater Service, unpublished data.

explained by the financial need of these students. The level of financial support needed by Black males and females in the ETS pool is summarized in Table 2-19. Over two-thirds of students (66.6% of the males and 69.7% of the females) indicated that as a minimum they needed not only tuition, but also support in their living expenses. Only 3.7% of the Black males and 1.9% of the Black females needed no financial support in order to go to graduate school. The current work patterns of these students indicated that over one-third (39.5%) worked from 11 to 20 hours each week. Only 14% of the students did not work.

The professional careers that the Black students in the graduate availability pool in 1973-74 planned to pursue, if admitted for training, did not differ significantly from the pursuits of Blacks who came before them. The social science professions, which included Education, Social Work, Psychology, and Law, were preferred over other possible fields by 39.6% of the Black students. In addition, in the transition from undergraduate to graduate training, there was a movement away from Humanities and Physical Sciences and toward Social and Biological Sciences by Black males and females in the ETS pool. (See figures 2-6 and 2-7.) For both sexes, however, Social Science was the undergraduate major of over 70% of the Blacks in the ETS pool.

In summary, Blacks in the ETS graduate availability pool needed financial assistance, and like other Blacks, they tended to prefer advanced training in Social Sciences and careers in Education, Law, Social Work, and Psychology.

Access Status in Graduate and Professional Schools

To assess the status of Blacks in advanced training, it is important to know whether Blacks in graduate and professional schools had achieved parity. The availability pool used to establish parity includes all people who have completed undergraduate schools by Spring 1973. As was the case with the undergraduate availability pool, an estimation of size was difficult on the basis of current data. However, using U.S. Census data for the age range 20 to 34 we can estimate the number of people who completed at least four years of college. In 1973, there were an estimated 6,851,000 people age 20 to 34 who had completed at least fours years of college, according to the U.S. Census. Of this group, 5.0% were Black. (See Table 2-20.) As a rough measure

TABLE 2-20. Blacks as Percent of Graduate/Professional Availability Pool by Age, March 1973.

Age	Total (In Thousands)	Percent Black
20 and 21	89	10.11
22 to 24	1,715	4.66
25 to 29	2,886	4.36
30 to 34	2,161	5.22
20 to 34	6,851	5.00

SOURCE: U.S. Census, *Educational Attainment in the United States: March 1973 and 1974*, Table 1.

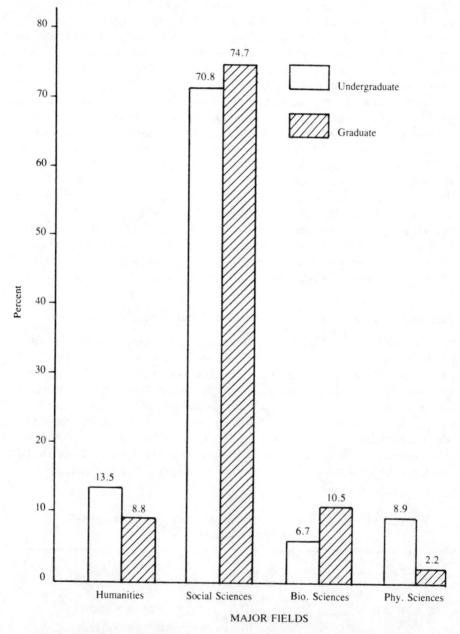

SOURCE: Educational Testing Service, Graduate Student Locater Service, unpublished data (1975).

FIGURE 2-6. Undergraduate and Proposed Graduate Majors of Black Males in the ETS Graduate Availability Pool, Spring 1974 (n=1,268).

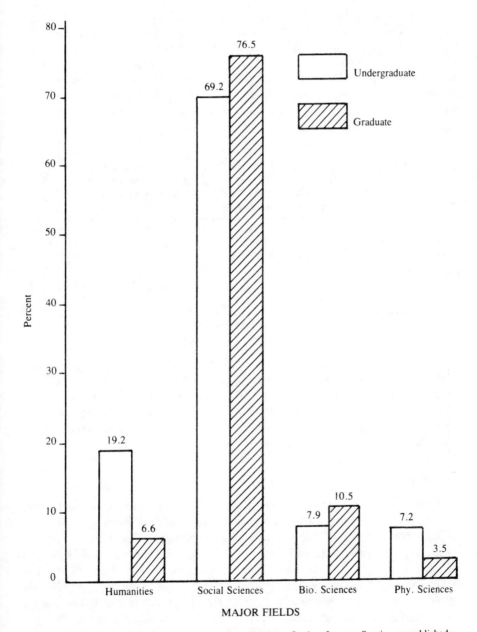

SOURCE: Educational Testing Service, Minority Graduate Student Locater Service, unpublished data (1975).

FIGURE 2-7. Undergraduate and Proposed Graduate Majors of Black Females in the ETS Graduate Availability Pool, Spring 1974 (n= 1,268).

of parity, therefore, Black enrollment in graduate and professional schools should have equaled 5.0% in Fall 1973.

Blacks were an estimated 4.4% of all students enrolled in the fifth year of college and beyond in Fall 1973. Assuming constant total enrollment, to achieve parity in the fifth year of college and beyond, Black enrollment would have to be increased by 8,250 (or 13.5% more Black students). (See Table 2-21.) Blacks were also 4.4% of all students in 154 Ph.D.-granting institutions in Fall 1973. Assuming constant total enrollment, to achieve parity within these 154 graduate schools approximately 2,238 (or 14% more) Blacks from the graduate and professional availability pool would have had to have been enrolled in 1973.

TABLE 2-21. Needed Black Graduate Enrollment in 154 Ph.D.-Granting Institutions and in 5th Year and Beyond to Achieve Parity with Graduate Availability Pool Age 20 to 34 Assuming Constant Total Enrollment, Fall 1973.

154 Ph.D.-Granting Institutions	Black Enrollment	5th Year of College and Beyond	Black Enroll- ment
Needed for parity	18,648	Needed for parity	69,250
Enrolled	16,410	Enrolled	61,000
Difference	2,238	Difference	8,250

SOURCE: Institute for the Study of Educational Policy Staff.

Because of the incompleteness in the data, the access status of Blacks in professional schools in 1973 was unknown. Based on OCR data for 1972, it would be expected that the underrepresentation of Blacks in professional schools is worse than that in graduate schools. (Using 5.0% Black enrollment as a yardstick for parity, the reader is encouraged to review the supplemental tables of enrollment in professional fields in the appendices of this report.)

Summary

"Equal educational opportunity is the chance for all students—Black and white, rich and poor, male and female—to attempt to realize their ambitions and aspirations through higher education" (Abramowitz and Abramowitz, 1975). It is evident that as a societal goal, equal educational opportunity has not been achieved in 1973. Neither all white nor all Black high school seniors, for example, who desire to enroll in college actually do so immediately following high school graduation. In 1973, less than one-half of the Black high school seniors aspiring to college actually enrolled the following Fall. In contrast, two-thirds of the white high school seniors aspiring to college actually enrolled the following Fall. At the graduate and professional level the racial differences between aspiration and enrollment increased.

High school non-completion was a major influence on Black undergraduate enrollment in 1973. High school dropout rates have been consistently overlooked in discussions of college access. But even when high school non-completion was taken into account, racial differences in college enrollment still exist.

As an immediate goal for equality of access, parity with the availability pool is desirable. To have achieved parity with the availability pool in Fall 1973, assuming constant total enrollment an additional 130,930 Black students age 16 to 34 should have been enrolled in college. At the undergraduate level, an additional 122,680 Black students (20% more) should have been in college. At the graduate level (that is, fifth year of college and beyond) an additional 8,250 Black students (13.5% more), should have been enrolled. At the 154 Ph.D.-granting institutions only 2,238 (or 14% more) Black students should have been enrolled for parity. Although the status of Blacks in higher education has improved over time, in the 1973-74 academic year equality of access had not been achieved.

DISTRIBUTION OF BLACK STUDENTS IN SCHOOLS AND PROGRAMS

Distribution refers to enrollment in a variety of higher educational institutions (college distribution) and in a variety of academic fields within an institution (field distribution). Equal distribution for Black (and all) students depends on equal choice: Black students must be able to choose where they will go to college and in which academic programs they will participate. Where there is equal educational opportunity, Black students have the opportunity to attend all colleges and to major in all subjects.

The college distribution of Blacks in 1973 is analyzed in relation to that of whites and other students attending the following types of institutions: public and private two-year and four-year colleges, and universities; land-grant colleges; and historically Black colleges. Academic field distribution in 1973 is analyzed by proposed freshmen majors, graduate majors, and professional fields for which data on Blacks were available.

College Distribution

Public and Private Colleges: Undergraduate and Graduate Enrollment

According to data provided by the U.S. Census, in October 1973, of the approximately 8 million people in higher education, white males equaled 49.7% of all persons enrolled in public and private institutions, white females 40.1%, Black males 3.9% and Black females 3.8%. (See Figure 2-8.) In addition, 60% of the estimated 322,000 Black students enrolled and 77% of the estimated 7,142,000 white students were in public undergraduate and graduate institutions. How these students were distributed among public and private colleges and universities is the focus of this discussion.

By control of the institution, the greatest number of students (75%) of all races were enrolled in public colleges. Black students were approximately equal proportions of the student bodies of all public and private colleges in 1973. Blacks were 8% of all students enrolled in public colleges and 7.4% of those in private colleges. (See Table 2-22.) By type and control, the greatest number of students of all races were enrolled in public universities. Public universities accounted for about 40% of the

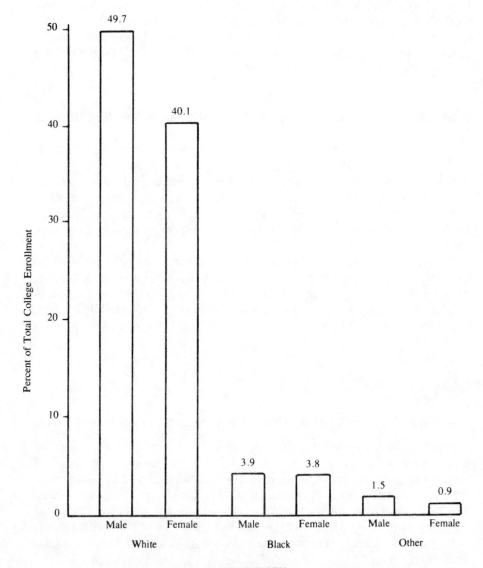

FIGURE 2-8. College Enrollment of Students 14 Years and Older by Race and Sex, October 1973.

total college enrollment (undergraduate, graduate, and professional schools combined) and about 55% of the public college enrollment. Private four-year colleges accounted for 9% of the total college enrollment in 1973.

Equal educational opportunity barriers were such that Blacks tended to be most underrepresented at large public universities where 6% of the total enrollment was Black and at private four-year colleges where 4.2% of the total enrollment was Black. At public four-year and private two-year colleges, Blacks were 13% and 11.5% of the total enrollment. Thus in public four-year colleges and private two-year colleges, the Black proportion of the total enrollment exceeded the Black proportion (9.0%) in the undergraduate and graduate availability pools combined. (See Table 2-23.)

TABLE 2-22. Total Enrollment in College and Percent Blacks Enrolled by Control and Type of Institution, October 1973.

Type of Institution	All Races (In Thousands)	% Black
PUBLIC		
University	3399	6.0
Four-Year	920	13.0
Two-Year	1839	9.2
Total Public	6158	8.0
PRIVATE		
University	889	9.2
Four-Year	763	4.2
Two-Year	131	11.5
Total Private	1783	7.2
TOTAL ENROLLED	7941	7.4

SOURCE: U.S. Census, (1975), unpublished data.

TABLE 2-23. Combined Undergraduate and Graduate Availability Pool and Percent Black, Age 18 to 34, Fall 1973.

	All Members In Pool	Black Number	Black Percent
Undergraduate Pool	34,452,000	3,376,296	10.0
Graduate Pool	6,851,000	328,000	5.0
Combined Undergraduate/ Graduate Pool	41,303,000	3,704,296	9.0

SOURCE: Tables 2-8 and 2-20.

Age Differences

In both public and private institutions, Black students were slightly older than whites, according to the U.S. Census data. In public colleges, 52.8% of the Black students in comparison to 54% of the white students were under 22 years of age. (See Tables 2-24 and 2-25.) In private colleges, 48.9% of the Black students and 60% of the white students enrolled were under 22 years old.

A possible explanation for these age differences is that the recent growth of Black and total enrollment in higher education has been in public colleges. In 1973, approximately one-half of the first-year Black students and even more first-year white students were recent high school graduates. Thus, the age differences in public and private enrollment in 1973 reflected the increased growth of public institutions, and the increased access of young Blacks, especially at the two-year college level.

TABLE 2-24. Estimated Enrollment of Black College Students by Age and Type of Institution, October 1973.

Type of Institution	Age Range				(in Thousands)			
	16-17	18-19	20-21	22-24	25-29	30-34	35+	Total
PUBLIC								
University	8	66	41	29	12	20	17	193
Four-Year	3	38	25	26	13	2	9	116
Two-Year	6	45	21	22	27	20	28	169
Total	17	149	87	77	52	42	54	478
PRIVATE								
University	2	15	16	20	16	4	8	81
Four-Year	0	4	13	3	2	4	7	33
Two-Year	4	6	3	0	2	0	0	15
Total	5	25	32	23	20	8	15	129
PUBLIC			PERCENT DISTRIBUTION					
University	4.1	34.2	21.2	15.0	6.2	10.4	8.8	100
Four-Year	2.6	32.8	21.6	22.4	11.2	1.7	7.8	100
Two-Year	3.6	26.6	12.4	13.0	16.0	11.8	16.6	100
Total	3.5	31.2	18.2	16.1	10.9	8.8	11.3	100
PRIVATE								
University	2.5	18.5	19.8	24.7	19.8	4.9	9.9	100
Four-Year	0	12.1	39.4	9.1	6.1	12.1	21.2	100
Two-Year	26.7	40.0	20.0	0	13.3	0	0	100
Total	4.7	19.4	24.8	17.8	15.5	6.2	11.6	100

SOURCE: U.S. Census, (1975), unpublished data.

TABLE 2-25. Estimated Enrollment of White College Students by Age and Type of Institution, October 1973.

Type of Institution	Age Range							(in Thousands)
	16-17	18-19	20-21	22-24	25-29	30-34	35+	Total
PUBLIC								
University	81	802	825	547	458	193	229	3136
Four-Year	21	226	218	98	95	30	76	764
Two-Year	41	563	206	188	273	142	217	1630
Total	143	1591	1249	833	826	365	522	5530
PRIVATE								
University	32	189	183	152	119	54	55	784
Four-Year	17	240	249	84	70	17	42	719
Two-Year	5	44	23	5	5	7	20	109
Total	54	473	455	241	194	78	117	1612
PUBLIC	PERCENT DISTRIBUTION							
University	2.6	25.6	26.3	17.4	14.6	6.2	7.3	100
Four-Year	2.7	29.6	28.5	12.8	12.4	3.9	9.9	100
Two-Year	2.5	34.5	12.6	11.5	16.7	8.7	13.3	100
Total	2.6	28.8	22.6	15.1	14.9	6.6	9.4	100
PRIVATE								
University	4.1	24.1	23.3	19.4	15.2	6.9	7.0	100
Four-Year	2.4	33.4	34.6	11.7	9.7	2.4	5.8	100
Two-Year	4.6	40.4	21.1	4.6	4.6	6.4	18.3	100
Total	3.3	29.3	28.2	15.0	12.0	4.8	7.3	100

SOURCE: U.S. Census, (1975), unpublished data.

Sex Differences

For Black and white students, sex differences in enrollment were small. The one exception was in private universities, where 63.4% of the whites enrolled were males. For white college students in 1973, males were more prevalent than females in all types of colleges, except private two-year. But no such consistent sex differences in enrollment were found in the college distribution of Black students. (See Tables 2-26, 2-27, and 2-28.) Within each race and sex group, about three-fourths of all college students were in public institutions. For Black and white males, 77% were in public colleges; for Black females, 80%, and for white females, 78%, were in public colleges in 1973.

(It should be noted that the college enrollment reported in Table 2-26 differs from that reported in Table 2-2 in previous section on Access. In Table 2-2 the Census data were based on the 50,000 household sample; they found that approximately 684,000 Black students were enrolled in college in 1973. The data reported in Table 2-26 were based on a smaller special follow-up survey of the same 50,000 households with family members in college. The small survey reported 608,000 Blacks in college in 1973, a difference of 76,000 Black students. The small sample of households in the follow-up survey (Table 2-26) increased the standard error and the likelihood that the reported statistics were unreliable. The data in Table 2-26 can be taken as a low

TABLE 2-26. College Enrollment of Students 16 Years and Older by Race, Sex, and Type of Institution, October 1973.

Type of Institution	All Races			White			Black		
(In Thousands)	Male	Female	Total	Male	Female	Total	Male	Female	Total
PUBLIC									
University	1819	1508	3399	1736	1380	3136	89	105	194
Four-Year	480	440	920	388	377	756	66	50	116
Two-Year	998	841	1839	887	743	1630	82	87	169
Total	3297	2789	6158	3011	2500	5522	237	242	479
PRIVATE									
University	556	333	889	497	287	784	46	36	82
Four-Year	394	369	763	377	343	720	15	17	32
Two-Year	57	74	131	48	61	109	9	6	15
Total	1007	776	1783	922	691	1613	70	59	129
TOTAL ENROLLED	4304	3565	7941	3933	3191	7135	307	301	608

SOURCE: U.S. Census, (1975) unpublished data.

TABLE 2-27. Percent Male and Female Enrolled in College by Race and Type of Institution, October 1973.

Type of INSTITUTION	White			Black *(Percent Within Race)*		
	Male	Female	Total*	Male	Female	Total*
PUBLIC						
University	56.0	44.0	100	46.0	54.1	100
Four-Year	51.0	49.0	100	57.0	43.1	100
Two-Year	54.4	45.6	100	49.0	51.4	100
Total	55.5	45.0	100	49.4	51.4	100
PRIVATE						
University	63.4	37.0	100	56.0	44.0	100
Four-Year	52.4	48.0	100	47.0	53.1	100
Two-Year	57.2	43.0	100	54.2	46.0	100
Total	57.1	43.0	100	54.2	45.7	100
ALL INSTITUTIONS						
University	57.5	43.0	100	49.0	51.0	100
Four-Year	51.4	48.5	100	55.0	45.2	100
Two-Year	54.0	46.2	100	49.5	51.0	100
TOTAL ENROLLED	55.3	45.0	100	50.5	50.0	100

SOURCE: Table 2-26.

*May not equal 100% due to rounding

estimate of Black college enrollment in 1973. The best that can be said is that total Black college enrollment in 1973 probably lay somewhere between 608,000 and 684,000 people. Percents based on data in both of these tables had greater similarity than do their absolute numbers.)

TABLE 2-28. Percent College Distribution of Black and White College Students by Sex and Type and Control of the Institution, October 1973.

Type of Institution	(In Thousands)	PERCENT OF TOTAL					
		White			Black		
		Male	Female	Total	Male	Female	Total
PUBLIC							
University	3,399	51.0	40.6	92.3	2.6	3.1	5.7
Four-Year	920	42.2	41.0	82.2	7.2	5.4	12.6
Two-Year	1,839	48.2	40.4	88.6	4.5	4.7	9.2
Total	6,158	49.2	40.6	89.8	3.8	3.9	7.8
PRIVATE							
University	889	55.9	32.3	88.2	5.2	4.0	9.2
Four-Year	763	49.4	45.0	94.4	2.0	2.2	4.2
Two-Year	131	36.6	46.6	83.2	6.9	4.6	11.5
Total	1,783	51.7	38.8	90.5	3.9	3.3	7.2
TOTAL ENROLLED	7,941	48.4	39.1	87.5	3.8	3.7	7.4

SOURCE: U.S. Census, (1975), unpublished data.

Land-Grant Colleges

Although the focus of this report is the 1973-74 academic year, the enrollment data on land-grant colleges are based on undergraduate figures for Fall 1972. The data are, therefore, not comparable with other enrollment data included in this section. But, nevertheless, they provide some valuable information on the college distribution of Black undergraduates in land-grant colleges.

According to data collected by the U.S. Office for Civil Rights (DHEW) and the National Association of State Universities and Land-Grant Colleges, there were 15 historically Black and 54 other land-grant colleges in 1972. These institutions combined equalled 3.1% of all higher educational institutions in the U.S. (See Table 2-29.) Of the 85,338 Black undergraduates in all land-grant colleges in 1972, 57.5% were enrolled in other land-grant colleges and 42.5% in the historically Black land-grant colleges.

The distribution of Black undergraduates in 1972 was such that Black land-grant colleges enrolled 7.8% of all Black undergraduates enrolled in all institutions. The other land-grant colleges enrolled 10.5% of all Black undergraduates. The total undergraduate enrollment in Fall 1972 at historically Black land-grant colleges was 41,529, of which 87.4% of the students were Black. At all other land-grant colleges, the total enrollment was 1,183,005, of which 4.1% of the students were Black. (At non-land-grant colleges reporting to the Office for Civil Rights, the total undergraduate enrollment was 4,318,670, in 1972, of which 0.8% were Black.)

While the college distribution of Black undergraduates in land-grant colleges was not solely determined by college costs, a factor contributing to that distribution was the difference in tuition and fee charges. Undergraduate institutions with predominantly white student bodies had higher fee charges than their Black counterparts. Thus, fees tended to contribute more than tuition to the college cost differentials of land-grant colleges. A survey by the National Association of State Universities and Land-Grant Colleges (1974) reported that member institutions with the lowest fees also had large Black enrollment. Of the ten member institutions with lowest resident tuition and fees, three had predominantly Black undergraduate enrollment in 1972. Of those with the lowest non-resident tuition and fees, five institutions had predominantly Black undergraduate student bodies. (See Table C-3 in Appendix C.)

Black Colleges

Categorical barriers based on race created the dual system in higher education, and this dual system continues to influence the college distribution and field distribution

TABLE 2-29. Black Undergraduate Enrollment in Land-Grant Colleges, Fall 1972.

	Land-Grant Colleges[1]			Other Colleges[2]	All Undergraduate Institutions
	Black	Other	All Land-Grant		
NUMBER OF INSTITUTIONS	15	54	69	2,131	2,200
Percent of Land-Grant Colleges	21.0%	78.0%	100%	NA	NA
Percent of All Undergraduate Institutions	0.8%	2.4%	3.2%	9.8%	100%
TOTAL UNDERGRAD ENROLLMENT	41,529	1,183,005	1,224,534	4,318,670	5,543,204
Percent of Land-Grant Colleges	3.4%	96.6%	100%	NA	NA
Percent of All Undergraduate Institutions	0.9%	27.3%	28.7%	77.0%	100%
BLACK UNDERGRAD ENROLLMENT	36,304	49,034	85,338	379,396	464,734
Percent of Land-Grant Colleges	42.5%	57.5%	100%	NA	NA
Percent of All Undergraduate Institutions	7.8%	10.6%	18.4%	81.6%	100%
Percent of Total Student Body	87.4%	4.1%	6.9%	8.8%	8.3%

SOURCE: [1]National Association of State Universities and Land-Grant Colleges, *Minority Undergraduate Enrollment, Fall 1972.*
[2]U.S. Office for Civil Rights (DHEW), *Racial and Ethnic Enrollment Data From Institutions of Higher Education, Fall 1972,* Section V.

of students. Until recently, the major responsibility for educating Black students fell on the traditionally Black colleges which are located primarily in the South. In 1973, these institutions still continued to educate a significant proportion (about 23%) of the Blacks in higher education. According to the Office for Civil Rights (DHEW), almost three-fourths of all undergraduate institutions receiving federal assistance in 1970 and 1972 had student bodies that were less than 6% Black. Thus, while Black students were found increasingly on predominantly white campuses in the 1970's they were still there in very small numbers on each campus.

According to data collected by the Institute for Services to Education, Black colleges enrolled 183,419 students in Fall 1973, of which 73% were enrolled in public Black institutions. (See Table 2-30.) Between Fall 1966 and Fall 1973, total

TABLE 2-30. Enrollment at Historically Black Colleges and Universities and First-Time Freshmen Enrollment by Control and Sex, Fall 1966, 1969, 1971, and 1973.

		Fall 1966	*Fall 1969*	*Fall 1971*	*Fall 1973*
PUBLIC COLLEGES					
Total Enrollment	Male	44,667	54,865	62,203	65,025
	Female	51,847	59,351	66,377	69,756
	Total	96,514	114,216	128,580	134,781
First-Time Enrollment	Male	13,251	13,532	13,804	12,973
	Female	14,928	13,557	14,926	13,641
	Total	28,179	27,089	28,730	26,614
PRIVATE COLLEGES					
Total Enrollment	Male	18,478	20,974	22,546	22,731
	Female	24,452	26,519	27,017	25,907
	Total	42,930	47,493	49,563	48,638
First-Time Enrollment	Male	6,157	5,720	6,553	5,837
	Female	8,279	7,215	7,531	6,921
	Total	14,436	12,935	14,084	12,758
ALL COLLEGES					
Total Enrollment	Male	63,145	75,839	84,749	87,756
	Female	76,299	85,870	93,394	95,663
	Total	139,444	161,709	179,143	183,419
First-Time Enrollment	Male	19,408	19,252	20,357	18,810
	Female	23,207	20,772	22,457	20,562
	Total	42,615	40,024	42,814	39,372
		PERCENT DISTRIBUTION			
Total Enrollment		100	100	100	100
Public		69.2	70.6	72.2	73.5
Private		30.8	29.4	27.8	26.5
First-Time Enrollment		100	100	100	100
Public		66.1	67.7	67.1	67.6
Private		33.9	32.3	32.9	32.4

SOURCE: Institute for Service to Education, *Degrees Granted and Enrollment Trends in Historically Black Colleges: An Eight Year Study*, Table IV.

enrollment at public Black colleges had risen by 38,267 students (or 39.6%). At private Black colleges the total enrollment dropped by 1,565 students (or 5.5%) at public Black colleges and dropped by 1,678 students (or 11.6%) at private Black colleges.

In 1973, Black colleges enrolled 2.2% of all students in higher education. At historically Black colleges, Black student enrollment was approximately 86% of 183,419 students. Using the U.S. Census figure of 684,000 total Black student enrollment in Fall 1973, Black colleges enrolled an estimated 23% of all Blacks in college that year.

Figure 2-9 illustrates the percent change in first-time freshmen enrollment between Fall 1972 and 1973 at historically Black and other institutions. At all Black colleges and universities, there was a decline in Fall 1973 enrollment over the previous academic year. The decline in first-time freshmen enrollment was sharpest at Black private colleges and universities. Compared to enrollment changes in all colleges between Fall 1972 and 1973, freshmen enrollment in Black colleges declined, while that in other public four-year colleges rose slightly. As was the case for Black private colleges, other private college freshmen enrollment declined, but only gradually. Combined with the data discussed previously in Access, it would appear that the drop in total student enrollment at historically Black public and private colleges contributed significantly to the drop in total Black student enrollment in 1973.

The dual racial system of public colleges was described by Mayhew (1971) as a waste of resources, both financial and educational. Although some students felt more comfortable attending institutions in which their race was a majority, the establishment of Black and white public colleges in the same neighborhood benefited whites more than Blacks.

When traditionally Black colleges began to attract white students in the early 1970's, new branches of predominantly white colleges were opened near the Black campuses. These state efforts to duplicate facilities in order to maintain a dual racial system increased the taxpayer's burden and were barriers to distribution. (This state policy decision continues to be a recurring source of debate, as "1202" state-wide planning commissions moved toward operation.)

The dual racial system influenced not only public funding policies but also private funding policies. The more heavily funded foundation programs for Blacks were on white campuses, not on Black campuses. Mayhew argued in favor of using public and private money to strengthen undergraduate programs at Black colleges, because it would result in aid to more concentrated numbers of Black students than was possible on individual white campuses.

Without public and private policies and practices which provided aid to Black colleges, Mayhew argued, the pattern of distribution would be one of continually weakened predominantly Black colleges and intensified expansion and competition from predominantly white colleges. The underfinanced Black colleges, according to Mayhew, needed equal treatment, so that they, like their white counterparts, could be given the opportunity to become centers of learning, not just for some students but for all students.

Within the private college community, Black and white institutions had different financial statuses that in turn had different impacts on Blacks in higher education (Jellema, 1972). Private Black colleges, which enrolled a higher proportion, but not

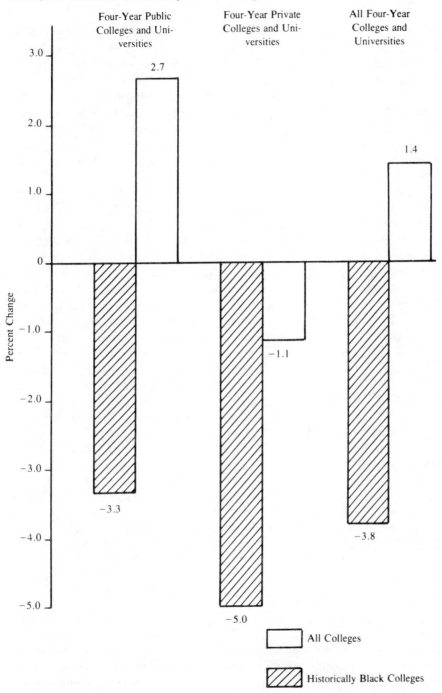

SOURCE: Institute for Services to Education, *Degrees Granted and Enrollment Trends in Histori-cally Black Colleges: An Eight Year Study*, p. 20.

FIGURE 2-9. Percent Change in First-Time Freshmen Enrollment, Fall 1972 to Fall 1973 by Type of Institution.

actual numbers, of Black students than private white colleges, were in worse financial condition because they carried heavier indebtedness. The precarious financial status of private Black colleges was most likely to affect Black students from low-income families, since low-income students tend to enroll in low-cost private colleges. According to Borgen's study of over 1,000 Black National Merit Scholarship candidates in 1970, private Black colleges were more likely to enroll bright Black students from low-income families, while private white colleges enrolled equally bright Black students from higher socio-economic status backgrounds. (Geography also was a factor in this study since virtually all bright Black students from the South enrolled in Black colleges.)

In October 1973, James Godard prepared for the Southern Regional Educational Board a paper on the use of state-wide planning to facilitate the development of a unitary state system. The paper was in part a response to *Adams v. Richardson*, a case which found that ten states, located in the South and Southeast, had maintained dual racial systems of public higher education. In defining a unitary system, Godard stated that it was one in which "predominantly white institutions increasingly share in the responsibility for providing higher education for larger numbers of Blacks and expand the employment of Blacks at all levels of institutions' operation. Likewise, traditionally Black institutions expand their efforts to enroll greater numbers of white students and to increase the employment of whites at all operations levels."

The ability of state-wide planning commissions to help solve the problems created by formerly dual racial systems of higher education has yet to be tested. Godard's paper, however, did suggest the future role of "1202" commissions not only in states which had formal dual racial systems, but also in states with informal dual systems of public higher education, so that the college distribution of Black students was disproportionately in two-year colleges.

The Higher Education Act of 1965 (amended) includes Title III, which provides financial assistance for two-year and four-year public and private colleges that qualify as developing institutions. The program grew out of the effort of presidents at historically Black colleges to meet the crisis that rapidly rising inflation posed for the survival of their institutions. Aid to Developing Institutions, however, was not limited to Black colleges. As the data in the appendices of this report indicate, of the 235 institutions receiving aid in Fiscal Year 1973, 41% (or 98) grantees were predominantly Black institutions.

Ph.D.-Granting Institutions

In the Fall of 1973, an estimated 4.5% of the 283,723 masters and doctoral students in 93 public Ph.D.-granting graduate schools were Black. And Black students comprised 4.0% of the 89,241 students in 61 private Ph.D.-granting graduate schools, according to a survey by the Higher Education Panel of the American Council on Education of 154 Ph.D.-granting institutions. (See Table 2-31.) Of the 16,338 Black graduate students enrolled in 154 Ph.D.-granting institutions in 1973, 78.1% were in public and 21.9% in private institutions. In contrast, of the 356,626 white students enrolled, 75.9% were in public institutions, and 24% were in private.

Compared to other students, a slightly higher proportion of Black graduate students enrolled in public Ph.D-granting institutions in the HEP survey.

Blacks, like all graduate students in the HEP survey, were most likely to be enrolled in the larger graduate schools. In 1973, 45.6% of all Blacks in the HEP survey were enrolled in institutions with total graduate enrollments over 5,000 students. This was partly due to the fact that the larger institutions were often public universities; these institutions offered more assistantships and/or fellowships and other forms of assistance than did smaller institutions. Moreover, as a percent of all graduate students enrolled, Black graduate students were 1.5% of all those in the smallest institutions, and 5.6% of those in the larger institutions. (See Table 2-32.)

TABLE 2-31. Public and Private Enrollment Patterns of Graduate Students in Ph.D.-Granting Institutions by Race, Fall 1973.

	Public	*Private*	*Total*
Number of Institutions	93	61	154
Graduate Enrollment			
All Students	283,723	89,241	372,964
Percent	76.1%	23.9%	100%
Black Students (Est.)	12,768	3,570	16,338
	78.1%	21.9%	100%
Percent of total enrollment	4.5%	4.0%	4.3%
White and Other Students (Est.)	270,955	85,671	356,626
	76.0%	24.0%	100%
Percent of total enrollment	95.4%	95.9%	95.5%

SOURCE: El-Khawas, Elaine H. and Kinzer, Joan L., *Enrollment of Minority Graduate Students at Ph.d.-Granting Institutions,* Higher Education Panel Reports, No. 19, ACE Table 1.

TABLE 2-32. Graduate Enrollment of Graduate Students in Ph.D.-Granting Institutions by Size of the Student Body and Race, Fall 1973.

Size of Graduate Student Body	*Number of Institutions*	*Total Graduate Enrollment*	*Percent Distribution*		
			White	*Black*	*Other*
Below 200	16	1,488	95.3	1.5	3.2
201 - 1000	36	21,867	93.9	3.9	2.2
1001-3000	57	114,512	92.5	4.2	3.3
3001-5000	26	102,318	94.9	3.1	2.0
Over 5000	19	132,779	91.4	5.6	3.0
TOTAL	154	372.964	92.8	4.4	2.8

SOURCE: El-Khawas, Elaine H. and Kinzer, Joan L., *Enrollment of Minority Graduate Students at Ph.D.-Granting Institutions,* Higher Education Panel Reports, No. 19, ACE, Table 1.

College Distribution Status

The relevant question in college distribution was how well enrollment in each type of graduate institution reflected the racial distribution of Blacks in the college availability pool age 16 to 34, which was 9% Black. Table 2-33 summarizes the number of Blacks that were needed to have achieved parity by type and control of institution in Fall 1973, assuming constant total enrollment.

A total of 127,000 Black students would have had to have been enrolled in college in the 1973-74 academic year in order to have achieved parity based on U.S. Census data. Of these 127,000 Blacks, 59% would have to have gone to public institutions and 41% to private. The greatest increase in Black student enrollment (112,000) was needed in public universities. No additional students were needed in public two-year and four-year colleges or in private universities and two-year colleges in order to achieve parity with the availability pool in Fall 1973. In these institutions the proportional Black enrollment in 1973 exceeded the 9% needed for parity with the combined undergraduate/graduate availability pool.

The graduate and professional availability pool (age 20 to 34) was 5% Black, according to U.S. Census data. The graduate enrollment of Blacks at the 154 Ph.D.-granting institutions was 4.4%. By size of the institution, Blacks were under-represented at all Ph.D.-granting institutions with student bodies under 5,000. Blacks were best represented at Ph.D.-granting institutions with student bodies over 5,000. (See Table 2-34.) To have achieved parity with the graduate and professional availability pool, assuming constant total enrollment in Fall 1973, an additional 2,238 Black students would have had to have been enrolled in the 154 Ph.D.-granting institutions in the HEP survey. The greatest increase in the number of Blacks needed for parity was in institutions with student bodies between 3,001 and 5,000 students. For these institutions, an additional 1,945 Black students would have had to have been enrolled for parity.

TABLE 2-33. Black Enrollment Needed For Parity In Combined Undergraduate/ Graduate Availability Pool by Type of Institution, Fall 1973[1].

| | *(In Thousands)* | | |
Type of Institution	*Current Black Enrollment*	*Black Graduate Enrollment at Parity (9%)*	*Increase Needed*
Public			
University	194	306	112
Four-Year	116	83	−33
Two-Year	169	166	−3
TOTAL PUBLIC	479	554	75
Private			
University	82	80	−2
Four-Year	32	69	37
Two-Year	15	12	−3
TOTAL PRIVATE	129	160	31
TOTAL ENROLLED	608	735	127

SOURCE: Institute for the Study of Educational Policy Staff.
[1]Figures assume constant total enrollment in Fall 1973.

TABLE 2-34. Black Graduate Enrollment Needed for Parity In 154 Ph.D.-Granting Institutions by Size of Institution, Fall 1973[1].

Size of Graduate Student Body	Current Black Enrollment	Black Graduate Student Enrollment At Parity (5%)	Increase Needed
Below 200	22	74	52
201-1000	852	1,093	241
1001-3000	4,809	5,726	917
3001-5000	3,171	5,116	1,945
Over 5000	7,435	6,639	—796
Total	16,410	18,648	2,238

SOURCE: Institute for the Study of Educational Policy Staff, Howard University (1975).
[1]Figures assume constant total enrollment in Fall 1973.

Because data on land-grant colleges for the 1973-74 academic year were not available, the distribution status of Blacks in land-grant institutions is not clear. Assuming constant total enrollment, based on Fall 1972 total enrollment and Spring 1973 Black availability, the following were found: (a) in Black land-grant colleges, the proportion of Blacks on campus exceeded their proportion in the availability pool by 114%; (b) in other land-grant colleges, Black enrollment would have to be increased by 59% to achieve parity with the undergraduate availability pool; and (c) for all land-grant institutions, the proportional Black enrollment to achieve parity would have to be increased by 31%.

Program Distribution

Distribution also refers to the presence of Blacks in academic fields within an institution. In 1973, as in previous years, academic fields in which Blacks had traditionally found greatest acceptance and employment opportunities, such as the Social Sciences and Education, were still selected more often than the recently opened technical and science fields. The current program distribution of Blacks in part reflects past and current efforts to recruit, admit, and encourage Blacks to enter and remain in these fields.

Academic Fields

According to the U.S. Census, racial differences in fields of study chosen by Black and white students in 1972 were small. In Fall 1972, for example, Education, Social Science, Business or Commerce, and other fields accounted for 52.7% of the majors of Black undergraduates and 55.9% of the majors of white undergraduates. Social Science fields accounted for slightly more than one-half of the Black and white undergraduates. Comparable data from the U.S. Census or other sources for Fall 1973 were not available. Although some change in major fields of undergraduates in 1973 would be expected, substantial movement by Black or white students out of the Social Sciences is unlikely. (See tables in appendices.)

At the graduate level, where future employment opportunities may be more carefully considered, the racial differences in choice of field were more evident in 1973. In a survey of 154 Ph.D.-granting institutions, Blacks were 7.2% of all students in Education, 5.5% in the Health field, 5.1% in the all other fields category. Black students were the smallest proportion of graduate students in the field of Engineering (1.2%), Physical Sciences (1.4%), and Life Sciences (1.5%). (See Tables 2-35 and 2-36.)

In the HEP survey, the type of institution attended produced insignificant differences in the fields of study of Blacks. In both public and private Ph.D.-granting institutions, Black graduate students were most numerous in Education and least numerous in Engineering and Physical Sciences.

TABLE 2-35. Distribution of Blacks in Graduate Programs of 154 Ph.D.-Granting Institutions, Fall 1973.

Field of Study	Total Enrollment	Black Enrollment Amount	Black Enrollment Percent
Arts and Humanities	53,920	1,516	2.8
Education	96,568	6,990	7.2
Engineering	31,238	368	1.2
Health Professions	13,238	727	5.5
Life Sciences	27,641	419	1.5
Mathematics	12,446	305	2.5
Physical Sciences	21,629	299	1.4
Basic Social Sciences	35,583	1,471	4.1
All Other Fields	80,666	4,146	5.1
Total, All Fields	372,964	16,241	

SOURCE: El-Khawas, Elaine H. and Kinzer, Joan L., *Enrollment of Minority Graduate Students at Ph.D.-Granting Institutions*, Table 3, and Table 7 (1974).

TABLE 2-36. Enrollment In Graduate Programs in 154 Ph.D.-Granting Institutions, by Type of Control, Race, and Field of Study, 1973.

Field of Study	Public Institutions Total Enrolled	Public Institutions Percent Black	Private Institutions Total Enrolled	Private Institutions Percent Black
Arts and Humanities	39,441	2.6	14,479	3.5
Education	78,178	7.3	18,390	6.9
Engineering	21,160	1.0	10,113	1.6
Health Professions	10,225	5.9	2,983	4.2
Life Sciences	23,257	1.5	4,384	1.9
Mathematics	9,872	2.5	2,574	2.2
Physical Sciences	16,530	1.3	5,099	1.5
Basic Social Sciences	28,130	3.9	7,453	5.0
All Other Fields	56,900	5.6	23,766	4.1
Total, All Fields	283,723	4.5	89,241	4.0

SOURCE: El-Khawas, Elaine H. and Kinzer, Joan L., *Enrollment of Minority Graduate Students at Ph.D.-Granting Institutions*, Tables 4 and 5, (1974).

How Black and white graduate students differed in their distribution across fields of study when race was held constant is summarized in Table 2-37. With the exception of Education, the racial differences in distribution across fields were small. Education alone accounted for 43% of all Black graduate students and 25% of all white students in graduate programs of Ph.D.-granting institutions in 1973, according to the HEP survey. Next to Education, Engineering produced the next largest difference (2.3% Black, 8.6% white enrollment in graduate programs).

TABLE 2-37. Program Distribution of Black and White Graduate Students in 154 Ph.D.-Granting Institutions, Fall, 1973.

	Percent Within Race		
Field of Study	*Black*	*White*	*Difference*
Arts and Humanities	9.3	10.8	−1.5
Education	43.0	25.1	17.9
Engineering	2.3	8.6	−6.3
Health Professions	4.5	3.6	0.9
Life Sciences	2.6	7.6	−5.0
Mathematics	1.9	3.4	−1.5
Physical Sciences	1.8	5.9	−4.1
Basic Social Sciences	9.1	9.5	−0.4
All Other Fields	25.5	21.6	3.9
Total, All Fields	100	100	100

SOURCE: El-Khawas, Elaine H. and Kinzer, Joan L., *Enrollment of Minority Graduate Students at Ph.D.-Granting Institutions*, 1974.

Wilburn (1972), in a discussion of Black Americans in the Sciences and Engineering, reported that there were 1.75 million scientific and engineering workers in the United States in 1971, of which 1.1 million were engineers and 650,000 were scientists. Of these, an estimated 12,000 were Black, equaling approximately 1.6% of all Black professional and technical workers in 1971. According to Wilburn, the educational and psychosocial barriers to increased participation of Blacks in scientific and engineering fields included the following:

(a) discouraging information about the degree of the need for such workers in the labor force,

(b) reduced federal support for graduate fellowships and traineeships due to predictions of oversupply,

(c) reluctance to enter a scientific field unless the probability is great that one will be a "star" (mediocrity remains a "white man's luxury" in many occupations—p. 149),

(d) inadequate engineering school facilities, especially for Black students attending predominately Black and less prestigious white colleges,

(e) inadequate preparation in mathematics and science courses in high school,

(f) peer, parental, and teacher pressure not to enter scientific or technical fields because of racism in employment opportunities, and

(g) the pressure to work part-time while in college, thus limiting time for laboratory classes and extra study hours.

In a related study, Skypek and Lee (1975), using Project Talent data, found that Black students equaled 3.6% of all students in the project survey, but only 1.0% of all high school students aspiring to science careers. (Black males interested in science careers were 0.3% of the 3,123 Black males in the survey, and Black females equaled 0.8% of the 2,060 Black females.)

(A discussion of the causes of differences in field distribution is included in the following chapter, "Barriers to Equal Educational Opportunity for Blacks.")

Professional Fields

Between 1900 and 1974, the proportion of Black professionals in the total Black population has risen from 0.5% to 2.9%, according to U.S. Census data. In 1900, there were 47,324 Black professionals, primarily in Education and Religion. In 1974, there were 710,000 Black professionals, primarily in Education. Although the proportion of professionals among all Blacks has increased in 74 years, it remains small. Moreover, with this increase, the types of fields Blacks entered as workers or students has not changed radically.

Blacks were a greater proportion of the student bodies at graduate (4%) than at professional (3.1%) schools receiving federal assistance in 1972, according to the Office for Civil Rights (DHEW). The recent increase in access to professional schools indicates that increased numbers of Blacks were entering professional training. However, not only were Blacks still a minuscule proportion of the professional school students, but also the gains in Black enrollment in recent years were surpassed by gains in white enrollment in the same period.

Because racial enrollment data for the academic 1973-74 year were not available for all professional fields, the most recent years for which these data were available were included. Based on the data, it was concluded that Black enrollment in professional schools was related to the length of training, to the historical participation of Blacks in the profession, and to the availability of professional training at historically Black colleges.

Length of training influenced Black enrollment by increasing the cost of completing training. Without financial assistance from either public or private sources, embarking on a career that required long-term training beyond a baccalaureate may be unrealistic for most Black students. As the tables on specific fields in the appendices indicated, Black enrollment drops off as the length of professional training increases. A notable exception to this is the enrollment of Blacks in professional schools at historically Black colleges, and in fields traditionally open to Blacks, such as Law and Medicine. Although these professions require advanced training, Black students were more likely to be in them than in Engineering or Public Administration, for example.

Howard University (1973) surveyed the enrollment of Black students in professional fields in Fall of 1971. They reported that in Law, Black students equaled 4.0% of the 93,500 students enrolled. In Medicine, Blacks equaled 4.5% of the 76,676 students enrolled. In Dentistry, Engineering, and Architecture, Blacks made up even smaller percentages of the total student enrollment. (See Table 2-38.)

In 1971, Black students were less than 5% of the students enrolled in Law, Medicine, Dentistry, and other professional undergraduate and graduate schools.

TABLE 2-38. Black Enrollments in Selected Professional Fields, Fall 1971.

	Enrollment		Percent
Field	*Total*	*Black*	*Black*
Law	93,500	3,732	4.0
Medicine	73,676	3,292	4.5
Dentistry	16,789	601	3.6
Engineering	229,047	4,831	2.1
		less than	3.5 (est.)
Architecture	25,000	1,000	
Communications	50,000	1,000	2.0

SOURCE: Howard University, *Four-Year Report Howard University, 1969-73.*

But, in 1973, including historically Black colleges, Blacks were approaching 5 to 10% of the students enrolled in these fields, especially in the first year of training. The enrollment data reported in the appendices were usually collected by professional associations from member institutions and students within each profession. For each field of study, the most recent data available were reported.

Black enrollment in the following professional fields is summarized in Appendix D: Health Professions, Dentistry, Nursing, Medical, Pharmacy, Engineering, Law, Business, Religion, Public Administration and Public Affairs.

Program Distribution Status

Compared to the proportion of Blacks age 20 to 34 in the graduate and professional availability pool, Black enrollment in academic fields, except Education, was below parity. For example, while Blacks were an estimated 5% of the availability pool, they were 7.2% of those in Education at 154 Ph.D.-granting institutions. In all other fields, including Arts and Humanities, Life and Physical Sciences, and Mathematics, Black graduate enrollment was lower than availability.

In professional fields included in the appendices of this report, Black enrollment in the 1973-74 academic year approached or exceeded parity with the availability pool in Dentistry, Medicine, and Business (undergraduate programs), but still remained small in terms of community needs for professional services. Black enrollment was below parity in Nursing, Pharmacy, Engineering, Law, Religion (graduate programs), and Public Administration.

Summary

Black students were most underrepresented as a proportion of total enrollment at large public universities and private four-year colleges and best represented in public four-year and two-year colleges in Fall 1973. Age differences between Black and white students were greatest at private institutions, where Blacks were slightly older than whites. Sex differences were such that for whites, males were more prevalent than females in all types of colleges (except private two-year), but for Blacks no consistent sex differences in college distribution were found.

Historically Black land-grant colleges enrolled 7.8% of all Black undergraduates and other land-grant colleges enrolled 10.5% of all Black undergraduates in 1972. In 1973, all historically Black colleges combined educated a significant proportion (about 23%) of the Black undergraduates in higher education. And, at selected (154) Ph.D.-granting institutions, Blacks were 4% of those enrolled in graduate studies.

Although the differences between Black and white distribution by field were small at the undergraduate level, Education accounted for 43% of the graduate majors for Blacks. (Education accounts for 25% of white graduate majors.) Blacks were underrepresented in scientific and technical fields, while in professional fields, other than Education, Blacks were best represented in Law and Medicine.

PERSISTENCE OF BLACK STUDENTS IN COLLEGE

Persistence is defined as staying in college and earning a degree. Access and distribution, though essential, are not enough to insure equality of educational opportunity for Black students. While they may be able to go to the college of their choice and major in the fields of interest to them, they may not finish school or enter more advanced programs.

The absence of data on how many Black students were completing college made assessment of the Black students' persistence needs difficult. Data on dropouts and the number of degrees awarded to Blacks are scarce. Indeed, no public or private data collector routinely records racial data on the number of associate arts, bachelor's, master's, or professional degrees awarded. In Spring 1973, the National Academy of Sciences National Research Council for the first time collected race and ethnicity data on its survey of doctorates awarded in U.S. universities.

In this section you will *not* find national data on the following:

(1) dropout rates for 1973-74 academic year by race, type of institution, or financial status;

(2) degrees earned by race: associate arts degrees, master's degrees, or professional degrees.

These statistics simply were not regularly collected nationally and, therefore, were not available.

In this section you *will* find the results of surveys of—

(1) dropouts of 1966 freshmen and college return rates of 1973 college students;

(2) baccalaureates awarded by race in the 1973-74 academic year;

(3) degrees awarded by historically Black colleges in the 1972-73 academic year; and

(4) doctorates awarded by U.S. institutions in the 1972-73 academic year.

Dropout Rates

"Dropout" as a term is in all probability a misnomer when applied to students who had not completed undergraduate work and who were not enrolled four years after college entry. Longitudinal studies by El-Khawas and Kinzer (1974) suggested that over a ten-year period almost three-fourths of the full-time freshmen do complete their baccalaureate training.

TABLE 2-39. National Persistence Rates for 1966 Black and Other Freshmen, Spring 1970 (Weighted Population Estimates).

Percentage of Students Who:	Two-Year Colleges			Four-Year Colleges and Universities		
	Blacks (N=30,769)	Whites[1] (N=504,484)	All Students (N=535,253)	Blacks (N=51,761)	Whites[1] (N=950,619)	All Students (N=1,002,380)
Returned for a second year	62.3	66.2	66.0	75.8	78.1	78.0
Received a degree*	29.4	39.0	38.4	42.1	47.0	46.7
Were still enrolled	1.2	2.1	2.1	14.1	11.6	11.8
Requested that a transcript be sent to another institution	26.3	25.3	25.4	16.8	22.9	22.7
Not enrolled	43.1	33.6	34.1	27.0	18.5	18.8

SOURCE: Astin, Alexander W., *College Dropouts: A National Profile*, Table 3.

*Associate degree for two-year colleges; bachelor's degree for four-year colleges and universities.

[1]Include other non-whites.

In a one-year follow-up study of 1966 freshmen, Astin (1972) found that fewer Blacks than whites returned for the second year of college. In addition, Black and white students in four-year colleges and universities had higher one-year rates than did students at two-year colleges. (See Table 2-39.) Astin found that four years later, 27.5% of the Black students in college and 27.4% of the white students in two-year colleges were either still enrolled or had requested that a transcript be sent to another institution. Among four-year colleges and universities, 30.9% of the Black students and 34.5% of the white students had requested transcripts or were still enrolled. Of the 1966 students not enrolled in 1970 (and without associate or bachelor degrees), the highest dropout rates were for Black and white two-year college students in that order. The lowest dropout rates were for white and Black students in four-year colleges and universities. According to Astin, the white dropout rate at two-year colleges was 77.9% that of the Black rate; at four-year colleges and universities it was 68.5% that of Black students.

Over a four-year period, only about one-third (38.4%) of all two-year college students had received associate degrees, and less than one-half (46.7%) of the four-year college students had received baccalaureates. The degrees-earned rate for Blacks (42.1%) was slightly lower than that of whites (39.0%) in two-year institutions in the Astin study. The Black degrees-earned rates at two-year and four-year colleges were 75.3%, and 89.5% that of whites at similar institutions.

TABLE 2-40. Proportion of College Returns Age 14 to 24, by Race and Years of College Completed, October 1973.

		Percent	
	Enrolled in 1972 (In Thousands)	Returned in 1973	Not Returned in 1973
All Races			
All Years	5,601	71.3	28.7
First Year	1,813	76.1	23.9
Second Year	1,527	76.1	23.9
Third Year	1,107	87.2	12.8
Fourth Year	845	32.4	67.6
Fifth Year or more	309	69.6	30.4
Blacks			
All Years	492	73.4	26.6
First Year	181	77.3	22.7
Second Year	143	76.2	23.8
Third Year	96	87.5	12.5
Fourth Year	60	31.7	68.3
Fifth Year or more	12	75.0	25.0
Whites			
All Years	5,003	73.5	26.5
First Year	1,603	75.9	24.1
Second Year	1,357	75.9	24.1
Third Year	978	87.6	12.4
Fourth Year	770	32.2	67.8
Fifth Year or more	295	69.8	30.2

SOURCE: U.S. Census, *Social and Economic Characteristics of Students: October 1973*, Table 6.

Because this study was based on 1966 freshmen and 1970 follow-up, its relevance for 1973 is open to question. The period covered by the Astin study predated the Education Amendments of 1972 and overlapped with initial enforcement of Title VI of the Civil Rights Acts of 1964. In addition, the study predated most institutional and state activities to expand equal educational opportunity for Blacks in college. Although more recent data might reflect the current dropout rates for Blacks, such national data are sketchy and limited.

According to the data provided by the U.S. Census, of 492,000 Blacks age 14 to 24, enrolled in college in October 1972, 73.4% returned in 1973. Of the 5,003,000 whites enrolled in 1972, 73.5% returned in 1973. (See Table 2-40.) A slightly higher

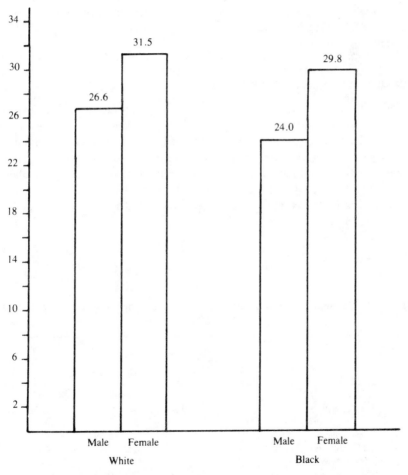

SOURCE: Table 2-40.

FIGURE 2-10. Proportion of College Students Age 14 to 24 Enrolled in October 1972 Who Did Not Return in October 1973, by Race and Sex.

proportion of Blacks (77.3%) than whites (75.9%) who completed one year of college continued their college education in 1973, according to U.S. Census data.

For both Blacks and whites, females were less likely to return in 1973 than were males. The highest one-year return rate was that of Black males (75%) and the lowest was that of white females (68%). (See Figure 2-10.)

Degrees Earned

The number of Blacks and whites with college degrees has increased along with their access and distribution. More Blacks and whites held higher education academic and professional degrees in 1973 than at any other time in history. Because racial data on all degrees awarded—associate arts, baccalaureates, masters, and professional degrees—were not routinely collected, the progress that has been made cannot be fully measured. The data included here come from private surveys designed to answer limited questions. They were also unique and often unduplicated. Thus, the validity of the statistics cannot be easily assessed.

Baccalaureate Degrees Awarded

In Spring 1974, an estimated 7.5% of the 954,000 baccalaureate degrees awarded went to all minority students. (See Table 2-41.) Black students received an estimated 5.1% of the baccalaureates awarded in Spring 1974. Compared with Black enrollment four years earlier, the proportion of Black baccalaureates was smaller than the estimated 6% Black full-time freshmen enrollment in two-year and four-year colleges in 1969 and 1970. (See Figure 2-11.) (Because of the possible undercounting of large institutions in the HEP survey, the actual proportion of total and Black baccalaureates may be higher.)

TABLE 2-41. Estimated Baccalaureate Degrees Awarded by Race and Ethnic Group, Spring 1974

	Estimated Baccalaureate Degrees, 1973-1974[1]
ALL PERSONS	100.0% (954,000)
White	92.5%
TOTAL MINORITY	7.5%
Black	5.1%
Spanish-surnamed	1.4%
Asian	0.8%
American Indian	0.2%

SOURCE: American Council on Education, Higher Education Panel, 1975 and National Board on Graduate Education of National Academy of Sciences, (unpublished date).
[1]Preliminary data.

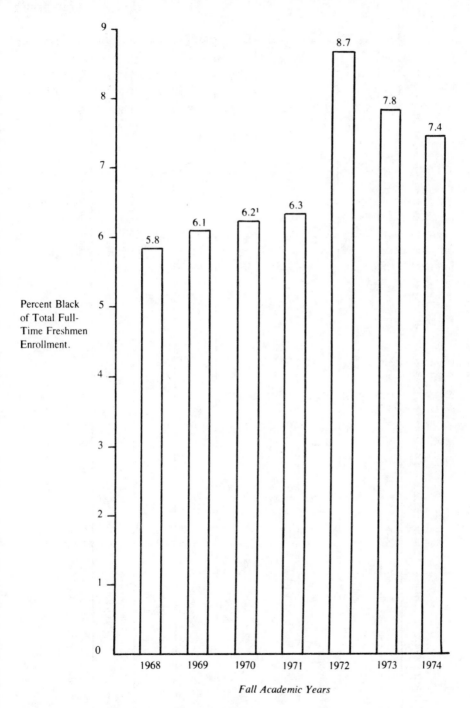

SOURCE: American Council on Education and National Board on Graduate Education.
[1]Not a published figure.

FIGURE 2-11. Proportion of Full-Time Black Freshmen, 1968-1974.

TABLE 2-42. Percentage of Bachelor Degrees Awarded by Selected fields in Historically Black Colleges and Nationally.

		1965-66	1966-67	1967-68	1968-69	1969-70	1970-71	1971-72[1]	1972-73[1]
Biological Sciences	Black Colleges	6.7	6.0	6.1	5.7	4.9	4.9	4.2	3.5
	National	5.2	5.1	5.0	4.8	4.7	4.3	4.4	4.4
Business & Management	Black Colleges	4.9	5.9	7.3	8.9	11.0	13.7	14.0	15.1
	National	12.1	12.4	12.6	12.9	13.3	13.8	13.4	13.1
Education	Black Colleges	44.9	43.3	40.2	37.6	36.1	35.1	34.6	33.4
	National	22.6	21.5	21.3	20.9	20.9	21.0	15.5	15.4
Physical Sciences	Black Colleges	2.6	2.4	2.2	1.9	2.0	1.6	1.7	1.6
	National	3.3	3.2	3.1	2.9	2.7	2.5	2.5	2.4
Social Sciences	Black Colleges	17.2	18.5	19.4	20.8	22.3	22.6	21.9	19.6
	National	17.9	18.6	19.1	19.3	19.4	19.9	19.7	20.2
Other	Black Colleges	23.7	23.9	24.8	25.1	23.8	22.1	23.6	26.8
	National	38.9	39.2	38.9	39.2	38.9	38.5	44.5	44.5
Total Bachelors	Black Colleges	100.0	100.0	100.0	100.0	100.0	100.0	100.0	100.0
	National	100.0	100.0	100.0	100.0	100.0	100.0	100.0	100.0

SOURCE: Institute for Services to Education, *Degrees Granted and Enrollment Trends in Historically Black Colleges: An Eight-Year Study*, Table 11.
[1] Projected national figures (Actual figures not available).

Degrees Awarded by Historically Black Colleges

Of the 4,216,896 baccalaureates awarded between Spring 1966 and 1971, 2.7% were awarded by historically Black colleges (Institute for Services to Education, 1974). Historically Black public colleges awarded 76,464 of the baccalaureates and historically Black private colleges 38,901 between 1967 and 1971. All other public colleges awarded 2,601,828 baccalaureates and all other private colleges 1,499,703 in this same time period.

An estimated one-half of the baccalaureates awarded to Black students in Spring 1974 were awarded by historically Black colleges. Nationally, however, Black colleges awarded only a small proportion of the total baccalaureates awarded in Spring 1974.

Although Education remained the field in which the greatest number and proportion of baccalaureates were awarded at historically Black colleges between 1966 and 1973, there was a decline in the proportion of Education degrees at both historically Black and other institutions. Of bachelor degrees awarded at historically Black colleges, baccalaureates in Education went from 44.9% in Spring 1966 to 33.4% in Spring 1973. Baccalaureates in Education at other colleges also declined in this same period from 22.6% to 15.4% of the degrees awarded. (See Table 2-42.) In addition, the proportion of bachelor degrees in Biological and Physical Sciences between Spring 1966 and Spring 1973 declined at both historically Black and all other institutions.

In the 1972-73 academic year, according to the Institute for Services to Education data, an estimated 25,094 baccalaureates were awarded at 86 historically Black colleges. This equaled 2.6% of the 954,000 estimated baccalaureates awarded by all U.S. colleges that year. Based on Fall 1972 enrollment data at historically Black land-grant colleges, an estimated 86% of the students enrolled in the largest historically Black colleges were Black. Using this estimate of Black student enrollment, approximately 21,581 (or 86%) of all baccalaureates awarded at historically Black colleges in Spring 1973 went to Black students. According to this estimation, Black students received an estimated 14,771 of the 17,175 baccalaureates awarded at publicly controlled Black colleges in Spring 1973.

Between the 1965-66 and 1972-73 academic years, historically Black colleges produced 3,527 professional degrees (72% in public universities), 25,603 masters degrees (75% in public universities), and 192 doctorates (95% in one public institution, Howard University). Law and Medicine were the primary professional degree programs at historically Black colleges in the 1972-73 academic year. In that year, 40.3% of the professional degrees awarded at historically Black colleges were in Law, 26.9% in Medicine (M.D.), and 19.9% in Dentistry. (See Table 2-43.)

In the 1972-73 academic year, 4,154 masters degrees were awarded at historically Black colleges (87.6% by public colleges). Of the masters degrees conferred by historically Black colleges, Education accounted for about 70% of the degrees, according to the Institute for Services to Education. (See Table 2-44.) Although the proportion of Black baccalaureates in Education has declined in recent years at historically Black colleges and other institutions, the number in graduate Education programs remains large. This was in part due to past enrollment patterns of Black students and to the fact that as Black students moved up into higher degree programs,

TABLE 2-43. Number and Percent of Masters, Doctorates, and Professional Degrees Awarded by Historically Black Public And Private Institutions, 1972-73 Academic Year.

	Public	Private	Total
Masters Degree			
Number	4,154	1,391	5,545
Percent	74.9	25.1	100.0
Professional Degrees			
Number	456	187	643
Percent	70.9	29.1	100.0
Doctorate Degrees			
Number	40	3	43
Percent	93.0	7.0	100.0
All Graduate and Professional Degrees			
Number	4,650	1,581	6,231
Percent	74.6	25.4	100.0

SOURCE: Institute for Services to Education, *Degrees Granted and Enrollment Trends in Historically Black Colleges: An Eight-Year Study*, Table 17.

TABLE 2-44. Professional Degrees Awarded by Historically Black Colleges in Selected Fields, 1972-73.

Degree	1972-73 Number	Percent
Law	259	40.3
Theology	67	10.4
(D.D.S. or D.M.D.) Dentistry	128	19.9
(M.D.) Medicine	173	26.9
(D.V.M.) Veterinary Medicine	16	2.5
Total Professional Degrees	643	100.0

SOURCE: Institute for Services to Education, *Degrees Granted and Enrollment Trends in Historically Black Colleges: An Eight-Year Study*, Table 19.

the number of students who transferred into Education increased. For white doctoral recipients, however, such a shift into Education did not occur, according to data provided by the National Academy of Sciences.

In the 1972-73 academic year, only two historically Black universities awarded doctorates—Howard University (listed as public in this report), and Atlanta University (private). (In this academic year, Texas Southern University started a doctoral program in Education, but awarded no degrees.) Howard University and Atlanta University, combined, awarded 192 doctorate degrees between the 1965-66 and 1972-73 academic years, according to the Institute for Services to Education. In the 1972-73 academic year, these institutions awarded 43 doctorates, which equaled 0.1% of all doctorates conferred that year. The fields in which the doctorates were awarded at the historically Black colleges were primarily the Physical and Natural Sciences and Liberal Arts. (See Table 2-45.) Only two doctorates were awarded in

TABLE 2-45. Doctorates Awarded by Historically Black Colleges, 1972-73 Academic Year.

	1972-73
Physical Sciences	
Zoology, General Biology	11
Pharmacology	1
Physiology	2
Natural Sciences	
Chemistry	9
Physics	2
Theology	4
Liberal Arts	
English	1
African Studies	2
Political Science	4
History	3
Psychology	2
Education	
Counseling and Guidance	2
Total Doctorate Degrees	43

SOURCE: Institute for Services to Education, *Degrees Granted and Enrollment Trends in Historically Black Colleges: An Eight-Year Study*, Table 20.

Education—Counseling and Guidance—both by Atlanta University.

Because the racial composition of the student bodies in professional and graduate programs at historically Black colleges differed significantly from department to department, it was not possible, with any degree of accuracy, to estimate the number of masters, professional, or doctoral degrees conferred on Black students attending historically Black institutions. A safe assumption is that at least one-half (3,115) of the combined graduate and professional degrees conferred by historically Black institutions in the 1972-73 academic year went to Black students. For graduate degrees only, the proportion of Black recipients is probably about 70%. For professional degrees only, Black recipients probably range from 66% to 33%, depending on the program.

Doctorates Awarded

In Spring 1973, the National Academy of Sciences included a race self-identification item in its survey of doctorates. Because of the high rate of enrollment of non-citizen minorities in doctoral programs in U.S. institutions, any description of minority participation must take citizenship into account. In Spring 1973, an estimated 2.0% of 33,727 doctorates from U.S. universities were awarded to Blacks who were U.S. citizens, according to the National Academy of Sciences.

As can be seen from Figure 2-12, in both the citizen and non-citizen groups, the largest proportion of doctorates went to whites. While Blacks received the largest

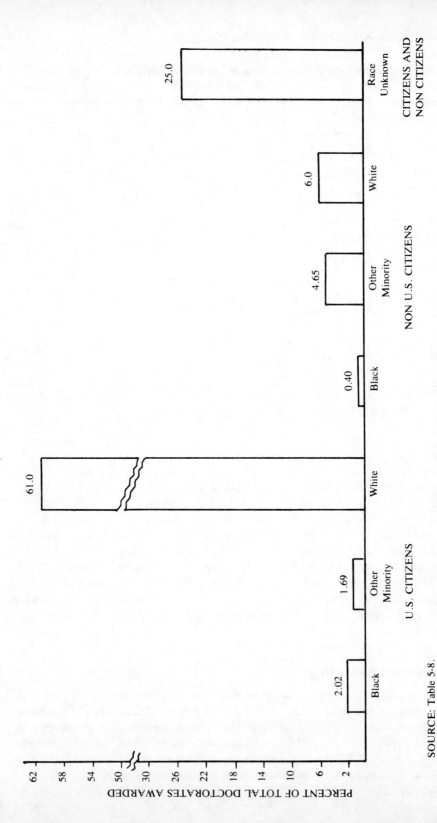

FIGURE 2-12. Doctorates Awarded by Race and Citizenship, Spring 1973.

SOURCE: Table 5-8.

number of doctorates (2.02%) awarded to U.S. citizen minorities, Orientals, which included Middle Eastern and Asian nationals, received the largest number of doctorates (4.3%) awarded to non-U.S. citizens.

A limitation of the National Academy of Sciences doctorate records data was that

TABLE 2-46. Doctorates Awarded by Race and Citizenship, June 1973.

Race/Citizenship	Number	Percent Within Race	Percent Of Total
Black			
U.S. Native	575	78.00	1.70
U.S. Naturalized	8	1.00	0.02
Non-U.S. Perm. Visa	41	6.00	0.10
Non-U.S. Temp. Visa	103	14.00	0.30
Unknown	10	1.00	0.02
Total Black	737	100.00	2.10
American Indian			
Total American Indian	108	100.00	0.30
Mexican-American/Span. Amer.			
U.S. Native	94	44.00	0.30
U.S. Naturalized	42	19.00	0.10
Non-U.S. Perm. Visa	17	8.00	0.05
Non-U.S. Temp. Visa	62	28.00	0.20
Unknown	1	0.50	—
Total Mexican-American	216	100.00	0.60
Puerto Rican			
Total Puerto Rican	29	100.00	0.09
Oriental			
U.S. Native	119	7.00	0.40
U.S. Naturalized	128	7.00	0.40
Non-U.S. Perm. Visa	778	45.00	2.30
Non-U.S. Temp. Visa	684	40.00	2.00
Unknown	12	1.00	0.03
Total Oriental	1,721	100.00	5.10
Other Minority			
U.S. Citizen	31	39.00	0.10
Non-citizen	48	61.00	0.10
Total Other Minority	79	100.00	0.20
White			
U.S. Native	19,731	89.00	59.00
U.S. Naturalized	671	3.00	2.00
Non-U.S. Perm. Visa	601	3.00	2.00
Non-U.S. Temp. Visa	1,192	5.00	4.00
Unknown	56	0.30	0.20
Total White	22,251	100.00	66.00
Race Unknown			
Total Race Unknown	8,586	100.00	25.00
(May include minorities)			
Total Doctorates Awarded			
U.S. Identified Minorities	1,134	—	3.40
All Doctorates Awarded	33,727	—	100.00

SOURCE: National Board on Graduate Education, National Academy of Sciences, National Research Council, Doctorate Records File, unpublished data.

19% did not get the questionnaire with the racial item and 6% did not report race or gave unusable responses. As can be seen from Table 2-46, 8,586, or 25% of the 33,727 doctoral recipients, did not report their race. Thus, for about one-fourth of the doctoral recipients, race was not known.

TABLE 2-47. Institutions awarding Doctorates to Native-born and Naturalized U.S. Citizens by Race, Spring 1973.

	Type of Control		
	Public	Private	Total
Number of Institutions[1]	154	119	273
Percent	56.4	43.5	100.0
Total Degrees Awarded[2]	15,213	7,581	22,794
Percent	66.7	33.2	100.0
Degrees by Race			
Black	409	171	580
Mexican-American/Span. Amer.	94	41	135
Puerto Rican	26	10	36
American Indian	78	29	107
Oriental	163	88	251
White[2]	13,791	6,584	20,375
Total	14,561	6,923	21,484
	Percent Distribution Within Race		
Black	70.5	29.4	100.0
Mexican-American/Span. Amer.	69.6	30.3	100.0
Puerto Rican	72.2	27.7	100.0
American Indian	72.8	27.1	100.0
Oriental	64.9	35.0	100.0
White	67.6	32.3	100.0
Total	67.7	32.2	100.0
	Percent Distribution Across Race		
Black	2.8	2.4	2.6
Mexican-American/Span. Amer.	0.6	0.5	0.6
Puerto Rican	0.1	0.1	0.1
American Indian	0.5	0.4	0.4
Oriental	1.1	1.2	1.1
White	94.7	95.1	94.8
Total	100.0	100.0	100.0

SOURCE: National Board on Graduate Education, National Academy of Sciences, National Research Council, Doctorate Records File, (1975) unpublished data.
[1]Each campus of multi-campus institutions is counted separately. Includes two predominantly Black institutions which awarded 43 doctorates (13 to Blacks).
[2]Less 27 for whom type of control was unknown.

Of the known Black doctoral recipients who identified race, 575 doctorates went to native-born Black Americans, 8 to naturalized Black citizens, 14 to Black non-citizens, and 10 to Blacks with unknown citizenship status. Therefore, 78% of the doctoral recipients who identified themselves as Black were native-born citizens.

Table 2-46 also includes the number of doctorates and citizenship status for other known ethnic and racial groups. For groups such as Orientals, Mexican-American, Spanish Americans, and "other" minorities, non-citizens receiving doctorates were a significant proportion of the awards to the racial/ethnic group. U.S. citizens in these "other" minority groups combined accounted for 1.69% of the doctorates awarded, while their non-citizen counterparts received 4.65% of the doctorates awarded in 1972-73.

Public colleges equaled 56.4% of the institutions that awarded doctorates in Spring 1973, and conferred two-thirds (66.7%) of the doctorates. (See Table 2-47.) Of the doctorates awarded to native-born Blacks, 70.5% were from public institutions. Of the total doctorates awarded by public and private institutions, native-born Blacks received 2.8% and 2.4% respectively.

For all races, doctorates were overwhelmingly awarded to males. (See Table 2-48.) The largest proportion of female recipients of doctorates within a racial group, however, were Black women, who received 26% of the doctorates awarded to native-born Blacks in Spring 1973.

Fields that had traditionally attracted Blacks continued to do so at the doctoral level in the 1972-73 academic year. At Black colleges, as was pointed out above, more

TABLE 2-48. Proportion of doctorates Awarded to Men and Women, by Citizenship Status, Race, and Ethnic Group, Spring 1973.

	Total	U.S. Native	*(In Percents)* U.S. Natural- ized	Non-U.S. Citizen Permanent Visa	Temporary Visa
Black					
Men	78	74	*	90	94
Women	22	26	*	10	6
White					
Men	81	81	71	81	89
Women	19	19	29	19	11

SOURCE National Board on Graduate Education, *Minority Group Participation in Graduate Education* (forthcoming).
*Less than 1%

than one-half (58.1%) of the doctorates awarded in Spring 1973 were in scientific fields. But at all colleges nationally, 60% of the doctorates awarded to native-born Blacks were in Education. (See Table 2-49.) Of the doctorates awarded to whites, 23% were in Education.

The greatest number of doctorates, for all U.S. citizens, were awarded to students in these fields: Education, Social Science, Arts and Humanities, Physical and Life Sciences. (Similar statistics for citizens and non-citizens combined are in Appendix D.)

Between undergraduate and doctoral training, many students shift their fields of study. But what was of special interest is the shift of Black students from technical and scientific fields to Education at the doctoral level. This shift, in part, accounted for the greater number of years it took Black students, compared with whites, between the baccalaureate and doctoral degrees. Only Black students with under-graduate degrees in Physical Sciences earned doctorates in the same field. Of the Black doctorates in Engineering, 70.6% held baccalaureate degrees in this field. Of the Black doctorates in Life Sciences, 80.4% held baccalaureates in the field. Of those in Social Sciences, and in Arts and Humanities, 62.7% and 74.0% respectively, held baccalaureates in these fields. Only 51.6% of the Black doctorates in Education held baccalaureate degrees in Education. (See Figure 2-13.) Professional fields also attracted Blacks with baccalaureate degrees in a wide range of fields.

As Black students moved into advanced training their distribution across fields of study narrowed. What is difficult to answer, based on available information, is why so many Black students shift into Education when they reach graduate schools. One explanation is that employment opportunities for Blacks have traditionally been greatest in Education fields.

Persistence Status

For Black students, one-year return rates were equal to those of whites in Fall 1973, according to U.S. Census data. In 1966, when the high school grade-point average was taken into account, the one-year return rate of Blacks was higher than that of whites for "A" and "B" students. For "C" students Black one-year return rates were lower than those of whites in 1966 (Astin, 1972).

In degrees awarded, the proportion of Blacks earning baccalaureate degrees in Spring 1973 approximated their undergraduate enrollment. Blacks were between 5.8% and 6.3% of the full-time entering freshmen between 1968 and 1971. They were also the recipients of about 5.1% of the baccalaureates earned in Spring 1974.

There is no simple answer to the question of whether the number of doctorates received by native-born Blacks approximates their enrollment in graduate school. According to the National Board on Graduate Education, both Black and white doctoral recipients spend, on the average, five years registered in doctoral programs. The obvious decision, therefore, would be to use the Fall 1968 graduate enrollment as a crude yardstick. In that year, Blacks were 3.4% of all 149,331 students enrolled in graduate and professional programs receiving federal assistance, according to the

Office for Civil Rights. Five years later, in 1973, Blacks made up about 2% of those receiving doctorates.

A factor that prohibits the conclusion that Black graduate school enrollment and Black doctoral degree completion were approximately equal is that Blacks went to

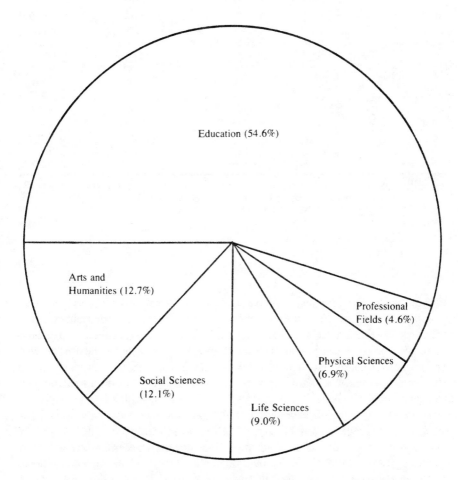

SOURCE: National Board on Graduate Education, National Academy of Sciences, National Research Council, Doctorate Records File, unpublished data.

FIGURE 2-13. Black (U.S. Native) Doctorates in Education by Baccalaureate Fields of Study, Spring 1973.

TABLE 2-49. Doctorates Awarded, by Field and Race, U.S. Native-Born Citizens, 1972-73 Academic Year (75% of all Awarded).

| Field | Native-Born U.S. Citizens Only (Number and Percent within Race) | | |
	Black	Other Minorities	White
Physical Sciences	32	43	2,976
& Mathematics	5.6%	12.0%	15.1%
Engineering	17	24	1,505
	3.0%	6.7%	7.5%
Life Sciences	51	82	2,790
	8.9%	22.8%	14.1%
Social Sciences	59	67	3,619
	10.3%	18.6%	18.4%
Arts and Humanities	50	53	3,409
	8.7%	14.8%	17.3%
Other Professional	17	4	852
Fields	3.0%	1.1%	4.3%
Education	346	86	4,559
	60.0%	24.0%	23.0%
Totals	572	359	19,710
	100.0%	100.0%	100.0%

SOURCE National Board on Graduate Education, National Academy of Sciences, National Research Council, Doctorate Records File, unpublished data.

graduate school intermittently. Compared to whites, Blacks took twice as many years to complete their doctoral training; however, field of study contributed to this difference. The difference was not in the number of semesters registered on a campus, but in how those semesters were spread out over time. For Blacks, the time between their bachelor's degree and their doctorate was on the average 13.25 years; for whites it was half as long. Comparing Black and white students in Education, the years between baccalaureate and doctorate averaged 15.27 years for Blacks and 12.51 years for whites. In non-Education fields, Blacks took 10.10 years and whites 7.61 years on the average to earn a doctorate. (See Table 2-50.) Consequently, the Fall 1968 enrollment of Blacks in graduate school does not necessarily relate to the doctorates awarded in 1973, since over one-half of the Black candidates for doctorates may not have been enrolled that year.

Compared with graduate school enrollment in Fall 1973, Black doctoral production was about proportional. Blacks were between 2 and 4% of the students in doctoral training in Fall 1973, based on estimates using Higher Education Panel and U.S. Census data. Thus, Black doctoral production in Spring 1973 roughly approximated their doctoral enrollment that same year.

TABLE 2-50. Number of Years Between Baccalaureate and Doctoral Degrees by Race, Spring 1973.

| | *U.S. Native-Born Only* | | | |
| | *Black* | | *White* | |
All Fields	*Number*	*%*	*Number*	*%*
0-1	0	—	1	—
2	1	0.2	16	0.08
3	6	1.1	278	0.40
4	19	3.3	1,307	7.00
5	25	4.4	2,072	11.0
6	35	6.1	2,321	12.0
7	32	6.0	2,231	11.3
8	30	5.3	1,829	9.3
9	37	6.5	1,594	8.1
10	25	4.4	1,191	6.0
11	29	5.1	1,030	5.2
12-13	53	9.3	1,555	8.0
14-15	53	9.3	1,070	5.4
16-17	53	9.3	796	4.0
18-19	46	8.1	577	3.0
20-24	80	14.0	1,165	6.0
25 or more	47	8.2	630	3.2
Total Known	571	100.0	19,663	100.0
Median Years (All Fields)		13.25		8.38
Education		15.27		12.51
Non-Education		10.10		7.61
Median Time in School		5.93		5.94

SOURCE: National Board on Graduate Education, National Academy of Sciences, National Research Council, Doctorate Records File, unpublished data.

Summary

Because no national data on dropout rates or on degree attainment of associate arts, masters, or professional school students were collected by race for the 1973-74 academic year, a complete picture of Black persistence is not possible. Based on available data on one-year return rates in 1973 on baccalaureates earned in Spring 1974, and doctorates earned in Spring 1973, it was concluded that once Black students gained access to four-year colleges and Ph.D.-granting institutions they were likely to persist. Persistence was lowest in two-year colleges. Compared with estimates of their enrollment, Black persistence and degree production in four-year colleges and Ph.D.-granting institutions was high. Blacks differed significantly from whites, not in whether they would complete training in these institutions, but in the number of calendar years it would require. For Blacks, it took longer to earn degrees than for whites because of the former's intermittent college attendance.

In Spring 1974, Black students received an estimated 5.1% of the baccalaureates awarded. Approximately one-half of these baccalaureates awarded to Black students were awarded by historically Black colleges. In the previous year, Blacks were recipients of approximately 2% of the doctorates awarded. The fields which traditionally attracted Blacks at the baccalaureate level continued to do so at the doctoral level in Spring, 1973. Of the doctorates awarded to Blacks, 60% were in Education. Between the baccalaureate and doctoral level Black students tended to shift away from technical and scientific fields into Education and professional fields, so that persistence of Blacks within scientific and technical fields was lower than their persistence within four-year colleges and universities.

CHAPTER 3

Barriers to Equal Educational Opportunity For Blacks

INTRODUCTION

As the previous discussion on Black enrollment in undergraduate and graduate schools in the 1973-74 school year demonstrated, the goal of equal educational opportunity for Blacks in higher education has not been achieved. The access, distribution, and persistence of Black students in higher education are still limited. Many barriers to equal educational opportunity (such as noncompletion of high school) were present before Black students even became eligible for college. Other barriers were deeply rooted in the racial and economic structure of this society. Although this discussion on barriers focused on Blacks in higher educational institutions, education is merely one indicator of the status of Blacks in American society. The relationship of barriers to equal educational opportunities for Blacks to the general societal status and treatment of Blacks cannot be overlooked.

High school noncompletion alone contributed to the unequal college attainment of Blacks. (An analysis of the barriers to high school completion is beyond the scope of this report.) The high percentage of high school dropouts and the quality of high school training severely restricted the size of the Black college availability pool. Indeed, for Blacks and other minority and disadvantaged groups in this society, noncompletion of high school and poor high school training may be the most significant barrier to college access.

Three classifications of barriers to equal educational opportunity are used to analyze the status of Blacks in college. These barriers are categorical (racial discrimination), educational (institutional policies and practices), and psychosocial (negative student attitudes) (Abramowitz and Abramowitz, 1975). Although the barriers are treated separately here, only for the purpose of this analysis, they do constantly interact, reinforce, or compete with each other. All three barriers, acting together, or

85

alone, negatively influenced the access, distribution, and persistence of Black students in college in the 1973-74 academic year.

Categorical Barriers

Categorical barriers arise when two groups are treated differently to the detriment of one group (Abramowitz and Abramowitz, 1975). Distinctions in treatment can be based on sex, race, national origin, or religion, to name a few. In this study, categorical barriers based on race were discussed. In higher education, categorical barriers included such things as quotas that limited college admission and eligibility requirements that limited the availability of financial aid to Blacks. Enforcement of Title VI of the Civil Rights Act of 1964 helped to reduce categorical barriers, especially in access. However, when income and aspiration differences had been accounted for, racial barriers to educational opportunity remained.

Educational Barriers

Educational barriers are policies and practices of institutions and individuals that seem neutral, but have an adverse impact on Blacks (Abramowitz and Abramowitz, 1975). A commonly cited example of an educational barrier is the use of the standardized tests for admissions or financial aid eligibility. All applicants take the same test and are judged by the same standards. But, because the test measures background and experiences as well as academic achievement, disadvantaged minority groups, and those more isolated from the mainstream American culture, tend not to score as well as others taking the test.

Educational and categorical barriers differ in that the latter are deliberate efforts to discriminate, whereas the racial impact of the former may be unintended. Their neutral appearance makes educational barriers more difficult to detect and easier to defend than categorical barriers. In addition, categorical barriers can simply be eliminated, but educational barriers must be replaced because they usually serve a legitimate function. Finding a replacement for an educational barrier is often difficult, because an institution may resist change, or because a satisfactory substitute cannot be found.

In addition to admissions tests, college costs, financial aid, educational preparation, transfer policies, counseling practices, recruitment, extracurricular activities, and student employment all constituted educational barriers for Black students. These seemingly neutral barriers produced negative impacts for Blacks.

Psychosocial Barriers

Psychosocial barriers arise from negative aspects of the life-styles individuals adopted voluntarily or through coercion (Abramowitz and Abramowitz, 1975). Clark (1934), in the now classic doll-preference study, found in young Black children feelings of inferiority both explicit and implicit in racially segregated systems in which they lived.

Psychosocial barriers influence distribution by the institutions and fields of study chosen by Black students, and persistence in those institutions. The discussion on psychosocial barriers included an analysis of the fields of study chosen by Black students, and their reactions to campuses of differing racial composition.

CATEGORICAL BARRIERS

Enforcement of Title VI of the Civil Rights Act of 1964 and other legislation, in addition to court decisions, has undoubtedly contributed to the increases in college enrollment of Black students by reducing categorical barriers to access, distribution, and persistence. Even with the widened educational opportunities for Blacks (and other disadvantaged groups), Black college enrollment in the 1973-74 academic year still reflected underrepresentation. (For discussion of racial differences in educational attainment in 1970, see Chapter 4.)

Although there has been an increase in the absolute numbers of Blacks and whites who attained some college education, there has been an uneven increase in the proportions. (See Table 3-1.) Comparing the percent of Black and white male high school graduates age 20 to 21 years old who completed one or more years of college between 1940 and 1974, it is evident that the racial gap between white and Black male educational attainment of youths has persisted over the 34-year period, without closing significantly in the 1970's. Indeed, the difference between the college attainment of white and Black male high school graduates age 20 to 21 was smaller in 1940 (3.4%) than it was in 1974 (13.7%). (See Figure 3-1.) Thus, it still takes Black youths longer than it takes white youths to complete one or more years of college.

The college attainment of white females was consistently lower than that of white males from 1940 to 1974. Until the 1960's, a higher percent of Black females than Black males attained some college education.

Sex differences in college attainment of Black and white female high school graduates age 20 to 21 years old were significantly smaller than those of their male counterparts. (See Figure 3-2.) In 1940, a higher proportion of Black female high school graduates had completed one or more years of college at age 21 than had their white female counterparts. By the 1950's however, this situation reversed itself as the number of white females with some college increased rapidly. In the 1970's, the racial gap between Black and white females that existed in the 1950's and 1960's had closed significantly to the extent that, in 1974, 46.1% of the white and 42.8% of the Black female high school graduates age 20 and 21, had completed one or more years of college, a difference of 3.3%.

Lack of aspiration on the part of Black students and lack of family financial resources to meet college costs are often cited as explanations for this unequal educational attainment of Black and white high school graduates. But the persistence of racial differences even when aspiration and income have been accounted for suggests continuing categorical barriers to education.

As a part of its enforcement of Title VI of the Civil Rights Act of 1964, the Office

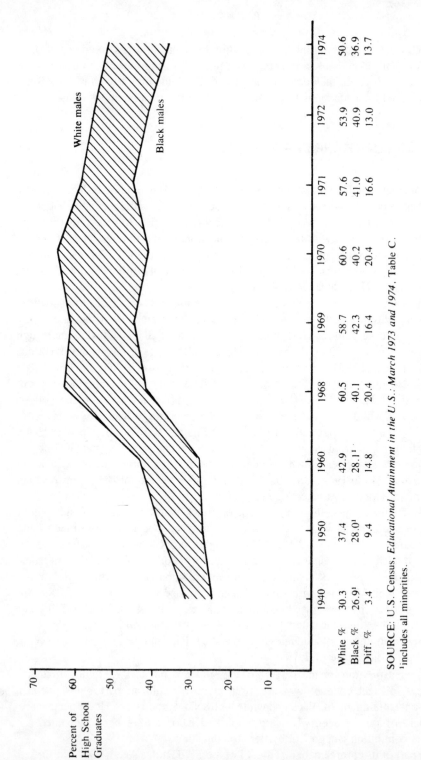

	1940	1950	1960	1968	1969	1970	1971	1972	1974
White %	30.3	37.4	42.9	60.5	58.7	60.6	57.6	53.9	50.6
Black %	26.9[1]	28.0[1]	28.1[1]	40.1	42.3	40.2	41.0	40.9	36.9
Diff. %	3.4	9.4	14.8	20.4	16.4	20.4	16.6	13.0	13.7

SOURCE: U.S. Census, *Educational Attainment in the U.S.: March 1973 and 1974*, Table C.
[1]includes all minorities.

FIGURE 3-1. Percent of Male High School Graduates 20 and 21 Years Old Who Completed One Year of College or More by Race, 1940 to 1974.

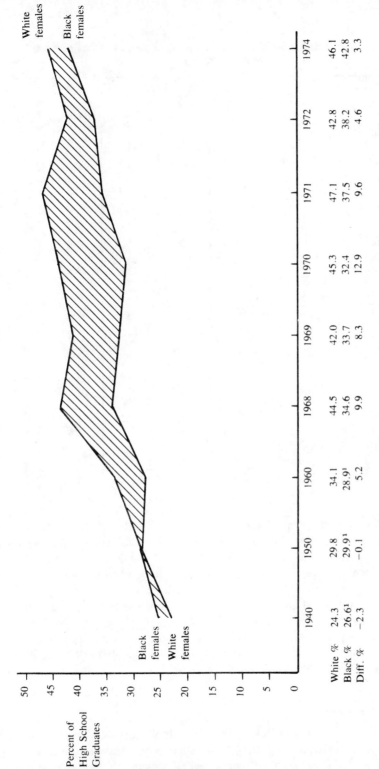

	1940	1950	1960	1968	1969	1970	1971	1972	1974
White %	24.3	29.8	34.1	44.5	42.0	45.3	47.1	42.8	46.1
Black %	26.6[1]	29.9[1]	28.9[1]	34.6	33.7	32.4	37.5	38.2	42.8
Diff. %	−2.3	−0.1	5.2	9.9	8.3	12.9	9.6	4.6	3.3

SOURCE: U.S. Census, *Educational Attainment in the U.S.: March 1973 and 1974*, Table C.

[1]Includes all minorities.

FIGURE 3-2. Percent of Female High School Graduates 20 and 21 Years Old Who Completed One Year of College or More by Race, 1940 to 1974.

TABLE 3-1. Percent Distribution of Years of School Completed by Race and Age, March 1973.

Years of School Completed	Age and Race					
	18 & 19		20 & 21		22 to 24	
	Black	White	Black	White	Black	White
Less than high school grad. only	52.8	35.2	28.5	14.5	28.9	15.0
High School grad. only	40.2	51.0	46.6	44.2	44.3	43.1
College						
1 year	6.2	12.5	10.5	14.7	7.9	7.9
2 years	0.7	1.2	9.2	17.1	7.9	9.9
3 years	0.2	0.2	4.1	8.1	4.4	6.5
4 years	—	0.1	0.6	1.2	5.5	14.6
5 or more years	—	—	0.5	—	1.0	2.9
Median school years completed	11.9	12.3	12.5	12.8	12.5	12.8

Years of school Completed	25 to 29		30 to 34		35 to 44	
Less than high school grad. only	35.7	18.0	42.0	22.5	52.4	28.1
High School grad. only	42.7	44.3	38.8	44.7	32.2	43.3
College						
1 year	6.2	6.8	5.3	6.0	3.6	5.1
2 years	4.0	7.5	4.7	6.1	4.0	5.5
3 years	3.2	3.6	0.7	2.6	1.2	1.9
4 years	6.6	12.8	5.9	10.2	3.7	9.2
5 years or more	1.5	7.0	2.7	7.8	2.8	6.8
Median school years completed	12.3	12.7	12.2	12.6	11.7	12.5

SOURCE U.S. Census,*Educational Attainment in U.S.: March 1973 and 1974, Table 1.*

for Civil Rights conducts biennial enrollment surveys. OCR does not, however, routinely collect data that would indicate the presence or absence of categorical barriers in state or institutional practices. To what extent, if any, race is a barrier in shaping recruitment or counseling, and to what extent race is a factor in determining student grades, in evaluating Black promise for graduate school, or in dispersing student aid from institutional funds is unknown. The continuing underrepresentation of Blacks in undergraduate, graduate, or professional schools (regardless of high school record, aspiration, or family income) does not allow us to readily dismiss race as a factor without objective data. As part of its enforcement of Title VI, these data should be collected by OCR.

Aspiration

The educational aspirations of Black high school and college students were equal to those of their white counterparts in the 1973-74 academic year. But the aspirations of Black students were higher than their own actual educational attainment. The immediate degree aspiration of about three-fourths of the Black and white college students enrolled in Fall 1973 was to earn a bachelor degree or higher. (See Tables 3-2 and 3-3.) More Black females than Black males wanted advanced degrees. However, compared to females of the same race, more white males in college wanted advanced degrees.

The proportion of high school graduates in college the following semester indicated the higher college-going rate of whites from 1970 through 1973. (See Figure 3-3.) The lower educational aspirations of Black high school students are often hypothesized as the reason for this difference in enrollment. However, Black high school seniors were slightly more likely than whites to want to go to college.

TABLE 3-2. Immediate Degree Aspirations of Black College Students by Sex, October 1973.

	Percent		
Degree Aspirations	*Male*	*Female*	*Both Sexes*
Associate	15.0	25.0	20.0
Bachelor	65.2	52.0	58.4
Masters	8.4	13.0	10.5
Doctorate	1.0	1.0	1.0
Professional	3.0	2.0	2.2
Other	3.0	4.4	4.0
No Degree	6.0	4.1	5.0
*TOTAL	100%	100%	100%

Source: U.S. Census, (1975), unpublished data.
*May not equal 100% due to rounding.

TABLE 3-3. Immediate Degree Aspirations of White[1] college Students by Sex, October 1973.

	Percent		
Degree Aspirations	*Male*	*Female*	*Both Sexes*
Associate	14.8	13.7	14.3
Bachelor	55.4	55.2	55.3
Masters	10.7	11.7	11.2
Doctorate	5.1	1.0	3.3
Professional	4.3	2.2	3.4
Other	2.3	3.3	2.7
No Degree	7.0	12.4	9.4
*TOTAL	100%	100%	100%

SOURCE: U.S. Census, (1975), unpublished data.
*May not equal 100% due to rounding.
[1]Includes non-Black minorities.

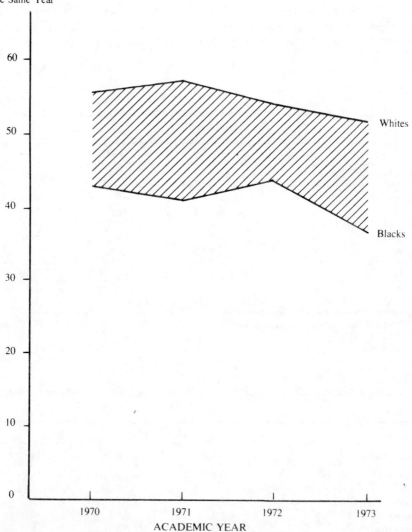

Percent of High
School Graduates
Who Attend College
the Same Year

Whites

Blacks

ACADEMIC YEAR

SOURCE: U.S Census, *College Plans of High School Seniors: October 1972*, Table E.

FIGURE 3-3. Percent of Spring High School Graduates Who Attend College the Following Fall by Race, 1970 Through 1973.

Data on educational aspirations of high school seniors in October 1972 were reported in Chapter 2. It will be recalled that 76.7% of the Black high school seniors and 71.5% of the white high school seniors in October 1972 stated that they planned to go to college the following Fall. Black and white high school seniors differed in the degree of certainty with which they felt they would go to college the following academic year. Of the Black seniors, 43.8% definitely planned to go to college in comparison to 45.6% of the white seniors. However, the remaining 32.9% of the Black and 25.9% of the remaining white high school seniors interested in college had less certain plans to attend college.

Based on October 1973 enrollment data, only 35% of the Black 1972-73 high school seniors actually enrolled in college. For whites, 48% enrolled in college. Thus, 42% of the Black and 24% of the white high school seniors in 1972-73 who wanted to go to college did not enroll in Fall 1973. Even when high school students with less certain plans to attend college were eliminated, the likelihood of immediate college enrollment for white and Black students aspiring toward college remained unequal: 97.1% of the Black high school seniors with more definite plans may have enrolled, compared to 104% of the whites.

At the graduate and professional school level, the aspirations of Black students also outstripped their actual attainment. Among college seniors, a higher proportion of Blacks than whites aspired for advanced training (Baird, 1973). (See Table 3-4.)

TABLE 3-4. Plans of College Seniors by Race, 1972.

	Black		White		All Students[1]	
Plan	No.	%	No.	%	No.	%
Continue further education next fall in Graduate Study	21	21.6	3.388	18.1	3.816	18.4
Continue further education next fall in Professional Study	195	19.1	3,725	18.9	4,152	20.1
Total planning further education the next fall	416	40.7	7,113	38.0	7,968	38.5
Continue further education after next fall						
Probably	214	20.9	5,100	27.2	6,157	29.7
Definitely	294	28.7	4,185	22.5	5,913	28.5
No plans for further education	27	2.6	1,225	6.5	1,469	7.1
Total	1,023		18,702		20,732	

SOURCE: Baird, Leonard, The Graduates, *A Report on the Characteristics and Plans of College Seniors* (1973), Table 2.2.

[1]Includes other ethnic groups and those who did not answer the race question.

However, the enrollment of Black seniors in graduate schools was lower than that of whites. Baird (1973) did a one-year follow-up of 27% (or 278) of the Black seniors and 35% (or 6,561) of the white seniors in this earlier study. He found that although 34.2% of all Black and 34.9% of all white college seniors in 1971 were enrolled in graduate school the following semester, fewer Black than white seniors engaged in the planned activity one year after graduation. (See Table 3-5.) Blacks in graduate school were more likely to be enrolled in a field other than the one planned. Because of the very small number of Black and white students in the one-year follow-up study, the generalizability of the findings is open to question without additional follow-up data on the other 745 Blacks and the 12,141 whites surveyed as seniors.

In a five- and ten-year follow-up study of freshmen by the American Council on Education, El-Khawas and Bisconti (1974) found that a slightly smaller proportion of 1961 and 1966 white than Black freshmen had enrolled in advanced training by 1972. Of the Black 1961 freshmen, 59.7% had enrolled in graduate or professional school by 1972. Of the white 1961 freshmen, 58.6% had enrolled in graduate or professional school by 1972. For the 1966 Black and white freshmen 32.6% and 31.1% respectively had at one time been enrolled in graduate or professional school by 1972. However, El-Khawas and Bisconti also found that aspirations were more likely to fall short of degree attainment for Black than for white 1961 and 1966 freshmen in 1972. (See Table 3-6.) In both 1961 and 1966 Black freshmen tended to have higher degree aspirations than their white counterparts. Five and ten years later, however, the distance between aspiration and attainment was larger for Black than for white freshmen. White students desiring graduate and professional degrees were more likely than Blacks to get them.

TABLE 3-5. Percentage of College Seniors Engaged in Planned Activity One Year Later by Race, Spring 1972.

	By Ethnic Group		
Plan	Black	White	Difference
Total in planned advanced study	39.7	52.3	−12.6
Total who planned to go who were in some other field	23.1	19.6	3.5
Total who planned to go in any advanced study	62.8	71.9	−9.1
	100%	100%	
Number	278	7,326	

SOURCE: Baird, Leonard, *Career and Curricula*, Table 1.4.

According to El-Khawas and Bisconti, the difference in graduate enrollment, degrees earned, and aspirations of Blacks and whites was larger five years after college entry than ten years after college entry. Although the racial difference was not eliminated completely over the ten-year period, it was reduced over time. In spite of equal or higher aspirations, it took Black students longer than whites to attain advanced degrees.

While aspiration was not a definite measure of commitment to a college education or the intensity of that motivation, Black students, contrary to racial stereotype, consistently expressed the desire for a college education. Aspiration alone, therefore, failed to explain differences in college enrollment and attainment of whites and Blacks.

TABLE 3-6. Highest Degrees Held and Planned by 1961 and 1966 Freshmen by Race, 1972.

	1961 (Percents)			*1966 (Percents)*		
Degrees	*Planned*	*Held*	*Differ-ence*	*Planned*	*Held*	*Differ-ence*
Black Students						
None	4	11	7	9	37	28
Associate	1	4	3	4	11	7
Bachelor's	17	57	40	18	49	31
Master's	48	23	−25	37	2	−35
Doctorate	25	4	−21	24	−	−24
M.D.	3	−	−3	3	−	−3
D.D.S. or D.V.M.	−	−	−	2	−	−2
L.L.B. or J.D.	2	−	2	2	−	−2
Other	−	−	−	2	2	0
Total (Weighted)	100	100		100	100	
	(9186)	(9128)		(68,080)	(63,351)	
White Students						
None	6	11	5	9	27	18
Associate	1	2	1	5	10	5
Bachelor's	29	53	24	27	59	32
Master's	39	23	−16	38	3	−35
Doctorate	15	4	−11	13	−	−13
M.D.	3	2	−1	2	−	−2
D.D.S. or D.V.M.	1	1	0	1	−	−1
L.L.B. or J.D.	6	3	−3	5	−	−5
Other	−	1	−1	1	1	0
Total (Weighted)	100	100		100	100	
	(400,505)	(401,573)		(1,236,033)	(1,214,682)	

SOURCE: El-Khawas, Elaine and Bisconti, Ann S., *Five and Ten Years After College Entry*, Table 13.

Family Income

Family income is also often used to explain racial differences in college access, distribution, and persistence. If the differences in college enrollment of white and Black high school graduates were due to family income, that is, the ability of families to pay college costs, racial differences in enrollment should disappear when income is held constant. When race was not considered, students from wealthier families were more likely to be enrolled in college. U.S. Census data on enrollment of students age 18 to 24 years old indicated that as income increased, the proportion enrolled also increased from 1967 to 1973. (See Table 3-7.)

When income was held constant, the proportion of family members age 18 to 24 enrolled in college full-time did not change significantly between 1967 and 1973. (See Figure 3-4.) Therefore, recent increases in the total number of family members age 18 to 24 enrolled in college from the lower income groups reflected population growth in low-income families, not increased rate of college enrollment of disadvantaged youths.

TABLE 3-7. Primary Families With Dependent Members 18 to 24 Years Old and Percent with Members Enrolled Full-Time in College by Family Income, October 1967 to October 1973.
(Numbers in Thousands. Income in Constant 1973 dollars. Civilian Noninstitutional Population).

Family Income and Enrollment status of family member	1973	1972	1971	1970	1969	1968	1967
Families with dependent members 18 to 24 years old							
Total	9,803	9,752	9,644	9,349	8,773	8,610	8,631
Total reporting income	8,900	8,979	8,933	8,614	8,053	7,979	7,833
Under $3,000	600	738	665	615	566	608	627
$3,000 to $4,999	832	808	792	723	650	640	631
$5,000 to $7,499	1,060	1,096	1,168	1,163	1,096	1,117	1,129
$7,750 to $9,999	945	1,118	1,284	1,274	1,198	1,240	1,279
$10,000 to $14,999	2,510	2,342	2,261	2,200	2,029	1,958	1,954
$15,000 and over	2,894	2,877	2,762	2,639	2,514	2,415	2,213
Median Income	$11,898	$11,557	$11,231	$11,210	$11,272	$10,981	$10,643
Percent with members enrolled full-time in college	*Percent Distribution*						
Total reporting income	36.2	37.8	38.4	39.8	42.0	40.1	39.1
Under $3,000	12.7	14.8	14.0	14.0	16.4	15.0	13.1
$3,000 to $4,999	18.0	19.8	21.0	19.1	22.5	20.9	19.7
$5,000 to $7,499	23.7	27.1	27.7	27.8	29.4	28.0	26.5
$7,500 to $9,999	28.9	31.4	32.2	34.6	36.0	34.4	32.4
$10,000 to $14,999	36.3	39.7	40.2	43.0	45.3	44.1	45.0
$15,000 and over	53.7	53.7	55.1	56.5	58.5	56.5	57.1
Median Income of families with members enrolled full-time in college	$14,679	$14,190	$13,947	$13,831	$13,798	$13,638	$13,481

SOURCE: U.S. Census, *Characteristics of American Youth: 1974*, Table 15.

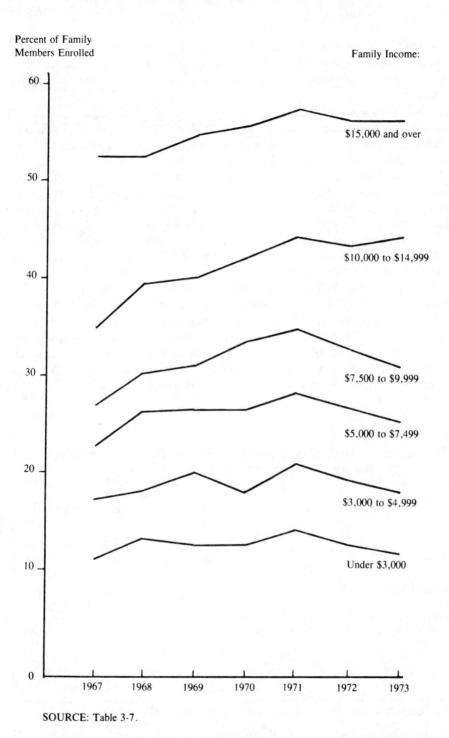

Percent of Family
Members Enrolled

Family Income:

$15,000 and over

$10,000 to $14,999

$7,500 to $9,999

$5,000 to $7,499

$3,000 to $4,999

Under $3,000

SOURCE: Table 3-7.

FIGURE 3-4. Percent of Family Members 18 to 24 Years Old Enrolled in College Full-Time by Family Income, 1967 to 1973.

Using U.S. Census data for the 1973-74 school year, enrollment was analyzed by race and family income of dependent students, age 18 to 24. Dependent students 18 to 24 accounted for 76% to 86% of Blacks and whites in college in Fall 1973. (See Table 3-8.)

When income was held constant, race was still a factor in college attendance of dependent students, age 18 to 24. (See Table 3-9.) At all income ranges, except $5,000 to $7,499, Black high school graduates were less likely than whites to have had any college experience. (See Figure 3-5.) The proportion of Black to white high school graduates with college experience was 78.1%. Thus, 21.9% of the difference in college experience of Blacks and whites was not due to income. If Blacks in the availability pool had the income distribution of whites, would the racial differences in college participation disappear? No, but redistributing the income of Blacks in the availability pool to equal that of whites reduced the difference of Black to white college experience by 61%, leaving 39% of the difference in Black-white college participation still unaccounted for.

If public policy set redistribution of Black family income in the college availability pool as the goal, college participation of Blacks and whites would still be unequal. The gap between Black and white college participation would be reduced if family incomes were redistributed, but the gap would not be closed. Even if incomes were distributed equally for Blacks and whites in the college availability pool, Black college participation would equal 91.2% that of whites in 1973. (See Table F-1 in Appendix F for calculations used to arrive at this conclusion.)

TABLE 3-8. Students 18 to 24 Years Old Enrolled in College Who Are Dependent (Members of Households), by race and sex, October 1973.

| | In Thousands | | | | | |
| | Black | | | White | | |
	Male	Female	Total	Male	Female	Total
Total Enrolled	267	231	498	3,032	2,405	5,437
Independent Students	64	33	97	591	464	1,055
*Dependent Students W/Income Reported	203	198	401	2,441	1,941	4,382
Percent Dependent Students W/Income Reported	76.0%	85.7%	80.5%	80.5%	80.7%	80.6%

SOURCE: U.S. Census, *Social and Economic Characteristics of Students, October 1973*, Tables 6 and 13.

*Less family income not reported.

TABLE 3-9. Percent of Blacks and Family Members Age 18 to 24 in College Availability Pool and With College Experience by Family Income, October 1973.

Family Income	All Family Members		Black Family Members		White Family Members	
	Availability Pool	College Experience	Availability Pool	College Experience	Availability Pool	College Experience
	(In Thousands)		(In Thousands)		(In Thousands)	
Under $3,000	781	289	211	59	560	228
$3,000 to $4,999	1,392	518	325	96	1,045	414
$5,000 to $7,499	2,621	948	390	147	2,206	793
$7,500 to $9,999	2,436	978	248	96	2,156	885
$10,000 to $14,999	5,479	2,875	373	159	4,525	2,150
$15,000 and above	4,383	2,999	209	124	4,105	2,817
Not Reported	1,395	793	136	58	11,231	718
Total	17,148	8,876	1,902	748	15,829	7,976
			Percent Distribution			
Under $3,000	37.0		28.0		40.7	
$3,000 to $4,999	37.2		29.5		39.6	
$5,000 to $7,499	36.2		37.7		35.9	
$7,500 to $9,999	40.1		38.7		39.7	
$10,000 to $14,999	52.5		42.6		47.5	
$15,000 and above	68.3		59.3		68.6	
Not Reported	56.8		42.6		6.4	
Total	51.8		39.3		50.43	

SOURCE: U.S. Census, *Social and Economic Characteristics of Students, October, 1973*, Table 13.

Figure 3-6 illustrates the effect on income of the college participation of dependent Black high school graduates age 18 to 24 using U.S. Census data. Black college participation expressed as a proportion of white was 78.1% in Fall 1973. If family incomes in the college availability pool were equalized, Black participation would increase from 78.1% of that of whites to 91.2%.

Income adjustments alone did not equalize college access for Black and white high school graduates age 18 to 24. If the emphasis of policies, to provide equal educational opportunity, were aimed exclusively at financial barriers, Blacks and whites would still have unequal college participation, regardless of whether the federal funds are aimed at the college availability pool or at students enrolled in college.

Racial differences in the likelihood of Black and white freshmen enrolling in certain types of institutions, even when high school grade-point average and family income were held constant, was also evident. (See Tables 3-10 through 3-13.) At each income level the greatest number of the bright Black freshmen in the ACE Survey (that is those with high school GPA of B+ or higher) were enrolled in public four-year colleges, which included historically Black institutions. And, at each income level, the greatest number of the bright white freshmen were in public universities and private four-year colleges.

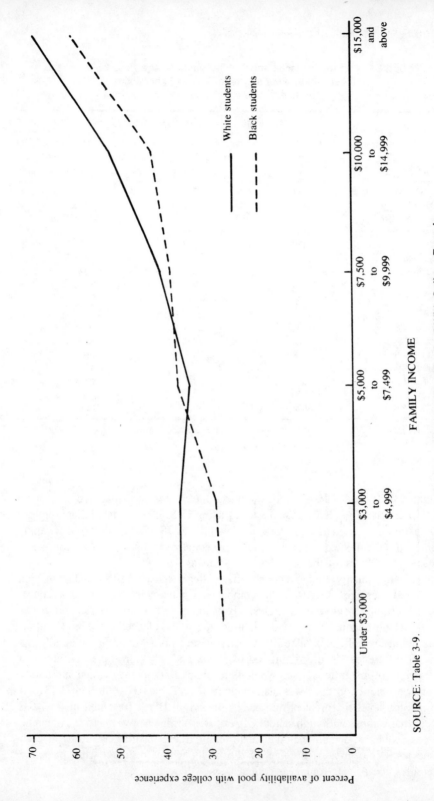

FIGURE 3-5. Percent of College Availability Pool With College Experience, Age 18 to 24, by Race and Family Income, October 1973.

SOURCE: Table 3-9.

As can be seen in Figure 3-7, as family income increased, public and private university enrollment of Black freshmen increased. For white freshmen, however, increases in white family income did not produce significant increases in public and private university enrollment.

For bright Black freshmen family income was also related to whether or not they enrolled in public two-year colleges. As can be seen in Figure 3-8, in Fall 1973, Black freshmen enrollment in public two-year colleges decreased as family income increased. For bright white freshmen, family income was unrelated to their enrollment in public two-year colleges.

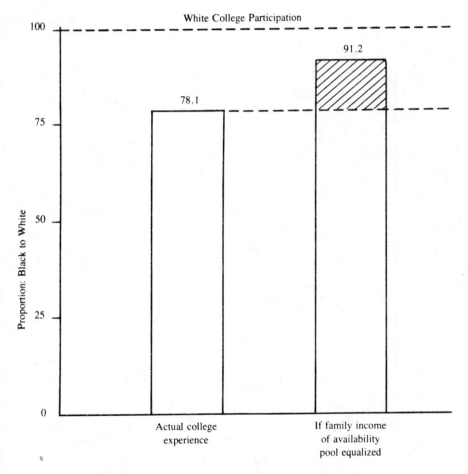

SOURCE: Table 3-9 and Tables F-1 and F-2 (in Appendix F).

[1]See text for explanation of adjustments (shaded areas) in figure.

FIGURE 3-6. Proportion of Black to White College Participation and Hypothetical Proportion if Black/White Incomes in the Availability Pool Were Equalized, October 1973.[1]

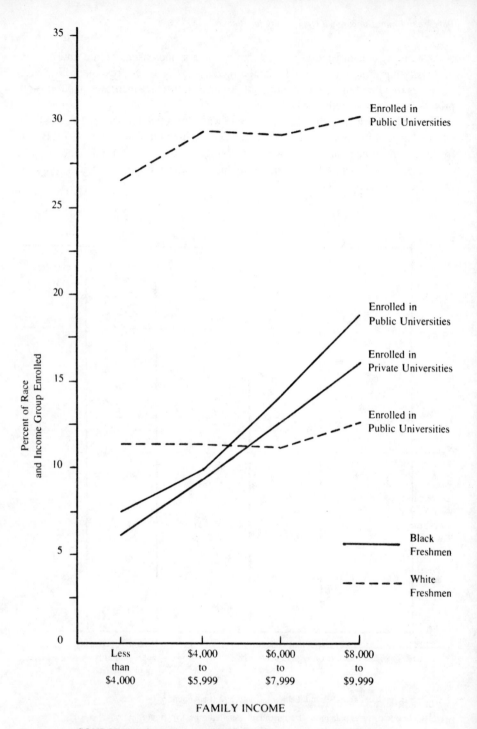

FIGURE 3-7. Percent of Bright Students by Income and Race Enrolled in Public and Private Universities, Fall 1973.

TABLE 3-10. Enrollment of Bright (High School GPA of B+ or Better)
Full-Time Freshmen From Low-Income ($4,000 or Less)
Families, by Race and Type of Institution, Fall 1973.

Type of Institution	*Percent Distribution (Unweighted Data)*			
	Black	*White*	*Other*	*All Students*
Public				
Universities	7.4	26.7	17.6	19.4
Four-Year	48.2	18.9	23.0	29.4
Two-Year	9.2	9.4	34.8	10.1
Total Public	64.7	55.0	62.5	58.9
Private				
Universities	6.4	12.5	10.2	10.2
Four-Year	27.7	29.2	25.9	28.5
Two-Year	1.1	3.0	1.2	2.2
Total Private	35.2	44.9	37.4	41.0
Race Totals	1,255	2,104	243	3,602

SOURCE: American Council on Education, CIRP Freshman Norms, (1973), unpublished data.

TABLE 3-11. Enrollment of Bright (High School GPA of B+ or Better)
Full-Time Freshmen From Low-Income ($4,000 to $5,999)
Families, by Race and Type of Institution, Fall 1973.

Type of Institution	*Percent Distribution (Unweighted Data)*			
	Black	*White*	*Other*	*All Students*
Public				
Universities	9.8	29.5	19.4	25.0
Four-Year	46.2	18.8	21.6	24.5
Two-Year	7.0	8.0	15.1	8.2
Total	(63.2)	(56.4)	(56.2)	(57.7)
Private				
Universities	10.0	11.5	20.2	11.7
Four-Year	26.2	29.6	20.5	28.4
Two-Year	0.4	2.3	2.1	1.9
Total	(36.7)	(43.5)	(43.7)	(42.2)
Race Totals	100%	100%	100%	100%
	(648)	(2,382)	(185)	(3,215)

SOURCE: American Council on Education, CIRP Freshman Norms (1973), unpublished data.

For both Blacks and whites the percent of bright freshmen enrolled in public (and private) two-year colleges was small. A greater proportion of the bright white freshmen in the ACE survey were enrolled in public two-year colleges than was true of their Black counterparts. As family income increased, the differences between Black and white enrollment in public two-year colleges also increased because of changes in Black enrollment.

TABLE 3-12. Enrollment of Bright (High School GPA of B+ or Better)
Full-Time Freshmen From Moderate-Income Families ($6,000 to $7,999)
by Race and Type of Institution, Fall 1973.

Type of Institution	*Percent Distribution (Unweighted Data)*			
	Black	*White*	*Other*	*All Students*
Public				
Universities	13.1	29.3	24.3	26.9
Four-Year	39.2	19.1	14.2	21.5
Two-Year	3.8	8.0	10.5	7.6
Total	(56.2)	(56.5)	(49.1)	(56.1)
Private				
Universities	14.5	11.1	15.1	11.7
Four-Year	28.0	29.6	33.6	29.5
Two-Year	1.0	2.7	2.1	2.4
Total	(43.7)	(43.4)	(50.8)	(43.8)
Race Totals	100%	100%	100%	100%
	(652)	(4,037)	(238)	(4,927)

SOURCE: American Council on Education, CIRP Freshman Norms (1973), unpublished data.

TABLE 3-13. Enrollment of Bright (High School GPA of B+ or Better)
Full-Time Freshmen From Lower Middle-Income Families ($8,000 to $9,999)
by Race and Type of Institution, Fall 1973.

Type of Institution	*Percent Distribution (Unweighted Data)*			
	Black	*White*	*Other*	*All Students*
Public				
Universities	16.3	30.3	21.2	29.0
Four-Year	30.2	18.3	15.8	19.1
Two-Year	3.6	7.2	14.1	7.2
Total	(50.2)	(55.9)	(51.2)	(55.3)
Private				
Universities	19.1	11.9	20.0	12.7
Four-Year	29.6	29.8	27.0	29.7
Two-Year	0.9	2.2	1.6	2.1
Total	(49.7)	(44.0)	(48.7)	(44.6)
Race Totals	100%	100%	100%	100%
	(543)	(6,432)	(240)	(7,206)

SOURCE: American Council on Education, CIRP Freshman Norms, (1973), unpublished data.

Summary

Income and aspiration were factors in the college enrollment attainment of Blacks. However, neither income nor aspiration alone adequately explained the racial differences in the college enrollment and attainment of whites and Blacks. When Blacks had higher educational aspirations and when income was equalized, racial differences in college enrollment and completion persisted. The remaining differences were due to other barriers to equal educational opportunity—categorical, educational, or psychosocial.

The influence of categorical barriers on the status of Blacks in higher education in 1973 was undoubtedly smaller than in previous years because of public laws and court decisions prohibiting racial discrimination in higher education practices and policies. Categorical barriers cannot be disregarded as causes of the continuous discrepancy in Black and white rate of college enrollment and level of attainment. Thus, expanded involvement of the Office for Civil Rights was discussed. Either alone or in combination with the educational and psychosocial barriers discussed below, categorical

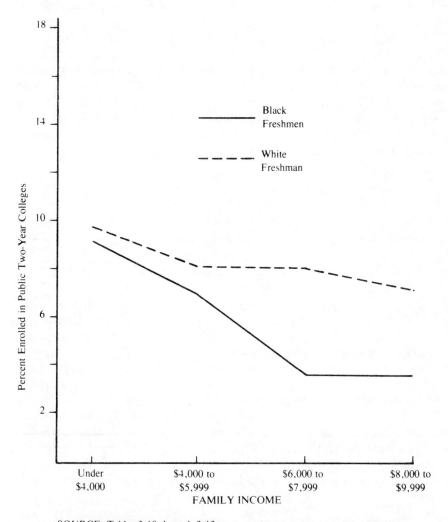

SOURCE: Tables 3-10 through 3-13.

FIGURE 3-8. Percent of Bright Freshmen Enrolled in Public Two-Year Colleges by Family Income and Race, Fall 1973.

barriers based on race influenced the status of Blacks in higher education in the 1973-74 academic year.

EDUCATIONAL BARRIERS

Educational barriers are policies and practices that are seemingly neutral, but have an adverse impact on the educational opportunities of Blacks. In this section the negative impacts of the following educational barriers are discussed: Admissions Tests, College Costs, Financial Aid, Family Income, Educational Preparation/ Academic Failure, Transfer Policies, Counseling Practices, Recruitment, and Extra-curricular Activities and Employment. Independently and together, these educational barriers tended to limit the educational opportunities of Blacks in higher education in 1973. In most instances removing educational barriers means developing alternative policies and practices because the barriers may have served a legitimate function. Developing alternative policies that are in fact racially neutral requires an adequate investment of time and research.

Admissions Tests

There was a powerful relationship between SAT scores and the parental income of the students taking the test. Although all students with the same parental income did not earn the same SAT scores, there was a greater tendency for students from low-income families to earn low scores and for students from middle-to-higher income families to earn high scores. In 1973, the College Entrance Examination Board reported that the average family income for students who earned 750-800 points on the Scholastic Aptitude Test (SAT) was $24,124. Students in the lowest SAT score range, 200-249, had a mean family income of $8,639. (See Figure 3-9.)

When educational institutions based their admissions decisions on such standardized test scores, they created a situation in which seemingly neutral standards had an adverse societal class impact that was not unrelated to race. There was an overlap between income and race, and the lower-income groups included the greatest proportion of Blacks. The median Black family income in 1973 was $7,269 or 60% that of the white family (according to the U.S. Census, 1974). Thus, if college admissions policies were based on standardized test scores, students from high-income families, a disproportionate number of whom were white, would be selected. And, under such a policy, low-income students, where Blacks are overrepresented, would be overlooked.

Why family income and test scores showed such a strong relationship was probably due to several causes, including the differences in the quality of high school experience offered among poor and more affluent communities; the differences in the test-taking facility; and the degree of confidence with which students from different family backgrounds approached testing situations. Regardless of the causes, the

SAT Scores

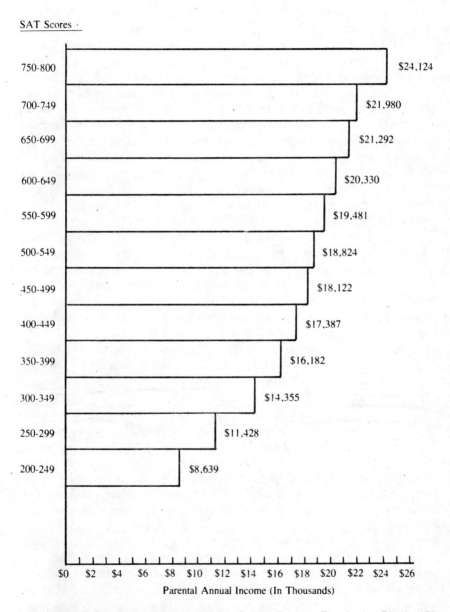

SOURCE: College-Bound Seniors, 1973-74. College Entrance Examination Board (1974),
Table 21.

FIGURE 3-9. Mean Parental Annual Income by SAT Score Ranges For High School Seniors, 1973-74 Academic Year.

outcome was that students from wealthier families were likely to score better than students from poorer families on standardized tests. Because these tests served a legitimate function (as gatekeepers) it was important to note they also discriminated on the basis of race and social class.

Admissions tests policies of undergraduate, graduate, and professional schools functioned as educational barriers to access (Bragonier and Ragin, 1970; Hull, 1970), and contributed to the underrepresentation of Blacks in college. In most undergraduate and graduate schools, tests were included in the selection criteria. In 1973, one or more standardized admissions tests were required by 80% of the graduate and professional schools. (See Table E-6 in Appendix E which summarizes the number of graduate and professional schools by field that required one or more admissions tests.) Sedlacek (1973) found that more institutions were relying on tests as selection criteria. However, according to the American Council on Education (Creager, 1973), many colleges and universities were supplementing test scores and high school grade-point averages with data provided through letters of recommendation and personal interviews. And a few institutions were using open admissions or special admissions programs targeted at minorities. (See Table E-5 in Appendix E.)

The value of admissions tests rested on their ability to predict reasonably well first-year grade-point averages in undergraduate, graduate, or professional schools. But admissions tests gave better estimates of the probable academic performance of white students than they did of Black students. Borgen (1971), for example, found that college grades of talented Black students were not only determined by their National Merit Test scores, but also by the selectivity of the colleges they attended. At highly selective colleges, which were predominantly white, the Black National Merit students earned lower grades than white National Merit students.

The general finding of the published research on admissions tests was that the tests were not barriers to access because they did not underestimate the ability of minority test-takers (Abramowitz, 1972; Linn, 1974). According to the research, the test scores of Black students predicted higher grade-point averages at the end of the first year than the students actually received. Thus, it was concluded that tests overestimated Black student performance. But the predictions of the first-year grade-point averages, based on the aptitude test scores, did not take into account the difficulties of adjustment for Black students on white campuses, as anecdotal data suggested. First-year grade-point averages, by themselves, may not have indicated the true academic ability of Black students. Research is needed to correlate second or third year grade-point averages with admissions test scores on campuses of various racial compositions.

Several alternatives to admissions testing have been proposed, and some were instituted in 1973. Among these alternatives were a policy of open admissions, which is used at City University of New York; a lottery, which was used in the first two years of Federal City College; and no admissions testing, which is the general practice at public two-year colleges. Another proposed alternative to aptitude tests, either alone or in combination, simply did not predict freshmen grade-point averages of Black students as well as aptitude tests and high school grade-point averages (Abramowitz, 1972).

Two other alternatives to standardized tests were special admissions for minorities, including Blacks, and open admissions for all students. The impact of these relatively new alternatives on Black access has been positive; their relationship to distribution and persistence, however, awaits further study.

In studying admissions policies at the leading graduate schools, Hamilton (1973) found that in the Spring of 1972 less than one-half (42.6%) of the 195 institutions in the graduate school survey gave special attention to minority disadvantaged graduate student applications as part of their admissions policies. (See Table 3-14 and 3-15.) In

TABLE 3-14. Special Attention to Minority/Disadvantaged Graduate Student Applications in the Admissions Process, 1972.

Institution	No. of Inst. in the Sample	No. Responding "Yes"	Percent "Yes"	No. Responding "No"	Percent "No"	No Response
Region						
NE/MA	78	42	53.8	31	39.7	5
MW	45	15	33.3	30	66.7	0
S/SE	39	12	30.8	24	61.5	3
W/SW/NW	33	14	42.4	14	42.4	5
Graduate Program						
Small	14	7	50.0	6	42.9	1
Medium	49	16	32.7	31	63.3	2
Large	50	26	52.0	17	34.0	7
Very Large	50	26	52.0	21	42.0	3
Location						
Town	53	25	47.2	26	49.1	2
City	45	17	37.8	25	55.6	3
Urban	34	18	52.9	15	44.1	1
Metropolitan	63	23	36.5	33	52.4	7
Highest Degree						
M.A.	39	12	30.8	26	66.7	1
Ph.D.	156	71	45.5	73	46.8	12
Type of Control						
Public	124	56	45.2	62	50.0	6
Private	71	27	38.0	37	52.1	7
Combined Degree and Control						
M.A./Public	23	7	30.4	16	69.6	0
M.A./Private	16	5	31.3	10	62.5	1
Ph.D./Public	101	49	48.5	46	45.5	6
Ph.D./Private	55	−22	40.0	27	49.1	6
TOTAL	195	−83	42.6	99	50.8	13

SOURCE: Hamilton, I. Bruce, *Graduate School Programs for Minority/Disadvantaged Students, Report on an Initial Survey*, Educational Testing Service, Table 16.

1973, Sedlacek found that, compared with 1970, 1973 showed a decline in the number of undergraduate major white universities offering special admissions for minorities. (See Figure 3-10.) The situation confronting Blacks in 1973, therefore, was one in which standardized tests were used with increasing frequency, while at the same time special admissions programs to increase minority enrollment were decreasing.

TABLE 3-15. Special Attention Given by Departments to Minority/Disadvantaged Graduate School Applications in the Admissions Process, 1972.

Institution	No. of Inst. in the Sample	No. Responding "Yes"	Percent "Yes"	No. Responding "No"	Percent "No"	No Response
Region						
NE/MA	78	47	60.3	23	29.5	8
MW	45	28	62.2	14	39.1	3
S/SE	39	19	48.7	17	43.6	3
W/SW/NW	33	20	60.6	7	21.2	6
Graduate Program						
Small	14	7	50.0	6	42.9	1
Medium	49	18	36.7	27	55.1	4
Large	81	50	61.7	19	23.5	12
Very Large	50	39	78.0	8	16.0	3
Location						
Town	53	28	52.8	21	39.6	4
City	45	30	66.7	13	28.9	2
Urban	34	25	73.5	6	17.6	3
Metropolitan	63	31	49.2	21	33.3	11
Highest Degree						
M.A.	39	13	33.3	21	53.8	5
Ph.D.	156	101	64.7	40	25.6	15
Type of Control						
Public	124	82	66.1	34	27.4	8
Private	71	32	45.1	27	38.0	12
Combined Degree and Control						
M.A./Public	23	11	47.8	10	43.5	2
M.A./Private	16	2	12.5	11	68.8	3
Ph.D./Public	101	71	70.3	24	23.8	6
Ph.D./Private	55	30	54.5	16	29.1	9
TOTAL	195	114	58.5	61	31.3	20

SOURCE: Hamilton, I. Bruce, *Graduate School Programs for Minority/Disadvantaged Students, Report on an Initial Survey*, Educational Testing Service, (1973), Table 17.

The dilemma confronting policy makers was that, on the one hand, tests served a legitimate function by providing an objective means of selecting students. Indeed, no better selection technique has been devised to date. But, on the other hand, since the performance of Blacks and low-income groups on standardized tests was generally lower than that of other groups, the tests were barriers to access.

If standardized tests are eliminated, as some have suggested, will more Black

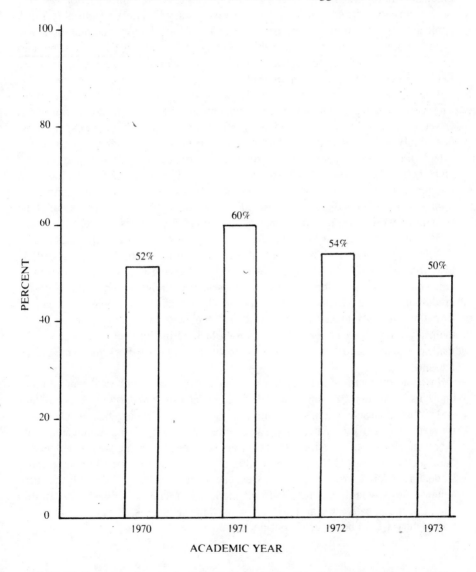

SOURCE: Sedlacek et al., *A National Comparison of Universities Successful and Unsuccessful In Enrolling Blacks Over A Five-Year Period.*

FIGURE 3-10. Percent of Public and Private Predominantly White Universities With Undergraduate Special Admissions Programs by Academic Year, 1970 Through 1973.

students be admitted to college? Perhaps not, if tests are not replaced with other objective criteria. Black students who received high test scores, especially in graduate and professional school admissions tests, might actually suffer if test scores were eliminated and not replaced with other objective criteria. Schools not wishing to admit Blacks, or any other group, would be better able to deny access to students who would have met objective testing criteria. For example, if high school (or undergraduate school) grade-point average plus three letters of recommendation were the only admissions criteria, it would be relatively easy to reject identifiable Black applicants by discounting their past grades at a Black institution, and ranking letters of recommendation on the basis of the prestige of the writer. Although testing does serve as some protection for Black students, for the majority of them, tests are more likely to serve as barriers, denying rather than facilitating access to college.

Are tests simply the messenger of bad news, as others have suggested? Perhaps so. The scores that Blacks and low-income students earned on standardized admissions tests (as well as other standardized tests) reflected the sum total of their experiences, not simply ability or aptitude. The tests also measured whether the high school offered the full range of courses in subject areas, such as mathematics and science, and whether the student was able to participate in advanced training. The tests also measured the quality of the social and cultural experiences that the community at-large and the immediate family provided the student. And, the tests measured the amount of work that the student had put into mastering the test content.

The question surrounding the use of admissions tests and their effects as educational barriers has no easy long-range or interim solution. Before abandoning aptitude tests forever, more validation studies are needed, taking into account a period of adjustment of Black students on white campuses, by including second- and third-year grade-point averages as prediction criteria. In addition, alternative objective means of assessing students must be devised so that the new admissions criteria do not themselves become categorical barriers for Blacks. Finally, every effort should be made to equalize across race and social class the non-ability factors that the tests also measure.

Two interim solutions to the testing problem may be to seek either (a) a moratorium on the use of standardized aptitude and achievement tests in undergraduate, graduate, and professional school admissions until the racial and social class factors inherent in the tests have been eliminated, or (b) a de-emphasis on aptitude and achievement test scores in admissions decisions. In the former solution, no testing would be done for admissions purposes. If tests were used at all, they would be used to diagnose the student's academic strengths, weaknesses, and interests after admissions. In the latter solution, tests would become minuscule elements in admissions decisions. In this solution, the negative racial and social class impact of tests on equal educational opportunity would be reduced, but not eliminated.

Family Income

The relationship between family income and equal opportunity for Black college students was not a simple one. Of all Black high school graduates in college in the

1973-74 academic year, lower-income Black families sent their members to college at a higher rate than more affluent Black families. Although all Black students were underrepresented in college in the 1973-74 academic year, the underrepresentation was greatest at higher, not lower, income levels. For whites, this was not the case. In the 1973-74 academic year, as white family income increased, so did white college enrollment.

The relationship of family income to distribution was such that low-income Black students were most likely to attend low-cost institutions, regardless of ability. In selecting college majors, Black students as a group, who also tended to be poorer, were more concerned than whites about potential earning power. In addition, within the Black group, those from wealthier families tended to select careers and fields involving advanced training, while less well-off Blacks selected other careers and fields of study. Finally, family income (and father's education) were related to persistence. Students from more affluent families entered advanced training as planned, while those from poorer families did not.

The negative impact of family income on the status of Blacks in college was greatest at the graduate and professional school level. Here the likelihood of entering advanced training was directly related to the family's ability to pay. At the undergraduate level, the existence of institutions with widely varying costs and the presence of federal and state student-aid programs had diminished the negative impact of low family income on access. Such compensations, however, do not exist in graduate or professional schools: advanced training costs more and few aid programs exist.

Following are detailed discussions of the relationships between family income and access, distribution, and persistence.

Family Income and Access

In Fall 1973, there were more affluent than poor white (but not Black) students enrolled in college, full- or part-time. (See Table 3-16.) The chances of going to college either full- or part-time increased for both Black and white students as their family incomes reached and surpassed the median incomes of their racial groups. The 1973 median annual Black family income of a male-headed household without a wife in the labor force was $7,148; with a wife in the labor force it was $12,226. For white families comparable incomes were $11,716 and $15,654 respectively (U.S. Census, 1974).

For Blacks with incomes above $15,000, the college enrollment was low. The more affluent Black families sent fewer of their eligible members to college in 1973 than did less affluent Black families. The disadvantages of students from low-income Black families were not absolute, since these Black students did enroll in college in higher proportions than their more affluent Black counterparts. Thus, white students from families with incomes $15,000 and above were 47% of all whites enrolled, while Blacks from the same income group were only 20% of all Black students enrolled in college in October 1973.

In 1973, the median annual income was $6,560 for white families and $4,226 for

Black families headed by females. Of all white students in college in Fall 1973, 10% came from families headed by females, although these families produced 13% of all white high school graduates. Of all Black college students, 32% came from families headed by females, which also produced 36% of all Black high school graduates in 1973. (See Figure 3-11.) Thus, students from both Black and white female-headed households were underrepresented in college in 1973. (See Table 3-17.)

Black freshmen, like all other Black college students, tended to have fewer family financial resources than their white counterparts in 1973. Figure 3-12 illustrates the percent distribution of full-time freshmen (unweighted numbers) by race and family income attending all types of institutions. Over one-half of the Black freshmen in the ACE Survey were from families with incomes of $7,999 or less. In contrast over one-half of the white freshmen were from families with incomes of $15,000 or more.

TABLE 3-16. Enrollment of Dependent College Students Age 18 to 24 by Race and Family Income, October 1973.

			Family Income				
	Under $3,000	$3,000 to $4,999	$5,000 to $7,499	$7,500 to $9,999	$10,000 to $14,999	$15,000 and Over	Total
Black Students							
Full-Time							
*Number	34	62	80	47	74	69	366
Percent	9%	17%	22%	13%	20%	19%	100%
Part-Time							
*Number	3	6	8	12	11	16	56
Percent	5%	11%	14%	21%	20%	29%	100%
Total							
*Number	37	68	88	59	85	85	422
Percent	9%	16%	21%	14%	20%	20%	100%
White Students							
Full-Time							
*Number	110	186	298	324	1,007	1,858	3,783
Percent	3%	5%	8%	9%	27%	49%	100%
Part-Time							
*Number	14	49	76	76	197	187	599
Percent	2%	8%	13%	13%	33%	31%	100%
Total							
*Number	124	235	374	400	1,204	2,045	4,382
Percent	3%	5%	9%	9%	27%	47%	100%

SOURCE: U.S. Census, *Social and Economic Characteristics of Students: October 1973*, Table 13.

*In Thousands

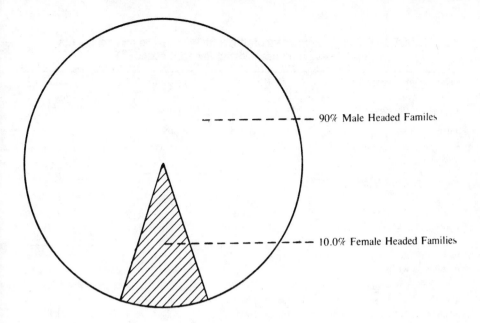

90% Male Headed Familes

10.0% Female Headed Families

White Students Enrolled in College

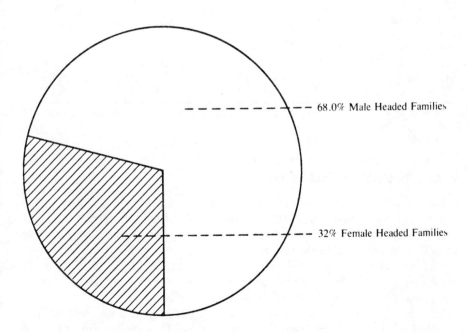

68.0% Male Headed Families

32% Female Headed Families

Black Students Enrolled in College

SOURCE: U.S. Census, *Social and Economic Characteristics of Students: October 1973*, Table 11.

FIGURE 3-11. College Enrollment of Black and White Students 34 Years Old and Younger by Sex of Head of Household, October 1973.

TABLE 3-17. College Enrollment of Students 34 Years Old and Younger by
Sex of Head of Household and Race, October 1973.

College Enrollments	White		Black		
	(In		*(In*		*% Difference*
Male Head of Household	*Thousands)*	*%*	*Thousands)*	*%*	*White-Black*
Total	4,043	100	288	100	—
Full-time	3,664	90.6	258	89.5	1.1
Part-time	379	9.4	30	10.4	–1.0
Females Head of Household					
Total	454	100	135	100	—
Full-time	399	87.9	125	92.6	–4.7
Part-time	55	12.1	10	7.4	4.7
Percent of all households with college students					
Total	4,497	100	423	100	
Male Head	4,043	89.9	288	68.1	21.8
Female Head	454	10.1	135	31.9	–21.8
Percent of all households with high school graduates					
Total	10,209	100	1,452	100	—
Male Head	8,854	87	934	64	23.0
Female Head	1,355	13	518	36	–23.0

SOURCE: U.S. Census (1974), *Social and Economic Characteristics of Students: October 1973*,
Table 11.

Family Income and Distribution

Family income was related to distribution by type of institution as can be seen in
Table 3-18 which summarizes American Council on Education 1973 freshmen survey
data collected from 579 institutions of which 196 were publicly controlled. As family
income increased, the proportion of full-time Black freshmen attending public
universities went from 10.5% from the poorest Black families to 28.4% from the
wealthiest Black families. For private universities, the proportion of Black freshmen
went from 14.8% to 36.3% as family income increased.

For white freshmen, family income had a smaller effect on distribution than it had
for Black freshmen. A significantly greater proportion of low-income white freshmen
were enrolled in the public universities, than were low-income Black freshmen. In
addition these differences in public, but not in private, university enrollment persisted
even though income increased. Black freshmen at all income levels were most likely
to be found in four-year colleges (including historically Black colleges), while white
freshmen at all income levels were in universities.

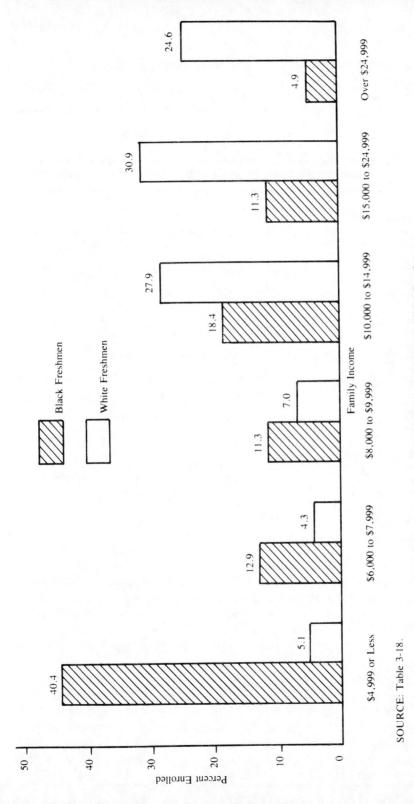

FIGURE 3-12. Income Distribution of Black and White Freshmen Enrolled Full-Time in College, October 1973.

SOURCE: Table 3-18.

Family income also affected distribution by field of study. As was seen in the description of NSSFNS students in Chapter 2, minority students from higher family incomes selected fields of study that involved longer training, such as Law, Medicine, and higher degrees, such as masters and doctorates. Minority students

TABLE 3-18. Percent Distribution of Black and White Full-Time Freshmen in Public and Private Institutions by Family Income, October 1973.

| Family Income and Race | Public Institutions (Percents) | | | |
	University	4-Year	2-Year	Total[1]
$5,999 or less				
Black	10.5	69.2	20.2	100 (4,257)
White	42.2	32.1	25.3	100 (5,994)
Difference	−31.7	37.1	−5.3	
$6,000 to $7,999				
Black	16.6	65.8	17.5	100 (1,261)
White	43.2	33.1	23.5	100 (5,162)
Difference	−26.6	32.7	−6.2	
$8,000 to $9,999				
Black	17.3	63.7	16.9	100 (1,041)
White	46.0	31.7	22.2	100 (8,311)
Difference	−28.7	34.0	−5.3	
$10,000 to $14,999				
Black	20.1	63.5	16.2	100 (1,626)
White	49.2	31.1	19.6	100 (32,757)
Difference	−29.1	32.4	−3.4	
$15,000 to $24,999				
Black	22.3	62.5	15.0	100 (901)
White	55.2	29.8	14.8	100 (34,149)
Difference	−32.9	32.7	0.2	
Over $24,999				
Black	28.4	59.4	12.0	100 (316)
White	65.8	22.1	10.4	100 (19,330)
Difference	−37.4	37.3	1.6	
	Private Institutions			
$5,999 or less				
Black	14.8	79.5	5.5	100 (2,166)
White	21.4	65.6	12.9	100 (3,846)
Difference	−6.6	13.9	−7.4	
$6,000 to $7,999				
Black	24.7	70.7	4.4	100 (801)
White	20.8	68.1	11.0	100 (3,216)
Difference	3.9	2.6	−6.6	

TABLE 3-18. (Continued)

Family Income and Race	University	4-Year	2-Year	Total[1]
$8,000 to $9,999				
Black	28.2	67.1	4.5	100 (765)
White	22.4	68.4	9.1	100 (5,140)
Difference	5.8	−1.6	−4.6	
$10,000 to $14,000				
Black	27.4	69.5	3.0	100 (1,355)
White	24.9	67.6	7.3	100 (20,871)
Difference	2.5	1.9	−4.3	
$15,000 to $24,999				
Black	30.4	67.2	2.3	100 (903)
White	29.7	64.8	5.4	100 (25,277)
Difference	0.7	2.4	−3.1	
Over $24,999				
Black	26.3	61.3	2.3	100 (473)
White	33.8	62.7	3.3	100 (27,970)
Difference	2.5	−1.4	−1.0	
	All Institutions			
$5,999 or less				
Black	11.9	72.7	15.3	100 (6,423)
White	34.1	45.2	20.6	100 (9,840)
Difference	−22.2	27.5	−5.3	
$6,000 to $7,999				
Black	19.7	67.7	12.4	100 (2,062)
White	34.6	46.5	18.7	100 (8,378)
Difference	−14.9	21.2	−6.3	
$8,000 to $9,999				
Black	21.9	66.3	11.6	100 (1,806)
White	36.9	45.7	17.2	100 (13,451)
Difference	−15.0	20.6	−5.6	
$10,000 to $14,999				
Black	23.4	66.2	10.2	100 (2,981)
White	39.7	45.3	14.9	100 (53,268)
Difference	−15.3	20.9	4.7	
$15,000 to $24,999				
Black	26.3	64.9	8.7	100 (1,804)
White	44.3	44.7	10.8	100 (59,426)
Difference	−18.0	20.2	−2.1	
Over $24,999				
Black	33.2	60.5	6.2	100 (789)
White	46.9	46.7	6.2	100 (47,300)
Difference	−13.7	13.8	0	

SOURCE: American Council on Education, CIRP Freshmen Norms, (1973), unpublished.

from lower family incomes selected fields of study that involved less training and few degrees, such as Associate Arts degrees and Business fields.

The 1973 American Council on Education freshmen norms found similar relationships between earning power and probable occupation. Black freshmen, who also tended to come from poorer families than their white counterparts, were less likely than white freshmen to regard earning power in probable career choice as unimportant. While 21.5% of the whites felt that earning power was unimportant in selecting an occupation, only 9.2% of the Black freshmen felt that way.

Family Income and Persistence

Socioeconomic status, which includes family income, was also found to influence persistence. Sewell and Shah (1967) defined socioeconomic status as the combination of father's and mother's occupation and educational level, family contribution to the student's college education and the sacrifice involved, and the approximate wealth and family income. In a follow-up study of high school seniors in Wisconsin, Sewell and Shah found that socioeconomic status influenced not only access but also persistence. Wealthier students were more likely to have enrolled in college and graduated, while their less affluent counterparts were not. When only those students who enrolled in college were studied, Sewell, and Shah found that among this more affluent cohort, income tended to be related to persistence.

In a study of the academic careers and social class of students at a Midwestern college ten years after their freshmen year, Ickland (1964) also found that socioeconomic status was a successful indicator of persistence. Moreover, parents' educational levels and occupations, in addition to the students' educational expectations, were significantly related to graduation at any time during the ten-year period of the study. Eckland asserted that the combined social class indicators were more powerful than intelligence in determining persistence. Thus, average ability students from wealthy families were more likely to persist in college than bright students from poorer families.

In a six-year follow-up study of 459 entering freshmen at North Texas State University, Kooker and Bellamy (1969) found that parents' educational attainment but not occupation were related to persistence. Of the two parents, according to a study by Warriner, Foster, and Trites (1966), the educational level of the father seemed to have more significant influence than that of the mother on the educational attainment of college males and females.

Among the Spring 1973 doctoral recipients, almost two-thirds (65%) of the Black students and one-half (51%) of the white students had fathers with high school education or less. (See Table 3-19.) Slightly more than one-half of both Black and white recipients had mothers with high school education or less. Among Blacks who received doctorates in Spring 1973, their mothers tended to have more education than their fathers. But for the overwhelming majority of both Black and white native-born students the educational opportunities open to them represent tremendous leaps over the educational attainment of their parents.

Panos and Astin (Lenning, et al., 1974), in a four-year follow-up study of 30,506 full-time freshmen at 246 four-year colleges, found that students who dropped out of college came primarily from lower socioeconomic backgrounds. In addition, the dropouts had lower high school grade-point averages, and lower levels of educational aspiration.

There was also a direct relationship between the parents' income and the likelihood that college seniors would be able to engage in their planned graduate activities, according to an ETS study. Baird (1972) found that one year after college graduation, over one-half (56.6%) of the college seniors from families with more than $20,000 were engaged in the graduate training they had planned in their senior year, compared to 41.3 of those from families with incomes less than $5,000. (See Table 3-20.) College seniors from poor families were more likely than wealthier students to have changed their planned fields of advanced study.

With the exception of those planning to work full-time or marry, the college seniors least able to fulfill their post-graduation plans were those from low to moderate family incomes. Similar findings were obtained by Baird on the basis of father's education. The more education the father had, the greater the likelihood that the students would be able to enter advanced study as planned.

Baird also found that family income made the greatest difference for those students

TABLE 3-19. Percentage Distribution of Doctorates Earned, by Native-Born Blacks and Whites, by Educational Level of Fathers and Mothers, Spring 1973.

	Percents		*Differences*
Father's Education	*Black*	*White*	*(Black-White)*
Below High School Grad	47.7	28.4	19.3
High School Grad Only	16.8	22.6	−5.8
1 to 3 Years of College	8.0	13.6	−5.6
Baccalaureate Degree (incl. LLB, BD)	5.8	15.0	−9.2
Master's Degree	7.9	.10.3	−2.4
Doctoral	1.4	3.6	−2.2
Postdoctoral	0.3	0.7	−0.4
Unknown	12.1	5.9	6.2
Total	100%	100%	———
Mother's Education			
Below High School Grad	39.2	20.8	18.4
High School Grad Only	20.3	34.7	−1.4
1 to 3 Years of College	12.1	18.1	−6.0
Baccalaureate Degree (incl. LLB, BD)	9.8	14.8	−5.0
Master's Degree	6.1	5.4	0.8
Doctoral	1.0	0.4	0.6
Postdoctoral	——	0.1	——
Unknown	11.5	5.8	5.7
Total	100%	100%	——

SOURCE: National Academy of Science, National Board on Graduate Education, National Research Council, Doctoral Records File, unpublished.

TABLE 3-20. Percent of College Seniors Engaged in Planned Activity a Year Later by Family Income and Father's Education, 1972.

	By Income					By Father's Education				
	Less than $5,000	$5,000-$7,999	$8,000-$11,999	$12,000-$19,999	$20,000 or more	Less than H.S. diploma	High School graduation	Some College	College Grad.	Adv. Work
Full-time work	77.1	80.0	88.0	86.8	81.4	81.9	86.3	85.7	80.6	82.9
Military service	41.7	67.9	45.9	63.9	58.3	46.5	66.2	64.2	60.0	51.4
Marriage only	100.0*	100.0*	75.0*	88.9*	95.0	100.0*	80.0	100.0*	90.9	88.9
Grad-arts and humanities	33.3	30.4	28.7	36.7	37.6	23.7	37.9	38.2	36.3	36.3
Grad-biological and Physical science	42.6	46.2	50.7	52.5	55.3	41.7	48.3	54.1	50.6	62.4
Grad-social science	29.4	27.9	39.0	40.2	39.6	37.3	35.3	38.7	40.6	40.3
Business school	46.2	46.4	45.7	50.0	60.3	38.2	44.9	49.5	63.7	69.1
Law school	65.2	52.8	63.9	72.1	73.2	52.7	68.8	72.1	70.3	80.4
Medical school	47.1	65.5	70.2	75.2	79.7	60.8	73.6	73.1	73.1	74.3
Other study	43.7	46.1	48.9	52.7	55.6	47.7	49.3	53.1	56.9	52.6
Total in planned advanced study	41.3	42.7	47.0	52.7	56.6	41.1	49.1	52.3	55.2	59.3
Total who planned to go who were in some other field of advanced study	23.3	21.9	19.8	28.6	19.2	21.0	18.8	19.5	20.4	19.4
Total who planned to go in any advanced study	64.7	64.6	66.8	81.4	75.5	62.1	67.9	71.8	75.6	78.7
	428	565	1619	2096	2841	1529	1930	1402	1482	1562

SOURCE: Baird, Leonard, *Careers and Curricula*. Table 1-6.

*N Less than 10

who planned to enter the most expensive training (medical school), but fathers' education made the greatest difference in likelihood of entering Business or Law Schools. Compared to family income, fathers' education seemed to produce greater differences in the likelihood of entering the planned field of study. However, family income produced greater differences in the desire to enter advanced study at all.

College Costs

The cost of going to college is the second of the three financial barriers to equal educational opportunity for Blacks: the first, family income, discussed previously, and the third, financial aid practices and policies, discussed later, are related to college costs. College costs determined the negative impact of low Black family income and current financial aid policies on access, distribution, and persistence of Blacks in undergraduate, graduate, and professional schools in the 1973-74 academic year.

While the interaction of family income and financial aid programs with college costs facilitated access, it did not produce the same success in distribution or persistence of Blacks in the 1973-74 academic year. The impact of college costs on Black distribution was such that Blacks were overrepresented in the low-cost public institutions and two-year and four-year colleges, and underrepresented in the more expensive private institutions and universities. In addition, the influence of college costs on persistence was such that Blacks were better represented in undergraduate than in graduate or professional schools. These points are developed in the discussion that follows.

College Costs and Family Income

In the 1973-74 school year the average direct cost of college tuition ranged from $533 in two-year colleges to $1,583 in four-year colleges, according to a survey by the American Council on Education (1973). (See Table 3-21.) The Black median annual income of a male-headed household without a wife in the labor force was $7,148, which was $4,568 less than comparable white family income in 1973. If the average Black family had to pay for the college education of their children out of current earnings, rather than savings or other sources, the Black family would have had to have spent 5% of its gross annual income on tuition to send one child to a public college for one year, and 27% of its gross income on tuition to send one child for one year to a private college. For the average white family, tuition cost of sending one child for one year to a public college would consume 3% of the gross family income, while tuition cost of sending a child for one year to a private college would consume 16% of the gross white family income.

If current earnings were the only source of funds to pay for college, few low-income families would have been able to afford it. Other sources of support for college costs included family savings. But, the differences in the wealth of Black and white families were significant. On the basis of data collected by the College Entrance Examination Board on people who took the Scholastic Aptitude Tests in 1973, the estimated parental average contribution of Black families was $713, while that of white families was $2,237 (a difference of $1,524). Over one-half (53%) of all Black College Entrance Examination Board applicants had expected parental contributions of under $625; less than one-quarter of the white applicants were in this category. (See Table 3-22.)

When college costs were compared with the expected family contribution of Black and white students who took the SAT, the influence of costs and family wealth on distribution was clear. If, for example, Black families had to pay for the cost of their children's education, 100% of the Black families would have been able to afford tuition at public colleges, but only 30% would have been able to afford tuition at private colleges. For whites, the proportion able to afford public and private tuition was 100% and 34% respectively based on their expected family contributions. (The residential costs were a larger drain on family financial resources.)

College attendance reduced the immediate income a family could produce by reducing the number of members seeking work or holding jobs. For Black families, unlike white families, this forgone income could have severe consequences because Black families were disproportionately in the lowest income groups. There were more Black wage earners in the family that together produced the same income as the single white workers. Thus, a higher proportion of Black than white families needed the wages from employment of the family members in order to maintain their economic well-being. The negative impact of forgone earnings, therefore, fell disproportionately harder on Black than on white families. Black families had to forgo not only the needed income of the college student in the family more often than

TABLE 3-21. Average College Costs as Percent of Family Income by Race and Type of Institution, Fall 1973.

Average College Costs	Type of Institution				
	Public	Private	Two-Year	Four-Year	Universities
Tuition	$ 377	$1,921	$ 533	$1,583	$1,282
Room and Board	$1,006	$1,135	$ 974	$1,116	$1,254
Total (Tuition Room and Board)	$1,383	$3,056	$1,507	$2,699	$2,536
*Percent Median Black Family Income ($7,148)					
Tuition	5%	27%	7%	22%	17%
Room and Board	14%	16%	14%	16%	18%
Total	19%	43%	21%	38%	35%
*Percent Median White Family Income ($11,716)					
Tuition	3%	16%	5%	14%	11%
Room and Board	9%	10%	8%	10%	11%
Total	12%	26%	13%	23%	22%

SOURCES: El-Khawas, Elaine H., and Kinzen, Joan L., *The Impact of Office of Education Student Assistance Program, Fall 1973*, Table 9. U.S. Census, *The Social and Economic Status of the Black Population in the United States 1973*, Table 7.

*Includes only male headed households with wife not in paid labor force.

whites, but also had to help the college student in the family by providing some support, such as room and board, books and supplies, or clothes. The strain on the family's well-being caused by forgone earnings of college members increased as the number of college students in the family without income increased. The likelihood of this happening was greater among Black families than white, because Black families had more children and were generally poorer.

College Costs and Distribution

It would be expected that as college costs increased, the proportional Black enrollment should have decreased in 1973. Table 3-23 summarizes the percent distribution of Black and all college students enrolled in public and private institutions in Fall 1973. The proportion of Black to total enrollment in public institutions was 102.5%, while that of Black to total enrollment in private institutions was 91.6%. For two-year and four-year colleges, the proportion of Black to all students enrolled was 119.8% and 114.6% respectively, while at universities the proportion of Black enrollment to total enrollment was 85.2%.

As college costs increased, the enrollment of Black students decreased in Fall 1973. Blacks were slightly overrepresented, in comparison to all students, in public institutions, and/or two-year and four-year colleges (which included historically Black institutions). Blacks were underrepresented in private colleges and universities in 1973. In part, this underrepresentation was due to the effect of college costs on

TABLE 3-22. Estimated Parental Contribution Toward College Education of High School Seniors by Race 1973-74 Academic Year.

Estimated Parental Contribution	Percent Distribution		
	Black	*White*	*Difference Black-White*
Under $635	53	21	32
$625 to $899	7	9	−2
$900 to $1,199	−6	−10	4
$1,200 to $1,499	5	11	−6
$1,500 to $1,799	2	7	−5
$1,800 to $2,099	2	−4	6
$2,100 to $2,399	2	6	−4
$2,400 to $2,699	1	2	−1
$2,700 to $2,999	1	5	−4
$3,000 to $3,299	0	−2	2
$3,300 to $3,599	1	3	−2
Over — $3,600	5	21	−16
TOTAL	100%	100%	—

SOURCE: *College-Bound Seniors, 1973-74,* College Entrance Examination Board, (1974), Table 20.

TABLE 3-23. Percent Distribution of Blacks and All Students Enrolled by Type of Institution, October 1973.

Type of Institution	Percents		
	All Students	Black	Ratio Black: All
Public	77.5	79.4	1.02
Private	22.5	20.6	1.91
Total	100.0	100.0	—
Two-Year	24.8	29.7	1.19
Four-Year	21.2	24.3	.14
Universities	54.0	46.0	.85
Total	100.0	100.0	—

SOURCE: U.S. Census, (1975), unpublished data.

distribution. If the student attended a two-year college, the financial strain on the family was reduced but not eliminated (Greene and Kester, 1970).

The importance of college costs and financial aid in college selection of full-time freshmen is summarized in Table 3-24. Regardless of race, more students in private four-year colleges and universities than in public four-year colleges and universities regarded the availability of financial aid as very important in their college selection. In both public and private four-year colleges and universities, financial aid was more important to Black than to white freshmen in their college selection. Black freshmen in public institutions were four times as concerned as white freshmen and twice as concerned as other minorities about financial aid in college selection. Racial differences in the importance of financial aid in college selection of freshmen attending private institutions were even larger.

One consequence of the inability to meet college costs was the lack of Blacks in fields requiring prolonged and/or expensive training. As of 1972, 1 out of every 560 white Americans was a doctor, but only 1 out of every 3,800 Blacks, according to Health Resources Administration (DHEW, 1974). In Dentistry, there was one Black dentist for every 11,500 Black people. Only 2.7% of the 700,000 RN's in 1970 were Black. A major contribution to the low representation of Blacks and other minorities in the health professions was the cost of instruction. (Tables E-1 through E-4 in Appendix E summarize the annual costs for health training at two-year colleges, four-year colleges, and universities.)

A 1973 study by the Health Resources Administration found that the highest annual expenses were for students in Dentistry, Podiatry, and Osteopathy, and lowest for students in Pharmacy. Black health-career students generally came from lower middle- or lower-class families, with the greatest proportion of poorer Black students in Optometry and Pharmacy programs. In addition, the educational expenses increased with each year in medical school. Single freshmen in medicine had average annual expenses of $4,059, while single sophomores in the same program had expenses of $4,166; for single juniors it was $4,612 and for single seniors, $4,630. With marriage and children, the average costs of education (primarily room and board) for health-career students increased markedly in all fields of study.

TABLE 3-24. The Importance of Financial Aid in College Choice of Freshmen Attending Public and Private Four-Year Colleges and Universities by Race, Fall 1973.

	Percents (Unweighted Number)			
Public Institutions	*Black*	*White*	*Other*	*Total*
Importance of Aid				
Very	40.4	10.5	20.7	12.9
Somewhat	21.0	12.1	17.6	12.8
Not	38.4	77.3	61.6	74.1
Total	100.0	100.0	100.0	100.0
	(7,546)	(93,440)	(2,367)	(103,553)
Private Institutions				
Importance of Aid				
Very	54.9	22.0	40.4	25.6
Somewhat	20.0	14.2	16.0	14.6
Not	25.0	52.6	43.4	59.0
Total	100.0	100.0	100.0	100.0
	(6,372)	(88,088)	(2,488)	(96,948)

SOURCE: American Council on Education Cooperative Instructional Research Program, Freshmen Norms (1973), unpublished data.

The high costs of higher education in general and of health fields in particular undoubtedly influenced the decision of low-income students, a disproportionate number of whom were Black, not to enter these fields unless financial aid was provided. Baird (1972) found that college seniors least likely to have fulfilled their graduate school plans to enter medical school were those from families whose incomes were under $3,000. The major federal sources of financial aid for health training included the National Direct Student Loan Program, Health Professions Student Loan Program, Nursing Student Loan Program, the Armed Forces Scholarships, and the Guaranteed Student Loan Program. (The funding levels of these programs for fiscal years 1973 and 1974 are included in Appendix A of this report.)

According to the Health Resources Administration Survey (1973), students paid for their health training programs primarily through their own, their parents', or their spouses' earnings. These sources provided about 50% of all income available to the students. Loans, both public and private, accounted for 15 to 20% of the income of health students. (Of those students receiving loans, the majority were enrolled in federal health-career loan programs.) The average indebtedness for medical students as of June 1971 ranged from $3,534 (Veterinary Medicine students) to $5,966 (Osteopathy students). In addition, significant proportions of the students in each health-career field were also living in debt. Thus, not only were they carrying a debt of several thousand dollars, they were also accumulating greater indebtedness as they remained in school. And, the majority of these medical students were from affluent families.

College Costs and Persistence

College costs were also barriers to persistence. Among bright Black college students, those from wealthier families, regardless of the college they were currently attending, aspired to and more often attended graduate and professional schools than did other Black college students (Borgen, 1970 and Watley, 1971).

In a one-year follow-up study of a small number of Black and white college seniors, Baird (1973) found that financial problems and the desire for practical experience were the most frequent causes of Blacks' not attending graduate or professional school immediately following undergraduate school completion. Of all Blacks in the follow-up study, 35.9% said that they did not go to graduate school because they wanted to get some practical experience before continuing, while 38.2% needed money to go. For white seniors, however, the desire to gain practical experience (37.1%) and not to be a student (35.1%) were the most frequent reasons given for not continuing their education.

El-Khawas and Bisconti (1974) also found that work and lack of financial support were more likely to account for the reasons that Blacks, rather than whites, interrupted their advanced studies. Among students who were freshmen in 1961, they found that ten years later, in 1972, 60% of the Black students, in contrast to 41% of the white students, interrupted advanced studies to work. In addition, 17% of the Black students and 5% of the whites discontinued their training because they were unable to find fellowships, scholarships, or grants to support graduate training.

The influence of college costs as a barrier to equal educational opportunity for Blacks, however, had not been overcome by financial aid or work. Because of costs, Black students could not go to graduate school as planned immediately after undergraduate school. Baird (1974) found that these Black students were more strongly motivated than their white counterparts similarly situated definitely to continue their education after a few years of work. Almost one-half (48.4%) of the Black students and 29.9% of the white students not in graduate school planned to enroll after a few years of work.

Black and white college seniors do not differ significantly in the amount of money that they expected to need to continue their education in graduate or professional school, according to Baird (1974). As Table 3-25 indicates, over two-thirds of the Black and white seniors needed $1,500 or more in order to go to graduate school. The differences between Blacks and whites were not in college costs, but in the public and private sources of financial aid available to them. Consequently, as was pointed out in Chapter 2, it took Black doctoral recipients on the average almost twice as many years from the time of their baccalaureates to the time of their doctorates as it did white students, according to the National Academy of Sciences data. Even when fields of study were held constant, it took Blacks on the average three years longer than it took whites to earn doctorates in Spring 1973. In those intervening years, Black students most often worked full-time and continued their education intermittently.

Financial Aid Practices and Policies

The negative influence of family income and college costs can be overcome through adequate financial aid. Therefore, how aid was allocated, to whom, what type of aid and for what purpose determined the extent to which aid practices and policies in 1973 constituted barriers to equal educational opportunity.

In the allocation of aid, independent white and dependent Black college students tended to receive the greatest amount of assistance. Among entering freshmen, Black and white freshmen from wealthier families received larger average amounts of aid than did their low-income counterparts. However, low-income freshmen participated in a greater number of aid programs than did wealthier freshmen.

Financial aid programs did facilitate access, but had a limited effect on distribution and persistence. Enrollment data on Blacks indicate that Black enrollment still followed college costs, as was discussed previously. Thus, Black access to only a limited number of institutions was facilitated by public and private financial programs in the 1973-74 academic year. Policies such as lack of full-funding and the 50% limit of the amount of aid under BEOGs, contributed to the limited access of Blacks.

The administration of the aid programs in 1973 was such that students seeking aid were required to complete separate forms for each aid program, or were given their aid money in lump sums that they had to budget over the year. Both practices were detrimental to equal educational opportunity.

In graduate schools, Black students had to rely primarily on their own resources, especially outside work, in contrast to white students who received family support in meeting graduate school costs. There were few institutional or public financial aid programs for graduate schools, with the exception of publicly funded fellowships and loans in Medicine, Education, Engineering, and Physical Sciences, and small institutional aid programs. Financial aid policies and practices were more favorable to undergraduate than to graduate or professional school students. Financial aid policies did not greatly facilitate persistence for Blacks in graduate and professional schools, because of their more limited scope.

In general, financial aid policies, especially in the federal aid programs, facilitated access of Blacks to undergraduate schools, but did not eliminate the ongoing financial programs of distribution and persistence. Thus, college costs and family income

TABLE 3-25. Amount Needed for Graduate School by 1971 Graduates Not Enrolled, by Race, Spring 1972.

| | Total Not Attending | By Race | | Difference Black-White |
		Blacks Not Attending	Whites Not Attending	
Amount needed to attend				
Less than $500	4.6	5.4	4.7	.7
$500-$1,000	10.7	12.9	10.7	2.2
$1,000-$1,500	16.0	14.0	16.4	-2.4
$1,500-$2,000	20.9	24.7	20.4	4.3
Over $2,000	47.8	43.0	47.9	-4.9
All Students	100.0%	100.0%	100.0%	—

SOURCE: Baird, Leonard, *Careers and Curricula,* Table 2.2.

continued to determine whether Black students would go to expensive institutions and whether they would enter advanced training.

Independent/Dependent Students

It is unlikely that all students who needed financial aid to facilitate their access, distribution, or persistence in college received it in Fall 1973. It is also unlikely that all students who had the same financial need received the same amount of aid dollars. In a special survey in October 1973, the U.S. Census asked households with members enrolled in college what their educational costs were that year. They found that the estimated median costs for full-time students differed as a function of type of institution attended and race.

Dependent Black students reported lower expenditures than dependent white students in meeting all college costs in 1973. Dependent Black students spent less than dependent whites on tuition and fees, books and supplies, and transportation costs (if they attended a two-year college).

Independent Black students reported greater expenses for tuition and fees than did their white counterparts attending the same type of institution. (See Table 3-26.) With the exception of independent students attending four-year colleges, Blacks reported higher costs for books and supplies. Transportation costs also differentiated Black and white independent students. Black students attending universities reported higher transportation costs than did their white counterparts, but white independent students attending four-year colleges reported higher transportation costs.

Why racial differences in college expenditures were obtained is not immediately apparent. Allowing for errors in reporting, these differences may in part reflect financial aid practices of public and private aid sources. The estimated median college expenditures of dependent and independent students less the estimated average tuition cost by type of institution are reported in Table 3-27. These differences between average tuition costs and median college expenditures may reflect the amount of aid received from public and private sources. If so, the greatest amount of aid on the average went to independent students, especially white students at four-year colleges ($624) and at universities ($602). The least amount of aid on the average went to dependent whites at four-year colleges (−$11) and at two-year colleges ($157). When Black and white students attending the same type of institution are compared, regardless of dependence status, white students received more aid, with the exception of those attending two-year colleges.

Based on these data, financial aid programs as a whole were less likely to have assisted independent Blacks, who tended also to be low-income Black males, and dependent white students, according to this analysis. The aid programs, however, seemed to have reached dependent Black students who tended to come from low-income Black families, and independent white students. If this were the case, then the definition of independence in qualifying for financial aid programs was critical. The U.S. Census data suggest that in competition for aid, the dependent Black and the independent white college students may have been the winners.

TABLE 3-26. Estimated Median Educational Costs of Financially Dependent and Independent Full-Time Students by Race and Type of Institution, October 1973.

Type of Expense and Institution	Independent White	Black	Dependent White	Black
Tution and Fees				
University	$680	$1,036	$782	$694
Four-Year College	$959	$1,054	$1,594	$1,074
Two-Year College	$253	$363	$376	$241
Books and Supplies				
University	$163	$182	$162	$149
Four-Year College	$163	$140	$162	$139
Two-Year College	$121	$153	$132	$ 86
Transportation				
University	$124	$160	$ 89	$109
Four-Year College	$135	$117	$ 81	$163
Two-Year College	$185	$148	$171	$137

SOURCE: U.S. Census, unpublished data, (1975).

TABLE 3-27. Estimated Differences in the Average Amount of Tuition Aid Received by Black and White Independent and Dependent College Students by Type of Institution, Fall 1973.

Type and average costs	Estimated Aid Received Independent White	Black	Dependent White	Black
Universities ($1,282)	$602	$246	$500	$588
Four-Year Colleges ($1,583)	$624	$529	*	$509
Two-Year Colleges ($533)	$280	$170	$157	$292

SOURCE: El-Khawas, Elaine H. and Kinzer, Joan L., *The Impact of Office of Education Student Assistance Programs,* Fall 1973, Table 9 and U.S. Census (1975), unpublished data.

*Aid received was slightly greater than the cost of average tuition at this type of institution.

Sources of Financial Aid

In Fall 1973, the type of financial aid packages used to meet college costs differed by family income and race for full-time freshmen attending the same public and private four-year colleges and universities. Tables E-7 through E-10 (in Appendix E) summarize how Black and white full-time freshmen financed their first year of studies according to American Council on Education data. (Table E-11 in Appendix E reports U.S. Census data on awards to all post-serondary students in Fall 1973 and percent of the awards to Blacks from public and private sources.)

Compared to more affluent Black freshmen attending the same type of institution, Black freshmen from poorer families relied more heavily on Social Security benefits, scholarships or grants and federally insured loans for financial aid. Wealthier Black students were more likely to use earnings from part-time or summer work, savings, and parents as sources of financial aid. (Tendency to use other sources of aid including G.I. benefits, spouse, full-time work, parents' military benefits, and other repayable loans were unrelated to family income of Black freshmen.)

Comparing the average amount of aid money actually received by wealthier and poorer Black freshmen attending the same type of institution, wealthier Black freshmen, with one exception, received on the average, larger amounts of money than did poorer Black freshmen from all sources of aid. The exception was earnings from part-time or summer work. In all other types of aid, the higher the family income the larger the average amount of aid received by Black freshmen. The same was also true of white students. Thus, even though poorer Black and white freshmen had heavier participation in a given type of student assistance program, on the average they received less money than wealthier students of the same race, attending the same type of institution.

Compared with Black freshmen in public four-year colleges and universities, those attending the costlier private colleges were more likely to have received aid. In addition, compared with white students from the same family income, Black freshmen were less likely to have received aid. (See Figures 3-13 through 3-16.)

Figure 3-17 plots the average amount of aid received by low-income Black and white freshmen ($5,999 or less) attending four-year colleges and universities. Individual Black low-income freshmen in public four-year colleges and universities received more money on the average than did their white counterparts from savings, parents' military benefits, scholarships or grants, federally insured loans, and other repayable loans. In all other types of financial aid, individual white freshmen on the average received more money.

Selby (1970) examined the relationships among race, financial aid, and persistence in college using thirty pairs of Black and white students matched on sex, aptitude test scores, and high school rank. All were enrolled in the University of Missouri at Columbia in the Fall of 1968. Selby found that the rates of completion of the freshmen (including those who transferred to other institutions) were not significantly different for Black and white students. But when financial aid was taken into consideration, he found that the greatest number of students who received aid but did not complete the freshman year were Black females. (Of the non-aid group, however, one-half of those who dropped out of college in the freshman year were white females.) Disregarding race, males were more likely than females to complete the freshman year. It should be stressed, as Selby did, that the number of cases in the study was exceedingly small and that the findings applied to conditions at only one institution.

Administration of Aid Programs

Administrative operations of financial aid programs, such as lump payments rather than regular payments in the loan programs, the complicated needs analysis in the federal grants programs, and the financial aid application process itself, have tended to defeat the purposes of the aid programs (College Entrance Examination Board,

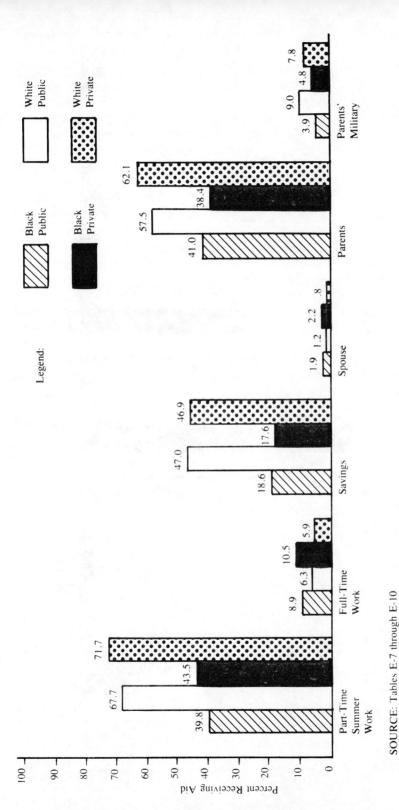

FIGURE 3-13. Percent of Full-Time Freshmen From Families With Incomes $5,999 or Less Receiving Aid by Race and Control of Four-Year College or University Attended, Fall 1973.

SOURCE: Tables E-7 through E-10

134

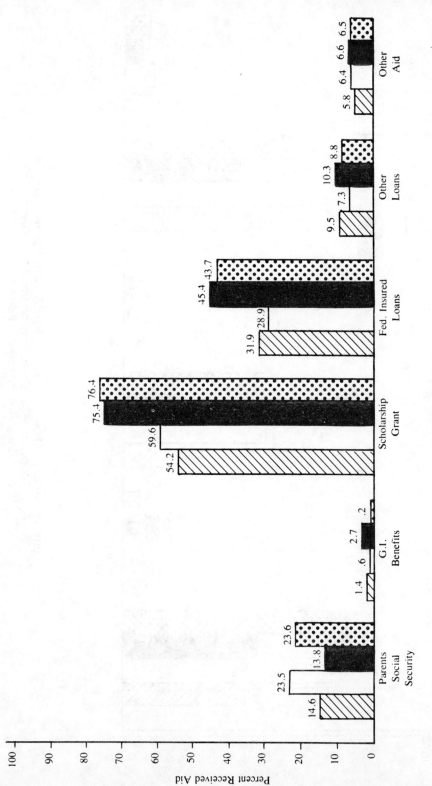

FIGURE 3-13. (Continued)

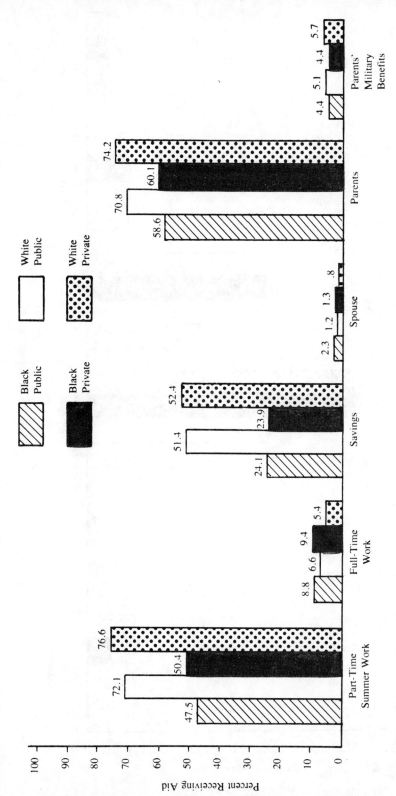

SOURCE: Tables E-7 through E-10.

FIGURE 3-14. Percent of Full-Time Freshmen From Families With Incomes $6,000 to $9,999 Receiving Aid by Race and Control of Four-Year College or University Attended, Fall 1973.

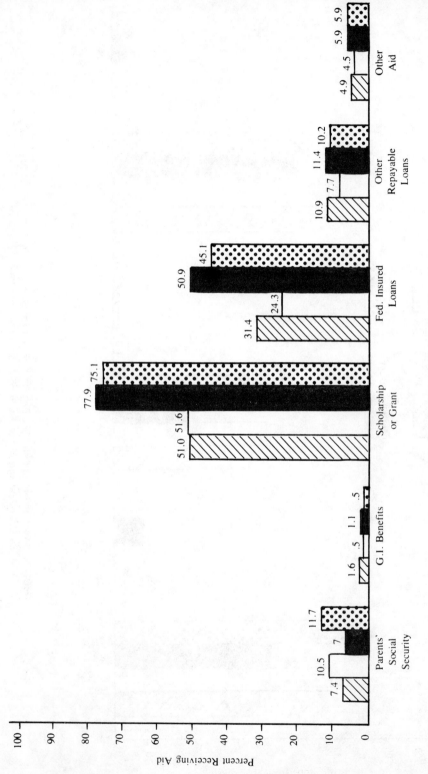

FIGURE 3-14. (Continued 2)

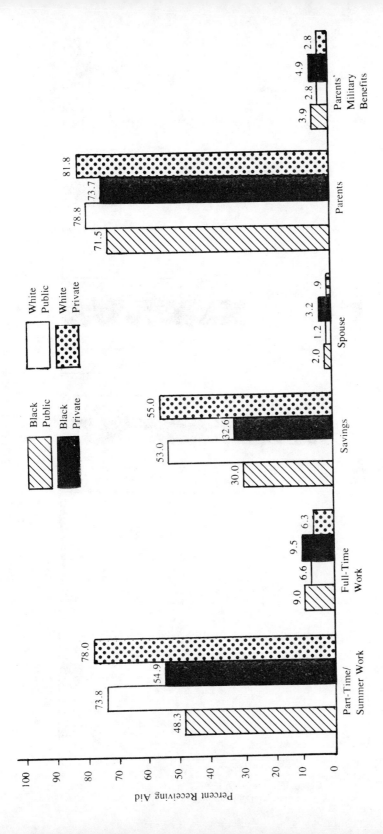

SOURCE: Tables E-7 through E-10.

FIGURE 3-15. Percent of Full-Time Freshmen From Families With Incomes $10,000 to $14,999 Receiving Aid by Race and Control of Four-Year College or University Attended, Fall 1973.

138

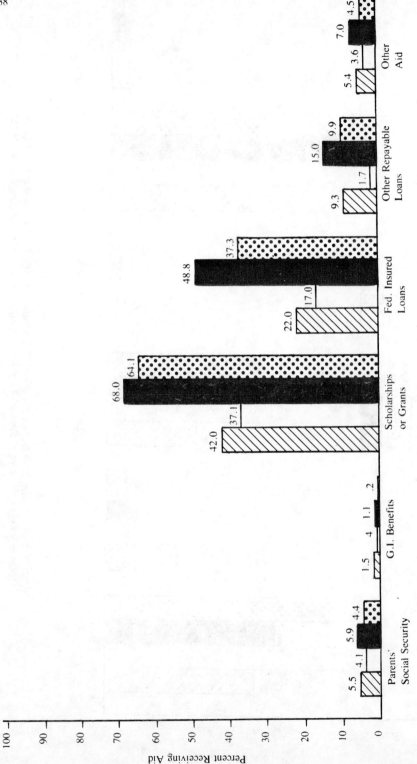

FIGURE 3-15. (Continued)

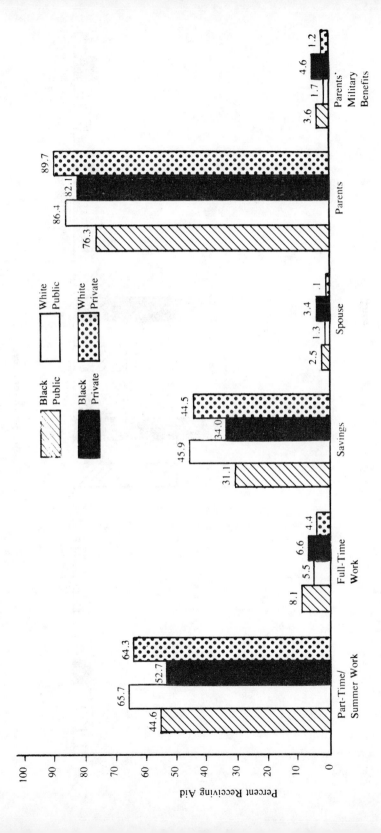

SOURCE: Tables E-7 through E-10.

FIGURE 3-16. Percent of Full-Time Freshmen From Families With Incomes $15,000 and Above Receiving Aid by Race and Control of Four-Year College or University Attended, Fall 1973.

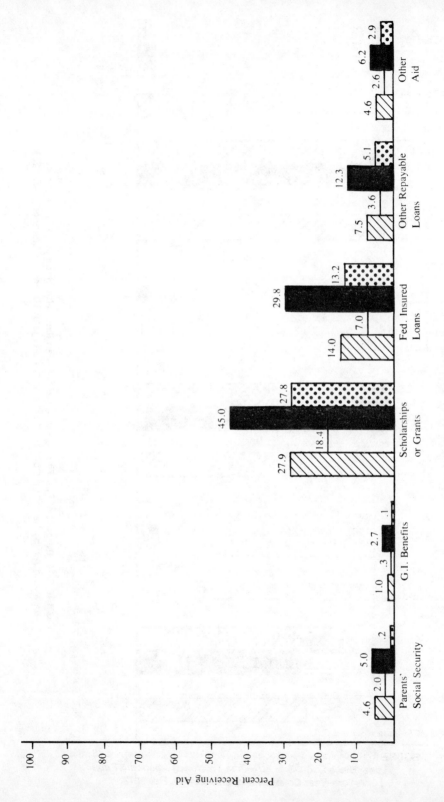

FIGURE 3-16../(Continued)

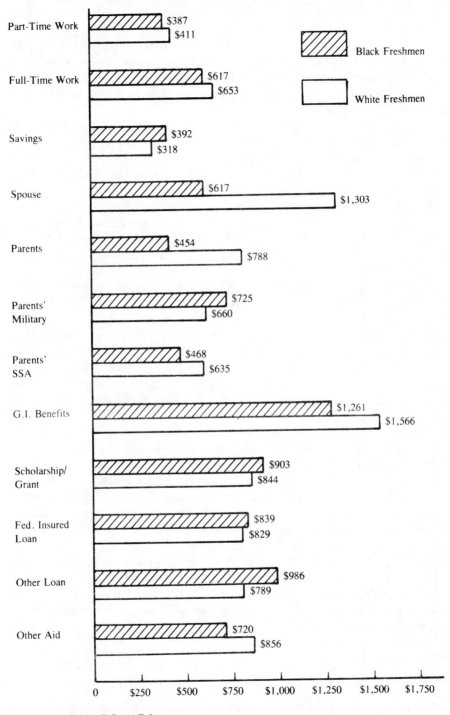

SOURCE: Tables E-7 and E-8.

FIGURE 3-17. Average Amount of Aid Received by Low Income ($5,999 or Less) Black and White Full-Time Freshmen Attending Public Four-Year Colleges and Universities, Fall 1973.

1971). McClennan (1969) described the difficulty of completing the Parents' Confidential Statement for families with low reading ability and generally no experience in completing financial information forms. For students in such a predicament, recruitment must be coupled with financial aid counseling by an aid officer, or well-versed high school counselors.

The creation of a common form, on which the parents' expected contribution to their child's college education can be determined for a variety of assistance programs, was also needed in 1973. (The differences between cost of education and the expected parents' contribution is defined as the financial need of the student.) Both the College Scholarship Service of the College Entrance Examination Board and the American College Testing Program, which was required for BEOG applicants, had financial needs tests which colleges used to disburse campus-based federal aid programs. Some colleges also developed their own financial needs tests in order to reflect the unique characteristics of their college cost structure and the expected rate of inflation that school year.

For students who came from homes in which they were the first generation college students, completing several financial aid applications was very difficult (National Task Force on Student Aid Problems, 1975). In 1973, the greater the student need, the greater the number of forms the student and his family had to complete in order to participate in federal, state, and other financial aid programs. The forms alone became formidable barriers that discouraged applicants. This cumbersome process of obtaining financial assistance had an adverse impact on Blacks: since Blacks were overrepresented among the disadvantaged, they were the people least able to cope with bureaucratic details.

If adequate financial assistance were at the end of the paper trails, then form filling per se would be a less significant barrier. But, since the application process simply determined the amount of aid, if any, the student could expect, the frustration that results from completing the forms and then not receiving adequate aid is obvious.

Special barriers also arose from the administration of BEOGs, the new federal student assistance program to facilitate access. Only six weeks were provided for students to receive and complete applications for BEOGs, placing a severe time constraint on students and their families. In addition, in determining parental contributions, problems arose in how to treat parental and student assets, social security and veterans' benefits, and the definition of independent students (ACE, 1974). In 1973, the BEOGs awards ranged from $50 to $452, with average awards of $270, which were inadequate to cover the college costs of low-income students. Finally, BEOGs awards were limited to first time, full-time freshmen, thus increasing the demand for other assistance programs.

Financial Aid and Graduate Education

In a study of financial barriers to graduate education for Black students, Cooke (1970) concluded that the Higher Education Act of 1965 discriminated against minority students who wanted to go to graduate school: (a) by placing heavy emphasis on loan programs (poor students in undergraduate school were already likely to have accumulated a large undergraduate debt and so would realistically hesitate to add to it by going to graduate school), and, (b) by placing the burden on family resources (poor families were neither able nor willing to assume the large financial burdens of graduate education, because of their own limited resources).

In 1972, about one-third (35.9%) of the 195 graduate institutions in a special survey by Hamilton (1973) allocated financial aid to minorities. (See Table 3-28.) The size of the graduate program seemed to be a significant factor in determining the presence of aid programs for minorities. Very large institutions were three times as likely as smaller ones to have such financial aid programs. In addition, special financial aid for minorities was more characteristic of doctoral institutions than masters level institutions. Region, location, and type of control were unrelated to financial aid for disadvantaged minority graduate students.

TABLE 3-28. Special Funds Allocated Solely for Financial Aid to Minority/Disadvantaged Graduate Students by Type of Institution, 1972.

Institution Subcategory	Number of Institutions in the Sample	Number Responding "Yes"	Percent "Yes"	Number Responding "No"	Percent "No"	No Response
Region						
NE/MA	78	36	46.1	40	51.3	2
MW/	45	15	33.3	29	64.4	1
S/SE	39	5	12.8	30	76.9	4
W/SW/NW	33	14	42.4	16	48.5	3
Graduate Program						
Small	14	0	0.0	14	100.0	0
Medium	49	11	22.4	35	71.4	3
Large	81	27	33.3	49	60.5	5
Very Large	50	32	64.0	16	32.0	2
Location						
Town	53	18	34.0	32	60.4	3
City	45	20	44.4	23	51.1	2
Urban	34	11	32.4	22	64.7	1
Metropolitan	63	21	33.3	38	60.3	4
Highest Degree						
M.A.	39	6	15.4	32	82.1	1
PH.D.	165	64	41.0	83	53.2	9
Type of Control						
Public	124	49	39.5	68	54.8	7
Private	71	21	29.6	47	66.2	3
Combined Degree and Control						
MA/public	23	5	21.7	17	73.9	1
MA/private	16	1	6.3	15	93.8	0
Ph.D./public	101	44	43.6	51	50.5	6
Ph.D./private	55	20	36.4	32	58.2	3
Total	195	70	35.9%	115	59.0%	10 (5.1%)

SOURCE: Hamilton, I. Bruce, (1973), *Graduate School Programs for Minority/Disadvantaged; Report on an Initial Survey*, Educational Testing Service, Table 5.

The sources of funds of those graduate institutions offering special aid for minority graduate students are summarized in Table 3-29. In 1972, Hamilton found about 62.8% of the funds for minority aid programs were from the university operating funds; 14.5% were from all sources of federal funds; and 13.7% from foundations. Hamilton also found that a small percent of the graduate schools (8.8%) awarded funds to minorities solely on the basis of need; most often, both need and merit usually were considered (74.9%). In the regular student aid programs at the same institutions, awards were made on the basis of merit with little need considerations by 78% of the institutions.

Since minority funds for graduate education came primarily from university income, only financially strong institutions were able to admit and support low-income minority students. Competition for such financial aid may have limited the number of Blacks and other low-income students who could consider graduate and professional schools as realistic alternatives.

The ability to draw upon financial resources facilitated persistence of college seniors into graduate and professional training without delay. It also differentiated Black and white doctoral recipients. Black native-born doctoral recipients in Spring 1973 were on the average 5.7 years older than their white counterparts. The Black median age for doctoral recipients was 36.7, in contrast to the white median age of 31.0, according to the National Research Council. The age differential reflected that Blacks had to spread out their doctoral training over a greater number of years; a fact also related to financial aid, as discussed previously.

As a part of his one-year follow-up study of college seniors, Baird (1973) found that Black and white graduate students financed their training differently. (See Table

TABLE 3-29. Approximate Percentage From Different Sources of Special Funds for Minority Graduate Student Aid, 1972.

Source	Mean Percentage from Each Source	Number of Responses Identifying the Source	Number of Times the Source is Indicated as the Sole Source
University operating funds	62.8	41	23
Special fellowship funds obtained through donations or assessment of students or alumni for this purpose	4.1	7	1
Special state appropriation	4.4	5	1
Federal funds (all sources)	14.5	16	3
Foundation funds	13.7	14	3
Other sources*	.5	2	0
Total	100.0%	85	31

SOURCE: Hamilton, I. Bruce, (1973), *Graduate School Programs for Minority/Disadvantaged, Report on an Initial Survey*, Educational Testing Service, Table 26.
*Dean's contingency Fund (1)
  Endowment Income

3-30.) While Black graduate students borrowed from banks and universities, and received scholarships or fellowships, white graduate students relied more heavily on their parents and personal savings to meet graduate school costs.

The overall patterns of financial support of Black and white (native-born) doctoral recipients were similar according to the National Research Council. Black doctoral recipients, however, most often used private earnings, federal programs, and teaching assistantships to pay for their doctoral training; whites used teaching and research assistantships and federal programs, in addition to private earnings. (See Table 3-31.) Few students, Black or white, borrowed as the primary support for doctoral training. Black graduate students, however, were in a less stable economic condition than their white classmates because the Black graduate students were more likely to have relied on loans which often extended from undergraduate through graduate training. After graduation, their salaries which were usually their only source of funds, were needed both to repay their loans and to meet the rising cost of living.

Educational Preparation and Academic Failure

Educational preparation and academic failure are separate but related barriers to access, distribution, and persistence in higher education. They interact with race and social class in limiting equal educational opportunity. Inadequate high school preparation and the resultant academic failure to which it contributes is not limited to Black students. But the probability that Black students will attend inferior high schools and receive inadequate academic training is related to (a) the disproportionate number of Blacks in poor inner city schools, (b) housing and employment discrimination that lead to a concentration of poor and unemployed Blacks, some in multiple problem families, in restricted areas, and (c) the scarcity of resources—financial and emotional—with which talented Black youths can compensate for the inadequate education their high schools and communities provide.

TABLE 3-30. Financial Characteristics of Students in Advanced Study by Race, 1972.

	Percents		
Amount of Loans	Black	White	Difference (Black-White)
Nothing	33.0	62.0	−29.0
Up to $2,000	35.0	21.0	14.0
More than $2,000	16.0	10.0	6.0
Amount of Indebtedness:			
Nothing	20.0	56.0	−36.0
Up to $2,000	35.0	20.0	15.0
More than $2,000	30.0	19.0	11.0
Source of Loans:			
Banks	23.0	18.0	5.0
University	20.0	12.0	8.0
Scholarship/Fellowships			
University	60.0	25.0	35.0
Other	37.0	13.0	24.0
Other Sources of Support:			
Parents	39.0	54.0	−15.0
Personal Savings	37.0	52.0	−15.0

SOURCE: Baird, Leonard, *Careers and Curriculum*, p. 137 to 140.

TABLE 3-31. Sources of Financial Support of Doctoral Recipients by Race, Spring 1973.

Sources of Financial Support	U.S. Native Born Only			
	Black		White	
	Number	Percent of Recipients	Number	Percent of Recipients
Federal Fellowship/Traineeships	219	38.3	8,997	45.6
G.I. Bill	93	16.3	2,308	11.7
University Fellow	107	18.7	3,616	18.3
Teaching Assistantship	178	31.1	9,508	48.2
Research Assistantship	94	16.4	6,035	30.6
Private Industry Funds	53	9.3	1,457	7.4
Institutional Funds	82	14.3	1,814	9.2
Private Earnings	241	42.1	8,038	40.7
Spouse Earnings	83	14.5	4,332	22.0
Family Contributions	17	3.0	1,408	7.1
Loans	104	18.2	2,564	13.0
Number Answering	552	96.4	19,304	97.8
Total Doctoral Recipients	572	—	19,731	—

SOURCE: National Board on Graduate Education, National Academy of Science, NRC, Doctoral Records File, unpublished data.

Educational Preparation

The level of high school preparation that Black high school students took to college determined not only the selectivity of the institutions they attended, but also the fields of study they selected. Equally bright Black students went to colleges of different selectivity because of other factors, such as location and costs. In Fall 1973, Black freshmen with the higher high school grade-point averages and aptitude test scores tended to enroll in the selective institutions, according to data from the American Council on Education.

The Association of American Medical Colleges Task Force (1970) found—as did studies on minority participation in Engineering and Physical Science—that a cause for the low enrollment of Blacks in medical training was inadequate educational preparation in Science and Mathematics. The effect of educational preparation in Mathematics and Science on distribution was greatest in determining whether students would enter Physical Science or technical fields. The quality of the science and mathematics training offered Black students in inner city or Southern high schools determined what they could major in at college.

Blewett (1974), in a follow-up study of special admissions of minority students in medical school, found that their cumulative grade point average was 2.61. But on the Medical College Admissions Test these students averaged 457, which was lower than the regular admissions average of 565. In 1970, while 1% of the students had to repeat the entire first year, 10% of the special admissions minority students did. While 3% of all medical students had to repeat one or more courses, 16% of the minority students did. Blewett suggested that a part of the problem that the minority students in the study had in medical school was due to the lack of supportive services and lack of a nurturing environment in the institutions to help the students overcome inadequate educational preparation. He pointed out that more psychosocial and educational assistance was offered to foreign students than was available to native Americans for cultural minorities. His recommendations were similar to those of the AMC Task Force: adequate and guaranteed financial aid, sensitized faculty to remove covert racism, academic reinforcement without stigma, and modernized medical school curricula.

Educational preparation was also related to aptitude and achievement test scores used to admit students. Where past preparation was poor, scores tended to be low. Because inner city high schools tended to offer fewer advanced training courses in Mathematics and Science than suburban high schools, students from inner city schools, especially in low-income Black neighborhoods, were likely to be less able to compete with better trained students for college space or course grades. It is not uncommon, for example, for both private and public high schools serving upper middle class students to include college level work in the junior and senior year required courses. A consequence is that the freshman year of college is a review of what had been learned in the last year of high school. Thus, the students earn respectable grade-point averages. For freshmen without such advanced high school training, that is Blacks and less affluent college students, the freshmen year curriculum is not review, but new work that they must master. Depending on their ability to compensate for the inadequacies in their past high school training and ability to compete with their better trained classmates, the disadvantaged freshmen persist or experience failure.

Academic Failure

As persistence studies have demonstrated, one significant reason for withdrawal from college is academic failure. Students who could not keep up with their classmates were likely to withdraw from college before being dismissed. And Black students who entered college with weak educational preparation were likely to become academic failures unless institutions intervened to provide compensatory tutorial or study skills centers and unless the students took advantage of the opportunities provided to overcome their weak educational preparation.

In a national study of 1966 full-time freshmen over a four-year period, Astin (1972) found that high school grade-point average was related to returning for the second year and receiving a degree in four years. Of the Black freshmen enrolled in four-year colleges and universities in Table 3-32, 83.5% of the Black students with the highest high school grade-point averages not only returned for the second year, but also 64.1% of them received their degrees in four years. Of Black students with the lowest high school grade-point averages, 64.0% returned for the second year, and 27.6% completed their degree work in four years. In addition, Black students with the lowest high school grade-point averages were more likely than any other group of Black students to still be enrolled in school at the end of four years or to have discontinued their education.

Compared with non-Black students of equal ability, Black students were as likely to have received their degrees, and slightly more likely to still be enrolled four years after college entry. For example, 4.6% of the Black students with high school grade-point averages of A, and 7% of the non-Black students had dropped out of college before graduation. (See Figure 3-18.) Only at the lowest ability level did Black attrition exceed that of non-Black students by less than 1%.

In a report on a conference on Black enrollment at eastern colleges including Bowdoin, Brown, Connecticut College, Mount Holyoke, Radcliffe, Vassar, University of Vermont, and Williams, Cobb and McDew (1974) included the enrollment and attrition rates of Black students at these institutions in 1972. According to the data supplied by the conference participants, the total student enrollment in 1972 was 20,003 students at the eight institutions listed above; of those enrolled 5.3% (or 1,065) were Black. The number of attritions for Blacks that same year was 79 students, which equaled 0.4% of the total enrollment and 7% of the Black enrollment. Approximately equal numbers of the Black students left for academic as for other reasons. Unfortunately, the total student body attrition rates at these same institutions in 1972 were not included in the Cobb and McDew report. Thus, it was impossible to determine whether Black students were more, or less, likely than all students to drop out of college because of academic failure or other reasons. What *is* known is that of the Black students who dropped out in 1972, personal reasons were as common as academic failure.

In a review of research on special admissions students at Michigan State University, Abramson (1968) reported that in one study a group of 22 high-risk students, some of whom were Black, were admitted to the University. They were provided financial aid through a student loan, a scholarship, and work-study. Of the original 22 high-risk students, nine graduated in four years. In another study, he reported that of 66 Black students admitted to the University in a different special admissions program, 27 completed their first year. Abramson concluded his report with recommendations for increased use of tutorial and counseling services for high-risk students and for revisions in university policies where needed to allow reduced course loads.

TABLE 3-32. Persistence of 1966 Freshmen Attending Four-Year Colleges and Universities by Race, Spring 1970.

		PERCENTS			
	Total	Returned for Second Year	Received Degree	Still Enrolled	Not Enrolled
Black Students:					
High School GPA					
A	201	83.5	64.1	31.3	4.6
B	1,262	67.4	40.5	45.6	13.9
C	831	64.0	27.6	50.4	22.0
Non-Black Students:					
High School GPA					
A	10,512	84.3	64.2	28.8	7.0
B	26,521	77.1	42.2	38.4	19.4
C	8,690	64.9	32.7	45.9	21.4

SOURCE: Astin, Alexander W., *College Dropouts: A National Profile.* Tables 4 and 5.

These recommendations were based on the assumption that the Black attrition was due primarily to academic reasons and that it was higher than that of non-Blacks, especially whites, of equal ability. But, as Cobb and McDew found, the reasons for Black students leaving selected eastern colleges were as likely to be personal as academic. Whether this was true of high-risk students who were Black is unknown.

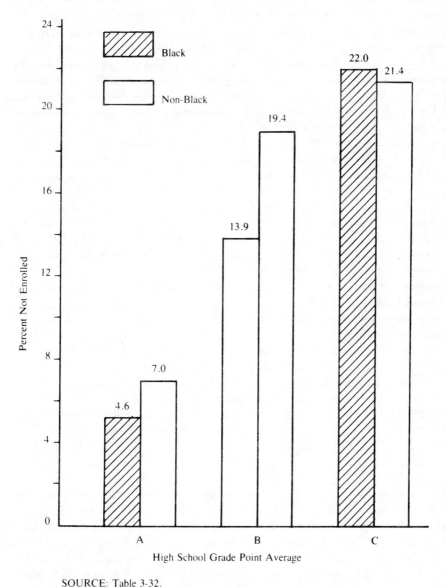

SOURCE: Table 3-32.

FIGURE 3-18. Percent of 1966 Full-Time Freshmen Not Enrolled (Without Degrees) by Race and High School Grade Point Averages, Spring 1970.

The existence of supportive services without stigma was related to academic failure and Black dropout: use of tutorial and related academic supportive services as integral parts of the educational programs offered academically weak Black students, especially on white campuses, while helpful, may also have produced an undesirable backlash. First, Black students may have begun to feel discriminated against by being required to take tutorial courses without the benefit of choice (Spurlock, 1974). Second, college professors may have begun to prejudge all Black students as educationally inadequate. Third, Black students who were unhappy in such circumstances may have transferred to other institutions or dropped out.

In Fall 1973, the existence of remedial programs (i.e., campus efforts to reduce academic failure) was not common on all four-year college and university campuses. While over three-fourths of the two-year colleges offered remedial programs, only half of the four-year colleges and universities did (Creager, 1973).

Academic failure was also a problem in graduate and professional schools. Bragonier and Ragin (1968), in a discussion of how to increase Black enrollment in graduate schools, found that not only was the presence of Blacks in research-oriented doctoral programs regarded as "experimental," but also there was little, if any, institutional effort to follow up the students, to identify and meet their academic and personal needs. Four years later Hamilton (1972) surveyed 195 graduate institutions of which 52.8% responded. He found that 51.7% of those who responded regarded the graduate department as the source of primary responsibility for any effort to assist minority/disadvantaged students enrolled in their graduate school. In addition, 70.3% of the responding institutions stated that they did not have an academic program "designed to reflect the needs and interests of minority/disadvantaged graduate students" on campus.

The importance of tutorial and other supportive services in avoiding academic failure in professional schools was studied as part of a survey of 98 law schools. Schrader (1973) examined the Committee on Legal Educational Opportunities Program (CLEO) of the American Bar Association, which provided tutorial assistance for Black and other minority law students who did not meet standard admissions criteria. In 1969, the CLEO law students were only slightly more likely than non-CLEO Black students to withdraw from law school for academic reasons. (See Table 3-33.) Thus, the supportive services offered to CLEO law students were sufficient to close, in part, the educational preparation gap, and prevent more academic failures.

Academic failure was also related to the type and amount of financial aid law students received. Schrader found that withdrawal for academic reasons was lowest among Black law students who had received greater amounts of financial support, which most often took the form of loans. (See Table 3-34.) Having sufficient financial aid that did not unduly obligate student time enabled the high-risk law students to devote their full attention to their studies. Without such aid, as Schrader suggests, the likelihood of completing law school diminished, and the likelihood of academic failure increased for high-risk law students.

Special support for minorities, financial or otherwise, as Spurlock (1974) observed, generally did not exist in graduate and professional schools in 1973. Under-

TABLE 3-33. Relation Between Participation in CLEO Program and Enrollment Status, 1969 Minority Entrants to 98 Law Schools.

Race and Year of Entry	Participation in CLEO Program	Withdrew: Academic Reasons	Withdrew: Other Reasons	Did not Withdraw	Number of Studetns
		Percents			
Total Minority Group (1969 Entrants)	CLEO	10.4	8.5	81.2	260
	non-CLEO	13.5	12.2	74.3	690
Black American (1969 Entrants)	CLEO	10.8	8.8	80.4	194
	non-CLEO	10.2	10.6	79.2	432

SOURCE: W. B. Schrader, *Relationships Between Characteristics of Minority Group Students Who Entered Law School in 1968, 1969, and 1970*, Table 41.

graduate supportive programs were not generally seen by graduate and professional school faculty and administrators as adaptable to their schools. But, where such adaptations had been made, the minority students experienced not only academic but personal benefits as well.

TABLE 3-34. Relation Between Kind and Amount of Financial Aid and Enrollment Status, 1969 Minority Entrants to 98 Law Schools.

Group		Percent in Each Enrollment Status:			
Total Minority Group (1969 Entrants)	Kind and Amount of Financial Aid	Withdrew: Academic Reasons	Withdrew: Other Reasons	Did Not Withdraw	Number of Students
	2/3 or more, mainly grants	10.4	9.5	80.1	423
	2/3 or more, mainly loans	2.4	19.3	78.3	83
	1/10 to 2/3 of expenses	15.9	6.9	77.2	189
	Less than 1/10 of expenses	20.0	13.5	66.5	155
Black Americans (1969 Entrants)	2/3 or more, mainly grants	10.1	8.8	81.1	307
	2/3 or more, mainly loans	3.1	17.2	79.7	64
	1/10 to 2/3 of expenses	15.2	6.4	78.4	125
	Less than 1/10 of expenses	14.9	14.9	70.3	74

SOURCE: W. B. Schrader, *Relationships Between Characteristics of Minority Group Students Who Entered Law School in 1968, 1969, and 1970*, Table 37.

Transfer Policies

Although not all transfers were from two-year to four-year colleges, the transfer barriers with the most significant racial impact occur in the transition from two-year to four-year colleges, because about 40% of all Blacks in college in 1973 were in two-year institutions. According to the American Association of Community and Junior Colleges, of 1,165 two-year institutions, 80% were publicly controlled, with a total enrollment equal to 96% of all two-year college students.

Four types of public and private two-year colleges were included in a survey by the American College Testing Program in 1973: junior, community, technical, and technical/vocational colleges. With the exception of junior colleges, the proportion of males enrolled in two-year colleges was greater than that of females regardless of the type of institution. (See Tables in Appendix D.) Less than one-half (42.8%) of all two-year college students were in transfer programs. In junior and community colleges respectively, 58.1% and 50.8% of the students were enrolled in transfer programs. For those students, continuing a college education at the senior college level may not be easy because of transfer policies (Association Transfer Group, 1974).

Table 3-35 summarizes the immediate degree aspirations of Black students attending two-year colleges in Fall 1973. Slightly more than half (54.2%) of the Black students in two-year colleges wanted associate arts degrees, while over one-third (36.6%) wanted to transfer to four-year colleges and universities to earn higher degrees.

Transferring from junior to senior colleges in one, and more typically, two years was not easy for some Black students. Table 3-36 indicates the number of years that Black students aspiring for bachelor degrees had been enrolled in two-year colleges in Fall 1973. Over one-half (55.2%) were in their second or third year in two-year colleges, according to U.S. Census data. For these estimated 47,000 Black two-year college students, transfer policies were important.

The barriers facing transfer students arose at the institutional level. They included (a) the articulation of their two-year college credits with the senior college curricula,

TABLE 3-35. Immediate Degree Aspirations of Black Students Attending Two-Year Colleges by Sex, October 1973.

Degree Aspirations	Percents		
	Male	Female	Both Sexes
Associate	44.6	62.8	54.4
Bachelor	36.2	18.0	26.5
Masters	2.4	2.1	2.2
Doctorate	0.0	0.0	0.0
Professional	0.0	0.0	0.0
Other	3.6	11.8	7.9
No Degree	13.2	5.3	9.0
Total	100.0	100.0	100.0

SOURCE: U.S. Census, Published data, (1975).

TABLE 3-36. Number of Years in School of Two-Year College Black Students Aspiring for Baccalaureate degrees or Higher by Sex, October 1973.

Years Completed	Male (n=30,000)	Percent Female (n=17,000)	Total (n=47,000)
First Year	50.0	11.8	36.2
Second Year	13.3	52.9	27.6
Third Year	30.0	23.5	27.6
Fourth Year	0.0	0.0	0.0
Fifth Year	0.0	0.0	0.0
Sixth Year or More	0.0	0.0	0.0
Unknown	6.7	11.8	8.6
Total	100.0	100.0	100.0

SOURCE: U.S. Census, unpublished data, (1975).

(b) the availability of financial aid, and (c) special orientation for transfer students (Willingham, 1972). Two-year college students were refused admission because their courses or grades were unacceptable for admission to a senior college. Of those accepted, some of their two-year college courses may not count toward course credit. Consequently, some transfer students would have to repeat courses they thought they had completed and to extend the time spent earning a degree. Because transfer students usually applied in the spring semester, their applications were often received later than those of new freshmen. As a result, they applied after many of the admissions and student financial aid decisions had been made. Finally, transfer student orientation programs analogous to those available to new students were generally not provided for transfer students. They often faced an unknown campus environment without the benefit of institutional supports provided new freshmen.

Thus, entering the four-year college from the two-year college was neither automatic nor simple. Because low-income students and those with marginal high school records did go to two-year colleges, and because a sionificant number of these students were Black, such transfer policies and practices constituted barriers with an adverse racial impact.

The racial inequalities in persistence were larger at the two-year college level, than at the four-year college level. According to Astin, it was estimated that 43% of the Black students enrolled in 1966 as full-time freshmen in two-year colleges had not completed training and were not enrolled in 1970. In contrast, 33% of their non-Black counterparts were not enrolled. Over 25% of the Black students at four-year colleges and universities in 1966 were enrolled in 1970, in comparison to 18.5% of the non-Black students attending the same type of institution.

If a hierarchical model of higher education is to be open to Black students without unintentional, but nevertheless real, racial bias, then appropriate transfer practices are needed. Under prevailing conditions, two-year colleges were likely to become a wasteland for Black intellect and talent desiring to transfer to four-year colleges and universities.

Counseling Practices

The counseling practice that most directly limits equal educational opportunity is the "cooling out process." This involves the counseling and eventual placement of students into levels of training below that to which they had originally aspired. The aim is to bring student aspirations more into line with their abilities as assessed by the institution. For unselective groups, such as two-year college students and some four-year college students, counseling and placement are used to screen and track students.

Because Blacks were the most likely students to aspire for degrees and fields of study inconsistent with their aptitude test scores, the cooling out process could have had an adverse racial impact in Fall 1973. Thus, Blacks were most likely to be encouraged to enter terminal degree programs in two-year colleges, or not to pursue advanced training in four-year colleges and universities.

Although the cooling out process has been most extensively researched and discussed in the context of two-year colleges, it also existed in four-year colleges and universities. Shea (1974) discussed the cooling out process as a means of tracking and social stratification designed to reduce attrition and academic failure in four-year colleges. After reviewing the literature, he concluded that the attrition rates of transfer and "native" students in four-year colleges were about equal. But, the survival rate of students at two-year colleges was lower than at four-year colleges. Two-thirds of the two-year college students who originally aspired to attend to four-year colleges either dropped out or moved into terminal career education programs in the same institution.

Beginning one's college education in a two-year college, as about 40% of all Black college students did in 1973, increased the likelihood that it would also end there. Regardless of aspirations, only a small number (about one-third) of the Black two-year college students eventually graduated from four-year colleges.

Low persistence could be due to factors other than the type of counseling services offered, but the cooling out process in all probability contributed to the low persistence of Blacks in two-year colleges. Through counseling and tracking practices, along with their own academic weaknesses, the educational attainment of Black students in two-year colleges was likely to fall below not only that of white students in the same type of institution, but also their initial degree aspirations.

Recruitment Practices

During the late 1960's college recruitment schedules were extended to include predominantly Black high schools. The National Scholarship Service and Fund for Negro Students conducted "college days" in several key cities to bring college recruiters into contact with substantial numbers of Black students. Some predominantly Black school districts, such as Washington, D.C., organized their own college day. Also, during this same period, national efforts (such as Project Access of the College Entrance Examination Board) developed rosters of minority students available to college recruiters.

Sedlacek, et al. (1974), in a five-year study on the successes and failures of minority recruitment at predominantly white public and private universities, found that there was a 1% gain in Black freshman enrollment over the previous year at predominantly white universities in Fall 1973. For the first time in five years, public universities nationally enrolled 7% of Black freshmen, while private universities enrolled 6%. Universities that were successful in recruiting more minorities to their campuses in 1973 differed from those that failed. The successful institutions stressed academic programs, offered special minority programs, employed minority recruiters, had more recruiters, and made admissions decisions at the time of recruitment. In addition, successful universities were able to finance minority recruitment programs out of their regular operating budgets, which suggested an institutional commitment to a minority recruitment program. Colleges that integrated special recruitment efforts aimed at minorities into ongoing recruitment policies and budgeting had larger minority enrollment than institutions that did not (Sedlacek, 1974).

In 1972, Hamilton found that only 53.8% of 195 graduate institutions engaged in special recruitment efforts to increase their minority enrollment. Ph.D.-granting institutions and those with large graduate programs were most likely to have these recruitment programs. Type of control was unrelated to whether the institution had special minority recruitment in 1972, according to Hamilton.

In 1973, minority recruitment activities for graduate schools had been cut back, in part as a result of general economic conditions within colleges. Spurlock (1974) found that those graduate minority recruitment activities in existence tended to be piecemeal and ill-defined, and that efforts in professional schools were often better than those in graduate schools. He suggested that this qualitative difference may in part have contributed to the more rapid increase in minority enrollment in professional schools, when compared with graduate schools.

Because of the recent economic crisis, however, only institutions with financial stability were able to spend money attracting minority students to their undergraduate or graduate schools. In graduate and professional programs, recruitment was done primarily at the departmental level, where the costs of aggressively seeking minority candidates could consume a significant proportion of the ongoing departmental budget (AACP, 1973). In addition, the minority graduate and professional recruitment programs could themselves create educational barriers. Institutions that concentrated their efforts on predominantly Black high schools and colleges, the former located primarily in inner cities, the latter in the South, achieved some *economy of scale* in minority recruitment. The negative impact, however, was that academically average or slightly below average Black and other minority students attending predominantly white institutions either in suburban communities or non-Southern states were likely to be overlooked as potential high (or moderate) risk students.

In the technical fields, recruitment barriers have also received attention. In a survey of deans of colleges of Engineering, Lantz (1970) found that of the 64 colleges reporting, about one-half had special recruitment and supportive programs for Black students. These same colleges also had one or more Black freshmen enrolled the year of the survey. Lantz concluded that colleges of Engineering could increase their non-white, undergraduate enrollment through special academic and social programs to attract Black high school students to the field of Engineering.

In another survey of Engineering schools, Kiehl (1970) examined the long-run employment demand for Black engineers. On the basis of a questionnaire sent to administrators of 263 Engineering and technical training institutions and the opinions of 295 Black graduates of schools of Engineering in 1968 and 1969, he concluded that there were widespread educational and employment opportunities for Blacks in Engineering. Despite this there were still very few Blacks in Engineering. He attributed this to high school guidance and counseling personnel not sharing this information with Black students. (Another barrier was the financial burden that went with the five-year Engineering undergraduate curriculum.) To increase the number of Black engineers, Kiehl recommended increased government support of Black as well as white Engineering colleges with Black students enrolled. He also recommended increased industry interest and participation in stimulating employment opportunities for Blacks in Engineering.

A significant but seldom mentioned aspect of the recruitment barrier in technical fields is that there is a finite pool of Black high school and college students interested in pursuing technical fields. For similar technical fields, the problem is to interest these students in entering a specific subject area (Planning Commission for Expanding Minority Opportunities in Engineering, 1974). The solution is to expand the pool of Black students interested in and able to undertake technical studies. Expanding the pool means up-grading grade school curricula in Mathematics and Science. In addition, expanding the pool means identifying and offering advanced work to talented and gifted Black junior and senior high school students. Expanding the pool also means that recruitment of Blacks into technical fields should begin in junior and senior high school. A recommendation of the Planning Commission for Expanding Minority Opportunities in Engineering (1974) stressed the need to stimulate interest in Engineering at the grade school level. Other technical, scientific and medical fields also have stressed the importance of such early recruitment.

Extracurricular Activities and Student Employment

Since both extracurricular activities and employment place demands on student time, it would seem that they could negatively affect distribution by field of study and persistence. Studies on extracurricular activities by Anderson (1966), Barger and Hall (1965), Vaughan (1968), Lenning et al. (1974), and others, however, conclude that participation in extracurricular activities was not negatively related to persistence. In fact, students who were involved in the campus activities were more likely to remain in school than those not involved. In addition, employment per se was found not to be negatively related to persistence. The research suggests that the conditions of employment rather than employment itself determined whether or not employment would have a negative effect on persistence.

Beyond the conditions of employment, faculty attitudes toward working students may also affect persistence. "Some faculty members may admire the initiative and fortitude of [students] who attend college while holding full and part-time jobs. Others may feel that working students, especially women, are not dedicated to, or interested in, academic [pursuits]'' (Abramowitz and Abramowitz, 1975). Because Black students were more likely to work than white students in 1973, negative attitudes toward working college students would have a disproportionate impact on Blacks.

In addition, Blacks were more likely to be negatively influenced by institutional policies that restricted student work. The College Work-Study program, for example, had limited student work hours. Yet, the financial burdens of some Black students in 1973 were such that additional work, even full-time work, was necessary. When institutional policies limiting work hours of full-time students were not compensated for by adequate evening programs for part-time students or sources of financial aid such as loans or grants, college opportunity was limited.

The relevance of the job to career goals and the demanding nature of the work (conditions of employment) determined the influence of employment on persistence. In 1973, full-time employment was a significant source of financial support for Black students. For example, the College Work-Study Program and Supplemental Educational Opportunity Grants were the most frequent sources of aid received by Blacks in the federal aid programs in 1973. (See Chapter 5.) In addition, a greater proportion of Black than white students were working full-time the year before they received their doctorates. (See Table 3-37.) White students, unlike Blacks, were more likely to be employed part-time, as teachers or research assistants, work likely to be relevant to later careers.

Of Black and white workers 35 years and older in the labor force also enrolled in school, over one-half were enrolled in college in Fall 1973. Although both Black and white workers in college were more likely to enroll as part-time students, a higher

TABLE 3-37. Employment Status in 1971-1972 Academic Year of Doctoral Recipients by Race, Spring 1973.

Employment Status 1971-72 Year	Native Born Only Percents		Difference (White-Black)
	White	Black	
Not employed	5.7	3.3	2.4
Fellowship	15.8	15.4	0.4
Own research grant	1.0	1.4	–0.4
Employed part-time	7.0	6.3	0.7
Assistantship	21.5	12.8	8.7
Full-time			
College teaching	25.1	28.1	–3.0
College non-teaching	4.7	8.0	–3.3
Grade school teaching	3.0	5.8	–2.8
Grade school non-teaching	3.5	8.4	–4.9
Other full-time	11.0	8.6	2.6
Unknown	1.7	1.9	–0.2
TOTAL	100.0	100.0	

SOURCE: National Board on Graduate Education, National Academy of Science, NRC, Doctoral Records File, unpublished data.

proportion of Blacks and other minorities (14.2%) than whites (8.4%) working full-time were also enrolled in college full-time. (See Table 3-38.)

Summary

The educational barriers arising from the interrelationship of college costs, financial aid program implementation and family income, together constituted the most significant educational barriers for Black students, and indeed, for all low-income groups in higher education. These financial barriers affected distribution and persistence, as well as access. For high school graduates, family financial condition and the availability of financial aid determined whether they enrolled in college (access) and what type of institution they chose and their career choices (distribution). Once in college, Black and other low-income students needed financial resources to remain and earn advanced degrees (persistence) especially in the more expensive graduate and professional fields of study.

Even with current financial aid, family income and college costs influenced the likelihood of Blacks going to undergraduate, and professional schools, as well as the type of institutions and fields Black and other students entered. The lower the family income, the less likely that Black college students would have the educational experiences and opportunities of whites from more financially advantaged families.

Admissions tests, when used as a basis for college admission, were access barriers to Black students, because admissions test scores were related to family income. Solutions lie in research on second and third year college students, improved grade school training, the elimination of class bias in tests and a moratorium on admissions tests.

Recruitment practices influenced access and distribution of Blacks in undergraduate, graduate, and professional schools in 1973. Many institutions had reduced their recruitment activities, undoubtedly in an effort to cut college costs. The result was that fewer institutions were aggressively seeking Black students. Recruitment in specific fields was adversely influenced by the limited number of students with ability

TABLE 3-38. Type of School Attended by Persons 35 Years Old and Over by Race, October 1972.

Race	Total		Elementary and High School	Percent Enrolled College		Trade or Vocational
	Number (In Thousands)	Percent		Full-Time	Part-Time	
Total	1,458	100.0	6.9	9.1	45.0	39.0
White	1,289	100.0	5.0	8.4	45.7	40.9
Black and Other Races	169	100.0	20.7	14.2	39.6	25.5

SOURCE: U.S. Department of Labor, *Going Back to School at 35*, Special Labor Force Report 159, Table 1.

and interest in them. Recruitment for distribution has to be coupled with expanding the number of Blacks in the college availability pool.

Both academic failure and withdrawal of Black students from college were related to the educational preparation the students received in high school. Students who entered college with weak educational preparation were less likely to persist in college.

Counseling practices and transfer policies affected the distribution and persistence of Black students. In certain screening and tracking processes, Black students were likely to be encouraged to enter terminal degree programs in two-year colleges. Existing transfer policies made it difficult for students at two-year colleges, where almost half of the Black students were enrolled in 1973, to pursue degrees at four-year colleges.

Sufficient financial aid was necessary to cover tuition, room and board, and travel costs for low-income students to attend colleges not located within commuting distances. One source of aid was work, discussed in the context of extracurricular activities. Both extracurricular activities and student work reduced the number of hours available for study; for Blacks and other low-income students who were academically weak, these demands on their time could increase the possibility of academic failure. Black students tended to work full-time, especially if they were enrolled in graduate and professional programs. The effect of work on Black persistence was to provide funds to meet college costs, but also to increase the number of years required to earn advanced degrees.

In addition to the categorical and educational barriers already discussed, Black underrepresentation in college was also the result of psychosocial barriers discussed in the following section of this chapter.

PSYCHOSOCIAL BARRIERS

Psychosocial barriers are the attitudes, values, and racial stereotypes that Blacks hold about themselves and that others use to limit the access, distribution, or persistence of Blacks in higher education. The most important influence of psychosocial barriers may be on college distribution, especially the racial composition of the student body.

White Students/Black Campuses

What happened when Black students went to white campuses, and what happened when white students went to Black campuses? The psychosocial aspects of the dual racial higher education system have received some attention. In 1973, the Southern Regional Education Board (SREB) published a study of the white students on the campuses of 18 traditionally Black public colleges. A stratified sample of the 5,579 white students (2,828 males and 2,751 females), who equaled 8.46% of the total enrollment of 65,966 on these campuses, was included in the study. Of 1,696 questionnaires sent to the white students, 626 had usable responses; this equaled 11% of all white students attending Black colleges in this study.

SREB found that two-thirds of the white students enrolled full-time in undergraduate and professional schools reported above average grades. Most white students commuted daily to campus, and only about 20% received financial assistance in grants or scholarships from Black colleges. Almost half of the white students had transferred to the Black campuses from predominantly white colleges, giving low tuition cost, convenience, and the availability of the desired degree programs as the reasons for transfer. Over half of the white students had little prior contact with Black students before enrolling in the Black colleges. Indeed one-third admitted having reservations about enrolling in the Black colleges. Yet, the white students did not feel that special orientation for whites was necessary and felt that such courses would create, not alleviate, anxiety and tension.

The white students on the Black campuses in the SREB study, while having limited participation in non-academic activities on campus, did receive the educational opportunities and experiences they wanted and needed. Over 80% of the white students indicated that they planned to take their degrees from the Black colleges in which they enrolled at the time of the study. They felt that the Black faculties were helpful, although some Black students were hostile. They also had increased contact with Black students of similar interests. These white students, however, tended to be older and not recent high school graduates. Military obligations, child rearing, time spent on predominantly white campuses, and the inclusion of graduate and professional school students in the survey increased the age range.

Black Students/White Campuses

In 1970, Jones, et al., studied the differences in perceived sources of academic difficulties of Blacks on predominantly white college campuses. His sample included 190 Black students (98 males and 92 females) at four Black universities, and 94 Black students (51 males and 43 females) enrolled in five white liberal arts colleges. Jones, et al., found Black students on white campuses ranked inadequate social life and lack of high school preparation as their most serious problems. These students were more likely than their counterparts on Black campuses to attribute their academic difficulties to these psychosocial factors. Black students on Black campuses tended to perceive inadequate high school preparation, competition, and other academic factors as those most likely to contribute to academic failure.

While it would be erroneous to generalize on the basis of Jones's study, it would seem that enrolling in predominantly white or Black colleges presented different barriers for Black students. For those on the white campus, the studies of Jones discussed above, Epps (1974), and others suggested the function of psychosocial barriers. Conversely, the barriers confronted by Black students on Black campuses tended to be educational.

Why this was so probably not only reflected the influence of the racial composition of the educational setting, but also the selection process by which some students went to white campuses and others to Black institutions. In order to isolate more effectively the consequences for a Black student attending a Black college as opposed to a white one, factors such as the academic preparation of the student, family income, high school grade-point average, age, and year in school would have to be taken into consideration. It may be that as well as the racial composition of the student body or faculty, age and social maturity also contributed to the differences in the perceptions of Black students on their respective white or Black campuses.

In another study of Black students on white campuses, Hedegard (Epps, 1972) reported the findings of his research at the University of Michigan. Hedegard examined the psychosocial characteristics of Black students admitted under a special admissions program to the University of Michigan undergraduate schools. He found that in their freshman year most of these Black students, who were for the most part recent high school graduates, tended to feel intense loneliness. This was especially true if they did not know other students on campus or if there was not a Black neighborhood near the campus. Compared with Black men, Black women had a more difficult and less pleasant time socially on white campuses.

In academic performance, unlike the older white students on Black campuses in the SREB study discussed above, younger Black students on white campuses tended to perform below their own academic expectations. As a result, some of the Black students began to question their intellectual abilities; others began to feel that they had been discriminated against by hostile, unfeeling white faculty. Black students admitted under the special program tended to feel less satisfied with themselves and their academic performance than white students on the same campus. When SAT scores were controlled, however, Black and white students with the same scores tended to obtain similar grades, although where differences occurred, white students tended to earn higher grades.

To some extent, these findings may be colored by the fact that social class and age interacted with satisfaction in college. As Hedegard pointed out, the size of an institution, such as the University of Michigan, tended to produce negative feelings in lower-class as opposed to middle-class students. Middle-class students were better able to cope and adjust to the relatively impersonal environment of a large college. As students got older, attitudes toward college improved. Black students who remained until the senior year tended to have positive attitudes toward their college education, their future, and themselves. In fact, according to Hedegard, the Black college seniors tended to hold attitudes more favorable to college than did white seniors.

In a study of 249 Black students attending 83 predominantly white institutions, Centra (1970) found that the incomes of the Black students, although lower than those of white students, were higher than the median Black family income. In addition, 82% of the Black students, compared to 74% of the whites, planned to attend graduate or professional school. White students were active in campus life, while Black students were active in the community. The Black students were more aware of their minority status on the white campuses and felt less absorbed into the college life than did their white counterparts.

A study of Black students on white campuses in North Carolina (Davis, 1973) found differences in attitudes. Black freshmen in two-year colleges were optimistic and hopeful of getting a good education and a good job by attending predominantly white two-year colleges. But Black upperclassmen on residential white campuses were hostile toward their college environment. The probable causes for the frustration of these Black students included unsatisfactory social life, social class differences in values and accepted behavior, and the absence of Black student leaders, Black faculty and counselors.

In a study of Black students on the campuses of five predominantly white junior colleges, the Southern Regional Education Board (1970) found that the three factors accounting for the presence of students on these campuses were cost, proximity, and program. The Black students elected to go to white junior colleges with low tuition, within commuting distance, and with the academic and vocational programs they wanted. In many cases, the Blacks not only attended junior colleges, but they also contributed to the support of their families by working while in school. Indeed, SREB found that a full expense grant would not solve their financial problems, because the grants would not cover their families' financial obligations.

In interviews with 148 Black students, SREB found that about 90% of these students felt that their courses met their needs, that they were satisfied with the quality of instruction they received, but that teachers held negative attitudes toward Blacks. The Black students tended to feel isolated and expressed the desire for more opportunities to become involved in the full range of campus life.

Of the Black students in the SREB survey, 55% planned to continue their education after junior college; 25% wanted to combine work and further post-secondary education; and 12% wanted to go to work full-time. Most of the Black students aspired to one or more college degrees.

The negative attitudes of the younger Black students on predominantly white university and junior college campuses toward white faculty and students were similar in nature, but more severe in degree, than the attitudes of older white students on predominantly Black four-year college campuses. While in most cases both the Black and white students felt satisfied with their experience, they were more dissatisfied with the non-academic social encounter with the opposite race. They tended to feel more negative toward fellow students of the opposite race than toward faculty of the opposite race.

While not fully describing the conditions of Black students on white campuses, or of white students on Black campuses, these studies suggested that in the integration of student bodies on campuses growing out of the dual racial system in higher education, white students who elected to go to predominantly Black colleges had more favorable experiences. Undoubtedly, the fact that the white students were older, had transferred from white campuses, and were enrolled as upperclassmen or in graduate or professional schools may have significantly reduced the number of problems that would have been encountered had the white students been recent high school graduates. For Black students, especially those in special admissions programs and junior colleges, with marginal academic skills and unfocused career expectations, attending white campuses may have intensified the psychosocial adjustment problems typical of their age group.

Psychosocial Barriers and Program Distribution

Psychosocial factors entered into the decision to enter a particular field of study. These factors included ability and personal interest, perceived employment opportunities, encouragement and guidance from interested others, and positive evaluations of one's abilities. In scientific and technical fields Wilburn (1972) identified two psychosocial barriers: reluctance to enter a scientific field unless the probability was great that one would be a "star"; and peer, parental, and teacher pressure not to enter scientific or technical fields because of racism in employment opportunities.

Fear of failure in entering not only predominantly white institutions but also fields with low Black participation remained a significant psychosocial barrier to distribution for Black college students in 1973. Because few Black families could absorb their failures by providing them with economic security, the consequences of failing were more devastating. Failing in college enhanced the probability that the Black male or female would hold lower-paying jobs and experience more unemployment than Blacks who succeeded. Fear of failure contributed, along with categorical and educational barriers, to the present distribution of Blacks in higher education.

The emotional climate of the school discouraged students from remaining there. Where the environment was hostile at worst and unsupportive at best, few Black students were likely to persist. Few students of any race would stay where they felt they were neither wanted nor fairly treated, and where the fields they wished to enter were not open to them.

Some students who wished to enter traditionally non-Black fields were also discouraged from doing so by two racially based notions: that Black students would not be able to handle rigorous work, and would not be able to delay gratification long enough to complete lengthy training. Fields requiring long-range preparation with less certain opportunities for training and employment were not attractive to most students. Low-income students, a disproportionate number of whom were Black, were the least able to afford the risk of entering training in which they perceived limited opportunities to complete their studies as well as future economic hardships.

In this way psychosocial barriers also contributed to the enrollment of Blacks in social science rather than science and technical fields. Since most students, Black and non-Black, expected to work after graduation, they entered fields in which they felt there would be employment opportunities. For Blacks, employment opportunities have been greatest in social service fields, such as Education, and smallest in technical and research-oriented fields. Consequently, most Black students set aside personal interests and followed the paths of opportunity, selecting fields of study in which employment opportunities seemed likely.

Beyond the barriers created by labor market conditions, psychosocial barriers were also controlled by college faculties that were 97% white. These categorical barriers arose out of the conscious and sometimes unconscious prejudgments and stereotypes about the abilities and interests of Black students, especially those who desired to enter fields in which Blacks were small in number.

The Association of American Medical Colleges Task Force (1970) found that only about one-fourth of the 6% of Black freshmen interested in medical careers would actually enroll in medical schools. In contrast, one-third of the white freshmen also interested in medical careers would actually enroll. Although the acceptance rate of Black medical school applicants was almost twice that of whites, racial bias on admissions committees was still a problem.

Psychosocial Barriers and Persistence

Psychosocial barriers were also related to persistence. In a one-year follow-up study of Black undergraduates at the University of Maryland, College Park, DiCesare, et al. (1970), found that about 13% of the Black undergraduates did not return the following year. (University-wide, 15% of all undergraduates did not return.) Blacks who did return differed significantly from those who did not in several psychosocial traits: the returning Black students were more certain about their degree aspirations, aspired to advanced degrees, and openly expressed their feelings about the racism they felt existed on the campus. DiCesare, et al., also found that Black students who persisted were more integrated into campus life; they tended to live on campus and to engage in extracurricular activities. The Black students who did not return were more likely to want to go to a Black college, and to be unsure of either their abilities or their future plans.

When students were able to develop a sense of self-worth and belonging on large campuses, their chances of persisting were enhanced. Students who felt isolated and alone tended to leave college. Nicholi (1967) in a study of personality factors related to dropouts at Harvard University found that over one-third of the dropouts had suffered some emotional disorders, especially depression, and had been treated by the university's psychiatric service.

Black and white graduate students differed in their perceptions of graduate school in Baird's study (1973). (See Table 3-39.) Black students felt that there were more student cliques and thus felt more isolated socially than did white students. Black graduate students were also more likely to be in favor of affirmative action to increase minority enrollment in graduate school. Because of their own financial need, Black graduate students also felt that tuition should be lowered, and that all students should receive scholarships with adequate funding in order to be able to concentrate on their studies.

Although Black graduate students were more satisfied than whites with the general academic environment, they were less satisfied with their interpersonal relationships with their professors according to Baird's study (1973). Black graduate students found their professors to be less friendly and less accessible. They felt they were not treated with respect, but rather like children. In addition, Black graduate students did not find their professors stimulating or able to explain the subject matter clearly.

Summary

Psychosocial barriers influenced distribution and persistence. They shaped how Black students perceived the institutions in which they were enrolled. The negative attitudes of white students and faculty, combined with the problems of adjusting to campuses of different racial compositions affected Black students' decisions to enroll or remain. How Black students perceived themselves and their future training and employment opportunities also determined the fields of study they chose.

The difference between Black students who dropped out and those who persisted in undergraduate or graduate school may have been in how they perceived their learning

TABLE 3-39. Differences in Perceptions of Graduate School by Black and White Students, 1972.

	PERCENTS		
Perception	Black	White	Difference
There are lots of student cliques	69.0	58.0	11.0
Do not like the required course work	36.0	49.0	13.0
Fulfillment of expectations about graduate school	47.0	58.0	−11.0
Liberal environment in department or school	43.0	57.0	−14.0
Satisfaction with:			
Formal degree requirements	43.0	53.0	−10.0
Opportunities for independent study	46.0	56.0	−10.0
Opportunities for teaching	23.0	33.0	−10.0
Relevance of courses to actual work in field	59.0	69.0	−10.0
Affirmation action:			
More minorities should be admitted to this department, even if they do not meet minimal requirements	61.0	36.0	25.0
More minorities should be admitted, even if qualified whites are excluded	61.0	29.0	32.0
Financial Aid:			
All students should receive scholarships so they can concentrate on studies	61.0	43.0	18.0
Scholarship should be based on need and ability	75.0	64.0	11.0
Tuition should be lowered	73.0	56.0	17.0
Relationship with prefessors:			
Professors were friendly and accessible	57.0	74.0	−21.0
Professors treat students like adults	63.0	80.0	−17.0
Professors had respect for most students	55.0	66.0	−13.0
Professors exercised a good deal of discipline in class	45.0	28.0	17.0
Professors clearly explained subject matter	48.0	65.0	−17.0
Professors stimulate student learning	39.0	53.0	−14.0

SOURCE: Baird, Leonard, *Careers and Curricula*, pp. 135-149.

environment. Black students who remained did not find their predominantly white colleges friendly, warm institutions. Rather, their ability to cope with and function adequately within indifferent and sometimes hostile environments may have determined their persistence.

Because of the high aspirations of bright Black students, their negative feelings about their institutions alone generally did not inhibit access, distribution, or persistence. For Black students with less ability and lower motivation, such feelings, however, created psychosocial barriers which operated with educational and categorical barriers to limit their opportunity for a college education.

CHAPTER 4

Impact Of Higher Education
On Black Income

INTRODUCTION

The previous chapters of this report have clearly indicated an increased participation of Blacks in higher education over the past twenty years. More Black people are currently enrolled and completing a college education, both absolutely and proportionately, than at any point in history. Clearly one of the principal motivations for this increased enrollment is the expectation that a college education will increase the economic well-being of the individual student. From the point of view of public policy two questions are also important: (1) Does the increased education promise to raise the *absolute* level of well-being for Blacks individually and collectively? (2) Does the increased education promise to raise the *relative* level of well-being for Blacks individually and collectively? In this chapter the effects of college education on the level of income of Black males and females are examined in an attempt to answer these questions.

This examination of the monetary returns on an investment in education in no way implies that increased income is the only valuable output of the educational process or that educational expenditures should be curtailed if the monetary benefits are small. There are other worthwhile returns to education and these must certainly be taken into account in deciding the total impact of college education on Blacks individually and collectively.

Our analysis is intended to investigate the economic benefit of a college education for Blacks, individually and collectively. The analyses concentrate directly on the income difference between groups with different quantities of education, using U.S. Census data from the 1970 Decennial Survey. The data provided in this survey were the most recent (1969) and complete available that relate income to education for Blacks. Although the focus of this report is the 1973-74 academic year, conclusions based on earlier income data are probably generally relevant. However, there have been recent indications of a decrease in the monetary returns to education (Freeman and Holloman, 1975) which suggest caution when extending these results into the future. But the just mentioned authors also found that while the returns to education may have dropped in recent years for the population in general, there is an indication that the returns may not have declined as yet for Blacks. If this holds up over time, the returns estimated for Blacks here will also hold up.

Overview

There was a significant income difference between the college-experienced and non-college-experienced populations of both Black males and Black females. The differences in income were largest for Black males with four or more years of college and fairly modest for education below four years of college. Black males obtained larger relative gains in income from five or more years of college than any other race, sex, or group. Black females obtained fairly large gains in incomes at all levels of college attainment, with the largest gain coming with the completion of four years of college.

Large differences in expected lifetime earnings favored Black males and females with a higher education compared to Blacks with less education. Discounted present value calculations show that all gains were significant at 6%, except returns to third year of college for Black males. Black males' rate of return to less than three years of college were under 6%; the rate or return to three years of college for Black females was also under 6%; while for four or more years of college, the rate of return was above 6% for females.

Relative to the all male population, Black males received smaller overall income gains from a college education. As the educational level increased, the relative disparity between Black males and all other males increased, except after five or more years of college. The Black male absolute position, however, improved continuously with college education. In the college-educated groups, the mean incomes of Black females exceeded those of all females in every region of the country.

Black males received little gains from experience and thus the relative position of Black males deteriorated with age. Experience appeared to interact strongly with college-level educational attainments below 5 years of college only for the all male population. Thus, the impact of experience on the relative incomes of Black males was felt only at five or more years of college. Black females also suffered some disadvantages with age; however, the deterioration for Black females was not so sharp as it was for Black males.

Over the last 40 years or so, the proportion of Blacks with some college experience has increased; however, for both males and females this increase has been accompanied by lower persistence. In fact, in the older age cohorts, Black females had a better persistence than all females.

Rough calculations indicated that college-educated Black males' mean incomes and aggregate Black male incomes increased modestly from improvements in persistence, while Black female incomes barely changed. Achieving equality in access produced significant income gains for Black males and females. Black male incomes increased significantly further by improving persistence and access simultaneously, whereas persistence had modest further effect on Black female incomes.

Black male incomes would be increased most dramatically by reducing income differentials between Blacks and all males with the same level of education. This resulted in a slight deterioration in the incomes of Black college-educated females. Black males achieved the most significant income gain from the joint effect of access, persistence, and income equality. For Black females, the effect of these three changes was somewhat smaller than the change of improved access alone.

College-educated Black males had significantly better occupational distributions than non-college-educated Black males. However, college-educated Black males had a significantly less favorable occupational distribution than all males.

Racial Discrimination

As much as 60% of the earnings differentials between Blacks and the rest of the population has been attributed to the impact of racial discrimination. Discrimination makes it difficult to predict the impact of Black educational gains on their future earnings. If education leads to increased earnings or occupational upgrading, then education will improve the situation of the Black population. The rough calculations below indicate the order of magnitude of potential income gains. However, these calculations do not indicate whether these benefits will be realized.

Since the Black population is only a small part of the entire labor force, it is unlikely that the increase in the total college-educated work force (created by equalizing the educational opportunities for Blacks) would lead to sharp declines, either in the income received by college-educated workers as a group, or in the marginal value of a college education to society. The important question, therefore, is whether or not the competitive position of Black workers would be improved relative to all workers by increased amounts of education.

The answer to this question depends essentially on how labor market discrimination works and the extent to which discrimination persists in the future. If one holds a strict dual labor market theory of discrimination, in which there are separate labor markets for Blacks and whites (Doeringer and Piore, 1971), then education might have little value in improving the situation of Blacks relative to other Blacks. The value of college education for Blacks would depend upon the marginal productivity of educated labor in the Black labor market only. In this isolated market, the marginal productivity of education could easily decline or even reach zero. This has been suggested to be the case for education in general.

If the marginal productivity is declining or near zero in a dual market, then college-educated Black workers would merely displace high school educated Black workers. Thus, in the strict dual labor market theory, the net effect on average incomes of the Black population could be insignificant. The gaps between the earning of Blacks with college educations and the other Blacks would persist. The gaps between the earning of college-educated Blacks and whites, however, would depend on the relative changes in the marginal productivity of educated labor in both the Black and white labor markets.

If one held a taste theory of discrimination in which the discrimination against

Blacks was based on a distaste for Blacks (Becker, 1971), improvements in education may not lead to increased employment for Blacks in a competitive labor market. However, the net gains would depend on the marginal product of education and the intensity of racial taste.

If one held a job competition model of discrimination, in which discrimination results from conflict over scarce jobs (Swinton, 1974), then the net effect of college education should be increased earnings. However, this also depends upon the degree of labor market imperfections and the relative power of racist coalitions. It is possible with a highly imperfect labor market or strong racist coalitions for the additional education of Blacks to be ineffective in producing income gains.

The ultimate gains from improved education cannot be accurately predicted without a better reading of the directions of racial discrimination in employment. Closer study of the labor market behavior of employers including higher educational institutions with respect to college-educated Black workers is required. Of course if racial discrimination should break down, the long run gains of a college education would approach the maximum indicated in the calculations below.

There is little question that increased education has at least prevented Black incomes from deteriorating in comparison to the total population. This is true in view of the rapid expansion of the college educational attainments of the total population. Thus, college education probably is a necessary factor to prevent increased deterioration of the relative Black position, and a permissive factor for absolute and relative improvement in the overall position of Black people.

Moreover, there is some limited evidence that the returns to very recent Black college graduates have improved relative to whites (Freeman, 1974). This could indicate a reduction in discrimination against Black college graduates. If the decline in discrimination against Black college graduates should continue and prove to be greater than the decline against Black high school graduates, the relative return to education for Black college graduates will be increased. However, it is still too early to interpret accurately these most recent data.

Methodology

Income was used as the indicator of well-being in this report because it is the most comprehensive measure of well-being readily available in published statistics. It is clear that there are other components of well-being that are less than perfectly correlated with income or bear the same relationship to education as does income.

The standard way of assessing the impact of education on income is to compare the incomes of similar individuals with different amounts of education. The differences in the incomes are then attributed to the effect of education. In this procedure, average incomes of the education groups are compared to the average incomes of those with less education. Because the distribution of income of the different educational groups overlapped considerably, and because some individuals with less education earned more than others with more education, the results of this analysis cannot be applied to individuals.

The objective of this study is to provide a fairly detailed description of the impact of education on the incomes of Blacks. We have therefore concentrated on developing data that present a comprehensive picture. As such we have used group means to represent the earnings of Blacks at different educational levels. The simple device of comparing the differences between group means was adopted as a suitable measure of the impact of education on expected earnings. These differences were calculated for different race, sex, and age groups and sometimes by region. These have been the most important variables in most analyses of the impact of education on income.

For the most part, the impact of these different factors is assessed by comparing the means of the stratified samples directly. For example, the impact of age on the earnings of those who have completed 1 to 2 years of college is determined by comparing the means for different age groups stratified by race and sex directly. This procedure is adequate to convey a general impression of the impact of age but does not provide so compact a summary as a regression coefficient might.

We have also estimated the aggregate impact of improved educational opportunity directly. These estimates were generally made by assuming a new distribution of educational attainment while holding all other factors including earnings, sex, and age constant. The same procedure has also been employed to assess the relative impact of income differences and educational differences in explaining the differences in the mean earnings of Blacks and non-Blacks.

There have been many studies in the literature concerned with this general question using different methods of analysis. (See, e.g., J.G. Haworth et al., 1975; F. Welch, 1973; R. Weiss, 1970.) For the most part our findings are consistent with the results obtained in these earlier studies.

In comparing the situation of different groups, it is preferable to discuss the entire distribution of income within the group rather than the average income of the group in order to assess accurately overall group well-being (Wohstetter and Coleman). However, the means were used as the best single indicator of the group income.

Education and the other factors controlled for are not the sole determinants of income differences. Other factors such as ability, racial and sex discrimination, family background, interest, and luck play important roles. If there were no correlation between these factors and education, then it would not be necessary to take them into account. However, these factors, especially ability as measured by standardized tests, family background, and interest, are related to college enrollment and educational attainment, as was pointed out in Chapters 2 and 3. Some of the income differences attributed to differences in education may be the result of these other factors. Unfortunately, there is no readily available methodology to separate the influences of these factors on income from the income data available from the U.S. Census. Thus, the traditional treatment of education as the causative factor behind the income differences in these types of studies, though somewhat arbitrary, is followed here. We have, however, been able to control for age, race, sex, and region of country in analyzing the impact of education on income. This was done by estimating the impact separately by age, sex, and racial group. In some instances the effect of region was also controlled.

The 1970 U.S. Census data which were used for the major analyses in this chapter report total income without regard to whether the person is a full- or part-time worker.

This is especially important in comparing the incomes of Black college-educated women with all college-educated women. Black college-educated women were more likely than all other college-educated women to be employed full-time regardless of the presence of children in the home, while all other college-educated women, especially white women, tended to work part-time. Consequently, the incomes of college-educated Black women were on the average larger than those of all other women with similar education, reflecting the differences in their participation in the labor market.

The income concept utilized by the U.S. Census includes both earned and non-earned income. Many of the sources of income included in the data below are not dependent upon college education. But because earnings account for better than 80% of most income, it is appropriate to base this analysis on all sources of income.

Theoretical Considerations

There is no question about the fact that educated groups have higher average incomes than uneducated groups. There is also little question about the fact that those who invest in education as a group receive a private net return on their investment that is comparable to the rates of return on other private investments, when we take the differential in expected earnings as their pay off. Despite the general agreement on these points, however, there is much less agreement about the degree to which education is a cause of the earnings differential or about the mechanism through which the increase in income is brought about. Yet these points are crucial for assessing the overall impact of education on aggregate income and for assessing the efficacy of educational investment as a strategy for improving the absolute and relative well-being of Blacks.

We shall not repeat the entire controversy concerning the measurement of the economic benefits of education here since it has been thoroughly discussed in the recent literature on the rate of return to education and human capital (Gordon, 1974; Eckaus et al., 1974; Thurow, 1974). We should, however, make a few points, especially in regard to the implications of this controversy for the impact of education on the economic position of Blacks. Essentially there are two views with respect to the role of education in determining income. One is held by human-capital/rate-of-return theorists and the other view by the critics of the human-capital/rate-of-return theory, especially the job competition theorists. Essentially the human-capital theorists view education as an investment in human beings that enhances the productivity of the human being. These theorists generally accept the marginal-productivity theory of wages and believe that higher earnings of the educated are attributed to their higher productivity.

The critics of the human-capital theorists point to flaws in the marginal-productivity (in human capital) theory. They conclude that the wage differentials cannot be attributed to differences in marginal product. The job-competition (or credential) theory offers an alternative explanation of the wage differences. This theory holds that education is used as a screening device. In this view, marginal productivities belong to jobs, not individual workers. Since workers must compete for these jobs, educational credentials are used as devices to ration the available supply of jobs. The educated may be preferred by the employer for sociological reasons (e.g., greater firm prestige), or because the employer believes the educated workers have lower training cost for any particular level of productivity. Such training-cost differences and sociological factors may well provide an incentive for the employer to hire the educated without explaining wage differentials.

The job-competition theory is not necessarily in conflict with the human-capital theory so long as the educated have lower on-the-job training cost than the uneducated, and so long as these differences in training costs are large enough to account for the wage differentials. However, advocates of the job-competition theory hold that training-cost differences are not large enough to explain observed wage differences. (See Swinton, 1974, for a discussion of factors determining wage differentials.) Moreover, the fact that the wage differentials have not declined over time, despite large increases in the supply of educated workers, has tended to cast doubt on the marginal-productivity theory. The marginal product of the educated labor depends both on the quantity of complementary factors and the quantity of educated labor already in existence. According to the theory of wages, as the quantity of educated labor increases, all other things being equal, the marginal product of the educated labor, and thus the wage differential, should fall. (See Thurow, 1974.)

The evidence appears to lean towards the credentialing theory of the role of education in the labor market. This is not to say that education is unimportant as a factor influencing productivity in some occupations. However, the differences in earnings across most occupations are not determined entirely by productivity differences that are attributable to education. In addition, there is mounting evidence that many workers are overtrained for their jobs. (See James O'Toole, *Change*, May/June 1975, for fuller discussion.) The educational requirements of jobs have increased although the contents have not significantly changed. (See references in M. Gordon, ed., 1974.) It also seems to be the case that when detailed occupations and other factors are controlled, the differences in earnings of different educational cohorts vanish. (See M. Gordon, ed., 1974.)

What are the implications of these theories for society? For one thing, if the human-capital/rate-of-return theory is false, then one cannot count on additional education to increase the aggregate income. The job-competition theory of the differential is consistent with a zero and even a negative marginal product of education. But, even under these circumstances, there would be differentials between the earnings of educated and non-educated individuals. The relatively favorable position of the educated would be simply a reflection of the deteriorated situation for the uneducated. In fact, at the margin, the income of those with more education would be no higher than it would have been with less education. Thus, the increments in expenditures on education would be completely ineffective in raising the incomes of the society, and thus would be a wasteful investment.

In a recent article by Freeman and Holloman (1975), new evidence was produced concerning the declining value of a college education. According to data presented in this article the overall return to education has declined dramatically in the past 5 years. Thus, the earnings of recent college graduates have declined relative to high school graduates for most college majors. Furthermore, the unemployment rates of college graduates have increased. These very recent data lend further support to the view that the marginal economic value of education may be low for the society as a whole.

What are the implications of the theories for Blacks? Education cannot be counted on to increase automatically the absolute and relative position of Blacks. If the job-competition theory is true, the opportunity for racial discrimination is maximal because discrimination would have little negative consequences on marginal productivity so long as at the margin there were no significant training-cost differences. Affirmative action in employment would be essential to ensure that the earnings of Black individuals reflected the earnings for their educational class. However, the differences in wages of educated and uneducated Blacks would have little or no meaning for the overall economic well-being of the Black community.

In an environment that is characterized by the use of education as a job-training device, attaining educational credentials is a necessity for individual economic prosperity. Thus, the expected value of an education for the private individual would remain high even though the marginal social value is low. This would hold doubly for Blacks if the environment is also characterized by racism and employment discrimination. Education will be a defensive necessity to prevent the Black relative position from deteriorating.

Although a college education does not guarantee relative income improvement, if there is to be any prospect at all for improvement under a credentialing regime, relative gains in education attainments are a must. This is obviously because without the appropriate credentials Blacks will be assigned to the lowest parts of the educated job structure under a discrimination regime. Whereas, with credentials, Blacks will be able to attain the lower rungs of the job set competed for by the educated group. If affirmative action proves successful, and as mentioned there is some evidence of limited success for younger Black college graduates, increasing the relative educational attainments of Blacks will be a necessary part of an effective strategy to eliminate the relative racial disparities. In addition, the recent article by Freeman and Holloman also indicates that the recent declines in the relative position of new college graduates have not affected young Black college graduates. Thus, the importance of increased education as a strategy for improving the economic situation of Blacks is not diminished by the finding that the job-competition hypothesis of wage differentials is correct.

EDUCATION AND INCOME

In what follows, we examine some statistics comparing the earnings of Blacks of different educational cohorts with each other and with the same educational cohorts for the population as a whole, after which we discuss some results from the literature on rates of return. This is followed by an analysis of the impact of unequal educational opportunities on the income of Blacks. This chapter has not undertaken an exhaustive analysis of this subject and our conclusions will of necessity be tentative and suggestive. Much future research will be required to assess the overall economic significance of recent and current development with respect to Blacks in higher education.

Annual Earnings of Black Males

Table 4-1 presents the 1970 U.S. Census data for the U.S. as a whole and the four census regions showing the average 1969 earnings of Black males and females by educational attainment. Education can be expected to increase the average earnings of both males and females in all regions. Male and female income data reveal systematic differences by race at all educational levels and in all regions. However, since our interest is in racial differences, we discuss the impact of education on income separately for each sex.

The differences in the mean incomes of Blacks with different levels of education can be taken as the expected increase in income (gain) for a Black who attains the higher level of education. These differences are shown in Table 4-2. Black males can expect to increase their income by an average of $388 a year over high school by completing one to three years of college. By graduating from college, or completing four years of college, Black males gained another $2,040 and if they attended graduate school or completed five or more years of college, they gained an additional $3,275. This same pattern of average gains is revealed in each region. It is evident that, for Black males, attending college up to three years added only a modest amount to their expected incomes in 1970. Expected incomes increased significantly by completing four or more years of college.

These expected gains can be viewed in terms of their percentage impact of the

TABLE 4-1. Mean Income for 1969 of Blacks by Year of School Completed, Sex and Regions.

	4 Years High School $	1 to 3 Years College $	4 Years College $	5 Years or more $
Males				
United States	5,397	5,785	7,825	11,100
Northeast	6,049	6,572	8,657	11,991
North Central	6,283	6,554	8,654	12,144
West	5,545	6,361	8,762	12,089
South	4,505	4,682	6,922	9,899
Females				
United States	3,256	3,680	5,812	7,916
Northeast	3,825	4,358	6,467	8,842
North Central	3,550	4,052	6,463	8,589
West	3,425	4,177	5,844	8,412
South	2,697	2,972	5,444	7,291

SOURCE: U.S. Census, *1970 Census of Population. Detailed Characteristics of the Population, U.S. Summary*, Tables 249 and 306.

TABLE 4-2. Gains in Mean Incomes for 1969 by Level of School Completed by Region and Sex of Blacks 18 Years and Older.

Males	1 to 3 Years College $	4 Years College $	5 Years or more $
United States	388	2,040	3,275
Northeast	523	2,085	3,334
North Central	271	2,100	3,490
West	816	2,401	3,327
South	177	2,240	2,977
Females			
United States	424	2,104	2,132
Northeast	533	2,109	2,375
North Central	502	2,126	2,411
West	752	1,667	2,568
South	275	1,847	2,472

SOURCE: Tables 4-1.

expected income. The average Black male's income in 1969 increased by only 7% for the U.S. as a whole over that of high school graduates as a result of completing one to three years of college. (See Table 4-3.) Moreover, the percentage increase for completing 3 or fewer years of college was small in all regions, ranging from 3.9% in the South to 14.7% in the West, whereas if a Black male completed four years of college, he gained 35.3% over those with one to three years of college, on the whole, and from 31.7% in the Northeast to 47.8% in the South. Of Black male incomes, the

TABLE 4-3. Percentage Gains in Mean Incomes for 1969 by Level of School Completed, Region, and Sex of Blacks 18 Years and Older.

Males	1-3 Years College %	4 Years College %	5 Years or more %
United States	7.1	35.3	41.9
Northeast	8.6	31.7	38.5
North Central	4.3	32.0	40.3
West	14.7	37.7	38.0
South	3.9	47.8	43.0
Females			
United States	13.0	57.9	26.6
Northeast	13.9	48.4	26.9
North Central	14.1	59.5	24.8
West	22.0	39.9	30.5
South	10.2	83.2	25.3

SOURCE: Tables 4-1 and 4-2.

percentage impact of completing five or more years of college was even greater than the impact of the fourth year. Their incomes increased by 41.9% over four years of college, and ranged from 38.5% to 43.0% in the regions. There was also a smaller range in percentage gains for graduate education in all regions. Compared to high school, four years of college increased Black male annual average incomes by 45%. Five or more years of college increased Black male annual income over that of high school graduates an average of 105.7% for the U.S. as a whole.

Lifetime Earnings of Black Males

In Table 4-4 the effect of education on average lifetime earnings is summarized. These figures are calculated on the assumption that the starting age for earnings of high school graduates was age 18, and that the starting age earnings for higher educational levels moved up by the number of years of college completed. The data in Table 4-4 are unadjusted lifetime earnings. Age earning profiles that existed in 1970 are assumed to continue to exist in the future. These lifetime earnings profiles are taken as the expected "income streams," that is, the flow of money to every individual who achieves the corresponding educational level. Unadjusted lifetime earnings data are simplistic in many respects, but they do provide a rough indication of the order of magnitude of expected lifetime earnings differentials related to educational differences. Adjustments could be made for economic growth, mortality, and taxes. All of these adjustments would change slightly the expected lifetime earnings reported in this chapter, but leave the order of magnitude of relative gains

TABLE 4-4. Total Average Lifetime Earnings in 1969 and Incremental Differences in Average Lifetime Earnings by Years of School Completed, Race, and Sex.

	Total $	4 Years High School $	1 and 2 $	3 $	College[1] 4 $	5 $	6+ $
ALL MALES	487,313	473,001	(75,144) 548,145	(56,907) 605,052	(119,178) 724,230	(13,157) 737,887	(198,119) 935,506
BLACK MALES	265,760	318,790	(27,217) 346,007	(1,954) 347,961	(56,737) 404,692	(72,081) 476,779	(154,700) 631,479
ALL FEMALES	200,782	209,420	(22,125) 231,545	(14,465) 246,010	(61,507) 307,517	(65,946) 373,463	(54,565) 428,028
BLACK FEMALES	154,065	182,793	(32,295) 215,088	(17,034) 232,122	(69,449) 301,571	(63,913) 365,484	(25,811) 391,295

SOURCE: U.S. Census, *1970 Census of the Population: Educational Attainment*, Tables 7 and 8.

[1]Earnings in parentheses are the incremental income gains.

basically unchanged. A more serious objection to our procedure would be the assumption that the differential currently reflected in the age earning profiles will be reflected in the future (Freeman, 1974).

The data in parentheses in Table 4-4 are the incremental effects on lifetime earnings for attaining that level of school completed. These data are another way of viewing the impact of education and reveal that for Black males there were significant differences in their lifetime incomes from each additional level of education. As was shown with annual average earnings, the most significant gains come from completing four or more years of college. The small gain in lifetime earnings from attending only through the third year of college is especially striking.

Black males' lifetime income was increased by $85,908 over that of high school graduates by completing four years of college and $312,689 by completing five or more years of college. Black males who completed six or more years of college could expect to earn $226,781 or 74% more income over their lifetimes than Black males with only four years of college.

In Table 4-5 the discounted value of lifetime incomes at a 6% discount rate is summarized. Discounting provides an estimate of the present value of the future earnings difference. On the assumption that a dollar in 1970 can earn 6% a year, these present value figures may be interpreted as roughly the amount that would have to be invested in 1970 to yield the corresponding income streams. The present values of future income streams are much smaller than the lifetime earnings. The differences in

TABLE 4-5. Discounted Present Value of Average Lifetime Earnings and Incremental Differences in Discounted Present Value of Average Lifetime Earnings in 1969 by Year of School Completed, Race and Sex.

| | Total | 4 Years High School | 1 and 2 | 3 | College[1] 4 | 5 | 6+ |
	$	$	$	$	$	$	$
ALL MALES	119,106	121,166	(7,858) 129,024	(898) 129,992	(31,268) 161,190	(11,647) 189,543	(22,771) 172,314
BLACK MALES	77,050	91,825	(184) 92,009	(–3,447) 88,562	(13,788) 102,350	(7,434) 109,784	(26,265) 136,049
ALL FEMALES	53,935	56,271	(–1,574) 54,697	(3,013) 57,710	(10,452) 68,162	(11,731) 79,893	(11,448) 91,341
BLACK FEMALES	54,307	53,228	(6,747) 59,975	(115) 60,090	(18,786) 78,876	(8,023) 86,899	(4,630) 91,529

SOURCE: U.S. Census, *1970 Census of the Population: Educational Attainment*, Tables 7 and 8.

[1]Earnings in parentheses are the incremental income gains.

the present values at different educational levels can be either positive or negative because of the shorter working lives of those with higher education. These differences may be interpreted as the present worth of the education at a 6% rate of interest.

The marginal value of a third year of college to Black males is negative at a 6% interest rate. The value of the first two years of college was very close to zero at a 6% interest rate. All other levels of higher education yielded substantial values to Black males at this interest rate, with very high benefits accruing to the earning of the Bachelor's degree and the attainment of more than two years of college.

These data also enable us to make inferences about the rates of return, a matter which is discussed further below. Taking average annual college cost to the student of $1,288 in the 1969-1970 academic year (Carnegie Commission on Higher Education, 1973), the present values in Table 4-5 indicated that the rate of return to Black education below four years of college is less than 6%, whereas the rates of return for four years of college and for graduate levels were much higher than 6%. The data in Table 4-5 indicates that if forgone earnings were the only cost, two additional years of college would yield a return much smaller than 6%. These data suggest that the earlier emphasis in this report on increasing persistence for Blacks was well justified since returns did not appear to be significant until at least four years of college had been completed.

Annual Earnings of Black Females

The situation for Black females is also shown in Tables 4-1 through 4-5. Females, in general, earned much less than males at all educational levels. Table 4-6 summarizes the percentage of Black male income received by Black females in each region in 1969. In all cases, Black females improved their status relative to Black males as their amount of education increased. This suggests that the relative gain in income from education for Black females was higher than the relative gain for Black males with up to five or more years of college.

The annual mean absolute gains to Black females from adding extra years of education tended to be absolutely higher for females after one to three years of college (See Table 4-2.) Gains were slightly higher than the Black male gains for completing four years of college, except in the West; however, Black female gains were absolutely smaller for five or more years of college.

The average percentage increase in annual incomes for Black females in the U.S. as a whole was 13% for one to three years of college, 57.9% for four years of college, and 26.6% for five years or more. The first two increases were substantially greater than the increases for Black males. However, the Black male gain in earnings was relatively greater than that of Black females from attaining five or more years of college. As was the case for Black males, the greatest percentage differences in the incomes of Black females with one to three years of college occurred in the South, where Black females with four years of college had average incomes 83.2% higher than those with one to three years of college, and more than double the incomes of Black female high school graduates, also in the South.

Black females who completed four years of college earned $2,556 or 78% more

TABLE 4-6. Percentage of Black Male 1969 Income Received by Black Females by Region of the Country and Educational Level.

	4 Years High School %	1 to 3 years %	College 4 Years %	5 Years or More %
United States	60.3	63.6	74.3	71.3
Northeast	63.2	66.3	74.7	73.7
North Central	56.5	61.8	74.7	70.7
West	61.8	65.7	66.6	69.7
South	59.9	63.5	78.6	73.7

SOURCE: Table 4-1.

than their high school graduate counterparts for the U.S. as a whole in 1969. These gains ranged from $2,419 in the West to $2,913 in the North Central; in percentages these gains varied from 69.1% in the Northeast to 102% in the South. For Black females who completed five or more years of college, the income difference over Black female high school graduates was $4,660 (or 143%) for the U.S. as a whole in 1969. The absolute gains ranged from a low of $4,594 in the South to $5,039 in the North Central; the percentage gains from 131% in the Northeast to 170% in the South.

Lifetime Earning of Black Females

Black females make significant lifetime income gains for every increase in the level of education. (See Table 4-4.) The effect of lifetime earnings was absolutely larger for Black females than for Black males at all levels except for five or more years of college, including graduate and professional schools. There was a larger difference in the impact of six or more years of college on the lifetime earnings of Black males than of Black females—$154,700 vs. $25,811 respectively.

The present value of the lifetime incomes of Black females is shown in Table 4-5 at a 6% rate of discount. The present value of the income differences was positive at all educational levels for Black females. The value, however, was small for the third year of college. The present values were higher than the corresponding values for Black males at all levels, below six years of college.

Accounting for forgone earnings, Black females received more than a 6% return at all levels of education. Even taking into account cost of attending college, the rate of return to Black females for a college education was substantially above 6% at all levels, except for the third year of college. Moreover, at all levels except six years or more of college, their gains were greater than the gains for their Black counterparts. This indicated a higher rate of return for a college education to Black females.

Summary

Four years of college made a substantial difference in both average annual and lifetime incomes for both Black males and Black females. The proportionate differences and the rate of return were higher for Black females. College education below four years made small differences in expected earnings for Black males and somewhat larger differences for Black females. The rates of return were clearly less than 6% for Black males and slightly greater than 6% for Black females. The largest impact on Black male income was made by six or more years of college. Black females also made significant gains in earnings from six or more years of college, but lower than the gains for Black males.

LIFETIME INFLUENCE OF EDUCATION

Age and Sex Differences

Education continues to influence income throughout the lifetime of an educated individual. Tables 4-7 and 4-8 show the mean average earnings for Black males and Black females for the U.S. as a whole by age and level of education, 1969. By looking at the earnings of each age education cohort, we can get some idea of the impact of experience on the returns to higher education. The pattern of changes in Black income with age was the same for all levels of education, except for five or more years of college. All of the annual income increased up to the 35-44 age group and decreased thereafter. Blacks with some college received very little gains to experience beyond 35-44 age grouping. Since the incomes of Blacks with below-college-level education also increased to the 35-44 age group, the position of Black college-educated persons with less than five years of college did not improve with age relative to Blacks with no college education.

For Black males the largest absolute and percentage differential was in the 35-44 age group. (See Table 4-9.) After that, both the absolute and percentage differential decreased. Thus, the relative and absolute advantage of college-educated Black males decreased after about age 40. This suggests that Black college graduates may have found themselves in jobs with fewer opportunities for promotion or advancement.

The Black female pattern was a little different from the Black male pattern. First, as noted earlier, the Black female gains from education were both absolutely and relatively greater than the gains to Black males. The larger absolute gains occurred at all age levels. Second, the reduction in absolute gains for Black females were modest for ages below 65. The relative gains for Black females showed no significant deterioration and, in fact, increased in the 55-64 age group. This indicates that college-educated Black females pretty much held on to or improved their relative advantage over non-college-educated Black females up until retirement.

TABLE 4-7. Mean Income in 1969 of Black Males 18 Years and Over by Years of School Completed and Age.

| | | YEARS OF SCHOOL COMPLETED | | | | | | | |
| | | Elementary | | | High School | | College | | |
Age	TOTAL $	Less than 5 Years $	5-7 $	8 $	1-3 $	4 $	1-3 $	4 $	5 or More $
18+	4,703	2,879	3,929	4,470	4,691	5,937	5,785	7,825	11,100
18-24	3,001	2,165	2,444	2,588	2,572	3,439	3,016	4,499	5,636
25-34	5,655	3,657	4,060	4,572	5,101	6,093	6,880	8,062	9,018
35-44	6,043	3,824	4,742	5,271	5,814	6,705	7,635	9,250	12,592
45-54	5,604	3,710	4,749	5,307	5,820	6,639	7,679	9,006	13,026
55-64	4,542	3,276	4,167	4,751	5,196	5,877	6,668	7,132	11,929
65+	2,319	1,807	2,251	2,599	2,948	3,572	3,739	4,555	7,934

SOURCE: Table 4-1.

TABLE 4-8. Mean Income in 1969 of Black Females 18 Years and Over by Years of School Completed and Age.

| | | YEARS OF SCHOOL COMPLETED | | | | | | | |
| | | Elementary | | | High School | | College | | |
Age	TOTAL $	Less than 5 Years $	5-7 $	8 $	1-3 $	4 $	1-3 $	4 $	5 or More $
18+	2,735	1,388	1,767	2,104	2,505	3,256	3,680	5,812	7,916
18-24	2,312	1,606	1,577	1,755	1,830	2,583	2,406	4,032	4,148
25-34	3,393	1,993	2,138	2,375	2,710	3,551	4,466	6,092	7,152
35-44	3,427	1,895	2,167	2,490	2,910	3,811	4,757	6,791	8,437
45-54	3,065	1,678	2,081	2,431	2,846	3,804	4,720	6,685	9,146
55-64	2,366	1,442	1,761	2,068	2,423	3,243	4,074	6,017	8,462
65+	1,384	1,102	1,254	1,380	1,546	1,953	2,174	3,151	4,959

SOURCE: Table 4-1.

The pattern of incomes also indicated that Black females with less than five or more years of college did not get many promotional opportunities. However, the income positions of Black females without college educations deteriorated more rapidly with age than did the positions of those with college educations.

The absolute and percentage difference in incomes between Blacks with four years of college and Blacks with five years or more of college are shown in Table 4-10. The incomes of Blacks with five or more years of college peaked later than the incomes of Blacks with less education. The peaks for both Black males and females occurred in the 45 to 54 age group indicating that Blacks with five or more years of college received greater returns to experience than those with less college education.

The absolute and relative advantages of Blacks with five or more years of college increased through the 55-64 age groups. (See Table 4-10.) And, the relative advantage continued to increase in the 65 and over age group. Thus, unlike the case for Blacks with four years of college, advanced training yields life-long advantages which become greater with age. The absolute and relative advantage of Black males obtained from five or more years of college were greater than the advantages received by Black females, with the single exception of the 25-34 age group.

Regional data tabulated from the same Census sources showed that this pattern of gains to experience was fairly consistent in all regions of the country. The southern region had slightly lower returns to experience than the other regions but the basic pattern was the same. There were modest or insignificant returns to experience for Blacks subsequent to age 35-45 for four years of college, and significant returns to experience for five or more years of college in all regions.

Private Rate of Return

Private rate-of-return analysis takes into account out-of-pocket private cost and forgone earnings. Based on our earlier discussion we found that the private rate of return was highest for Black males with five or more years of college. The implied rate of return for attending college less than four years was low and the implied rate of return for completing four years of college was fairly high. Black females received modest rates of return for education below four years of college, substantial returns for completing four years of college, and great returns from even further training.

TABLE 4-9. Difference in Mean 1969 Incomes Between Blacks With Four Years of College and Black High School Graduates by Age and Sex.

	MALES		FEMALES	
Age	Absolute Difference $	Percent Difference %	Absolute Difference $	Percent Difference %
18-24	1,060	30.8	1,449	56.1
25-34	1,972	32.4	2,541	71.6
35-44	2,545	39.0	2,980	78.2
45-54	2,367	35.7	.2,881	75.7
65+	983	27.5	1,198	61.3

SOURCE: Tables 4-7 and 4-8.

TABLE 4-10. Difference in Mean 1969 Incomes Between Blacks With Five or More Years of College and Blacks With Four Years of College by Age and Sex.

	BLACK MALES		BLACK FEMALES	
	Absolute Difference	*Percent Difference*	*Absolute Difference*	*Percent Difference*
Age	*$*	*%*	*$*	*%*
18-24	1,137	25.3	116	2.9
25-34	956	11.9	1,060	17.4
35-44	3,342	36.1	1,646	24.2
45-54	4,020	44.6	2,461	36.8
55-64	4,197	54.2	2,443	40.6
65+	3,379	74.1	1,808	57.3

SOURCE: Tables 4-7 and 4-8.

These conclusions were generally consistent with the estimates in the literature for the past several decades. Becker (1964) noted returns to four years of college of 8.3% in areas other than the South and 12.3% in the South for non-whites in 1940. This is consistent with our observation that the impact of four years of college education on income in the South was higher for both males and females in 1969. Data reported by Kaun (1974) in "The College Dropout and Occupational Choice" for the U.S. as a whole indicated that returns for a college degree were substantially higher than returns for attending college short of a degree. For 1939, the returns were estimated to be 14.5% vs. 9.5%; for 1949, 13.0% vs. 8.0%; and for 1960, 13.6% vs. 12.1%. Although the exact magnitude of these differences in rates of return was not precise, the direction was clear.

The rate of return to Black education at the below-college level was even lower than Kaun's figures. Unadjusted figures reported by Eckaus et. al. (1974) in "An Appraisal of the Calculations of Rates of Return to Higher Education" showed significant difference between returns to one to three years of college and the fourth year of college. Eckaus et al. eliminated most of this differential by adjusting for hours worked; however, such an adjustment is of questionable validity. (See comments by Margaret S. Gordon, 1974, in "Introduction to Higher Education and the Labor Market.")

Eckaus et al. also summarized the results of rate-of-return estimates from several other studies. These results showed substantial variation in calculated rates of return. But the general range was from 10-15% for four years of college and generally smaller returns for less than four years of college and post graduate work. However, most of these results were not specifically for Blacks or other minorities.

The results of studies on rate of returns specifically for non-whites showed even wider variation than was true of whites. In general, the rates of return to Blacks for a college education were lower than those for non-Blacks at the below graduate school (five years of college) level. With five years of college or more, Black rates of return were slightly higher than those of non-Blacks.

Freeman (1974) reported crude rates of return to Blacks based on 1969 data of 20% for four years of college, which was significantly higher than the 10% rates of return reported for whites in 1969. According to Freeman, rates of returns to Blacks were obviously much higher than the returns on private investment; however, the validity of these crude rates was not clear.

Summary

The private rate-of-return calculations in the literature generally substantiated the analysis done in this chapter. There was a significant difference between the incomes of Blacks with college education and Blacks without college education. If these differentials were taken as returns to the expenditures to attain a higher education, the returns compared favorably with other forms of private investment.

BLACK AND TOTAL POPULATION INCOME COMPARISONS

Black Males vs. All Males

The relative impact of education on Black earnings as compared to the total population was also examined, as well as the impact of education on the relative status of Black educational cohorts. Tables 4-11 and 4-12 show the gain in income in absolute and percentage terms respectively for the total population. Comparing Table 4-11 and Table 4-2 shows that, in general, the absolute increases in mean earnings for Black males were significantly greater than for the total population at the five years of

TABLE 4-11. Absolute Gains in Mean 1969 Earnings by Level of School Completed, Region, and Sex, for Total Population 18 Years and Older.

	YEARS OF COLLEGE COMPLETED		
	1 to 3 Years *College*	*4 Years* *College*	*5 Years* *or More*
Sex and Region	*$*	*$*	*$*
Males			
United States	280	4,825	2,576
Northeast	384	5,627	2,610
North Central	84	4,849	2,166
West	387	4,244	2,603
South	576	4,451	2,989
Females			
United States	142	1,667	2,119
Northeast	153	1,775	2,274
North Central	10	1,846	2,009
West	253	1,350	2,221
South	181	1,635	1,923

SOURCE: Table 4-1.

college level in every region, except the South. In the South, total population male gains were absolutely higher at all levels.

From a comparison of Tables 4-12 and 4-3 it can be seen that the percentage gains for Black males were greater at the one to three years and at the five years of college level. This is heightened by the fact that high school educated Blacks started off with a relatively lower income. However, the absolute gains for total population male college graduates over all male high school graduates were sufficiently large, so that the relative gain of this group was larger than the relative Black gains. This suggests a significantly higher rate of return for males as a whole from four years of college.

Black Females vs. All Females

The female pattern was different. Black females achieved both higher absolute and relative gains in all regions for levels of education below five years of college than did the total female population. At the equivalent of graduate level (five years or more of college) Black females received higher absolute returns than the total female population in all regions, except the South. Since the Black female average incomes were higher after four years of college, their relative return to further college education was lower than that of all females in each region.

Regional Differences

The impact of education on the relative mean incomes of Blacks to the total population by region and level of education is shown in Table 4-13. If Black means

TABLE 4-12. Percentage Gains in Mean 1969 Incomes by Level of School Completed, Region, and Sex, for Total Population 18 Years and Older.

	YEARS OF COLLEGE COMPLETED		
	1 to 3 Years College	4 Years College	5 Years or More
Sex and Region	$	$	$
Males			
United States	3.6	59.4	19.9
Northeast	4.7	65.7	18.4
North Central	1.0	59.0	16.6
West	4.9	51.3	20.8
South	8.2	58.8	24.9
Females			
United States	4.1	46.0	40.1
Northeast	4.1	46.0	40.4
North Central	0.3	54.6	38.4
West	7.1	35.2	42.9
South	5.5	46.8	37.5

SOURCE: Table 4-11.

TABLE 4-13. Index[1] of Black to Total Mean 1969 Incomes by Sex, Years of School Completed, and Region

Sex and Region	YEARS OF SCHOOL COMPLETED			
	4 Years High School	1 to 3 Years College	4 Years College	5 Years or More College
Males				
United States	69	72	60	71
Northeast	74	78	61	71
North Central	76	79	66	80
West	70	777	70	80
South	64	62	58	66
Females				
United States	94	101	109	107
Northeast	103	113	115	112
North Central	105	120	124	119
West	96	109	113	114
South	81	85	106	103

SOURCE: Table 4-1.

[1]Index equals the Black mean income divided by the total population mean multiplied by 100.

were equal to total means, the index would have a value of 100. When Black means were less, the value is less than 100. And, when Black means were greater, the value is greater than 100. For the U.S. as a whole and in all regions except the South, the index of Black male to all male mean incomes was less than 100. The index increased with the completion of one to three years of college, then decreased significantly with completion of four years of college. In all cases except in the West, the index was significantly lower for Black males who had completed four years of college than for Black males with a high school degree.

In the South the index decreased for both the one to three years of college group and the four years of college group. For all regions the index increased for the five year or more group. And for all regions, except the Northeast, the increase put the five years or more group higher than the high school group.

The same data can be expressed in ratios where a value of 1 indicates equality, less than 1 indicates lower incomes for Blacks, and greater than 1 indicates higher incomes for Blacks. The ratio declined steadily for the U.S. as a whole (see Table 4-14) and in all regions from the lowest educational level to the highest level with the exception of the one to three year category. Thus, as Black males gained more college education below the five year level, they fell further behind their non-Black male counterparts in earnings. Black male incomes rose with additional education but at a lower rate than all male incomes, indicating further the lower absolute and relative return to education for Black males compared with all males.

The picture for Black females relative to all females was different. In Table 4-13 we see that the relative position of Black females compared with all females improved steadily in all regions with increases in college education, until five years of college was reached. In the West, there was a further slight gain to Black females with five or

TABLE 4-14. Ratio of Mean Incomes in 1969 of Black Males to All Males 18 Years and Older by Years of School Completed and Age.

| Age | Total | YEARS OF SCHOOL COMPLETED | | | | | | | |
| | | Elementary | | | High School | | College | | |
		Less than 5 Yrs	5-7	8	1-3	4	1-3	4	5 or More
18	.0650	.8096	.7987	.7583	.6977	.6878	.7118	.6042	.7125
18-24	.8616	.8500	.7720	.7161	.8640	.8852	.9898	1.022	1.253
25-34	.6826	.7518	.7565	.7333	.7319	.7487	.7842	.7549	.8280
35-44	.5873	.7807	.7575	.7130	.7012	.6932	.6610	.5886	.7022
45-54	.5437	.8063	.7669	.7187	.6841	.6508	.5977	.5097	.6260
55-64	.5186	.7965	.7401	.7044	.6585	.6209	.5551	.4194	.5761
65+	.5097	.7535	.7173	.6983	.6278	.6129	.5071	.4112	.5835

SOURCE: Institute for the Study of Educational Policy staff.

more years of college, but in all other regions there was a slight deterioration in their relative position at this college attainment level. However, in all regions, the relative position of Black females compared to all females in their educational group remained substantially higher after five years of college than after high school graduation only.

At four years of college and above, the Black female mean 1969 income was higher than the all-female income for the same educational level. And, with the exception of the South, the Black females' relative income was higher for all college-educated groups. Unlike Black males, Black females' relative position improved steadily in all regions as their educational level increased from the very lowest to highest levels. Thus, the Black female income relative to the white and all other female income was improved appreciably by gaining additional college education.

Age Differences

At the lowest levels of education (below high school), there was no significant difference between the ratio of relative income for different Black male age cohorts. (See Table 4-14.) All males gained no more from experience at their lower level of education than did Black males. However, for educational levels at high school or above an entirely different picture emerged. (See Table 4-15.) For all of these levels the ratio declined continuously as age increased. The declines in the ratio were sharper at higher levels of education up through four years of college. The declines in the ratio were also significant for Black males at the graduate level of education. All males gained significantly more from the interaction of education with experience than Black males. The most experienced Black male with four years of college had a lower income status relative to his age education cohort than did any other age education group.

The declining ratios of incomes as educational levels increased were caused

TABLE 4-15. Ratio of Mean Income in 1969 of Black Females to all
Females 18 Years and Older by Years of School Completed and Age.

| | | YEARS OF SCHOOL COMPLETED | | | | | | | |
| | | Elementary School | | | High School | | College | | |
Age	TOTAL	Less than 5 yrs	5 to 7 yrs	8 yrs	1 to 3 yrs	4 yrs	1 to 3 yrs	4 yrs	5 yrs or more
18	.8392	.8228	.8897	.9148	.9008	.9356	1.0160	1.0989	1.0686
18-24	.9222	.8858	.8547	.9060	1.0603	.9592	1.0371	1.0055	.9604
25-34	.9309	.8092	.8938	.9263	.9727	1.0240	1.1074	1.1954	1.1421
35-44	.8952	.8087	.8335	.8554	.8934	1.0053	1.1024	1.2691	1.1112
45-54	.7412	.7708	.7949	.7916	.8202	.8976	.9503	1.0460	1.0351
55-64	.6218	.7601	.7714	.7536	.7428	.7720	.8177	.8815	.9200
65+	.6251	.8175	.8360	.8009	.7187	.6779	.6305	.6548	.7750

SOURCE: Institute for the Study of Educational Policy staff.

entirely by the failure of Black males to receive the gains from experience that all males received. In fact, at the below 35 age group, the relative income of Black male college groups was slightly higher than the relative incomes of Black male groups who had less than a college education. Therefore, it was the failure of the older college-educated groups to maintain their relative income position which caused these declines.

These phenomena are subject to two interpretations with different implications for the future returns to Blacks for education. One interpretation is that the higher relative incomes of younger Blacks are evidence of a permanent improvement in the labor market positions of these groups. If this were true, the gains might be expected to hold up as these cohorts aged suggesting higher relative incomes for the older cohorts in the future.

The other interpretation is that the gains are non-permanent. They are a reflection of the lack of experience on the part of both white male and Black male workers and specific reactions on the part of employers to pressure by civil rights law enforcement. In this view, as the cohorts age, white males will gain the more valuable training opportunities and experience. Therefore, white males will get the more valuable positions. Thus, in the long run the income differentials of Blacks and whites with a college education will be reestablished as the younger cohorts age.

As mentioned earlier, there is some limited evidence that labor market discrimination has lessened somewhat (Freeman 1974). An analysis by Haworth, Gwartney, and Haworth (1975) suggests that the relative positions of each Black age cohort will be maintained over time. They compared the ratio of non-white to white mean earnings by age cohort in 1960 and in 1970. They found that between 1960 and 1970, there were slight increases in the ratio of non-white to white mean earnings for each age cohort. They also found that between 1960 and 1970 the increase in the ratios of non-white to white mean earnings was greater for the college-educated age cohorts.

While the evidence from these studies is inconclusive, it does indicate that the relative income gains made by younger college-educated Black workers will be maintained as they grow older. Therefore, the first interpretation of the relationship of age and education to the ratio of Black to white mean incomes may be valid.

Again the situation for Black females was different. The relative deterioration in the income position with age also occurred. However, the deterioration was not as sharp for Black females compared to all females, as it was for Black males compared to all males. And in the highest educated groups, the deteriorations started at the 45-54 age group, as opposed to the 35-44 age group for Black males. The relative ratio for below-college-educated females declined steadily with age also, whereas there were no declines of significance in these groups for Black males.

The relative position of Black females with most education and experience was still higher than the relative position of Black females of the same age cohorts but with less education. Throughout the age groupings, the relative income of Black females tended to increase with the level of education except for the over 65 age groups. However, over the 45-54 age groups, there were significant relative declines for Black females.

Summary

The discussion of relative position, to this point, has indicated that in general the Black male position deteriorated relative to the equivalent educational group, as the level of education increased (below five or more years of college). At each higher educational level, the Black male position was significantly lower than the total male population position. The attainment of five or more years of college lifted the relative position of Black males. The deterioration in the relative position with increases in educational attainment was caused by the failure of educated Black males to match the experience gains of all males. The Black female position was improved, overall, relative to the total female population by each increase in educational level up to five years of college. Black females suffered less relative deterioration compared to all females from the advantages produced by education with increases in age. At higher educational levels, the Black female generally had a higher relative income than did their total female population counterparts because of the greater number of Black female full-time workers.

UNEQUAL EDUCATIONAL OPPORTUNITY AND INCOME LOSS

Educational Attainment in 1970

As was indicated in Chapter 2, the absolute number and the proportion of all Blacks with some college education has been increasing over the past several decades. As a result, each succeeding age cohort has a larger percentage of individuals with some college education. In 1970, the overall percentage of Black males with some college was 11.5%; this varied from 3.8% in the 75+ group to 20.4% in the 20-21 group. The overall percentage of Black females with some college education was 13.0% and varied from 4.9% for the 75+ age group to 22.0% for the 20-21 age group. For each age cohort in 1970, the absolute number and proportion of all Black females with some college experience exceeded the proportion of all Black males. However, the sex gap appears to be narrowing over time.

Although there was an increase in the number of Blacks with some college education, there was no such increase in the number of Blacks completing four or more years of college. While Black access had increased, Black persistence rates as of 1970 had not. As was pointed out in Chapters 2 and 3, it took more years for Blacks than for whites to complete four or more years of college. Thus, Blacks with advanced training tended to be older than whites with equal training. In the analyses that follow, age groups are compared. At each age level, the persistence of Blacks was lower, undoubtedly because of the categorical, educational, and psychosocial barriers to equal educational opportunity discussed in Chapter 3.

In 1970, the relative position of Blacks in college attainment was well below that of the total population, both overall and at each age cohort. The ratio of the overall proportion of Blacks with some education relative to the total population was 58.9% for females and 44% for males. (See Table 4-16.) (If the proportions of Blacks were equal to the proportions of the total population, these ratios would equal 100%.)

There was some improvement with time in the ratio of Black to total population with college experience for succeeding age cohorts. For males there was no significant difference in the ratio for cohorts from age 20 to 34, and for females no significant differences for cohorts from age 20 to age 45. This indicates that there was probably not much relative improvement in equal education opportunity for Blacks relative to the total population in the two decades prior to 1968. However, there was a significant increase in the ratio for the 18-19 year cohort for both sexes with some college experience, indicating that some relative gains occurred in the late 1960's. Nonetheless, the proportion of Blacks with some college was, in 1970 and in 1973, signific-

TABLE 4-16. Total and Proportion of Black Individuals With at Least One Year of College by Sex and Age Group for the Total U.S., 1970.

AGE	Total Number		Percentage of Cohort		Ratio of Black to Total Percentage	
	Females	Males	Females	Males	Females	Males
18 and 19	27,411	23,747	10.5	8.9	63.6	58.6
20 and 21	65,514	59,246	22.0	20.4	56.0	46.4
22 and 24	88,433	73,326	21.4	18.5	55.4	45.9
25 and 29	109,113	104,456	18.7	17.3	57.0	46.9
30 and 34	80,260	81,319	15.3	15.1	61.2	46.3
35 and 44	143,882	132,065	14.5	12.7	66.8	43.3
45 and 54	85,515	83,624	10.2	9.0	52.6	39.0
55 and 64	52,527	40,921	8.2	5.8	44.1	33.0
65 and 74	28,420	18,461	5.7	4.2	41.0	31.3
75+	12,909	7,969	4.9	3.8	44.5	35.8
TOTAL	693,984	625,134	13.0	11.5	58.9	44.0

SOURCE: U.S. Census, *1970 Census of the Population: Educational Attainment.* Tables 7 and 8.

antly below the proportion for the population as a whole, even among the youngest cohorts. (See Table 4-17.)

For both Black males and females, the proportion of Blacks with college experience has increased in each succeeding age cohort, but the proportion attaining at least four years of college has not. The proportion of the Black male college group with only one and two years of college has increased from 38.9% in the 75+ age group to 52.5% in the 25 to 29 year old age group. (See Table 4-18.) While the proportion of Black college educated males with four years of college declined from 29.3% to 23.5%, the proportion of the group with six years or more of college also declined from 16.1% in the 65 to 74 age group to 9.6% in the 30 to 34 age group in 1970.

For Black females, the proportion with less than three years of college experience in the 75+ age group was 41.1% in 1970; whereas the proportion was 46.4% in the 25 to 29 age group. (See Table 4-19.) The proportion with four years of college held

TABLE 4-17 Distribution of Total Males Above High School by Age Group, 1970.
(In Percents)

AGE	YEARS OF COLLEGE COMPLETED				
	1 and 2	3	4	5	6+
18-19	98.7	.8	.3	—	—
20-21	77.7	19.5	.2	—	—
22-24	41.4	17.1	30.3	9.2	2.0
25-29	35.8	8.9	28.2	13.3	13.3
30-34	33.7	7.4	27.9	11.7	19.0
35-44	32.4	7.2	29.7	9.9	20.5
45-54	37.2	7.8	27.7	8.2	19.0
55-64	38.1	9.1	26.1	8.0	18.0
65-74	38.8	9.7	28.4	6.7	16.4
75+	39.6	10.4	29.2	5.7	15.1

SOURCE: U.S. Census, *1970 Census of the Population: Educational Attainment*, Tables 7 and 8.

TABLE 4-18. Distribution of Black Males Above High School by Age Group, 1970.
(In Percents)

AGE	YEARS OF COLLEGE COMPLETED				
	1 and 2	3	4	5	6+
18-19	98.0	1.7	.2	—	—
20-21	83.8	12.9	2.9	.2	.14
22-24	58.5	17.5	19.1	4.1	.8
25-29	52.5	10.9	23.5	7.9	5.3
30-34	48.4	9.8	23.3	8.9	9.6
35-44	45.5	10.3	21.6	8.8	13.8
45-54	47.3	10.1	20.3	6.8	15.4
55-64	43.1	10.2	22.2	8.0	16.4
65-74	41.8	8.1	26.9	7.0	16.1
75+	38.9	12.4	29.3	7.4	12.0

SOURCE: U.S. Census, *1970 Census of the Population: Educational Attainment*, Tables 7 and 8.

TABLE 4-19. Distribution of Black Females Above High School by Age Group, 1970.
(In Percents)

	YEARS OF COLLEGE COMPLETED				
AGE	1 and 2	3	4	5	6+
18-19	97.7	2.0	.3	—	—
20-21	80.9	15.5	3.3	.2	.1
22-24	54.9	12.7	28.2	3.3	.9
25-29	46.4	1.0	34.4	5.6	3.6
30-34	48.8	7.7	29.4	7.6	6.5
35-44	43.8	8.0	29.4	8.2	10.6
45-54	40.4	8.0	27.5	10.0	14.1
55-64	38.2	8.3	30.4	9.6	13.5
65-74	43.3	9.3	30.4	7.3	9.7
75+	41.1	12.2	34.8	5.6	6.4

SOURCE: U.S. Census, *1970 Census of the Population: Educational Attainment,* Tables 7 and 8.

steady and even increased from the middle age groups. While the proportion of college educated Black females with six years or more declined somewhat from the 65-74 age cohort, to the 30-34 group. (See Table 4-20.)

The relative deterioration in the structure of the educated population was slightly less for Black females than for Black males. There was a larger proportion of Black males than females leaving college with less than four years at all age groups. Relative to the population, the structure of the Black college-educated group was worse for Black males. However, this appears to be changing in the younger age cohorts. This implies that at the same time that the proportion of Blacks going to college relative to the total population was increasing, relatively fewer Blacks completed college in comparison to the total population. Thus, part of the relative gains in access were lost because of low persistence by the age group.

The relative decline in the Black female structure compared to the total Black

TABLE 4-20. Distribution of Total Females Above High School by Age Group, 1970.
(In Percents)

	YEARS OF COLLEGE COMPLETED				
AGE	1 and 2	3	4	5	6+
18-19	98.8	1.0	.2	—	—
20-21	76.2	19.7	3.8	.2	.1
22-24	40.7	14.5	38.2	5.3	1.3
25-29	36.1	9.0	38.1	10.3	6.6
30-34	38.4	9.9	32.9	10.0	8.7
35-44	41.8	9.4	30.1	9.4	9.3
45-54	45.2	9.3	26.6	8.8	10.0
55-64	41.9	10.6	28.3	8.9	10.3
65-74	48.5	10.7	26.6	6.8	7.4
75+	51.2	11.2	27.0	4.8	5.8

SOURCE: U.S. Census, *1970 Census of the Population: Educational Attainment,* Tables 7 and 8.

structure has been greater than the relative decline for Black males. This has been caused by a decline in the Black female persistence accompanied by a fairly sharp improvement in total female persistence. Older Black female cohorts have a more favorable college persistence than did the total female population.

At ages below 35-44 the total female population had better persistence than Black females in the same age ranges. Thus, Black female persistence (compared to total female persistence) has worsened relatively and absolutely with increasing enrollments.

Total Black Income Loss

As a first step in assessing the improvement to be expected from continued increases of the Black college-educated population, some rough calculations were made estimating the income loss to Blacks from their less favorable educational status. These calculations are only to be taken as rough indications of income loss due to educational status.

In Table 4-21, a summary of the income statistics was reported. The group means were calculated as weighted averages of the means of each age group. The group weights were based on the population with income and, therefore, the means were somewhat overstated for the population as a whole.

As can be seen in Table 4-21, Black males were relatively disadvantaged with respect to the total population at each educational level and overall. At high school and below, the Black male mean was 3.4% of the total male mean in 1969; whereas for those with some college the Black male mean was 62.9% of the total male mean. The overall Black male mean income was 65.7% of the overall mean for all males. Using the means to estimate the aggregates, Black males had an aggregate income of $27.9 million in 1969 which was 5.9% of total aggregate income.

The Black female was also disadvantaged relative to the total female population. The overall Black female mean income was 83.5% of the overall mean income for all

TABLE 4-21. Mean 1969 Incomes and Aggregate Incomes by Race, Educational Level and Sex, and Ratio of Black to Total U.S. Income.

	Educational Level			
Sex	High School or Below	Some College	Overall	Aggregate Income
Black Males	$4,881	$ 6,925	$5,115	$ 27.877 million
All Males	$6,646	$11,009	$7,786	$473.933 million
Ratio of Black male/all male	63.4%	62.9%	65.7%	5.9%
Black Females	$2,426	$ 4,723	$2,725	$ 14.494 million
All Females	$2,888	$ 4,586	$3,264	$156.603 million
Ratio of Black Female/all Female	84.0%	103.0%	83.5%	9.3%

SOURCE: U.S. Census, *1970 Census of the Population: Educational Attainment* Tables 7 and 8.

females. However, for females with some college, the average Black female income was relatively higher than the average all female income; the Black female mean being 103% of the all female mean. Below high school Black females tended to receive only 84.0% of the mean income of all females with the same amount of education. Black females received $14.5 million in income in 1969 which was roughly 9.3% of the all female income.

Relative Status of Black Male vs. Black Female

The relative income position of Black females vs. all females was better than the position of Black males vs. all males. The reasons for this include (1) the structure of jobs traditionally held by females and (2) the participation of females in the labor market (Swinton & Ellison, 1973).

The structure of jobs influenced the relative well-being of all females because there is less variation in the wages of female-held jobs than in the wages of male-held jobs. Both the range and the variance are significantly lower in the jobs females hold. Thus, there is less room for differences in female incomes given such sex discrimination in employment. This appears to be an important cause of the differences in the relative disparity of Black males to all males and Black females to all females, but the magnitude of this effect is unknown.

The other principal reason has to do with the fact that employment had not been the traditionally preferred role of females in the U.S. economy. Females worked principally to supplement earnings. Thus, the more well-off females tended not to work as often. Given the relatively disadvantaged position of Black males and given the high incidence of female-headed households in the Black community, the Black female had to work more often. The Black female had a higher labor force participation rate than other females, and was more likely to work full-time and all year round. She was also more likely than other females to work in the prime child-rearing years and to pursue a career. All of these factors helped account for the relatively higher incomes of educated Black females who tended to use their educations to improve the economic position of their families. The advantages of Black females did not hold up when the incomes of only full-time year-round workers are compared.

Reasons for Lower Black Incomes

The overall lower incomes of Black workers were due to many factors that operated both at the college level and below. At higher educational levels, these factors were of three types. (1) The first resulted in the Black group's having an unfavorable distribution of their college-educated group. Thus the fact that fewer Blacks attained degrees or attended graduate school (out of the Blacks with some college) led to lower mean incomes for the college-educated group; this was the persistence factor. (2) The second factor was that fewer Blacks of each age cohort actually attended college; this was the access factor. (3) The third factor was the tendency for Blacks to earn less money at equivalent educational levels than the total population; this was the earning differential factor.

Each one of these factors was the result of a complex set of determining circumstances: background disadvantages, previous poverty, and racial discrimination, to name only three of the barriers discussed in Chapter 3.

Persistence and Income Loss

Table 4-22 summarizes an estimate of the effect of the persistence factor on overall Black income. This estimate was based on the assumption that the Black sub-group earnings were not affected by shifting the composition of the Black educated class. This calculation estimates what the impact on Black income would have been if Blacks had the same proportions above the high school level at each age group, but had the distribution among years of college completed equivalent to the same age all male group.

Such a distribution would have resulted in a fairly significant improvement in the incomes of Black males and a small improvement for Black females. The Black male college mean would have increased from $6,925 (or 62.9% of the all-male college mean), to $7,211 (or 65.5% of the all-male college mean). This would result in an additional $179.3 million in aggregate Black male income (an increase of 0.6% of previous Black male incomes). The gap in Black male college mean income would have closed 2.6 points (or 7.0%). The gap in the overall mean would have been reduced by .04 points (or 1.2%).

For Black females on the other hand, the increase in income from increased persistence was fairly small. The mean for Black females with college would have increased by $17.00 (or 0.3%). The change in overall Black female income would have been approximately $11.8 million dollars (or 0.1%).

Thus, if Black males had had the same persistence as the total male population, their incomes would be 0.6% higher in the aggregate. And, the mean incomes of Blacks with some college would have been roughly 4.1% higher. For Black females, the gains were much smaller. These figures can be taken as rough estimates of long term income gains from equalizing persistence.

The data in Table 4-22 are somewhat misleading, because the smaller female differences were caused by the method of estimation. It will be recalled that Black

TABLE 4-22. Mean 1969 Incomes of Blacks With College Persistence Equal to Persistence of Total Population by Sex.

Sex	New Mean Some College	New Mean Overall	New Aggregate Income	% Aggregate Income	Aggregate
Black Males	$7,211	$5,148	$28,056.6 million	0.6%	$179.3 million
Ratio of Black males/ All males	65.5%	66.1%	5.9%		——
Black Females	$4,740	$2,728	$14,510.2 million	0.1%	$ 11.8 million
Ratio of Black females/ All females	103.4%	83.6%	9.3%		——

SOURCE: U.S. Census, *1970 Census of the Population: Educational Attainment* Tables 7 and 8.

females had a better distribution than total females at the 35-45 and higher age groups. Our procedure in effect resulted in losses in the older Black age groups which offset most of the gains to be had by improving the persistence in the younger age groups.

Access and Income Loss

Table 4-23 summarizes some calculations that provided a rough estimate of the income loss due to a lower access to college education. The proportions of Blacks in each age cohort with some college experience were equalized while holding the persistence constant. This calculation was made on the assumption that incomes earned by particular Black education age cohorts would not be affected by increasing the number of individuals in the cohort.

The impact of this change on the mean incomes of Black males with some college was smaller than the impact of improving Black male persistence—adjusting for quantity increases the average income by only $7,026 (or 1.5%). However, equalizing the number of college educated Black males increased the ratio of the overall Black to the whole male mean income by 4.3%. This gap in the relative income of college-experienced Black males was reduced by 2.5%.

For Black females, equalizing access to a college education raised the average income of all Black women, but caused a slight decline in the mean income of college-educated Black females. The total Black female mean increased from $2,725 to $2,948 (a rise of 8.2%). The gap between Black and all females in total relative income dropped 6.8%. Thus, 41.2% of the disparity in the relative incomes of all Black females compared to all females would have been eliminated by equalizing the quantity of education.

The equalization of the access can be expected to have positive effects on aggregate income. The Black male and female losses combined from lower education were on the order of $3 billion a year in 1969. If the simple assumptions made here were roughly correct, long-run percentage gains from 6 to 8% in Black income could be expected from equalizing the quantity of higher education alone.

TABLE 4-23. Estimated 1969 Mean Incomes of Blacks With College Access Equal to Access of Total Population and Persistence Held Constant, by Sex.

Sex	New Mean Some College	New Mean Overall	$\triangle$Aggregate Income	%$\triangle$Aggregate Income	$\triangle$Aggregate Income
Black Males	$7,026	$5,449	$29,697.1 million	6.5%	$1,820.1 million
Ratio of Black Males/ All Males	63.8%	70.0%	6.3%		——
Black Females	$4,667	$2,948	$15,680.4 million	8.2%	$1,186.4 million
Ratio of Black Females/ All Females	101.8%	90.3%	10.0%		——

SOURCE: U.S. Census, *1970 Census of the Population: Educational Attainment*, Tables 7 and 8.

Combined Effects of Persistence and Access On Income Loss

Table 4-24 summarizes the results of equalizing access and persistence on Black income in 1969 by giving Blacks both the access and persistence of all students. As can be seen, this leads to additional income gains. These additional gains were relatively large for Black males and more modest for Black females. The Black male college mean income increased to 66.4% of the total male college mean; the average income of all Black males increased to 71.0% of the total male mean.

The percentage change in aggregate income was 8.0% for Black males and 8.4% for Black females. Thus, equalizing persistence and equalizing access resulted in an additional $414 million for Black males and $31.9 million for Black females. This roughly indicates the joint loss in Black income due to lower persistence and lower access, an annual loss of incomes of 8 to 8 1/2%. At 1969 income levels, this loss equalled $3,453 million a year.

Employment Discrimination and Income Loss

Table 4-25 shows the results of equalizing the rate of income of Black college-educated males without changing the persistence or quantity of education. This calculation was not done for Black females since at the level of aggregation of this study Black females have mean incomes at the college level higher than that of all females. Thus, this calculation would have resulted in a net loss for Black females. However, we know that inequalities in Black female income exist at a more disaggregate level.

Equalizing rates of income of college-educated males has a significant effect on Black male income. The mean income of college-educated Black males increased to $9,384 (or 35.5%). The overall Black male mean increased less, to $5,691 (or 11.3%). Moreover, 59.6% of the gap in the mean earning of Black males with some college was accounted for by disparities in rates of income. These income differences also accounted for 21.6% of the overall disparities in Black male mean and all males' incomes in 1969. In the aggregate, Black male incomes were 11.3% lower because of

TABLE 4-24. Estimated Mean 1969 Incomes of Blacks With Black College Access and Persistence Equal to Access and Persistence of Total Population, by Sex.

Sex	New Mean Some College	New Mean Overall	$\triangle Aggregate$ Income	$\% \triangle Aggregate$ Income	$\triangle Aggregate$ Income
Black Males	$7,314	$5,525	$30,111.3 million	8.0%	$2,234.3 million
Ratio of Black Males/ All Males	66.4%	71.0%	6.4%	——	——
Black Females	$4,674	$2,954	$15,712.3 million	8.4%	$1,218.3 million
Ratio of Black Females/ All Females	101.9%	90.5%	10.0%	——	——

SOURCE: U.S. Census, *1970 Census of the Population: Educational Attainment* Tables 7 and 8.

TABLE 4-25. Estimated Mean 1969 Income of Black Males With Income Distribution Equal to Distribution of Total Population.

Sex	New Mean Some College	New Mean Overall	△Aggregate Income	%△Aggregate Income	△Aggregate Income
Black Males	$9,384	$5,691	$31,015.9 million	11.3%	$3,139.0 million
Ratio of Black Males/ All Males	85.0%	73.1%	6.5%	——	——

SOURCE: U.S. Census, *1970 Census of the Population: Educational Attainment* Tables 7 and 8.

differences in rates of income between Black males and all males. This resulted in an annual loss in Black income at 1969 income levels of $3,139 million.

The impact of equalizing income differences was greater than the impact of equalizing access or persistence combined. Thus, significant short-run gains in Black economic well-being can be obtained by reducing labor market discrimination for college-educated Black workers. Moreover, without reducing labor market discrimination, gains were more limited, especially in the short run, as the previous calculations would have to be taken as potential long-run gains.

Combined Effects of Access, Persistence and Employment Discrimination on Income Loss

Finally, Table 4-26 shows the effect of combining all three types of improvements—access, persistence, and wages—for Blacks. The impacts were quite large. The combined impact exceeded the sum of the gains to be had from the three separate changes, indicating interaction between all three types of changes. The gap between Black male college-educated and all male college-educated income was almost eliminated. The remaining small differences were due to differences in the age structure of the Black male and the total male population. College-educated Black male structure is more heavily weighted towards the younger workers who have lower incomes. The combined access, persistence, and income differences led to a slightly lower mean income for college-educated Black females, because they tended to be younger workers, and because the total mean income for college-educated females was somewhat lower than that of Black college-educated females.

The impact of all three factors reduced the gaps in the overall means between Blacks and all people by 39.4% for Black females and 50.7% for Black males. These large reductions in the disparity indicated the magnitude of income losses currently incurred by Blacks. Black male incomes were 26.5% lower than they would have been with complete equality of opportunity in higher education and non-discrimination in the labor market, while Black female incomes were 7.8% lower. The effect of unequal educational and employment opportunity was an annual loss at the 1969 income level of $8,507 billion a year to Blacks. This figure provides an estimate of potential long-run gains to the Black community from equalizing higher

TABLE 4-26. Estimated 1969 Incomes of Blacks With College Access,
Persistence and Income Distribution Equal to That of Total Population, by Sex.

Sex	New College Mean	New Overall Mean	New Aggregate Income	Δ Aggregate Income	% Change in Aggregate Income
Black Males	$10,842	$6,469	$35,256,100	$7,379 million	26.5%
Ratio of Black Males/ All Males	98.5%	83.1%	7.4%	—	—
Black Females	$ 4,638	$2,937	$15,621,903	$1,127.9 million	7.8%
Ratio of Black Females/ All Females	101.1%	90.0%	10.0%	—	—

SOURCE: U.S. Census, *1970 Census of the Population:* Educational Attainment, Tables 7 and 8.

educational opportunity and eliminating labor market discrimination against Blacks
with some college training.

EDUCATION AND OCCUPATION

The data in the following tables show that, in general, increases in average
educational attainment improved the occupational status of the worker. In a job
competition theory, the higher incomes of workers are produced by their ability to
obtain higher paying jobs. In Table 4-27, the job categories were listed roughly in the
order of their desirability and their mean income. The table shows the distribution of
each educational cohort across occupations. As can be seen, the better-educated
cohorts tended to be concentrated in the better jobs, which in turn helped to explain
their higher incomes.

Not only did the higher-level jobs tend to produce higher earnings, but they also
tended to be regarded as more desirable by the population. Thus higher education
increased the probability of what is generally considered to be an all-round better life
style. This broad occupational classification system understates the relative occupational disadvantage of the less educated.

Relative Occupational Standing of Black Males

The occupational distribution of Black males and all males aged 25 to 64 with some
college experience is summarized in Table 4-28. Black workers with college experience were more concentrated than all workers in unfavorable occupations. This was
brought out clearly by the ratio formed by dividing the Black proportion in each
classification by the corresponding all-male proportion which is shown in the last

**TABLE 4-27. Occupational Distribution of Black Males
Age 25 to 64 by Highest Level of School Completed.**

OCCUPATION	All Black Males	Elementary 0-8	High School 1-3	High School 4	College 1-3	College 4	5 or more
Managers and Administrators Except Farm	3.2	1.3	2.2	3.7	7.7	10.7	16.5
Professional Technical and Kindred Workers	6.0	.7	1.6	4.3	15.5	54.4	68.5
Sales Workers	1.7	.7	1.4	2.5	4.6	4.5	2.1
Clerical and Kindred Workers	7.4	2.6	6.8	12.2	18.8	10.8	4.5
Craftsmen and Kindred Workers	16.7	16.3	18.2	18.9	14.9	6.7	2.7
Operatives Except Transport	19.7	19.6	23.2	21.6	12.8	3.6	1.6
Transport Equipment Operatives	10.7	11.3	13.0	10.8	5.9	2.0	.4
Service Workers Except Private Household	14.5	15.5	15.5	14.5	12.3	5.3	2.3
Labor Except Farm	15.6	22.8	15.4	10.3	5.5	1.7	1.3
Private Household Workers	.4	.6	.4	.2	.1	.1	.0
Farmers and Farm Managers	.9	1.7	.5	.3	.2	.2	.1
Farm Laborers and Foremen	3.3	6.8	1.9	.7	.4	.1	.1
Total	100.0%	100.0%	100.0%	100.0%	100.0%	100.0%	100.0%

SOURCE: U.S. Census, *1970 Census of the Population: Earnings by Occupation and Education,* Tables 1, 2, 7, and 8.

column. The data indicate that in the preferred occupations, Black participation was smallest. In all of the top three occupations, college-experienced Blacks were underrepresented, which is indicated by the ratio values less than one. In the less desirable occupations the Black males were employed at a rate up to three times the all-male participation rate. Seventy-five percent of all male workers with some college were in the professinal, managerial, and sales occupations; however, only 49% of the Black male college-educated workers are so employed. When this fact is combined with the underrepresentation of Black males in the college-educated group, the relative occupational disadvantage of Black males is even more striking.

TABLE 4-28. Occupational Distribution of Males Age 25 to 64 Who Have Completed One or More Years of College, by Race, 1970.

OCCUPATIONS	All Males		Black Males		Ratio of Black Male/All Male	Percent Black of All Male
	Number	Percent	Number	Percent		
Managers and Administrators Except Farm	2,228,414	21.3	40,533	10.2	.48	1.8
Professional Technical and Kindred Workers	4,583,856	43.8	139,396	35.2	.80	.30
Sales Workers	1,095,160	10.5	16,105	4.1	.39	1.4
Clerical and Kindred Workers	770,138	7.4	56,158	14.2	1.92	7.2
Craftsmen and Kindred Workers	917,561	8.8	42,780	10.8	1.23	4.6
Operatives Except Transport	309,305	3.0	33,649	8.5	2.83	10.8
Transport Equipment Operatives	129,452	1.2	15,658	4.0	3.33	12.0
Service Workers Except Private Household	310,450	3.0	35,061	8.9	2.97	11.2
Labor Except Farm	108,758	1.0	15,298	3.9	3.90	14.0
Farm Laborers and Foremen	16,362	.2	1,063	.3	1.33	6.4
Total	8,469,456	100%	395,701	100%	——	4.6

SOURCE: U.S. Census, *1970 Census of the Population: Earnings by Occupation and Education*, Tables 1, 2, 7, and 8.

The occupational data for Black males by level of college completed is reported in Table 4-29 with the corresponding data for all males. In general, the same patterns that were evidenced by the aggregate data hold at each level of college education. At each level of attainment, Black males were generally underrepresented and the ratio of the Black male to the all-male participation was lowest for the most desirable occupations, and highest for the least desirable occupations. Black males were least represented in the managerial, sales, and professional occupations at all educational levels. However, Black males who had completed four or more years of college were as well represented in the professional group as were all males. For Black males with five or more years of college, the representation in the managerial occupations reached parity.

Below five years of college, the Black representation in lower sales and managerial jobs, which were the two highest-paid occupations at these levels, was poor. Even at

TABLE 4-29. Percentage Distribution of Males Age 25 to 64 Years Old by Broad Occupational Groups, Years of College Completed and Race, 1970.

	Years of College Completed[1]								
	1 to 3 years			4 years			5 or more years		
Occupation	Black	All	B/A	Black	All	B/A	Black	All	B/A
Managers and Administrators except farm	7.7	21.1	.36	10.7	25.5	.42	16.5	16.4	1.01
Professional Technical and Kindred workers	15.4	22.2	.69	54.4	45.5	1.20	68.5	72.7	.94
Sales Workers	4.6	12.8	.46	4.5	12.9	.35	2.1	4.1	.51
Clerical and Kindred workers	18.8	10.9	1.72	10.8	6.3	1.71	4.5	2.9	1.55
Craftsmen and Kindred workers	14.9	15.8	.94	6.7	4.8	1.40	2.7	1.7	1.59
Operatives except Transport	12.8	5.6	2.29	3.6	1.3	2.77	1.6	.5	3.2
Transport Operatives	5.9	2.4	2.46	2.0	.5	4.0	.4	.2	2.00
Service Workers	12.3	5.2	2.37	5.3	1.5	3.53	2.3	.8	2.88
Laborers except farm	5.5	1.9	2.89	1.7	.5	3.4	1.3	.3	4.33

SOURCE: *U.S. Census, 1970 Census of Population: Earning by Occupation and Education*, Tables 1 and 2.

[1]Percentage will not add to 100 due to rounding and omission of Farm workers.

five years of college, the representation of Black males in the sales occupations was poor. Sales occupations were much less important for those with five or more years of college than for those with four years or less. The relative occupational standing of Black males improved as the level of education increased. The proportion of Black males with less than four years of college in the top three occupations was 49% of the all-male proportion. It rose to 83% of the all-male proportion for those with four years of college and 93% of the all-male proportion for those with five or more years of college. With more detailed disaggregation of the occupational data, the situation of Blacks would look less favorable. Within each broad occupational category, Blacks tended to be disproportionately represented in the least desirable positions.

Occupation and Earnings

The mean earnings of Blacks with college experience were generally lower than the mean earnings of all males for every broad occupational classification and level of education in 1970. In general, the higher the salary of the occupation, the less well-off the Black male, relative to all males. This general pattern held at each education level. The overall mean earning of Black males with one to three years of college in 1969 was $7,722, which was 69% of the total male mean. The mean earnings of Blacks with four years of college in 1969 was $9,287, or 63% of the corresponding all-male mean. The mean earning of Black males with five or more years of college in 1969 was $12,596, which is 74% of the all-male mean. (See Table 4-30.)

Education obviously increased the earnings of Black males, which was reflected in the impact of education on income discussed earlier. The relationship of earnings and occupation to education is the same as that discerned in the relationship of income to education: The earnings of Black males with four years of college were lowest relative to all males with the same amount of education. Black male earnings were highest relative to all males for those with five or more years of college. This general pattern tended to hold for each broad occupational group. Blacks in the managerial and sales occupations earned less relative to all males at each educational level, than Black males in any other occupation. The all-male sales worker earned more on the average than did their all-male professional worker counterparts with less than five years of college; the opposite was true for Black males.

The fact that Black males in professional occupations earned so much less than their all-male counterparts combined with the gross underrepresentation of Blacks in these occupations noted earlier, further explains the lower total mean incomes of Black males. Thus, the lower overall earning of Black males is due to their occupational differences and to wage differences within occupational fields.

Impact of Occupational Distributions on Earnings

The overall mean earnings of college-educated Black male workers aged 25 to 64 were 63.4% of the mean earnings of all college-educated males. Mean incomes were used to calculate an index of occupational similarity for Black males and all males. By assuming that Black males had the same earnings at each occupation as all males with the same amount of education, a new weighted mean was calculated. The index was

TABLE 4-30. Mean Earnings in 1969 of Male Workers Age
Selected by Broad Occupational Groups, Race and Years of College Completed, 1970.

	Years of College Completed											
	1 to 3 years			4 years			5 or more years			All College		
Occupation	Black	All	B/A	Black	All	B/A	Black	All	B/A	Black	All	B/A
Managers and Administrators except farm	$9,543	$14,184	.67	$10,432	$18,182	.57	$13,543	$18,909	.72	$11,068	$16,678	.66
Professional Technical and Kindred workers	8,687	11,591	.75	9,672	13,799	.71	13,129	17,089	.77	10,823	14,540	.74
Sales Workers	8,353	12,390	.67	9,393	15,242	.62	12,178	16,159	.75	8,991	13,443	.67
Clerical and Kindred workers	7,739	9,226	.84	8,582	11,285	.76	9,527	12,165	.78	7,984	9,747	.82
Craftsmen and Kindred workers	7,873	10,178	.77	8,228	12,327	.67	9,144	13,248	.69	7,980	10,630	.75
Operatives except Transport	7,270	8,724	.83	8,530	10,382	.82	8,530	9,890	.86	7,430	8,924	.83
Transport Operatives	7,343	8,784	.84	7,551	9,140	.83	N/A	9,166	—	7,151	8,830	.81
Service Workers	7,102	8,094	.88	7,152	10,034	.72	7,813	10,878	.72	7,137	8,975	.80
Laborers except farm	6,660	7,789	.86	6,428	8,701	.74	N/A	8,031	—	6,519	7,906	.82
All Workers	7,722	11,239	.69	9,287	14,675	.63	16,971	12,596	.74	8,834	13,934	.63

SOURCE: *U.S. Bureau of the Census, Washington, D.C., 1970 Census of Population: Earnings by Occupation and Education, PC (2) – 8B, Table 1.*
N/A—Not available

formed by taking this new weighted mean relative to the actual all-male mean. The index calculated for the occupational distributions in 1970 equaled 84. (A value of 100 indicates occupational equality.) This index indicated that roughly 42% of the disparity in 1969 earnings of Black males and all males with some college in the 25 to 64 age group could be attributed to occupational dissimilarity. A similar index was calculated for 1959 income data and equaled 81, which indicated that about 43% of the disparity in 1959 income of non-white and all males was due to occupational dissimilarity.

The questions of the ability of education to enhance the occupational mobility of Blacks is crucial for assessing the potential of investment in college education to lead to future improvement in the economic situation of Blacks. The very close values of the occupational similarity index indicated that there was minimal relative occupational upgrading for college-educated Blacks as a whole from 1960 to 1970. There was no deterioration in the status of Black males despite the fact that the proportion of Black males with some college increased. However, these rough calculations did not permit us to assess fully the impact of increasing education on employment of Blacks. A study of more detailed occupational groups, perhaps by regional grouping, is desirable.

Summary

The preceding discussion of occupation and earnings concentrated on the Black male population. Increases in education clearly improved the occupational standings of Black males. The proportions in the three highest occupations rose from less than 3% for those with only an elementary education to 87% for those with five or more years of education. Educational attainment generally improved the occupational standings of Black males relative to all males. In the top three occupations, the representation of Black males relative to white males was 49% for one to three years of college, 83% for four years of college and 93% for five or more years of college.

The earnings of Black males generally rose with education at each major occupation. However, relative to all males, the position of Black males declined at the four years of college level and was highest in the five or more years of college level. Overall, Black males with college experience earned 63.4% of that earned by all males. About 42% of the gap in Black male earnings is explained by their occupational and educational distribution. The remaining 57% is explained by difference in rates of earnings within each broad occupational category and other factors.

CHAPTER 5

Federal Policies Related To Equal Educational Opportunity

INTRODUCTION

This chapter briefly discusses the federal role in the removal of barriers to equal educational opportunity. Although many excellent reviews and analyses of current federal and state higher-education legislation are available, they tend to focus only on the legislative efforts to remove financial barriers for low-income students of all racial and ethnic groups, while other barriers have been slighted or ignored. Since a substantial number of Blacks seeking access to undergraduate, graduate, and professional schools come from low-income families, there is an obvious overlap between legislation to provide equal educational opportunity for low-income students and that to widen opportunities specifically for Black students. However, as explained in the discussion of barriers to access, distribution, and persistence in Chapter 3 of this report, not all barriers are financial. Some equal educational opportunity problems are unique to Blacks, and to similarly disadvantaged non-white minorities.

Discussions of policies needed to facilitate equal educational opportunity for Blacks, therefore, must consider all four of the following:

(a) policies that attempt to remove educational barriers based on family income that Blacks and other minority groups share with others of similar socio-economic status or situation;

(b) policies aimed at categorical barriers based on racial and ethnic discrimination and patterns of exclusion;

(c) policies aimed at psychosocial barriers that emerge from the life situations of Blacks; and

(d) the degree of coordination and integration of all three types of policies.

Although this policy discussion focuses on the federal role in meeting the need for equal educational opportunity for Blacks in higher education through student assistance and enrollment, it is clear that the status and the needs of Blacks in higher education, as discussed throughout this report, were not determined by federal action in isolation. State, institutional, and private action also shape the educational opportunities of Blacks. Categorical barriers based on race, in addition to educational and psychosocial barriers, can be, and are, constructed by individual colleges, by isolated state governments, and by professional associations and individual families. The size of the Black availability pools for undergraduate and graduate or professional schools, Black college enrollment, dropout rates, and degrees earned were all determined by the interaction of state, federal, institutional, and private action. Therefore, brief discussions of the state/federal relationship, the institutional role, and the private sector in equal educational opportunity for Blacks are included.

State/Federal Relationship

State governments, through their control of public institutions, the determination of licensure and certification requirements, and through other state regulatory functions, are the primary agents in determining higher educational policies. States vary widely in their commitment to equal educational opportunity, in the size and scope of special programs for furthering Black access, distribution, and persistence, and in the number and location of Black residents. They also differ in their implementation of higher education policies, and the consequences these policies have for Black and other disadvantaged students. This variability may be necessary to meet unique state needs and respond to state political, social, and economic pressures. It also contributes, however, to the difficulty of developing a coordinated state/federal approach to equal educational opportunity.

In the 1973-74 school year, the federal government increased its direct involvement in higher education with the implementation of the Education Amendments of 1972. In Fiscal Year 1974, federal funds for student assistance campus-based programs (SEOGs, College Work-Study, and NDSL) were distributed among the states as summarized in Tables A-5 through A-7 in Appendix A. (The 1973-74 school year preceded implementation and funding of the State Student Incentive Program and therefore has not been included in this discussion.)

States differed in the amount of federal money they received and in the size of the average awards they made. Federal money for campus-based student aid programs was allocated to the states, who in turn distributed the money among colleges and universities located there. The funds were unequally, but perhaps equitably, divided among institutions within a state. Depending on the number of awards made, the average awards for each assistance program varied. In Fiscal Year 1974, $692 was the national average award under the SEOG program; this program aided an estimated 300,300 students. States such as Montana, Louisiana, and Alaska gave average awards of $881, $745, and $798 respectively. (See Table A-5.) These states awarded individual students more money than California ($678), New York ($626), and Illinois ($685). However, California, New York and Illinois not only aided more students, but also received more federal dollars. Similar patterns were also found in NDSL and College Work-Study programs. However, in these federal programs the differences between average awards by state were small. (See Tables A-6 and A-7.)

How the differences in the amount of federal money allocated to states, the number of students aided, the average awards made, and the types of institutions disbursing the funds shaped or influenced state-funded programs is unknown. We do know that, in addition to federally funded programs, states operated their own student assistance programs. The amounts and number of awards made in state programs in Fiscal Year 1974 are summarized in Table A-8 in Appendix A. In the 1973-74 academic year, Georgia, Kentucky, Oklahoma, Puerto Rico, South Dakota and the Trust territories had no state-funded student assistance programs. Of the remaining states that had programs in both the 1972-73 and the 1973-74 academic year, 29 states increased the number of awards, 29 increased the number of dollars awarded, and 18 increased the average award. During the same time period, 3 states decreased the average awards. No states remained unchanged. (See Table A-9 in Appendix A.)

As was found in the federal student assistance programs, the average size of the awards, the number of awards, and the total amount awarded in the state student assistance programs were not always related. While we do not know the actual number of students assisted in each state, we do know that states with fewer dollars tended to give more of the money to fewer students. Thus, such states had the largest average awards. In the 1973-74 academic year, New York state student assistance programs gave out the greatest number of awards and awarded the greatest amount of money, compared to all other states. (New York state program average awards were ranked 29th nationally. Tennessee state student assistance programs gave the largest average award in the 1973-74 academic year. See Table A-10.) Five states— New York, Pennsylvania, Illinois, California, and Ohio awarded 67% of the $364,204,427 student aid money awarded by all states in the 1973-74 academic year. In both the state-funded and the federally funded campus-based student assistance programs, the state the individual lived in could affect the size of the award he would receive, the amount of competition for assistance, and ultimately the likelihood of access to college.

The federal/state relationship in student assistance programs is poorly defined and underresearched. In California, for example, a total of $79,164 flowed to the state from SEOGs, College Work-Study, and NDSL in Fiscal Year 1974. At the same time, California itself awarded $31,338,543 in state funds for student assistance programs. How do—and should—these state and federal student assistance programs work together to facilitate minority access, distribution, and persistence in higher education? Who was served and who was missed by these state and federal programs? Did the funding levels and regulations of the various state and federal programs complement each other? Finally, how will the future funding levels and regulations in federal programs, such as BEOGs and SEOGs, increase or decrease the need to expand or revise similar state programs?

The data with which to answer such policy questions about the state/federal relationship have not been adequately developed, but are greatly needed. Without the delineation and integration of state and federal higher education policies and practices built upon reliable data bases, government policy planning at all levels suffers, as do efforts, such as this report, to evaluate equal educational opportunity for minorities.

Institutional Role and the Private Sector

As shown in Chapter 3 of this report, barriers for Blacks arose from institutional as well as governmental policies and practices. Whether colleges were committed to equal educational opportunity for minorities on their campuses profoundly influenced whether or not the goals could be achieved there. It will be recalled that in 1968, immediately following the death of Dr. Martin Luther King, individual colleges decided to increase opportunities for minorities on their campuses. This independent action by colleges, along with federal, state, and private foundation action, contributed to the sharp increase in the total minority enrollment in the late 1960s and early 1970s. The role of colleges in meeting equal opportunity goals has not been passive. Where the commitment existed, as in 1968, minority access, distribution, and persistence were facilitated.

It is, therefore, important to know how state and federal roles in securing equal educational opportunity for minorities interacted with the institutional role. Not all colleges participated in federal campus-based student assistance programs aimed at removing financial barriers to access in the 1973-74 school year. Not all colleges were required to report racial enrollment to the U.S. Office for Civil Rights. The federal role in such instances was limited, while state and institutional roles were crucial for minority access, distribution, and persistence.

The institutional response to equal educational opportunity goals shaped the emotional climate, quality of instruction, and supportive services, including recruitment and counseling, that a college offered Black students.

Revisions in institutional practices can be either *additive* or *institutional* reform (Abramowitz and Abramowitz, 1973). The former involves a limited or peripheral modification of institutional practice; the latter, a systemic change in which the new policies are integrated into institutional life. The distinction is important when assessing how institutions respond to the needs of Blacks and others for equal educational opportunity. Institutions have the choice of selecting additive or institutional reforms as responses. If they choose the former, then educational barriers are only temporarily removed. If they choose the latter, then the affected barriers may be permanently removed. Additive reform is the peripheral and temporary institutional response to barriers to equal educational opportunity. Programs for minorities that are not understood by the faculty or are poorly integrated into the mainstream of the college's operations and budget are examples of additive reform.

Unfortunately, the lack of adequate data severely limited the assessment of the institutional response to equal educational opportunity for Blacks in the 1973-74 academic year. Since all goals for equal educational opportunity required an institutional response, the lack of such data was crucial. While studies of minority recruitment and of tutorial and related supportive programs on specific campuses were useful (and are included in this report), a comprehensive assessment of the institutional response of a representative cross-section of colleges and universities is needed. Research is needed to answer basic questions: How are institutions currently responding to these goals? What should their responses be? How do institutional policies and practices interface with federal and state actions in equal educational opportunity?

In addition to the roles of the public sector (federal and state government) and the colleges themselves, there was also a role that the private sector played in shaping, implementing, and evaluating policies for equal educational opportunity for Blacks. The private sector includes business and foundations; professional, educational, civil rights, and church-related associations and organizations; higher education policy study centers; and individual families and communities. The private sector, as the term is used here, therefore, includes a variety of groups and individuals. Some have overlapping memberships and common concerns; others have competing interests and divergent perceptions of the equal educational opportunity needs of minorities, especially Blacks.

The methods the private sector used to influence minority goals for equal educational opportunity varied. They included policy research and conferences; publicized resolutions and position statements; special minority training, counseling, and recruitment programs; legal and political pressure on state and federal government; and financial and professional support of college programs to facilitate access for Blacks and other minorities.

The several areas of the private sector's influence on equal educational opportunity for Blacks and other minorities in need of further study beyond the scope of this report are (1) how the different entities within the private sector can and should work together to achieve equal educational opportunity goals; (2) how public, private, and institutional policies and practices could interface to facilitate efforts to achieve minority access, distribution, and persistence; and (3) the various methods used by the private sector to shape public policy and institutional responses toward equal educational opportunity.

FEDERAL FACILITATORS OF EQUAL EDUCATIONAL OPPORTUNITIES FOR BLACKS IN HIGHER EDUCATION

Federal policies did not operate in isolation from state, institutional, or private sector activities. Because of this complex interrelationship, the lack of data with which to disaggregate the contributions of each, and the absence of evaluative studies on federal higher education policies, a simple cause-effect analysis of federal policies and equal educational opportunity for Blacks was not possible.

Categorical, Educational, and Psychosocial Facilitators

Appendix A of this report briefly summarizes all federal higher education legislation as of 1973. In examining these laws and their underlying policies, the distinction is made between the *legislative intent*, on the one hand, and their *operation*, on the other hand, as categorical, educational, and psychosocial facilitators of equal educational opportunity for Blacks.

Federal policies that were intended to enhance or support access, distribution, or persistence of Black students in higher education are defined here as facilitators of equal educational opportunity. These facilitators operated independently and in concert with each other to affect the access, distribution, or persistence of Blacks in higher education in the 1973-74 academic year. In analyzing federal policy intent and practice, therefore, it was difficult to isolate the categorical from the educational and psychosocial facilitation of a single program or law.

Categorical Facilitators

Higher educational activities, programs, and policies available only to people previously excluded on the basis of race are categorical facilitators. Categorical facilitators correct for past patterns of racial discrimination by enhancing or supporting the treatment of Blacks so that their participation in higher education is increased. Affirmative action and preferential admissions, in theory if not in practice, are examples of categorical facilitators. (In the context of this report, only those categorical facilitators applying to Blacks in higher education are discussed. While other categorical facilitators do exist, such as those based on sex or cultural heritage, they are beyond the scope of this report.)

Educational Facilitators

Educational facilitators are programs, practices, and policies that arose from higher-education laws or institutions, and had a positive racial impact on the equal educational opportunities of Blacks. The effect of educational facilitators, like that of categorical facilitators, was to increase the access, distribution, and persistence of Blacks in higher education. But educational facilitators differed from categorical facilitators in that the former, unlike the latter, were not limited to Blacks. For example, student assistance programs based on need are available to all qualified low-income students interested in college attendance. Because a disproportionate number of low-income families are Blacks, such financial aid programs had an indirect racial impact, while categorical facilitators produced a direct racial impact.

Psychosocial Facilitators

An individual carries with him from childhood into adulthood both the positive and the negative effects of his life situation. The positive attitudes, beliefs, values, and motivations that are already within the student facilitate educational attainment. These are defined as psychosocial facilitators of equal educational opportunity.

Psychosocial facilitators differed from both categorical and educational because they arose from within the individual. However, external realties, such as the attitudes of whites toward Blacks, undoubtedly helped shape the self-perceptions of Black students. Certainly one by-product of racial segregation has been an unrealistically inflated sense of worth in white children, and an equally unrealistically deflated sense of worth in Black children.

Federal Programs

Some federal programs in operation may have contributed to the attainment of qual educational opportunity because of their legislative intent. Other programs funded through the following federal higher education legislation may have facilitated equal educational opportunity, especially for Blacks, in their operation, although such was not the intent of the legislation: Education Professions Development Act, Title I of the Higher Education Act of 1965 (amended), and the First and Second Morrill Acts of 1862 and 1890.

The Education Professions Development Act was enacted to meet manpower shortages in the field of education with no expressed or understood concern for minority needs or problems. Because education is a profession that included a significant proportion of all Blacks in college, some Blacks also benefited from EPDA-funded programs. According to a recent study by the National Advisory Council on Education Professions Development (1975), 34% of the Teacher Corps interns in 1972 were Black; 17% were of Spanish heritage/surnames; 9% native American; and 1% other. Title I of the Higher Education Act of 1965 funded two-year college adult education and extension programs, at a time when a growing number of Blacks were enrolled in two-year colleges. Finally, the First and Second Morrill Acts provided some federal support to colleges designated as fulfilling the land-grant function for the state. Although the federal funds were unequally distributed among the land-grant institutions (the Black land-grand colleges in particular), the Morrill Act of 1890 influenced college opportunities for Blacks. Thus, the operation of EPDA, Title I, the Morrill Acts, and possible other higher-education programs undoubtedly facilitated equal educational opportunity for at least some Black students, even though that was not their specific legislative intent. (Without adequate data on Black participation in these higher education programs, more definite conclusions about their actual roles as facilitators of access, distribution, and persistence for Blacks cannot be made.)

The federal involvement in Black higher education (other than the founding of Howard University) can be dated from the Second Morrill Act of 1890, which created Black land-grant colleges under the then accepted doctrine of separate-but-equal. But equal educational opportunity for Blacks in higher education as a national objective is very recent.

Two federal policies in particular–the Civil Rights Act of 1964 and the Education Amendments of 1972–have shaped the federal position toward equal educational opportunity. Both were intended to function as categorical, institutional, and/or psychosocial facilitators of access, distribution, or persistence.

Civil Rights Act of 1964

● Desegregates dual racial systems of public and nonprofit educational institutions, including colleges (Title IV)
● Prohibits racial discrimination in the administration of all federally assisted programs (Title VI)

Education Amendments of 1972

● Amends Title III of the Higher Education Act of 1965 to strengthen the efforts of developing institutions (which include historically or predominantly Black colleges) to provide quality education

● Amends Title IV of the Higher Education Act of 1965 to provide student financial assistance and some supportive services:

The Title IV programs include *Basic Educational Opportunity Grants (BEOGs)*, which went directly to students who applied to the U.S. Office of Education. Awards were limited to one-half of the actual cost of attending college, less expected family contributions. Although all qualified full-time undergraduate students were eligible under Title IV to receive a BEOG, a congressional rider to the programs appropriation made the grants available only to entering freshmen in the 1973-74 academic year. In the 1973-74 school year, the maximum grant was $452, with an average grant of $270. The average size of the grants varied with the type and control of the institution. All students obviously did not receive the average grant award since need was based on family wealth and college costs. According to a survey of the American Council on Education, the average amount of federal assistance through BEOGs and other programs was greater at private institutions. (See Table 5-1.) The average BEOG grant in the 1973-74 academic year at higher educational institutions was $349, based on ACE data.

The first year of operation of the BEOG program was undoubtedly hindered by the short time for applications. Application forms were issued by USOE on March 31, 1973, to be returned May 31, 1973, in order to be considered for 1973-74 awards.

Another Title IV program is *Supplemental Educational Opportunity Grants (SEOGs)*, formerly known as Educational Opportunity Grants. SEOGs were multiple-year awards of federal funds disbursed by colleges to needy students. They were limited to one-half of all student aid provided by the institution, with the maximum total multiple-year award of $4000 for four-year undergraduate degrees and $5000 for five-year under graduate programs. In the 1973-74 academic year a total of $207,677,000 was disbursed to an estimated 3,000,000 students, with an average grant of $692, according to USOE data. (According to ACE data, the average SEOG award was $646 in the 1973-74 academic year.)

Title IV also includes the *College Work-Study Program*, which authorizes the federal government to pay up to 80%, and under special conditions 100%, of the costs of jobs for full-time and part-time undergraduate, graduate, or professional school students with financial need. Students were paid a maximum of $3.50 per hour. The

TABLE 5-1. Estimated Average Amount Awarded by Type of Institution and Assistance Program, 1973-74 Academic Year.

	Institutions (Higher Education)					
Type of Program	*All*	*Public*	*Private*	*Two-Year*	*Four-Year*	*Universities*
BEOG	$349	$284	$418	$287	$404	$308
SEOG	$646	$469	$827	$448	$783	$748
College Work-Study	$582	$560	$601	$531	$601	$708
NDSL	$653	$517	$793	$515	$738	$805

SOURCE: American Council on Education, *The Impact of Office of Education Student Assistance Programs,* Fall 1973, pp. 21-24.

average College Work-Study grant was $582 in 1973. Like BEOGs, and SEOGs, Work-Study grants at private institutions were higher than those at public institutions.

Another Title IV program is *Special Programs for the Disadvantaged*. Two of the "Trio" Programs, Upward Bound and Talent Search, originated as part of the Economic OPPORTUNITY Act of 1964 and in Fiscal Year 1970 were transferred from the Office of Economic Opportunity to the U.S. Office of Education. These two complementary programs were intended to overcome deficiencies in secondary school counseling and to provide tutorial and enrichment programs. Upward Bound provided a variety of supportive services for disadvantaged students and high school graduates interested in college. Talent Search offered enrichment to junior or senior high school students. The third program, Educational Opportunity Centers, began operation in 1973. E.O. Centers were located in low-income neighborhoods to disseminate information on academic and financial assistance for college.

● Amends Title IX and Title IV (Part E) of the Higher Education Act of 1965 which includes the Insured Student Loan Programs–the state and federal *Guaranteed Student Loan Programs* and the *National Direct Student Loan Program*, formerly part of the National Defense Education Act.

Of the three, NDSL is the oldest loan program. Together these three loan programs assisted student borrowers in undergraduate, graduate, and professional schools. GSLP was also open to proprietary school students. The programs, however, differed in repayment requirements and in the type of lenders participating in the loan programs. (See Appendix A for description of each loan program.)

A LIMITED ASSESSMENT OF THE FEDERAL ROLE IN EQUAL EDUCATIONAL OPPORTUNITY FOR BLACKS IN HIGHER EDUCATION

Current federal (and some state) policies have at least temporarily answered fundamental questions: Who should pay the costs of a college education and how should public resources be channeled to meet equal educational opportunity goals? In answering the first question, the federal government concluded: (a) that a college education–especially in undergraduate school–involves both private and public benefits and, therefore, (b) that college costs are shared by the individual, to the extent that he is financially able, and by society through public funds.

Federal higher-education policies, especially the student assistance programs coming out of the Education Amendments of 1972, set the removal of financial barriers to equal educational opportunity as the primary social goal and reflected the acceptance of shared public and private benefits and responsibility for the cost of a college education. However, this position did not extend to graduate and professional schools.

In answering the second question, a bifurcated approach has been chosen by federal and state governments. Through the political process, what emerged, particularly in the Education Amendments of 1972, was a position that both students and higher educational institutions should be direct recipients of public funds intended to facilitate equal educational opportunity in higher education.

Before passage of the Education Amendments of 1972, the federal legislation to achieve equal educational opportunity for Blacks involved the Civil Rights Act of 1964. This act was intended to function as a categorical facilitator to higher education. Through the Office for Civil Rights (DHEW), institutions receiving federal assistance are required to complete a biennial racial census of fall enrollment. The census, which began in 1968, is published with the name of the institution and its undergraduate, graduate, and professional racial enrollment.

Although racial discrimination continued to be a barrier for Blacks in higher education, other barriers–educational and psychosocial–contributed to the lack of status of Blacks in higher education. With passage of the Education Amendments of 1972, the federal role was expanded to include the removal of some educational and psychosocial barriers to equal educational opportunity for disadvantaged students. Taken together, therefore, the Civil Rights Act of 1964 and the Education Amendments of 1972 delineate the current federal approach to facilitating equal educational opportunity for Blacks (and other disadvantaged people) in higher education.

Comprehensive, formative, and aggregate evaluations of higher education policies per se are needed to determine whether the programs as operated are in reality meeting their legislative intent. For those policies with equal educational opportunity intent– the Civil Rights Act of 1964 and the Education Amendments of 1972–the need for program evaluations is even greater.

Unfortunately, the inadequacy of data with which to assess the status of Blacks in higher education extended to the federal role in providing equal educational opportunity for Blacks. While we can describe the level of participation of Black students in selected higher education programs, the data were unavailable to assess this participation in the context of similar state and private policies. Although we can relate Black participation in a particular student assistance program to the number of needy Black college students, we did not know their level of participation in other federal, state, or institutional student assistance programs. While it was possible to estimate the total number of awards made in individual Title IV programs in the 1973-74 academic year, the actual number of students served was unknown.

Despite these data limitations, we shall try to assess the influence of Titles IV and VI of the Civil Rights Act of 1964, and Titles III, IV, and IX of the Higher Education Act of 1965 on meeting the needs of Blacks in higher education. First, we examine Title VI of the Civil Rights Act of 1964 and higher education opportunity for Blacks, then the Education Amendments of 1972, and finally, the federal role in graduate and professional educational opportunities for Blacks.

Civil Rights Act of 1964

The major federal law prohibiting racial discrimination against students in higher education is the Civil Rights Act of 1964, Title VI. As it applies to higher education, Title VI is enforced by the Office for Civil Rights, Department of Health, Education, and Welfare, in 1973. As it applies to proprietary schools with VA-approved courses, Title VI is enforced by the Veterans Administration. In addition to Title VI, Internal Revenue Service Ruling 71-447 requires that private tax-exempt schools not discriminate against students on the basis of race. The IRS ruling overlaps Title VI, higher education enforcement, but is limited to private tax-exempt colleges and universities.

The discussion that follows focuses on the impact of the enforcement of Title VI of the Civil Rights Act of 1964 on the access, distribution, and persistence of Blacks in higher education. The most recent year for which data collected by the Office for Civil Rights were available is Fall 1972. This was, it will be recalled, a peak year in the proportional college enrollment of Blacks between 1968 and 1974.

Before passage of the Civil Rights Act of 1964, the opportunity for Blacks to attend college had been almost exclusively limited to historically Black public and private colleges. Racially non-discriminatory colleges, located primarily in the North and West, did not enroll Blacks in large numbers. Fall enrollment data were collected by the Office for Civil Rights on even-numbered years from colleges receiving federal funds as part of implementation of Title VI.

The distribution of Black students among the colleges receiving federal assistance is summarized in Table 5-2. In 1970, 86% (or 1,817) of all colleges reporting to the Office for Civil Rights had Black undergraduate enrollments less than 10%. In 1972, 80% (or 2,141) of the institutions reporting had Black undergraduate enrollments less than 10%. In 1970, 25.1% of the institutions and in 1972, 18.7% reported Black enrollments of less than 1% of their total undergraduate student body. Between 1970 and 1972 the number of institutions with small Black enrollments (less than 1%) decreased by one-fourth.

There was an increase in the number and percent of institutions with Black enrollments of over 60% between 1970 and 1972. In 1970, 95 colleges (4.4% of all

TABLE 5-2. Distribution of Undergraduate Institutions Receiving Federal Assistance by Percent Blacks Enrolled, Fall 1970 and 1972.

| | *Undergraduate Institutions* | | | |
| | 1970 | | 1972 | |
Percent Black in Student Body	*Number*	*Percent*	*Number*	*Percent*
0.0 - 0.9%	531	25.1	498	18.7
1.0 - 1.9	363	17.2	362	13.6
2.0 - 2.9	273	12.9	295	11.1
3.0 - 3.9	200	9.5	238	8.9
4.0 - 4.9	136	6.4	209	7.8
5.0 - 9.9	314	14.8	539	20.2
10.0 - 20.9	161	7.6	265	9.9
21.0 - 40.9	29	1.4	98	3.7
41.0 - 60.9	14	0.7	28	1.1
61.0 - 80.9	3	0.1	24	0.9
81.0 - 100.0	92	4.3	110	4.1
TOTAL	2,116	100.0	2,666	100.0

SOURCE: U.S. Office for Civil Rights (DHEW), *Racial and Ethnic Enrollment Data From Institutions of Higher Education, Fall 1972*, Section I, and *Racial And Ethnic Enrollment Data from Institutions of Higher Education, Fall 1970*, Part II.

institutions) were over 60% Black. But in 1972, 134 colleges (5.0% of all institutions) were over 60% Black. This increase in the number of institutions with over 60% Black undergraduate full-time enrollment in 1972 was largely due to an increase in Black enrollment at two-year public institutions reporting to the Office for Civil Rights.

Table 5-3 summarizes the number and percent of full-time Black undergraduates by region in Fall 1968, 1970, and 1972. (See Table A-11 in Appendix A for list of states in each region.) Between 1968 and 1972 three trends emerged: first, total Black undergraduate enrollments increased; second, Black enrollment in all three years was largest in Region IV (Southern States); and third, Black enrollment increased most rapidly in Region II (New York and New Jersey). While colleges in the southern states, which included most of the historically Black institutions, continued to enroll the largest number of full-time Black undergraduates nationally, there was increased proportional Black enrollment between 1968 and 1972 in all regions of the country (except the South and Far West).

A limitation of OCR regional data is that, within a region, institutions differed in the number of Blacks enrolled. Indeed, the point was made in *Adams v. Richardson*, that in 10 southern and southeastern states where Black enrollment was most numerous, Black students were not evenly spread out over the institutions within each state. In Region IV, for example, Blacks were 15.6% of all undergraduates enrolled within the region in 1972. (Nationally, Blacks were 8.4% of all undergraduates in 1972.) But, as the *Adams v. Richardson* case decided, the states in Region IV, in addition to states in Region III, maintained dual racial systems of public higher education. Thus, equal access did not exist for Black students.

The importance of *Adams v. Richardson* for assessing the impact of Title VI of the Civil Rights Act of 1964 is that enforcement of the law may have contributed to increased Black enrollment within the regions as seen in Table 2-2. But the current enforcement practices had not removed access, distribution, or persistence barriers due to race constructed by individual institutions within each region or state. (For further discussion of the limitations of current Title VI enforcement see *The Federal Civil Rights Enforcement Effort 1974, Volume III, To Ensure Equal Educational Opportunity*, by the U.S. Commission on Civil Rights, January 1975.)

Further limitations of OCR data are that not all higher educational institutions were required to report their racial enrollments, and that not all institutions were covered by Title VI in 1972; however, 2,666 colleges (or 92.7% of the covered institutions) were included in the OCR Fall 1972 enrollment report. In addition, the problems involved in conducting a racial census that was tied to civil rights law enforcement undoubtedly introduced some error into the reported enrollment figures. If institutions were to err in reporting the number of Blacks enrolled, it would be in their self-interest to err in favor of inflating, rather than deflating, Black enrollment, a point discussed in Chapter 1 above.

Unfortunately, data were not collected by OCR on other aspects of Title VI enforcement. Educational barriers that had adverse racial impacts (such as financial aid practices, recruitment and housing practices, counseling and guidance services, and other aspects of institutional response that affected not only access, but also distribution and persistence) were not collected as part of Title VI monitoring. When

TABLE 5-3. Full-Time Undergraduate Black Enrollment by Region of the Country, Fall 1968, 1970, and 1972.

Region[1]	Number Blacks Enrolled			Percent Blacks Within Region			Percent Blacks of all Enrolled		
	1968	1970	1972	1968	1970	1972	1968	1970	1972
I	4,067	8,590	13,180	1.9	2.7	3.5	1.9	2.6	2.8
II	4,891	31,431	52,997	2.8	6.1	8.8	2.3	9.5	11.4
III	31,481	41,000	59,211	9.5	9.5	9.9	15.0	12.4	12.7
IV	78,359	98,938	120,351	16.1	14.1	15.6	37.5	29.9	25.9
V	27,635	56,160	88,213	4.3	5.0	7.4	13.2	17.0	19.0
VI	37,026	48,069	67,882	10.8	9.6	11.7	17.7	14.5	14.6
VII	6,927	10,504	14,034	2.8	3.4	3.9	3.3	3.2	3.0
VIII	1,057	2,051	2,510	0.8	1.1	1.2	0.5	0.6	0.5
IX	15,405	30,328	41,117	6.0	5.0	6.0	7.4	9.2	8.8
X	2,357	3,580	5,239	1.5	1.7	2.1	1.1	1.1	1.1
TOTAL	209,205	330,651	464,734	7.1	6.8	8.4	100.0	100.0	100.0

SOURCE: Office for Civil Rights (DHEW), *Racial and Ethnic Enrollment Data From Institutions of Higher Education, Fall 1972.* (1975) Section 11-1 and Section 12-1.

[1] See Table A-11 in Appendix A for list of states in each region.

in-depth compliance studies of individual colleges were done, an interview schedule prepared by OCR asked questions about possible educational barriers to equal educational opportunity. However, routine collection and analysis of data on educational barriers were not included as part of Title VI enforcement.

Education Amendments of 1972

Of the programs in the Education Amendments of 1972, the student assistance programs, which included the Guaranteed Student Loan, Basic Educational Opportunity Grants, Supplemental Educational Opportunity Grants, National Direct Student Loans, and College Work-Study programs were the major higher education programs. These programs in Fiscal Year 1973 received 69.4% of the appropriated $1,287.2 million for higher education programs administered by USOE. The next year, FY 1974, these same programs received 76% of the $1,763.68 million appropriated for Higher Education Programs administered by USOE. The largest increase between FY 1973 and 1974 was in appropriations for BEOGs, which in the first year of operation, FY 1973, was $122.1 million, but was increased to $475.74 million the following fiscal year. (The funds appropriated for FY 1973 were spent in the 1973-74 academic year for the student assistance programs.)

Table A-2 in Appendix A gives FY 1973 and 1974 appropriations for all higher education programs administered by USOE. Tables A-3 and A-4 describe the programs and appropriation levels for higher education programs administered by other federal offices outside of DHEW.

In the discussion that follows, participation of Blacks in the federal student assistance programs is described. Because of their significance in higher education funding and their legislative intent to remove financial barriers, BOEG, SEOG, NDSL, CW-S, and GSLP were analyzed as facilitators of opportunities for Blacks in higher education. First, however, census data on what college costs are for Black and white independent and dependent students are summarized. As was discussed in the previous chapter on financial aid practices, the estimated median cost of education for financially dependent and independent full-time students differed as to function not only of the type of institution attended, but also the race of the student (U.S. Census, 1975). Except for four-year colleges, independent Black students in the 1973-74 school year reported greater personal expenses than did their white counterparts attending the same type of institution. Thus, independent white students may have received greater financial assistance from public or private sources than did their Black counterparts. Similarly, dependent Black students may have received greater financial aid from public or private sources than did dependent white students in meeting college costs.

The differences in the reported college costs of Black and white students attending the same types of institutions require further study. Of special interest here was the extent to which these differences in college costs reflected differences in participation in federal student assistance programs or other types of financial aid.

If the allocation of federal financial aid did contribute to the differences in the costs of college for Black and white dependent and independent students, then the definition of independence and other criteria for qualifying for aid becomes important. Federal student assistance programs were open to both independent and dependent students in financial need in 1973. The newly emancipated students from wealthy families could compete with dependent and independent low-income students for the federal student aid dollars. The impact that newly emancipated wealthy students may have had on the equal educational opportunities of Blacks and other disadvantaged students requires special study. In the following discussion, the participation of Black and other students in each of the federal student assistance programs is described without regard to their family income or independence.

Basic Educational Opportunity Grants Program (BEOGs)

The student-based BEOGs program began operation in the 1973-74 academic year. According to a special U.S. Census survey, of the estimated 3,643,000 college students who had heard of BEOGs, 88% were white and 10% were Black. And of the 733,000 who applied for BEOGs, 81% were white and 18% were Black. (See Figures 5-1 and 5-2.)

Approximately 19% of the white and 36% of the Black college students who had heard of BEOGs actually applied for grants. Based on full-time first-year enrollment, Black applicants for BEOGs equaled 84.6% of the Black first-year enrollment while white applicants equaled 38.2%. (See Table 5-4.)

The greatest number of college students, regardless of race, who had heard of the BEOGs program were between the ages of 16 and 21. (See Tables 5-5 and 5-6.) White students in universities were more likely to have heard of the BEOGs than other white students enrolled in Fall 1973. For Blacks such differences did not emerge. (See Table 5-7.) With the exception of older Black and white students attending two-year colleges, as student age increased the likelihood of having heard of BEOGs decreased.

Because the BEOGs survey was limited to enrolled college students, we cannot fully describe the size of the group that actually heard of and applied for BEOGs. In addition, income data on the college students in the BEOGs survey were not available; therefore, it is not possible to determine whether college students with the greatest financial need were also the most likely ones to have heard of or applied for BEOGs.

According to racial data in the special U.S. Census survey, Black first-year college students were probably more likely than white students to have heard of and applied for BEOGs, in 1973. Of all Black college students, age 16 to 21, regardless of year in college, an estimated 5.4% to 6% had heard of BEOGs, and 23 to 43% had applied for grants. In contrast, of all white students in this age range, 40 to 45% had heard of BEOGs, and between 9 and 21% had applied for grants. (Because of the standard errors resulting from the small sample size in the survey, greater precision in the data was not possible. Therefore, ranges rather than signal numbers are reported here.)

In addition to who heard of and applied for BEOGs, how they heard about the

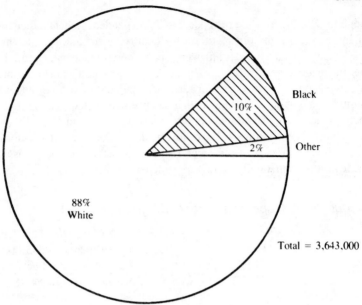

SOURCE: U.S. Census, (1975), Unpublished.

FIGURE 5-1. Percent of College Students (16 Years and Older) Who Have Heard of BEOGs by Race, October 1973.

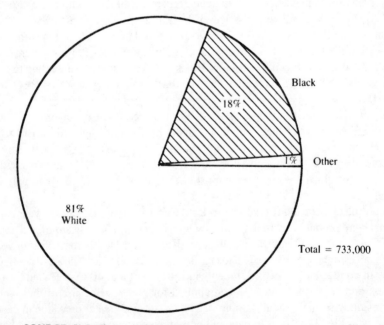

SOURCE: U.S. Census, (1975), Unpublished data.

FIGURE 5-2. Percent of College Students (16 Years and Older) Who Applied for BEOGs by Race, October 1973.

program was important because the participation rate in the first year of the BEOG program was lower than what was anticipated by the program planners. One-third of all college students who knew of BEOGs learned about the BEOG program through their colleges. College offices, high school counselors, and public communication (radio or television or mail) were the three most common means of learning about BEOGs. The least effective means were the state employment offices and post office displays. Moreover, neither the race of the student nor the type of institution attended appeared to determine significantly how students heard about BEOGs. (See Table 5-8.)

Unless the college students had access to a high school counselor or to a college admissions or financial aid officer, the chances of learning about the BEOGs program

TABLE 5-4. BEOGs Applicants as Percent of all First-Year Full-Time College Students and all High School Graduates by Race, Fall 1973.

	RACE	
	BLACK	*WHITE*
Number of BEOGs applicants	131,940	593,730
Number of full-time first-year students	155,900	1,551,100
Percent of full-time first-year students and BEOGs applicants	84.6%	38.3%

SOURCE: Institute for the Study of Educational Policy Staff (1975).

TABLE 5-5. Number of Black College Students Who Had Heard of BEOGs by Age, and Type of Institution Attended, Fall 1973. (Numbers in Thousands)

Type of Institution	*AGE*				
	TOTAL	*16 to 21*	*22 to 24*	*25 to 34*	*35 & Above*
All Colleges					
Heard of BEOGs	375	214	65	56	40
Not Heard of BEOGs	238	102	32	67	37
Total	613	316	97	123	77
Universities					
Heard of BEOGs	171	100	39	19	13
Not Heard of BEOGs	100	45	9	32	14
Total	271	145	48	51	27
4-Year Colleges					
Heard of BEOGs	97	60	19	11	7
Not Heard of BEOGs	46	22	9	8	7
Total	143	82	28	19	14
2-Year Colleges					
Heard of BEOGs	107	54	7	26	20
Not Heard of BEOGs	92	35	14	27	16
Total	199	89	21	53	36

SOURCE: U.S. Census, (1975), Unpublished data.

TABLE 5-6. Number of White College Students Who Had Heard of BEOGs by Age, and Type of Institution Attended, Fall 1973. (Numbers in Thousands)

Type of Institution		AGE			
	TOTAL	16 to 21	22 to 24	25 to 34	35 & Above
All Colleges					
Heard of BEOGs	3,206	1,799	483	618	395
Not Heard of BEOGs	4,021	2,151	615	880	375
Total	7,227	3,950	1,098	1,498	681
Universities					
Heard of BEOGs	1,787	948	322	375	142
Not Heard of BEOGs	2,160	1,162	381	466	151
Total	3,947	2,110	703	841	293
4-Year Colleges					
Heard of BEOGs	664	440	83	87	54
Not Heard of BEOGs	827	519	106	129	73
Total	1,491	959	189	216	127
2-Year Colleges					
Heard of BEOGs	755	411	78	156	110
Not Heard of BEOGs	1,034	470	128	285	151
Total	1,789	881	206	441	261

SOURCE: U.S. Census, (1975), Unpublished data.

TABLE 5-7. Proportion of College Students 16 to 21 Years Old Who Applied for BEOGs by Type of Institution and Race, Fall 1973.

Type of Institution	White	Black	Difference (White-Black)
Number	374,000	92,000	282,000
*Total	100.0	100.0%	—
University	53.0%	39.0%	14.0%
Four-Year College	32.0	37.0	–5.0
Two-Year College	14.0	24.0	–10.0

SOURCE: U.S. Census, Unpublished data.
*May not equal 100% due to rounding.

were limited. Because almost one-half of the first-year Black college students, unlike the white students, in Fall 1973 were not recent high school graduates, the methods used to disseminate information about BEOGs could adversely affect Black access.

According to another U.S. Census survey, 18% of the 105,000 awards made in the BEOGs program went to Black post-secondary students. (See Table E-11 in Appendix E.) The number of BEOG awards to Blacks in Fall 1973 equaled 12.1% of the Black first-year college enrollment. Thus, while 84.6% of the full-time first-year Black college students could have applied for BEOGs, which is encouraging, only 12.1% of them could have received BEOGs grants. How well the total number of Black BEOGs applicants and recipients reflected the number of needy Black college

TABLE 5-8. How College Students Heard About BEOGs by the Type of Institution Attended, October, 1973.

	PERCENT			
	University	Four-Year College	Two-Year College	Total
All Races				
Through mail	9.0	11.0	8.0	9.0
Post Office Display	5.4	6.2	5.5	6.0
State Employment Service	2.0	2.0	3.0	2.0
Radio or TV	12.0	9.3	13.0	12.0
College Office	37.5	39.3	36.5	38.0
H.S. Counselor	19.0	21.0	20.0	19.4
Pre-college Program	4.0	3.0	4.2	3.4
Other sources	13.0	9.0	11.1	12.0
*Total	100.0%	100.0%	100.0%	100.0%
Black Only				
Through mail	9.4	14.4	6.4	10.0
Post Office Display	5.0	6.3	6.0	5.3
State Employment Service	3.0	4.0	3.0	3.2
Radio or TV	14.2	9.2	8.3	11.5
College Office	31.1	43.1	46.2	38.0
H.S. Counselor	19.0	13.0	17.0	17.0
Pre-college Program	10.0	6.3	8.0	8.3
Other Sources	9.4	4.0	6.4	7.3
*Total	100.0%	100.0%	100.0%	100.0%

SOURCE: U.S. Census, (1975), Unpublished data.
*May not equal 100% due to rounding.

students in the undergraduate availability pool is unknown; such analysis must await improved and expanded data collection. Based on enrollment, however, only a small proportion of the Black first-year college students were aided by BEOGs grants in the 1973-74 academic year. Of all Blacks who applied for BEOGs that year, only 20.6% could have received them.

SEOG, College Work-Study, NDSL

With the exception of the Basic Educational Opportunity Grants Program, the other student assistance programs were campus-based and operational before the 1973-74 school year. Between 1968 and 1970, Black students went from 14% of the students receiving financial assistance from SEOGs, CW-S, and NDSL programs in FY 1968 to 16% in FY 1969 and 18% in FY 1970, according to the U.S. Office of Education. (See Table A-12 in Appendix A and Table 5-9 below.) During those years, Black students were less than 10% of the total college enrollment.

The growth rate of participation by Blacks in these federal student assistance programs between 1968 and 1970 was 48%. These gains in Black participation in these federal programs should be assessed in the context of overall Black college enrollment growth and the accompanying increased financial need. Total Black

**TABLE 5-9. Participation in SEOGs, College Work-Study, and NDSL
by Race, Fiscal Years 1968 Through 1970.**

	FISCAL YEARS			
All Students	1968	1969	1970	TOTAL
Black	94,278	115,026	140,875	350,179
American Indian	1,740	2,669	3,340	7,749
Asian American	4,586	6,576	7,728	18,890
Spanish Surnamed	17,996	28,900	28,900	75,796
White (incl. other)	574,229	588,772	591,832	1,754,833
TOTAL	692,829	741,943	772,672	2,207,444
	Percents Across Races			
Black	13.6	16.0	18.0	16.0
American Indian	.3	.4	.4	.3
Asian America	.7	.9	1.0	.9
Spanish Surnamed	2.6	4.0	3.7	3.4
White (incl. other)	82.9	79.4	76.6	79.4
TOTAL*	100.0%	100.0%	100.0%	100.0%

SOURCE: U.S.O.E. (DHEW) *Institutional Fiscal Operations Report for Federal Student Financial Aid Programs.*
*May not equal 100% due to rounding.

college enrollment increased by about 40% between the late 1960s and early 1970s,
according to U.S. Census data. One result of this increased enrollment was increased
financial need, because increasing numbers of Black college students came from
low-income families (U.S. Census, 1974). As more Black students entered college,
the need for financial assistance such as that provided by the federal programs
increased.

Tables 5-10 and 5-11 summarize the type of federal assistance Black and white
students received in FY 1968 and 1970. In all fiscal years Black students were more
likely to receive assistance through the College Work-Study Program (either alone or
combined with SEOGs or NDSL) while whites were more likely to be in the NDSL
program (either alone or combined with another federal program).

Participation in SEOGs was low for both Black and white students in FY 1968
through 1970. Although the numbers were small, Black students were more likely
than their white counterparts to have received SEOGs in the early years of the
program.

The significant difference in the type of assistance Black and white college students
received was their participation in NDSL. This loan program whether alone or in
combination with another federal program, was used more often to assist white
students. Black students in FY 1968 through 1970 were more likely to receive either
work or grant assistance.

Data on the number of awards to Blacks in College Work-Study, SEOG, and
NDSL from FY 1968 through 1973 are summarized in Table 5-12. Since some
students received a financial aid package that included two or more student assistance

TABLE 5-10. Financial Assistance to Black Students by Type of Program, Fiscal Years 1968 Through 1970.

| Type of Assistance | FISCAL YEARS (In Percents) | | | |
	1968	1969	1970	TOTAL
College Work-Study Only	32.1	26.2	25.0	27.2
SEOG Only	10.5	13.0	10.4	11.1
NDSL Only	21.2	15.2	14.0	16.3
College Work-Study and SEOG	4.0	7.4	12.0	8.3
College Work-Study and NDSL	8.4	8.0	8.1	8.0
SEOG AND NDSL	14.6	17.2	15.5	16.1
Work-Study, SEOG, and NDSL	9.2	13.0	15.0	13.0
TOTAL*	100.0% (94,278)	100.0% (115,026)	100.0% (140,875)	100.0% (350,179)

SOURCE: Tables A-12 and 5-9.

*May not equal 100% due to rounding.

TABLE 5-11. Financial Assistance to White Students by Type of Program, Fiscal Years 1968 Through 1970.

| Type of Assistance | FISCAL YEARS (In Percents) | | | |
	1968	1969	1970	TOTAL
College Work-Study Only	27.2	29.1	30.0	28.2
SEOG Only	6.2	6.0	5.0	5.7
NDSL Only	37.2	33.5	33.0	34.5
College Work-Study and SEOG	2.3	3.2	5.1	4.0
College Work-Study and NDSL	8.1	3.2	5.1	4.0
SEOG and NDSL	13.2	14.5	11.4	13.0
Work-Study SEOG and NDSL	6.0	7.3	7.0	7.0
TOTAL*	(574,229) (100%)	(588,772) (100%)	(591,832) (100%)	(1,754,833) (100%)

SOURCE: Tables A-12 and 5-9.

*May not equal 100% due to rounding.

programs, the total number of *awards* across all three programs is higher than the number of *students* actually assisted.

More awards were made under NDSL and College Work-Study than under SEOG in all Fiscal Years. The largest average award in FY 1973 was in NDSL, followed by SEOG. (See Table 5-1.) The proportion of the total number of awards that went to Black students in all fiscal years is plotted in Figure 5-3. The Black proportion of all awards in SEOGs went from 18% in FY 1968 to 34% in FY 1973. The Black proportion of College Work-Study awards went from 16% in FY 1968 to 31% in FY 1973. But, the Black proportion of NDSL awards went from 12% in FY 1968, to 22% in FY 1973. Thus, Black participation remained relatively low in NDSL.

For all three programs, the percent of awards to Blacks exceeded the percentage to all other students enrolled. While Black participation has increased, were either the levels of participation or the amounts received sufficient to meet the financial need of Black students?

As a percent of 242,000 dependent Black college students with family incomes under $7,500, the number of awards to Blacks under College Work-Study in Fiscal Year 1973 would accommodate 66% of the Blacks enrolled in October 1972. The number of awards to Blacks under SEOGs and NDSL would cover 35% and 59% respectively of all low-income dependent Black students enrolled. Thus, Work-Study and loans were the types of aid in which Black participation could have served the greatest number of low-income students in 1972.

For whites, the number of students who received awards in the College Work-Study Program in FY 1973 would accommodate 41.2% of the 755,000 white students from families with incomes under $7,500 SEOG and NDSL awards to whites would accommodate 23.2% and 57.2% respectively of all low-income whites (under $7,500) enrolled in college in October 1972.

Figure 5-4 illustrates the distribution of all 1,211,000 low-income dependent college students (under $7,500) by race in Fall 1972 in comparison to their participation in SEOGs, NDSL, and College Work-Study in 1973. Black participation in NDSL and College Work-Study was about equal to their proportion of the total low-income enrollment; but Black participation in SEOGs exceeded their proportion of low-income enrollment. For white students, only NDSL approached their proportional low-income enrollment. For the other ethnic groups, participation in SEOGs, CW-S, and NDSL exceeded their proportion of the total low-income enrollment.

Guaranteed Student Loan Program (GSLP)

Borrowers

Loans under GSLP were made by colleges, banks, and state agencies in the program. Some data were available on the number and size of insured loans to Black students in post-secondary education and their default rate. In FY 1973, of the 576,720 federally insured loans, 73% went to white students, 14% to Blacks, and 13% to others. In the state program, of the 95,333 loans, 80% went to white students, 10% to Black, and 10% to other students, according to USOE (1974).

In both the federal and state operated programs, the average size of the loans to

TABLE 5-12. Awards in College Work-Study, SEOG, and NDSL by Race of Recipient, Fiscal Years 1968, 1969, 1970, 1972, and 1973.

Student Assistance Program	1968 n	1968 %	1969 n	1969 %	FISCAL YEARS 1970[1] n	1970[1] %	1972[1] n	1972[1] %	1973[1] n	1973[1] %
College Work-Study										
Black	50,442	16	62,452	18	83,654	21	143,914	29	161,000	29
White	249,313	80	272,871	77	301,296	74	277,904	56	311,000	56
Other	13,176	4	20,686	5	22,579	5	74,439	15	84,000	15
Total	312,931	100	355,009	100	407,502	100	496,257	100	556,000	100
SEOGs										
Black	36,152	18	58,649	23	74,762	29	105,722	33	113,000	34
White	157,279	78	180,821	71	164,840	64	172,999	54	175,000	53
Other	8,463	4	16,755	6	19,033	7	41,648	13	43,000	13
Total	201,894	100	256,225	100	258,635	100	320,369	100	331,000	100
NDSL										
Black	50,552	12	61,963	14	74,563	16	135,596	21	144,000	22
White	368,752	85	372,346	82	357,622	79	432,616	67	432,000	66
Other	12,618	3	18,696	4	19,765	5	77,484	12	79,000	12
Total	431,922	100	453,005	100	451,950	100	645,696	100	655,000	100

SOURCE: Table A-12 in Appendix A and Division of Student Support and Special Programs, USOE (unpublished data).

[1] Preliminary data.

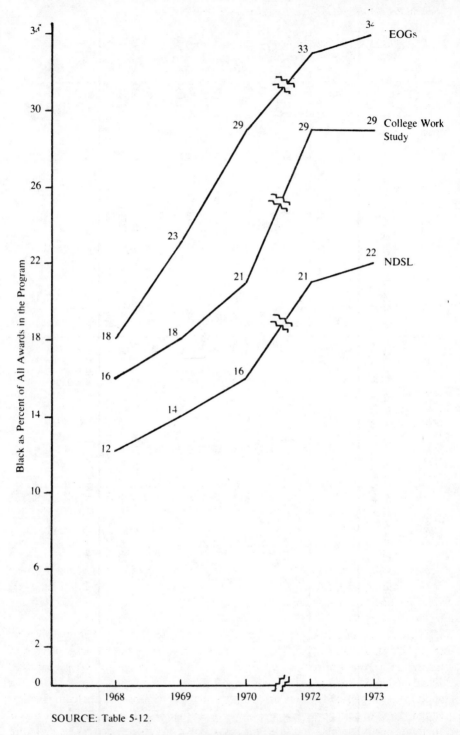

SOURCE: Table 5-12.

FIGURE 5-3. Percent of Awards to Black College Students in SEOGs, College Work-Study, and NDSL in Fiscal Years 1968, 1969, 1970, 1972, and 1973.

TABLE 5-13. Average Student Loan Amounts for Blacks and Whites for Fiscal Years 1968 through 1973 in the Federally Insured Student Loan Program.

Fiscal Year	White	Black	Difference (Black-White)
1968	$ 749	$710	$39
1969	826	746	80
1970	911	853	58
1971	959	936	23
1972	967	909	58
1973	1,040	988	52

SOURCE: U.S. Office of Education. *Guaranteed Student Loan Program*, Chapter VIII, "Loan and Borrower Characteristics (FISLP)," p. VII-22.

TABLE 5-14. Average Student Loan Amounts for Blacks and Whites in Fiscal Years 1967 Through 1973 in the State Guaranteed Agency Programs.

Fiscal Year	White	Black	Difference (Black-White)
1967	$ 728	$ 524	$204
1968	818	567	251
1969	856	649	207
1970	864	649	215
1971	921	760	161
1972	992	938	54
1973	1,139	1,034	105
1974			

SOURCE: U.S. Office of Education, *Guaranteed Student Loan Program*, Chapter X, "State Guarantee Agency Loan and Student Borrower Characteristics," p. x-19.

whites was larger than those to Blacks each year of the program. (See Tables 5-13 and 5-14.) In total, of $557,105,000 in federally insured loans, $79,772,108 (or 14%) went for loans to Blacks. In the state-insured loan program, of the $107,440,291 insured in FY 1973, $8,941,954 (or 8%) went for loans to Blacks.

The meaning of this is unclear for Blacks in higher education because all post-secondary students are treated together. Loan data controlled by costs or type of institution were not provided by USOE. In addition, how well the loans received actualy covered need is also unknown, based on available data from USOE. In applying for loans, students indicated other sources of financial aid (including family) and the costs of college attendance. The difference between costs and resources was an unmet need. Students applied for loans to cover this unmet need. Whether or not the dollar amounts of actual loans approved equaled the unmet need was unknown. In both the state and federal student loan programs, lending institutions were not

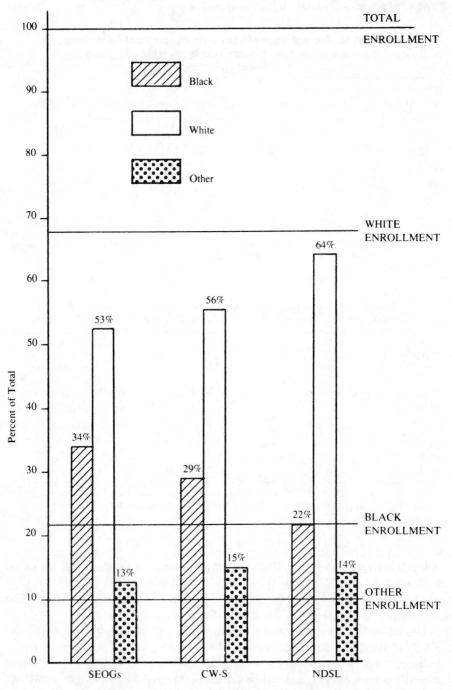

SOURCE: U.S. Census, *Social and Economic Characteristics of Students: October 1972*, Table 12.

FIGURE 5-4. Participation in SEOGs, CW-S, and NDSL in FY 1973 in Comparison to Low-Income (Under $7,500) Dependent College Enrollment in Fall 1972 by Race.

required to report: (a) the number of rejected student loan applications, (b) the number of rejected Black applicants, or (c) the amount of rejected loan requests.

That the average loans to Blacks were smaller than those to whites has raised questions. One possible explanation is that Blacks attended less costly institutions and thus had less financial need than white students. According to ACE data, the size of the average federally insured loan to full-time freshmen varied with the type and control of the institution attended and with family income, but not with the race of the borrower. In Fall 1973, wealthier freshmen received larger average loans than poorer students attending the same type of institution. In addition, students in more expensive private colleges had larger loans than those in less costly institutions. These data, however, included all federally insured loans, not just GSLP. In spite of this limitation, the data offered some description of the borrowing behavior of entering freshmen in Fall 1973.

Using the midpoint of the ranges for the amount borrowed, and using $5,000 for the top range, the estimated amount of money borrowed by freshmen, whether through GSLP or NDSL or both, was calculated. At each family income level, public college freshmen borrowed less on the average than private college freshmen. (See Table 5-15.) Also, as family income increased, freshmen, on the average, were likely to borrow more money. This suggests that individual private college students and individuals from higher income groups were relying on the federal loan programs to cover more of their college costs than were either public college students or those from low-income groups.

Racial differences in the estimated average amount borrowed were smaller among public college students than private college students. With the exception of "other minority" groups, Black and white students differed only slightly in the amount of money borrowed. "Other minority" students, however, tended to borrow the least amount of money when compared with white or Black freshmen from similar family incomes attending the same type of institution.

The GSLP program was initially conceived as a means of facilitating distribution of the middle class into private colleges. In 1973, however, although the size of the federally insured loans were, on the average smaller, entering full-time freshmen from low-income groups and Black freshmen were more likely to use loans than were higher-income students to meet some of their college costs (Holstrom and Smith, 1974). Consequently, more low-income Black freshmen accumulated debt after only one year of college than did either white or wealthier freshmen. (The distributions of the federal loans to full-time freshmen are summarized in Tables E-12 through E-15 in Appendix E.) For each income group, regardless of the type of institution attended, Black students were most likely to have borrowed money to meet college costs. As the costs were reduced, and as family income increased, borrowing declined. Thus, for full-time freshmen from more advantaged families or those attending public colleges, there was a lower debt burden than for other freshmen in 1973.

As can be seen in Figure 5-5, the groups least likely to borrow to meet college costs were "other minority" and white freshmen attending public institutions. The group most likely to borrow were Black freshmen attending private colleges. The effect of family income in reducing the incidence of borrowing was most pronounced for white

TABLE 5-15. Estimated Total and Average Amounts Borrowed in Federal Loans (NDSL and GSLP) Full-Time Freshmen Attending Four-Year Colleges and Universities, by Control of Institution, Family Income, and Race, Fall 1973.

Family Income	Private Colleges			Public Colleges		
	Black	White	Other	Black	White	Other
$5,999 or less						
Total Amount Borrowed	$960,850	$1,586,700	$154,400	$906,350	$1,079,900	$ 57,800
Number of Borrowers	915	1,47.	156	1,080	1 302	75
Average Amount Borrowed	$1,050	$1,076	$989	$839	$829	$770
$6,000 to $9,000						
Total Amount Borrowed	$797 ·'0(	53,662,350	$213,400	$523,800	$2,212,400	$ 67,050
Number of Borrowers	758	3,402	215	398	2 526	89
Average Amount Borrowed	$1,051	$1,076	$992	$875	$875	$753
$10,000 to $14,999						
Total Amount Borrowed	$679,850	$8,167,850	$266,750	$291,450	$4,385,750	$ 89,550
Number of Borrowers	627	7,223	248	229	4,482	103
Average Amount Borrowed	$1,084	$1,130	$1,075	$974	$978	$869
$15,000 and Above						
Total Amount Borrowed	$483,250	$9,256,600	$267,500	$194,700	$3,944,050	$100,500
Number of Borrowers	376	6,768	210	145	3,258	81
Average Amount Borrowed	$1,285	$1,367	$1,273	$1,342	$1,210	$1,240

SOURCE: American Council on Education, CIRP, Freshmen Norms, 1973, unpublished data.

and "other minority" freshmen, and least pronounced for Black freshmen, especially those enrolled in private colleges. Thus, both NDSL and/or GSLP loans were a significant part of the means by which low-income students, especially Blacks attending private institutions, were able to meet college costs.

Defaults

As of May 1974, 91% of all claims (or $225,534,000) in both the federally insured and guarantee (state) agency programs, were paid by loan defaults, especially loans made to students attending proprietary schools. Defaults as of May, 1974 equaled

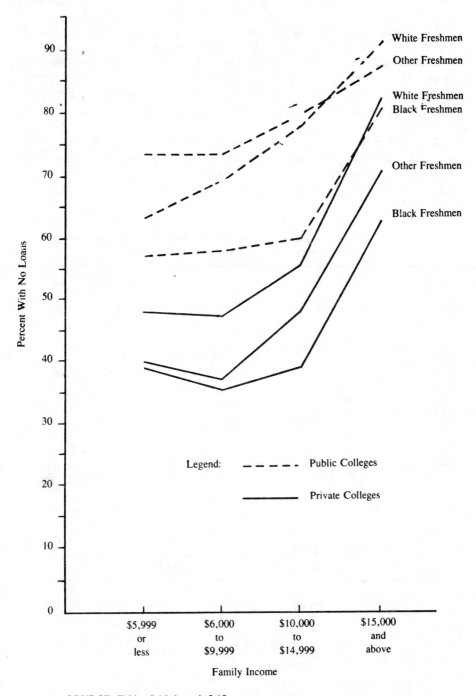

SOURCE: Tables 5-16 through 5-19.

FIGURE 5-5. Distribution of Entering Full-Time Freshmen in Public and Private Four-Year Colleges and Universities With No Loans by Family Income and Race, Fall 1973.

19.8% of the volume ($) of loans made in FY 1974. Bankruptcy, which was higher in the federally insured program than in the state programs, equaled 0.8% of the value of loans made in FY 1974. (See Tables 5-16, 5-17, and 5-18.) Death and disability equaled 1.1% of the volume of loans in FY 1974.

The average amount defaulted was $1,220 as of May 1974. In the federal program, $960 was the average default amount. In the state program $1,170 was defaulted, on the average.

Of special concern was whether Black college students made good borrowers. Recent data from the U.S. Office of Education did not answer this question. In its study of student defaults in GSLP, the USOE did not separate post-secondary school students on the basis of the type of institutions they attended. Consequently, Black

TABLE 5-16. Total Annual Loans Under the Guaranteed Student Loan Program, Fiscal Years 1966 Through 1974.

Year	Volume $	Number	Growth over Prior Fiscal Year Volume	Number
1966	77,492,058	48,495	—	—
1967	248,494,327	330,088	—	—
1968	435,884,721	515,408	75.3	56.1
1969	686,675,781	787,344	57.6	52.8
1970	839,666,044	921,896	22.3	17.1
1971	1,043,933,551	1,081,286	24.3	17.3
1972	1,301,576,723	1,256,299	24.7	16.2
1973	1,198,523,248	1,088,286	−7.9	−13.4
1974*	1,138,640,973	938,342	−5.0	−13.8

SOURCE: U.S. Office of Education, Office of Guaranteed Student Loans, *Monthly Report*, June 1974.

*Preliminary Data.

TABLE 5-17. Claims Paid Summary for the Guaranteed Student Loan Program as of May 1974.

	All Claims	Defaults	Bankruptcy	Death & Disability
Federally Insured Program				
Total Amount	$112,755,000	$102,618,000	$5,292,000	$4,845,000
Percent of Total	100%	91%	4.7%	4.3%
Guarantee Agency Program				
Total Amount	$134,628,000	$122,916,000	$4,054,000	$7,658,000
Percent of Total	100%	91.3%	3.0%	5.7%

SOURCE: U.S. Office of Education, Office of Guaranteed Student Loans, *Monthly Report*, June 1974

**TABLE 5-18. Claims Paid as of May 1974 as Percent of
the Volume ($) of Guaranteed Student Loans in FY 1974.**

	$	*Percent of Loan Volume ($)* *($1,138,640,973)*
All claims	247,383,000	21.7
Defaults	225,534,000	19.8
Bankruptcy	9,346,000	0.8
Death and Disability	12,503,000	1.1

SOURCE: Tables 5-20 and 5-21.

students in proprietary schools were combined with two-year and four-year university Black students. The influence of college costs on the size of the loan, as was found in the ACE study, also was not taken into consideration in the USOE study.

Black students in post-secondary schools accounted for 22% of the defaults and 14% of the loans in the federal program in FY 1973; they accounted for 13% of the defaults and 10% of the loans in the state program in the same year.

Careful analysis of the USOE default data indicated that most Black defaulters were proprietary school students, not higher education students. There were several causes for defaulting: graduates were unable to find work and to repay on time; lenders differed in the vigor with which they attempted to collect the loans; students felt cheated if they dropped out of the programs or the programs were terminated or misrepresented to them by the school. Based on such data it appeared that defaults, like size of loans, depended on the type of institution attended.

Federal Responsibility in Graduate and Professional Education of Minorities

Federal activity in graduate and professional education is based primarily on the national need and public interest. When the national security was thought to be threatened, the federal government supported research and training of scientists and technicians in defense-related fields. When manpower shortages threatened the schools, the federal government supported programs to increase the supply of trained educators. And, when the distribution of trained medical personnel was such that people in rural and low-income neighborhoods were without adequate health care, the federal government supported medical students interested in working in poorly served areas. When the public interest and the nation's needs (as opposed to local) are deemed sufficient to warrant federal action, federal programs have been created. These federal programs supported graduate and professional training in such fields as Education, Engineering, Medicine, and National and Physical Sciences.

As was pointed out in Chapter 2, Blacks (and other minorities) are underrepresented in all academic fields and professions at the graduate level. The recurring question in all discussions of the federal role in graduate and professional opportunities for minorities is: Is it in the national interest to increase access, distribution, and persistence of minorities in graduate and professional fields? Those who answer "Yes" generally based their discussion on the moral necessity of assisting minorities, especially Blacks, because of past and enduring patterns of racial discrimination. Their argument focuses on low minority enrollment in graduate and professional schools. Those who answer "No" generally based their discussion on the oversupply of highly trained manpower in the labor force. For them, the problem is not one of increasing the number of minorities in graduate and professional schools, but of the oversupply of highly trained people and its effect on the labor market. Their argument tends to focus on labor market needs and the well-being of the economy as a whole. Both positions have merit.

In this report it is contended that, accepting academic standards of excellence, federal support for minorities in graduate and professional education is justified and necessary in order to expand the supply of highly trained workers who are aware of and sensitive to the problems confronting the society. In this way, the federal government could facilitate the access and distribution of minorities to leadership positions in the society. Federal support is needed to expand the supply of able students, of sufficiently varied backgrounds, to conceive as yet untried alternative solutions to pressing social problems. There is a shortage, not in the number of credentialed people per se, but in the number of credentialed people who have the insight and sensitivity necessary to provide leadership in solving the problems of the cities, the reservations, and rural pockets of poverty—a shortage of credentialed people who share the same racial, ethnic, and cultural backgrounds as those who disproportionately bear the brunt of the unsolved social and economic problems. There is also a shortage of highly trained personnel who can develop curricular offerings and course materials appropriate for addressing the societal problems from a new perspective, with sensitivity and understanding. And there is a shortage of highly trained people who can serve as models of success and can give emotional support to the disadvantaged high school students and discouraged minority undergraduates.

The cause of these manpower shortages is the lack of equal educational opportunity. In its recent report on federal policy alternatives toward graduate education, the National Board on Graduate Education (1975) concluded:

> Minorities largely attend colleges where graduate study is not encouraged, and they are often unfamiliar with careers based on graduate education and regard these careers as not open to them. Moreover, the stability of our society does depend in part on our making progress in raising the proportion of minority people pursuing certain careers for which graduate education is prerequisite, and only by increasing their numbers in the professions will we be able to tap a large reservoir of unused talent.
>
> Examples of two professional fields where minorities are underrepresented are medicine and college teaching. Unless the proportion of minority persons in these fields rises, our society will be worse off. This will be especially so if we continue to insist on affirmative action programs for college faculties, without ensuring an adequate supply of trained minorities to make such programs viable. (p. 49)

The major by-product of increased minority participation in graduate and professional training is the spread of effect of minority leaders with advanced training. That is, the type of expertise that minorities bring as instructors and as graduate students would be shared with non-minority instructors and graduate students. The ideas minorities bring, therefore, would spread and could become part of the organized body of knowledge, part of the curricula, the theories, the values, and the methodology that shape advanced training in a discipline.

While we do not contend that having more Black Ph.D.s in and of itself will solve urban ghetto problems, or that having native American technicians will alone solve the problems on Indian reservations, or that Black professors alone would automatically revise long-standing curricula, we do contend that one cause contributing to the persistence of these societal problems has been the lack of minority perspective and sensitivity in the training and practice of professionals and experts. It is in the public interest to meet this national need by creating programs for equal educational opportunities to graduate and professional education for Blacks and other disadvantaged groups.

Of the barriers to equal educational opportunity, the greatest is financial; for the people most likely to be able to solve the pressing social problems are also those least able to afford the cost of graduate and professional training. Addressing financial barriers of minorities can and should be done without threatening the academic standards of graduate and professional schools. As was pointed out in the discussion of financial barriers in Chapter 3, family income and college costs severely limit opportunities of able Black undergraduates for graduate and professional training. Federal student aid programs could fill this void and make talented minorities from disadvantaged backgrounds part of the solution to our social problems rather than part of the problems themselves.

Beyond rigorous enforcement of Title VI of the Civil Rights Act of 1964, federal student aid programs are needed for minority access, distribution, and persistence in all fields of graduate and professional study, including Education. Blacks and other minorities are needed as lawyers, administrators, doctors, college teachers, program and budget planners, and as specialists, such as economists, chemists, architects, and systems analysts, who can integrate their advanced training with their unique social and cultural experiences.

The federal government could do much to insure equal educational opportunities for Blacks and other minorities in graduate and professional schools by removing financial barriers, through a combination of institution-based grants, loans, and fellowships. Federal student assistance packages for minorities entering or enrolled in graduate and professional schools are needed. This financial aid package could include the following: (a) flexible grant awards based on financial need, with a maximum annual award of about $5,000 and average annual award of about $3,000; (b) fellowships with provisions for research and teaching assistantships for minority students; (c) cost-of-education allowances to institutions in the program; and (d) guaranteed loans with graduate institutions as the primary leaders.

Specific alternative means of funding federal assistance for graduate and professional education have been proposed by the Carnegie Council on Policy Studies in Higher Education (1975) and the National Board on Graduate Education (1975). All of the approaches they recommend, while not specifically aimed at minority access distribution, or persistence, could be adapted to meet the financial barriers of Blacks and other minorities to advanced training. (In the forthcoming *Minority Participation in Graduate Schools*, the National Board on Graduate Education recommends federally funded programs to increase minority access to graduate schools.)

Summary   •

The Education Amendments of 1972 and the Civil Rights Act of 1964 are federal laws whose combined legislative intent is to increase equal educational opportunity. These policies were designed to function as categorical, education and/or psychosocial facilitators.

On the basis of available data on federal student assistance programs in the Education Amendments of 1972, BEOGs, SEOGs, NDSL, College Work-Study, and GSLP, the number of Blacks participating in these programs was greater than their proportion of the college students enrolled. Compared to the number of needy Black students enrolled, however, the level of Black participation was not high enough to assist all needy Black students. These programs did assist more than half of them, and met some of the financial needs of Black college students.

Black college students were most likely to have received SEOGs and College Work-Study assistance; whites were most likely to have received NDSL support. In the guaranteed loan programs (NDSL and GSLP combined), Black and low-income freshmen were more frequent borrowers than other students. However, the larger loans went to the wealthier students, regardless of institution or race. Data on defaults of college students in GSLP were not available. Defaults as of May 1974 equaled $225,534,000, or 21.7% of the loan volume of that year.

The influence of the Civil Rights Act of 1964 enforcement contributed to the increased access of Blacks to previously all-white college campuses. However, within states and regions of the country, the access of Blacks to colleges remained unequal. In addition, current enforcement of the Civil Rights Act of 1964 did not include the routine collection and analysis of data on educational practices and policies that could adversely affect Black access, distribution, and persistence. In the area in which there had been enforcement, entering enrollment, there was increased proportional Black enrollment between 1968 and 1972 nationally.

Taken as a whole, both the legislative intent and the program operation of the Education Amendments of 1972 and the Civil Eights Act of 1964 positively influenced equal education opportunity for Blacks in higher education, especially in undergraduate school. Federal student assistance, with the exception of the loan programs, was aimed primarily at removing financial barriers to undergraduate, rather than graduate or professional, schools. Thus, while categorical barriers to advanced training may be reduced through vigorous enforcement of Title VI of the Civil Rights Act of 1964, financial barriers to graduate and professional schools remain.

The role of the federal government in facilitating access, distribution, and persistence of Blacks and other minorities in graduate and professional schools is currently being debated. The position taken here was that it was in the public interest to facilitate equal educational opportunities for Blacks and other minorities in advanced training. Minorities are needed among the ranks of highly trained professionals because of the understanding, sensitivity, and leadership that they can bring to the solution of societal problems, and because of the nation's commitment to equal educational opportunity, and affirmative action in college employment.

Federal Higher Education Legislation

**TABLE A-1. Summary of Federal Higher Education Laws
Affecting the 1973-74 School Year, in Chronological Order.**

First and Second Morrill Acts of 1862 and 1890 (As Amended)	Donates public lands to several states and territories to provide colleges of agriculture and mechanic arts, provided that no mineral lands are selected. Appropriates to each state a quantity equal to 30,000 acres for each Senator and Representative in Congress based on 1860 Census, to be sold or used for the establishment of public colleges. Authorizes the use of Federal funds to support land-grant colleges, including colleges in the Virgin Islands and Guam.
Bankhead-Jones Act (1935)	Provides for research in agriculture and support for land-grant colleges.
National Defense Education Act of 1958 (As Amended)	Authorizes the use of federal funds to assist post-secondary institutions, including proprietary institutions, in establishing, equipping, and operating undergraduate and graduate centers and programs for teaching modern foreign languages. Also provides stipends to individuals undergoing advanced training in such foreign languages.
Higher Education Facilities Act of 1963 (As Amended)	Authorizes federal aid to public and private non-profit institutions to finance the construction, rehabilitation, or improvement of needed school facilities. Provides loans to institutions for facilities.
Civil Rights Act of 1964 Title IV	Requires that public colleges operated by the state or with public funds properly desegregate. Provides technical assistance to state or local school boards, funds to higher educational institutions to run training institutes, grants to school boards for staff development to resolve desegregation problems.
Civil Rights Act of 1964 Title VI	Requires nondiscrimination on the basis of race, color, or national origin by a contractor under any program or activity receiving federal financial assistance.
Education Professions Development Act Part A (As Amended)	Provides federal funds to state or local educational agencies, higher education institutions, or other public or non-profit agencies to improve the quality of teaching and to help meet critical shortages of adequately trained personnel. Also provides for National Advisory Council on Education Professions Development and periodic appraisal of personnel needs in education by the U.S. Commissioner of Education.
Education Professions Development Act Part B (As Amended)	Establishes the Teacher Corps to attract people into education and to train them as classroom teachers, interns or aids, or as supportive personnel in remedial education, communication

Table A-1 (continued)

	skills, juvenile problems, or basic education. Provides funds to local educational agencies or higher educational institutions to carry out these activities.
Education Professions Development Act Subpart 2 (As Amended)	Provides funds to states that submit a state plan and designate a state agency for administration of the state plan funds to attract and train teachers to meet critical teacher shortages.
Education Professions Development Act Part C (As Amended)	Provides federal funds as fellowships for graduate study in higher educational institutions to individuals who plan to pursue a career in elementary, secondary, or vocational education.
Education Professions Development Act Part E (As Amended)	Provides grants to higher educational institutions to assist in training persons who plan to work as college instructors, administrators, or specialists.
General Education Provisions Act	Provides for the Education Division of the Department of Health, Education and Welfare and related organizational entities. Authorizes funds to post-secondary educational institutions (public and private) to improve educational opportunities by: creation of new institutions and programs, including programs in technology of communications, internal structural and operational changes of post-secondary institutions and other institutional reforms including those in graduate education. Requires that no grants or contracts be made available unless the institution has submitted its proposed program for review and recommendation to the appropriate state commission established under section 1202 of the Higher Education Act of 1965.
Higher Education Act of 1965 Title I (As Amended)	Authorizes the use of federal funds by colleges and universities to assist in the solution of community problems, including continuing and extension education. Provides for allotments to states which designate or create a state agency or institution which has special qualifications with respect to solving community problems, and which is broadly representative of higher educational institutions in the state competent in community service programs. Also provides for direct grants to higher educational institutions to carry out special programs and projects to solve community problems.
Higher Education Act of 1965 Title II (As Amended)	Provides funds to assist the development of libraries, and to increase the number of trained personnel in librarianship, through Basic and Supplemental Grants and through Special Purpose Grants to meet special national or regional needs in library or information sciences. Awards funds to individual or consortia of higher educational institutions.
Higher Education Act of 1965 Title III (As Amended)	Provides for assistance to strengthen developing institutions, defined as 2-year and 4-year colleges and universities, publicly or privately controlled, making reasonable efforts to improve the quality of its teaching and administrative staff, in financial distress, and isolated from the mainstream. Provides funds for cooperative arrangements between developed and developing institutions. Authorizes special consideration to applications from developing institutions for grants and contracts under Titles II, IV, or VII of the Higher Education Act of 1965.
Higher Education Act of 1965 Title IV Part A (Subpart 1) (As Amended)	Provides federal financial assistance to qualified full-time and part-time students attending higher educational institutions.

Table A-1 *(continued)*

	Provides direct financial aid as Basic Educational Opportunity Grants to students, covering no more than one-half of the actual costs of attendance at the institution. Limits Basic Grants to the difference between the expected family contribution for the student and the actual cost of attendance at the institution.
(Subpart 2) (As Amended)	Provides Supplemental Educational Opportunity Grants directly to the higher educational institutions to be disbursed by them to eligible students. Limits grants to one-half of all aid provided by the institution to the student.
(Subpart 3) (As Amended)	Provides matching funds to states to assist them in providing financial aid to students under State Student Incentive Grants. Funds to states are allocated on the basis of student enrollment.
(Subpart 4) (As Amended)	Provides funds for grants and contracts to post-secondary institutions including those with vocational and career educational programs for planning, developing, or carrying out one or more of the following special programs for students from disadvantaged backgrounds: Talent Search, Upward Bound, and Special Services for Disadvantaged Students. Also provides funds for 75 percent of the cost of establishing Educational Opportunity Centers to serve low-income populations seeking post-secondary education.
(Subpart 5) (As Amended)	Provides each higher education institution with annual cost-of-education payments. Payments are based on undergraduate student enrollment and the number receiving Basic Grants (Subpart 1), in addition to a proportion of Supplemental Educational Opportunity Grants, Work-Study payments and loans to students. Also provides for federal payment to institutions offering training for veterans receiving vocational rehabilitation or educational assistance.
Higher Education Act of 1965 Title IV Part C (As Amended)	Stimulates and promotes part-time employment of students with great financial need through the Work-Study Program. Allocates federal money to states so that one-third is based on full-time student enrollment in higher educational institutions in the state; one-third is based on the number of high school graduates; and one-third is based on the number of children under eighteen years old living in families with annual incomes less than $3,000. Also provides matching grants to post-secondary education institutions to assist in the operation of Work-Study Programs. Enables students to work in community service operations of non-profit organizations which receive money from the Federal government. Gives special preference to Vietnam-era veterans in community service Work-Study Programs.
Higher Education Act of 1965 Title IV Part D (As Amended)	Makes Federal grants to higher educational institutions to plan, establish, and carry out Cooperative Education Programs that alternate periods of full-time work with periods of full-time college enrollment. Provides grants for training and research related to cooperative education.
Higher Education Act of 1965 Title IV Part E (As Amended)	Provides for the establishment of Direct Student Loan Programs (originally established 1958). Provides matching funds under this program on the basis of full-time student enrollment in higher educational institutions. Authorizes funds for under-

Table A-1 *(continued)*

graduate, graduate, and professional training programs. Cancels loans in return for services as: full-time school teacher in a school district eligible for Title I assistance under the Elementary and Secondary Education Act of 1965; full-time teacher in a pre-school carried under the Economic Opportunity Act of 1964; full-time teacher of the handicapped; or member of the Armed Forces of the United States in Service who then qualifies for special pay under Section 310 Title 37 of the U.S. Code. Also provides for reduced payment of the loan in varying amounts, depending upon the length and type of service.

Higher Education Act of 1965 Title IV Part F (As Amended)

Defines Higher Education Institution Act to include schools of nursing and proprietary institutions (with the exception of Subpart 5 of Part A and the exception of Part B). Prohibits the award of student assistance funds to individuals convicted by a court of any crime committed after June 30, 1972, which involved the use of force, disruption, or seizure of property under control of the institution. Establishes Advisory Council on Financial Aid to Students.

Higher Education Act of 1965 Title IX Part B (As Amended)

Encourages states and non-profit organizations and institutions to establish adequate loan insurance programs for students in eligible post-secondary educational institutions. Provides a Federal program of student loan insurance for students without reasonable access to state or non-profit institutional programs. Pays a portion of the interest on loans to qualified students made under state-operated or non-profit institution loan program. Guarantees a portion of the loans made under the state student loan program. Establishes a student loan insurance fund to make default payments and to receive loan payments. Limits interest on loans to 7 percent. Requires Commissioner of Education to repay loan defaults due to death or disability of the borrower. Creates a Student Loan Marketing Association, a federally sponsored, privately financed, secondary market and warehouse facility for student loans insured by the federal or state governments or private non-profit organizations.

International Education Act of 1966

Provides grants to higher education institutions and non-profit agencies and organizations individually or in consortia to establish, strengthen, and operate undergraduate comprehensive programs and graduate centers in international studies. Authorizes the use of Federal funds to cover costs of teaching and research resources for international educational centers.

Higher Education Amendments of 1968

Provides that Federal financial aid to students in higher education not be treated as income.

Emergency Insured Student Loan Act of 1969 (As Amended)

Authorizes the Commissioner of Education to pay up to three percent of the average unpaid balance to holders of student loans eligible under Title IV of the Higher Education Act of 1965.

Emergency Assistance for Institutions of Higher Education

Provides direct financial assistance to two-year and four-year colleges and universities which demonstrate extreme financial need. Funds are to be used to help institutions determine the cause of their financial crisis, develop plans to eliminate it, and improve their capability to deal with financial distress.

Table A-1 *(continued)*

Title IX of Education Amendments of 1972 Prohibits discrimination on the basis of sex in participation of, or benefits from, any educational program or activity receiving federal financial assistance. Applies to vocational, professional, graduate, and public undergraduate post-secondary institutions. Does not apply to: educational institutions controlled by a religious organization if application is not consistent with religious tenets; educational institutions whose purpose is to train individuals for military service in the United States, or merchant marines; or public undergraduate schools that traditionally and continually from establishment have admitted only students of one sex.

SOURCE: Committee on Education and Labor, House of Representatives, and Committee on Labor and Public Welfare, U.S. Senate, November 1972, *Compilation of Higher Education Laws, 1972*.

TABLE A-2. Authorized Appropriations for Higher Educational Programs Administered by U.S.O.E., Fiscal Years 1973 and 1974.

Name of Program	Authorized Appropriations (In Millions)		
	FY 1973	FY 1974*	Difference
College Work-Study Program	$270.2	$270.2	$ 0.0
Interest on Insured Loans	245.0	310.0	65.0
Supplemental Educational Opportunity Grants	210.3	210.3	0.0
Basic Educational Opportunity Grants	122.1	475.74	353.64
Educational Professions Development Act:			
Elementary and Secondary Teachers	54.6	46.2	−8.4
Teacher Corps	37.5	37.5	0.0
Fellowships	2.8	1.5	−1.3
Institutes	0.5	0.286	−0.214
Aid to Developing Institutions	87.4	99.9	12.5
Programs for the Disadvantaged (incl. Talent Search, Upward Bound, and Special Services)	67.3	70.3	3.0
Student Loan Insurance Fund	46.6	88.7	42.1
Veterans Cost-Of-Instruction	25.0	23.7	−1.3
College Personnel Development (incl. fellowships for colleges teachers and disadvantaged)	20.0	6.55	−13.45
Land-Grant Colleges	16.0	9.5	−6.5
Community Service and Continuing Educational Programs	15.0	14.2	−0.8
Loans for Construction of Academic Facilities	14.0	31.4	17.4
Foreign Language and Area Studies	13.8	12.7	−1.1
College Library Resources	12.5	9.9	−2.6

Table A-2 (continued)

	Authorized Appropriations (In Millions)		
Name of Program	FY 1973	FY 1974*	Difference
Cooperative Educational Programs	10.7	10.7	0.0
Fund for Improvement of Post-secondary Education	10.0	10.0	0.0
State Post-secondary Education Commissions	3.0	3.0	0.0
Undergraduate and Graduate Facilities Grants	2.9	2.4	–0.5
State Student Incentive Grants	——	19.0	19.0
TOTAL:	$1,287.2	$1,763.68	$476.48

SOURCE: U.S. Office of Education.

*Less 5% witheld by President

TABLE A-3. Summary of Domestic Assistance Programs Affecting Higher Education, 1973-74 Academic Year by Department in Alphabetical Order.

Alcohol, Drug Abuse, and Mental Health Administration, Department of HEW
—Mental Health Training Grants

Disburses funds to public and private institutions for training in the mental health disciplines of psychology, social work, and psychiatric nursing, in the biological and social sciences, and in other areas relevant to mental health. Funds may be used to defray institutional costs of training programs or to provide training stipends and other allowances.

Atomic Energy Commission
—Nuclear Science and Technology: Faculty Training Institutes and Workshops

The Atomic Energy Act of 1954, secs. 31a and b, sets up funds to provide colleges and university science and engineering faculty and students with research training and experience in nuclear research.

—Traineeships for Graduate Students

The Atomic Energy Act of 1954, secs. 31a and b as amended, allocates funds to any U.S. college or university for the purpose of training and updating the training of college science and engineering faculty in energy development and environmental effects.

Center for Disease Control, Department of HEW
—Occupational Safety and Health Training Grants

The Public Health Service Act, secs. 301 and 311 as amended, provides funds to institutions involved in training at the technical, professional, or graduate level to develop specialized professional personnel in occupational safety and health problems with training in solution techniques.

Extension Service, Department of Agriculture
—Cooperative Extension Service

The Smith-Lever Act as amended makes grants to land-grant institutions for the provision of educational programs, rural development, home economics, and youth development.

Food and Drug Administration
—Research Grants

The Public Health Service Act, Title III, Sec. 301d, and the Radiation Control for Health Safety Act of 1968 provide grants to colleges, universities, and other non-profit institutions for use

Table A-3 *(continued)*

	in establishing, expanding, and improving research activities concerned with foods, shellfish sanitation, poison control, drug and cosmetic hazards, veterinary drugs, medical devices, biological and radiological health.
—Food Research Training Grants	The Public Health Service Act, sec. 309a, provides support to non-profit institutions through training grants to enable them to establish or improve training opportunities for individuals interested in careers in research, teaching, and administration in the food science and technology fields. Training is at Master and Ph.D. degree levels.
Forest Service, Department of Interior —Forestry Research Grants	Under the Basic Research Grants (P.L. 85-934), the Forest Service makes grants for basic research to non-profit institutions of higher education. Grants are used for research in the fields of timber management, watershed management, forest range management, forest recreation, forest fire protection, forest insect and disease control, and forest engineering.
Health Resources Administration, Department of HEW —Hill-Rhodes Grants	The Public Health Service Act, Title III, sec. 309c, provides money for formula grants to assist schools of public health in providing comprehensive professional public health training and specialized consultative services in addition to technical assistance to state and local public health programs.
—Nursing Training Improvement	The Public Health Service Act, Title VIII, sec. 805a, awards project grants to diploma, associate, baccalaureate, and higher degree programs of nursing education for salaries of personnel, consultant fees, supplies and equipment, essential travel expenses and other operating expenses in order to help schools of nursing improve the quality and availability of nursing education through projects in special areas of concern.
—Nursing Student Loans	The Public Health Service Act, Title VIII, sec. 822, allocates funds to be dispersed by public and private schools of nursing (meeting accreditation requirements as defined by the Nurse Training Act of 1971) to assist students in need of financial assistance to pursue a course of study in professional nursing education by providing low-interest loans.
—Capitation Grants	The Comprehensive Health Manpower Training Act of 1971, sec. 770, Public Health Service Act, awards project grants to public and private schools of medicine, veterinary medicine, optometry, pharmacy, dentistry, and podiatry to be used to increase student enrollment, to train physician assistants and dental therapists and to aid and shorten curricula.
—Health Professions: Student Loans	The Public Health Act, Part C, Title VII sec. 740, as amended awards project grants to accredited schools of medicine to increase educational opportunities for students in need of financial assistance, enabling them to pursue a course of study in specified health professions by providing long-term low-interest loans.
—Training in Expanded Auxiliary Management (TEAM)	The Public Health Service Act, Title III, sec. 301d, provides funds for the support of existing approved Training in Expanded Auxiliary Management programs (TEAM), which teaches dental students how to function effectively as managers and organiz-

Table A-3 (continued)

ers in multiple auxiliary dental health care delivery teams. Accredited dental schools are eligible.

—Dental Health Continuing Educational Grants

The Public Health Service Act, Title III, sec. 301d, as amended, provides funds to accredited dental schools to assist in the establishment and expansion of organized programs of continuing education.

—Allied Health Professions: Special Project Grants

The Public Health Service Act, Title VII, sec. 792, awards money in the form of project grants to institutions to support the planning, establishment, development, demonstration, or evaluation of programs, methods, or techniques for the training of allied health personnel.

—Health Services Research and Development

The Public Health Service Act, sec. 301 and 304, as amended provides funds to colleges and universities for the purposes of establishing, improving, or expanding programs designed to train investigators in methods and techniques of conducting health services research.

—Health Services Research and Development: Grants and Contracts

The Public Health Service Act, secs. 301 and 304, as amended, awards funds to universities and non-profit private agencies to support research, development, demonstration and evaluation designed to improve health services. Priority is given to improve availability and quality of services.

—Health Manpower Education Initiative Award

The Public Health Service Act, sec. 774a and b, as amended by the Comprehensive Health Training Act of 1971, awards project grants to improve the distribution, supply, quality, utilization and efficiency of health personnel and the health services delivery system; and to recruit into the health professions: (1) students likely to practice in areas with shortage of health personnel and (2) students who are financially or otherwise disadvantaged.

—Health Professions: Financial Distress Grants

The Public Health Service Act, sec. 773e, Title VII, as amended, provides funds to schools of medicine, pharmacy, dentistry, optometry, and veterinary medicine, which are accredited but are in serious financial strains, to meet costs of operation.

Law Enforcement Assistance Administration, Department of Justice
  —Law Enforcement Research and Development Grants

The Omnibus Crime Control and Safe Streets Act of 1968, as amended by the Omnibus Crime Control Act of 1970, provides funds to be used to conduct research and development of new approaches to crime prevention or reduction. The National Institute of Law Enforcement and Criminal Justice is authorized to make grants to, or enter into contracts with, institutions of higher education to accomplish the just mentioned objectives.

—Law Enforcement Assistance: Educational Development

The Omnibus Crime Act of 1970, sec. 406e, as amended by Crime Control Act of 1973, awards grants to higher educational institutions that demonstrate an ability to coordinate comprehensive programs of criminal justice education, research, evaluation, and curriculum development.

—Law Enforcement Assistance: Internships

The Omnibus Crime Control and Safe Streets Act of 1968, sec. 406f, as amended, provides financial assistance in the form of internships to students pursuing careers in the criminal justice system, providing them with opportunities to have practical work experience relevant to their studies. Participating students must be enrolled full-time and have completed the first year in a degree program.

Table A-3 *(continued)*

Manpower Administration, Department of Labor –Manpower Research and Development Grants	The Manpower Development and Training Act of 1962, as amended, awards project grants to academic institutions to support manpower studies needed to develop policy and programs for achieving the fullest utilization of the nation's manpower, and to demonstrate the effectiveness of specialized methods in meeting the manpower, employment, and training problems of particularly disadvantaged worker groups.
—Manpower Institutional Grants	The Manpower Development and Training Act of 1962, in conjunction with the Comprehensive Employment Training Act of 1973 (PL 93-203), provides for project grants awards to be used by accredited institutions of higher education to strengthen their manpower activities (i.e., augmenting staff, introducing new manpower curricula, conducting manpower research).
National Aeronautics and Space Administration —Space Science Education Project	The National Aeronautics and Space Act of 1950, sec. 203a, as amended, awards funds to colleges and universities and other teacher training institutions for the purpose of providing information about U.S. aeronautics and space research, development activities and their results, enhancing the knowledge of students and teachers, and enriching regular science curricula.
National Institute of Education —Educational Research and Development	Part A, sec. 405 of the General Educational Provisions Act as amended by the 1972 Education Amendments, allocates funds for educational research to be conducted by public and private, profit and non-profit organizations to help solve problems associated with American education.
National Institutes of Health —Biotechnology Research	The Public Health Service Act, Title III, sec. 301d and i, allocates funds to be used to assist academic and other non-profit institutions in developing and sustaining sophisticated technological capabilities (i.e., computer centers, biochemical instrumentation resources, and biological material preparation resources).
—Cancer Research Manpower	The Public Health Service Act, Title III, sec. 301c, provides support for non-profit institutions interested in providing biomedical research training opportunities for individuals interested in careers in particular specified areas of shortage in health sciences and related fields. Individuals selected are at the level of post-doctoral academic and research training only.
National Oceanic and Atmosphere Administration, Department of Commerce —Sea Grant Support	The National Sea Grant College and Program Act of 1969 provides funds to support establishment of major university centers for marine research, education, training, and advisory services within universities, colleges, junior colleges, and technical schools.
Office of Minority Business Enterprise, Department of Commerce —Coordinating Management and Technical Assistance	Title III of the Public Works and Economic Development Act of 1965, as amended, provides funds to private firms, trade and business associations, universities and colleges, to promote full participation of socially and economically disadvantaged individuals through successful business ownership. In addition, OMBE maintains a national clearinghouse for information on minority business enterprise.
Social and Rehabilitation Service, Department of HEW —Public Assistance: State and Local Training	The Social Security Act, sec. 3, 403, 603, 1003, as amended, makes grants to educational institutions to train personnel employed or preparing for employment in state agencies or in local agencies administering approved public assistance plans.

Table A-3 (continued)

Urban Mass Transportation Administration, Department of Transportation —Grants for University Research and Training	The Urban Mass Transportation Act of 1964, as amended, awards funds to non-profit institutions of higher learning to assist in the establishment or continuation of programs of training and comprehensive research in the problems of transportation in urban areas.

SOURCE: U.S. Government, *Catalog of Federal Domestic Assistance*, 1974 edition.

TABLE A-4. Authorized Appropriations by Agency Programs, Research and Training Grants to Colleges, Fiscal Years 1973 and 1974.

	Authorized Appropriations (in millions)		
Agency and Program	*FY 73*	*FY 74*	*Difference*
	$	$	$
Alcohol, Drug Abuse, and Mental Health Administration			
—Mental Health Training Grants	73.5	119.4 est.	45.9
Atomic Energy Commission			
—Nuclear Science and Technology Faculty Training Institutes	0.66	0.485 est.	–0.175
—Traineeship for Graduate Students	1.2	0.520 est.	0.68
Total (AEC)	1.86	1.0	.86
Center for Disease Control			
—Occupational Safety and Health Training Grants	1.2	1.2 est.	0.0
Extension Service (Agriculture)			
—Cooperative Extension Service	162.9	169.2	6.3
Food and Drug Administration			
—Research Grants	3.175	4.194	0.01
—Food Research Training Grants	0.047	0.006	0.041
Total (FDA)	3.222	4.2	0.97
Forest Service			
—Forestry Research Grants	1.46	2.0 est.	0.54
Health Resources Administration			
—Hill-Rhodes Grants	6.0 est.	5.7 est.	–0.3
—Nurse Training Improvement	25.0 est.	19.0 est.	–6.0
—Nurse Student Loans	20.8	25.8	5.0
—Capitation Grants	165.9	185.5	19.6
—Health Professions-Student Loans	36.0	36.0	0.0
—Training in Expanded Auxiliary Management	6.751 est.	5.188 est.	–1.56
—Dental Health Continuing Education Grants	0.199	0.2 est.	0.001
—Allied Health Professions Special Project Grants	15.745 est.	14.158 est.	1.587
—Health Services Research and Development	4.610	4.9	0.29

Table A-4 *(continued)*

Agency and Program	Authorized Appropriations (in millions)		
	FY 73	*FY 74*	*Difference*
—Health Services Research and Development—Grants and Contracts	40.4	51.0 est.	10.6
—Health Manpower Education Initiative Awards	42.0	46.5 est.	4.5
—Health Professions— Financial Distress Awards	42.0 est.	46.5 est.	4.5
Total (HRA)	372.7	400.9	28.2
Law Enforcement Assistance Administration			
—Law Enforcement Research and Development Grants	31.5	40.0	8.5
—Law Enforcement Assistance— Education Development	2.0	2.0 est.	0.0
—Law Enforcement Assistance Internships	0.5	0.5	0.0
Total (LEA)	34.0	42.5	8.5
Manpower Administration (Labor)			
—Manpower Research and Development Grants	19.5	19.2	0.2
—Manpower Institutional Grants	2.35 est.	1.45 est.	–0.9
Total (MA)	21.8	20.7	–0.7
National Aeronautics and Space Administration			
—Space Science Education Project	0.795	0.795 est.	0.0
National Institute of Education			
—Educational Research and Development	106.8	75.7 est.	–31.1
National Institutes of Health			
—Biotechnology Research	10.7	11.9 est.	1.2
—Cancer Research Manpower	0.0	5.4 est.	5.4
Total (NIH)	10.7	17.3 est.	6.6
National Oceanic and Atmospheric Administration			
—Sea Grant Support	18.8	18.8 est.	0.0
Office of Minority Business Enterprise			
—Minority Business Enterprise— Coordination, Management and Technical Assistance	35.2	53.4 est.	18.2
Social and Rehabilitation Service			
—Public Assistance—State and Local Training	35.76	44.64	8.8
Urban Mass Transportation Administration			
—Urban Mass Transportation			

Table A-4 (continued)

	FY 73	FY 74	Difference
Grants for University Research and Training	2.497	2.25 est.	−0.24
TOTAL	$883.63	$974.37	$90.74

SOURCE: U.S. Government, *Catalog of Federal Domestic Assistance Programs*, 1974 Edition.

TABLE A-5. Supplemental Educational Opportunity Grants in Rank Order of Federal Funds Allocated by State, Fiscal Year 1974.

Rank Order	State	Federal Funds Allocated (000)	Number of Students Aided*	Average Grant
	Total	$207,677	300,300	$692
1	California	23,719	35,000	678
2	New York	17,336	27,700	626
3	Illinois	10,550	15,400	685
4	Texas	10,054	15,500	649
5	Michigan	9,846	14,100	698
6	Pennsylvania	9,207	12,700	725
7	Ohio	8,831	12,600	701
8	Wisconsin	8,626	12,300	701
9	Massachusetts	6,741	9,800	688
10	Minnesota	6,083	8,100	751
11	Florida	5,327	7,700	692
12	North Carolina	5,312	7,600	699
13	New Jersey	4,491	6,400	702
14	Indiana	4,479	6,300	711
15	Washington	4,296	6,000	716
16	Missouri	4,081	5,800	704
17	Iowa	3,640	5,200	700
18	Alabama	3,454	5,000	691
19	Virginia	3,452	5,000	690
20	Louisiana	3,278	4,400	745
21	Tennessee	3,241	4,700	690
22	Mississippi	3,169	4,500	704
23	Georgia	3,116	4,500	692
24	Maryland	3,098	4,400	704
25	Colorado	2,824	4,000	706
26	Connecticut	2,683	3,800	707
27	Oklahoma	2,612	3,700	706
28	Oregon	2,581	3,700	698
29	Kansas	2,436	3,500	696
30	Maine	2,365	3,400	696
31	Kentucky	2,362	3,400	695
32	Arizona	2,259	3,200	706
33	District of Columbia	2,239	3,200	700
34	South Carolina	1,984	2,900	684
35	Utah	1,891	2,700	700
36	Nebraska	1,528	2,100	728
37	West Virginia	1,492	2,000	746
38	New Mexico	1,476	2,000	738

Table A-5 (continued)

Rank Order	State	Federal Funds Allocated (000)	Number of Students Aided*	Average Grant
39	North Dakota	1,338	2,000	669
40	South Dakota	1,332	1,900	701
41	New Hampshire	1,315	1,800	731
42	Arkansas	1,313	1,900	691
43	Vermont	1,180	1,600	738
44	Rhode Island	1,034	1,500	689
45	Idaho	823	1,100	748
46	Hawaii	800	1,100	727
47	Montana	705	800	881
48	Delaware	561	800	701
49	Alaska	455	600	758
50	Wyoming	365	500	730
51	Nevada	297	400	743

SOURCE: American Council on Education, Policy Analysis Service. Based on unpublished information from the U.S. Office of Education, Bureau of Post-secondary Education, Office of Student Assistance, Division of Student Support and Special Programs, Program Support Branch, April 1974. (From: American Council on Education, *Diversity Among the Fifty States in Higher Education*. July 1974.)

*Estimated

TABLE A-6. National Direct Student Loans in Rank Order of Federal Funds Available by State, Fiscal Year 1974.

Rank Order	State	Federal Funds Available (000)	Number of Students aided*	Average Grant
	Total	$283,744	668,800	$424
1	California	30,974	73,000	424
2	New York	23,770	56,100	424
3	Texas	15,330	36,100	425
4	Pennsylvania	14,267	33,600	425
5	Illinois	14,260	33,600	424
6	Ohio	13,591	32,100	423
7	Michigan	12,718	30,000	424
8	Massachusetts	10,537	24,800	425
9	Florida	7,857	18,500	425
10	Indiana	7,506	17,700	424
11	Wisconsin	7,314	17,200	425
12	North Carolina	6,784	16,000	424
13	Missouri	6,672	15,700	425
14	Minnesota	6,351	15,000	423
15	Washington	5,823	13,700	425
16	New Jersey	5,714	13,500	423
17	Tennessee	5,322	12,500	426
18	Iowa	5,081	12,000	423
19	Virginia	4,919	11,600	424
20	Georgia	4,913	11,600	424
21	Louisiana	4,850	11,400	425
22	Oklahoma	4,482	10,600	423

Table A-6 (continued)

Rank Order	State	Federal Funds Available (000)	Number of Students aided*	Average Grant
23	Maryland	4,450	10,500	424
24	Alabama	4,339	10,200	425
25	Colorado	4,164	9,800	425
26	Kansas	4,116	9,700	424
27	Kentucky	4,107	9,700	423
28	Oregon	3,946	9,300	424
29	Connecticut	3,788	8,900	426
30	Mississippi	3,287	7,800	421
31	Arizona	3,024	7,100	426
32	Nebraska	2,710	6,400	423
33	South Carolina	2,695	6,400	421
34	West Virginia	2,688	6,300	427
35	Arkansas	2,279	5,400	422
36	Utah	2,266	5,300	428
37	District of Columbia	2,169	5,100	425
38	New Mexico	1,569	3,700	424
39	Rhode Island	1,507	3,600	419
40	North Dakota	1,343	3,200	420
41	South Dakota	1,324	3,100	427
42	Hawaii	1,245	2,900	429
43	New Hampshire	1,237	2,900	427
44	Montana	1,229	2,900	424
45	Idaho	1,216	2,800	434
46	Maine	1,189	2,800	425
47	Vermont	903	2,100	430
48	Delaware	747	1,800	415
49	Wyoming	577	1,400	412
50	Nevada	443	1,000	443
51	Alaska	182	400	455

SOURCE: American Council on Education, Public Analysis Service. Based on unpublished informa-
tion from the U.S. Office of Education, Bureau of Post-secondary Education, Office of
Student Assistance, Division of Student Support and Special Programs, Program Support
Branch, April 1974. (From: American Council on Education, *Diversity Among the Fifty
States in Higher Education*, July 1974.)

*Estimated

**TABLE A-7. College Work-Study Programs in Rank Order of
Federal Funds Allocated by State, Fiscal Year 1974.**

Rank Order	State	Federal Funds Allocated (000)	Number of Students Aided*	Average Grant
	Total	$266,257	551,800	$483
1	California	24,471	50,300	407
2	New York	19,263	39,800	484
3	Texas	14,207	29,500	482
4	Illinois	13,721	28,400	483
5	Pennsylvania	12,091	25,100	482
6	Massachusetts	11,392	23,600	483

Table A-7 (continued)

Rank Order	State	Federal Funds Allocated (000)	Number of Students Aided*	Average Grant
7	Ohio	11,059	22,900	483
8	Michigan	9,584	19,900	482
9	North Carolina	8,181	17,000	481
10	Florida	7,377	15,300	482
11	Wisconsin	7,240	15,000	483
12	Georgia	6,390	13,300	480
13	Minnesota	6,295	13,100	481
14	New Jersey	6,230	12,900	483
15	Louisiana	6,076	12,600	482
16	Tennessee	5,964	12,400	481
17	Alabama	5,802	12,000	484
18	Virginia	5,606	11,600	483
19	Missouri	5,426	11,300	480
20	Indiana	5,403	11,200	482
21	Mississippi	4,885	10,100	484
22	Kentucky	4,772	9,900	482
23	Washington	4,667	9,700	481
24	South Carolina	4,483	9,300	482
25	Maryland	4,036	8,400	480
26	Iowa	3,926	8,100	485
27	Oregon	3,924	8,100	484
28	Colorado	3,539	7,300	485
29	Oklahoma	3,522	7,300	482
30	Arkansas	3,358	7,000	480
31	Connecticut	2,953	6,100	484
32	West Virginia	2,934	6,100	481
33	Kansas	2,847	5,900	483
34	Maine	2,726	5,700	478
35	Arizona	2,502	5,200	481
36	Montana	2,101	4,400	478
37	Nebraska	2,023	4,200	482
38	District of Columbia	1,879	3,900	482
39	New Mexico	1,798	3,700	486
40	Utah	1,714	3,600	476
41	New Hampshire	1,514	3,100	488
42	North Dakota	1,314	2,700	487
43	South Dakota	1,185	2,500	474
44	Rhode Island	1,150	2,400	479
45	Hawaii	1,093	2,300	475
46	Idaho	930	1,900	489
47	Vermont	749	1,600	468
48	Delaware	623	1,300	479
49	Wyoming	564	1,200	470
50	Nevada	450	900	500
51	Alaska	328	700	469

SOURCE: American Council on Education, Policy Analysis Service. Based on unpublished information from the U.S. Office of Education, Bureau of Post-secondary Education, Office of Student Assistance, Division of Student Support and Special Programs, Program Support Branch, April 1974. (From: American Council on Education, *Diversity Among The Fifty States in Higher Education,* July 1974.)

*Estimated

TABLE A-8. State Scholarship Programs by State and Type of Program for the 1972 and 1973 Academic Years.

	No. of winners enrolled		Dollars paid out		Average Award Amount	
	1972-73	1973-74	1972-73 $	1973-74 $	1972-73 $	1973-74 $
California						
State Scholarships	28,283	34,080	20,828,904	25,655,400	736	753
College Opportunity Grants	3,811	4,762	3,871,738	5,291,733	1,016	1,111
Occupational Training Grants		198		391,410		1,977
All California programs	32,094	39,040	24,700,642	31,338,543	770	803
Colorado						
Student Grants	12,066	13,056	5,127,890	5,875,104	425	450
Connecticut						
State Scholarships	2,010	2,127	1,287,900	1,419,300	641	667
Higher Education Grants						
College Continuation Grants	492	318	190,000	107,500	386	338
Restricted Education Achievement Grants	482	508	228,000	237,100	473	467
All Connecticut programs	2,984	2,953	1,705,900	1,763,900	572	597
Delaware						
Higher Education Scholarships	112	117	73,210	72,650	654	621
Florida						
Student Assistance Grants	337	3,151	360,000	3,537,400	1,068	1,123
Georgia						
Incentive Scholarships	—	—	—	—	—	—
Idaho						
State Student Incentive Grants	—	—	—	—	—	—
Illinois						
Monetary Awards	69,588	72,246	51,091,125	53,767,000	734	744
Indiana						
State Scholarships	10,981	10,842	7,567,244	7,602,206	689	701
Educational Grants	989	1,551	688,037	971,958	696	627

Freedom of Choice Grants		954		521,240		546
All Indiana programs	11,970	13,347	8,255,281	9,095,404	690	681
Iowa						
Scholarships	432	595	231,979	321,587	537	540
Tuition Grants	4,500	6,612	3,999,998	5,893,083	889	891
Vocational-Technical Tuition Grants						
All Iowa programs	4,932	7,207	4,231,977	6,214,670	858	862
Kansas						
Tuition Grants	1,118	2,703	1,000,000	2,329,086	894	862
State Scholarships	309	305	145,992	147,500	472	484
All Kansas programs	1,427	3,008	1,145,992	2,476,586	803	823
Kentucky						
State Student Incentive	—	—	—	—	—	—
Maine						
Tuition Equalization Grants	237	328	147,522	183,217	622	559
Maryland						
General State Scholarships	650	545	296,500	327,300	456	601
Massachusetts						
General Scholarships	13,000	15,849	8,000,000	9,498,350	615	599
Michigan						
Tuition Grants	7,920	7,703	5,563,002	7,865,521	702	1,021
Competitive Scholarships	15,581	13,953	8,035,056	8,712,904	516	624
All Michigan programs	23,501	21,666	13,598,058	16,578,425	579	766
Minnesota						
State Scholarships	3,776	4,498	2,491,427	3,026,056	660	673
Grants-in-aid	3,236	4,207	2,168,595	2,673,800	670	636
All Minnesota programs	7,012	8,705	4,660,022	5,699,856	665	655
Missouri						
Student Grants	172	7,489	56,172	8,299,006	327	441

Table A-8 (continued)

	No. of winners enrolled		Dollars paid out		Average Amount Award	
	1972-73	1973-74	1972-73	1973-74	1972-73	1973-74
Nebraska			$	$	$	$
State Student Incentive Grants	—	—			—	—
New Jersey						
State Competitive Scholarships	16,130	13,742	7,088,067	511,826	439	474
Educational Incentive Grants	3,400	8,630	1,516,000	1,467,993	446	170
Tuition Aid Grants	51,000	4,283	3,570,000	3,263,769	700	762
County College Graduate Scholarships	650	491	313,300	240,080	482	489
Tuition Remission Grants		8,200		2,824,513		344
Educational Opportunity Grants	12,662	13,131	10,058,990	11,049,250		
All New Jersey programs	37,942	48,477	22,546,357	25,357,431	594	523
New York			$	$	$	$
Regents Scholarships (1972-73 & 1973-74)						
Scholarship Incentive Awards	67,681	67,700	28,612,378	28,600,000	423	422
Tuition Assistance Program	203,174	205,400	45,300,000	49,400,000	223	241
All New York programs	270,855	273,100	73,912,387	78,000,000	273	286
North Dakota						
Grants	—	625	—	144,708	—	232
Ohio						
Ohio Instructional Grants	36,561	40,682	15,594,988	16,700,000	427	411
Oklahoma						
Tuition Aid Grants	—	—	—	—	—	—
Oregon						
Seed Grants	2,845	3,523	1,029,053	1,537,617	362	436
Cash Awards	669	695	264,759	285,709	396	411
All Oregon programs	3,514	4,218	1,293,812	1,823,326	368	432
Pennsylvania						
State Scholarships	105,501	106,474	62,759,544	63,639,614	595	598
Puerto Rico						
State Student Incentive Grants	—	—	—	—	—	—
Rhode Island	2,429	2,400	1,914,835	1,933,525	788	777

South Carolina Tuition Grants	129	3,284	147,500	3,849,600	1,143	1,172
South Dakota State Student Incentive Grants	—	—	—	—	—	—
Tennessee Tuition Grants	2,002	3,888	1,177,093	2,146,628	588	552
Texas Tuition Equalization Grants	6,550	10,002	3,000,000	5,000,000	458	500
Trust Territories Education Assistance Grants	—	—	—	—	—	—
Vermont Incentive Grants	3,422	3,972	2,380,343	2,525,126	696	636
Virgin Islands Territory Scholarships	308	372	284,100	317,635	922	854
Virginia Scholarship Assistance	—	195	—	53,686	—	275
Washington Seed Giving	1,600	4,422	887,193	1,400,000	554	316
West Virginia Scholarships	1,363	1,649	425,000	500,000	312	303
Wisconsin Tuition Grants	6,873	7,079	4,762,414	4,625,205	547	653
Talent Incentive	498	730	411,416	650,807	826	892
Honor Scholarships	1,130	864	748,363	557,150	662	645
Higher Education Grants	—	10,983	—	4,398,727	—	401
Indian Student Assistance	895	1,064	766,850	853,845	857	802
All Wisconsin programs	9,396	20,720	5,689,043	11,085,734	605	535
TOTALS	661,654	733,267	$315,462,476	$364,204,424	$477	$497

SOURCE: National Association of State Scholarship Programs, *The Chronicle of Higher Education,* 1974.

**TABLE A-9. Numbers of Increases and Decreases in State Student
Assistance Programs Between 1972-73 Academic Year and the 1973-74 Academic Year.**

	Number of States		
	Increase	Decrease	Unchanged
Number of Awards	28	3	0
Dollars Awarded	29	2	0
Average Award	18	13	0

SOURCE: Table A-8.

**TABLE A-10. Rank Order of States by Number of Awards, Total Dollars
Awarded, and Average Award for 1973-74 Academic Year.**

	Ranks (1 = highest)		
States (and Territories)	Number of Awards	Total $ Awarded	Average $ Size
New York	1	1	29
Pennsylvania	2	2	16
Illinois	3	3	9
New Jersey	4	5	21
Ohio	5	6	26
California	6	4	6
Michigan	7	7	8
Wisconsin	8	8	20
Massachusetts	9	9	15
Indiana	10	10	10
Colorado	11	12	23
Texas	12	14	22
Minnesota	13	13	11
Missouri	14	17	24
Iowa	15	11	3
Washington	16	24	27
Oregon	17	22	25
Vermont	18	18	12
Tennessee	19	20	19
South Carolina	20	15	1
Florida	21	16	2
Kansas	22	19	5
Connecticut	23	23	17
Rhode Island	24	21	7
West Virginia	25	25	28
North Dakota	26	29	31
Maryland	27	26	14
Virgin Islands	28	27	4
Maine	29	28	18
Virginia	30	30	30
Delaware	31	31	13

SOURCE: Table A-8.

TABLE A-11. OCR Regional Categories of the States Used in Table 2-2.

Region I	Kentucky	Missouri
Connecticut	Mississippi	Nebraska
Maine	North Carolina	
Massachusetts	South Carolina	*Region VIII*
New Hampshire	Tennessee	Colorado
Rhode Island		Montana
Vermont	*Region V*	North Dakota
	Illinois	South Dakota
Region II	Indiana	Utah
New Jersey	Michigan	Wyoming
New York	Minnesota	
	Ohio	*Region IX*
Region III	Wisconsin	Arizona
Delaware		California
D.C.	*Region VI*	Hawaii
Maryland	Arkansas	Nevada
Pennsylvania	Louisiana	
Virginia	New Mexico	*Region X*
West Virginia	Oklahoma	Alaska
	Texas	Idaho
Region IV		Oregon
Alabama	*Region VII*	Washington
Florida	Iowa	
Georgia	Kansas	

SOURCE: Office for Civil Rights (DHEW), *Racial and Ethnic Enrollment Data From Institutions of Higher Education,* Fall 1972, pp. 134-135.

TABLE A-12. Students Receiving Financial Assistance by Type of Federal Campus-Based Programs and Race, Fiscal Years 1968 Through 1970

Program and Race	Fiscal Year			
College Work Study Program Only	*1968*	*1969*	*1970*	*Total*
Black	30,230	30,209	34,897	95,336
American Indian	582	868	1,017	2,467
Asian American	1,428	1,930	2,108	5,466
Spanish Surnamed	6,840	8,951	8,244	24,035
White	156,752	162,344	175,631	494,727
TOTAL	195,832	204,302	221,897	622,031
Educational Opportunity Grant Program Only (SEOG)				
Black	9,877	14,337	14,543	38,857
American Indian	156	226	377	799
Asian American	411	738	523	1,672
Spanish Surnamed	1,475	4,286	3,100	8,861
White	35,747	34,947	28,482	99,176
TOTAL	47,666	54,574	47,125	149,365

Table A-12 (continued)

Program and Race	1968	1969	1970	Total
National (Defense) Direct Student Loan Program Only				
Black	19,974	17,495	19,740	57,209
American Indian	348	530	568	1,446
Asian American	1,352	1,734	1,700	4,786
Spanish Surnamed	3,682	5,095	4,558	13,335
White	213,436	196,967	194,870	605,273
TOTAL	238,792	221,821	221,436	682,049
College Work Study and Educational Opportunity Grant (SEOG) Programs				
Black	3,619	8,517	16,772	28,908
American Indian	58	231	452	741
Asian American	126	352	1,308	1,786
Spanish Surnamed	628	1,837	3,074	5,529
White	12,978	19,135	30,097	62,210
TOTAL	17,409	30,062	51,703	99,174
College Work Study and National(Defense) Direct Student Loan Programs				
Black	7,922	8,673	11,476	28,071
American Indian	227	169	251	647
Asian American	299	478	573	1,350
Spanish Surnamed	1,101	1,635	1,916	4,652
White	46,762	48,640	56,491	151,893
TOTAL	56,311	59,595	70,707	186,613
Educational Opportunity Grant (SEOG) and National Defense (Direct) Student Loan Programs				
Black	13,985	20,742	22,838	57,565
American Indian	232	402	387	1,021
Asian American	671	922	975	2,568
Spanish Surnamed	2,819	4,486	5,201	12,505
White	75,733	83,987	67,211	226,931
TOTAL	93,440	110,539	96,612	300,591
College Work Study, SEOG and National Defense Loan Programs				
Black	8,671	15,053	20,509	44,233
American Indian	137	203	288	628
Asian American	299	422	541	1,262
Spanish Surnamed	1,451	2,620	2,807	6,878
White	32,821	42,752	39,050	114,623
TOTAL	43,379	61,050	63,195	167,624

SOURCE: U.S.O.E. (DHEW), *Institutional Fiscal Operations Report for Federal Student Financial Aid Programs*, 1968, 1969, 1970.

SURVEY OF NATIONAL DATA COLLECTORS

Elizabeth A. Abramowitz
Institute for Study of Educational Policy

The systematic sources of variance in racial statistics due to the methodological problems discussed in Chapter 1 are significant. The unsystematic sources of variance come from the emotion-laden factors underlying racial surveys. This unsystematic variance is the residual variance inherent in any data collection situation.

As an initial attempt to isolate the causes of the discrepancies in racial enrollment statistics, a telephone survey of national data collectors was undertaken by the Institute for the Study of Educational Policy in July 1974.

The purpose of the telephone survey was twofold: first, to obtain 1973 enrollment statistics and, second, to determine methodological differences in the derivation of the enrollment statistics that were included in the survey. Of the fourteen, nine were private and five public. All but two of the organizations were located in Washington, D.C. The organizations and respondents were as follows:

I.D. No.	Name
01.	Engine Holmstrom American Council on Education
02.	Sherri Levine DHEW, Office of Civil Rights
03.	Linda Lambert Institute for Services to Education
04.	Mark Littman U.S. Bureau of the Census
05.	Robert L. Stein Department of Labor, Division of Labor Statistics
06.	Iris Garfield U.S. Office of Education, NCES National Assessment of Educational Progress
07.	Phil Rever American College Testing Program
08.	Nancy Greenberg College Entrance Examination Board, D.C.

09.	Renee Licht
	National Council on Graduate Education

10.	George Wade
	National Center for Educational Statistics
	Higher Education Survey Branch

11.	Clarebeth M. Cunningham
	National Research Council

12.	Penny Edgar
	NSSFNS, Research Department

13.	Ken Wilson
	Educational Testing Service
	New Jersey

14.	Elaine El-Khawas
	Higher Education Panel
	American Council on Education

TABLE B-1. Do you Collect Racial Statistics on Enrollment?

TYPE OF INSTITUTION	YES	NO	TOTAL
Public	2	3	5
Private	3	6	9
TOTAL	5	9	14

Five of the fourteen respondents reported that they regularly collected racial enrollment data (See Table B-1). Table B-2 describes the institutions from which racial statistics are collected.

TABLE B-2. From Which Institutions Do You Collect Racial Statistics?

I.D. No. of Respondent	Type of Institution
01	Sample of 600
02	2,700 receiving federal assistance
03	113 traditionally black colleges
04	Based on 50,000 households. Collect from all types of post-secondary institutions.
07	2,300 institutions

Each data collector used a different number of institutions on which to base its statistics. Two organizations used most of the higher education universe as defined by the *Education Directory*. Another used an unknown distribution across types of institutions. And, the remaining two used samples of which one collected from a sample of all institutions, and the other from traditionally black colleges exclusively.

The data collectors also differed in the sources of the racial data they obtained. One collected from heads of households in voluntary personal interviews. The others were mandatory; one collected by mail survey, the other by group testing of students. No two collectors used the same source or method of obtaining racial enrollment (See Table B-3).

TABLE B-3. How Are Your Racial Statistics Collected?

I.D. No.	Sources Mandatory/Voluntary		Collection Method	Informant
04		x	Interview (October)	House of household
03		x	Mail (September)	Institutional personnel
01	x		Testing Session (September)	Students at institution
02	x		Mail (September)	Students & Institutional Personnel
07	x		Testing Session (December)	Students at Institution

Like the size of the sample, the mandatory nature of the survey, plus the type of informant and method of data collection vary across major data collectors of racial statistics.

Because the number of institutions in the samples of the data collectors did vary, the usable response rates were critical. As can be seen in Table B-4, the response rates ranged from a low of 55% to a high of 96% for enrollment items.

TABLE B-4. What Were the Usable Response Rates for Enrollment Statistics?

I.D. No.	Rate	Total Usable Responses
04	96%	48,000*
01	92%	552
02	90%	2,430
03	77%	87
07	55%	1,265

*Proportion of 50,000 households responding.

On the basis of response rate alone, the data collectors vary significantly. The last column in Table B-4 gives the actual number of usable responses the data collectors used to generate 1972 racial enrollment statistics. The number of respondents ranged from a high of 2,430 to a low of 87.

Table B-5 summarizes the percent of Black enrollment obtained by each data collector. As would be expected, the higher percentage of Black enrollment was reported for data collected at traditionally Black colleges, followed by data volunteered by a national sample of households. The lowest percent of Black undergraduate enrollment was reported by data collectors who administered their questionnaire in December. Their statistics, therefore, were not opening fall enrollment, but rather final fall enrollment, which usually is lower because of within-semester attrition.

TABLE B-5. What Percent of the Total Entering Fall Enrollment in 1972 was Black?

I.D.	Institution Type 2-Yr.	4-Yr.	All Under-grad	Graduate	Prof.	Grad. and Prof.
01	NA	NA	8.7%	NA	NA	NA
02	NA	NA	8.5%	5%	4.8%	NA
03	NA	NA	Over 90%	NA	NA	Over 90%
04	10.5%	11.5%	NA	NA	NA	6%
07	NA	NA	7.9%	NA	NA	NA

NA=not available

In summary, the data collection methods influenced the obtained racial statistics in these ways:

1. Racial statistics expressed as percents derived from representative sample institutions did not differ significantly from the same racial statistics derived from the total population of higher education institutions. While whole numbers vary, the proportion of minority enrollment is equivalent, regardless of the use of a representative sample of the universe.

2. When completion of the survey is mandatory or has subtle coercion, e.g., personal interviews, the obtained statistics from these sources agree.

3. When the survey is completed at an institution by either students or institutional personnel, the obtained racial statistics on enrollment are *lower* than statistics obtained from noncollegiate settings, such as households.

4. When students are the informants, the time of data-collection is more critical than when institutional personnel are the informants.

Enrollment in Selected Institutions

TABLE C-1. Land-Grant Colleges and Universities.

Land Grant Institution	Location	Date Established as a Land Grant College
Alabama:		
1. Auburn University	Auburn	1872
*2. Alabama Agricultural & Mechanical College	Normal	1891
Alaska:		
3. University of Alaska	College	1922
Arizona:		
4. University of Arizona	Tucson	1885
Arkansas:		
5. University of Arkansas	Fayetteville	1871
*6. Agricultural, Mechanical and Normal College	Pine Bluff	1875
California:		
7. University of California	Berkeley	1866
Colorado:		
8. Colorado State University	Fort Collins	1879
Connecticut:		
9. University of Connecticut	Storrs	1862
Delaware:		
10. University of Delaware	Newark	1867
11. Delaware State College	Dover	1891
District of Columbia:		
12. Federal City College	Washington, D.C.	1968
Florida:		
13. University of Florida	Gainesville	1870
*14. Florida Agricultural & Mechanical University	Tallahassee	1893
Georgia:		
15. University of Georgia	Athens	1866
*16. Fort Valley State College	Fort Valley	1874
Guam:		
17. University of Guam	Guam	1935

Table C-1 *(continued)*

Hawaii:
| 18. University of Hawaii | Honolulu | 1907 |

Idaho:
| 19. University of Idaho | Moscow | 1890 |

Illinois:
| 20. University of Illinois | Urbana | 1867 |

Indiana:
| 21. Purdue University | Lafayette | 1865 |

Iowa:
| 22. Iowa State University | Ames | 1862 |

Kansas:
| 23. Kansas State University | Manhattan | 1863 |

Kentucky:
| 24. University of Kentucky | Lexington | 1863 |
| *25. Kentucky State College | Frankfort | 1893 |

Louisiana:
| 26. Louisiana State University | Baton Rouge | 1869 |
| *27. Southern University & Agricultural & Mechanical College | Baton Rouge | 1890 |

Maine:
| 28. University of Maine | Orono | 1863 |

Maryland:
| 29. University of Maryland | College Park | 1864 |
| *30. Maryland State College | Princess Anne | 1890 |

Massachusetts:
| 31. University of Massachusetts | Amherst | 1863 |
| 32. Massachusetts Institute of Technology | Cambridge | 1863 |

Michigan:
| 33. Michigan State University | East Lansing | 1863 |

Minnesota:
| 34. University of Minnesota | Minneapolis | 1863 |

Mississippi:
| 35. Mississippi State University | State College | 1866 |
| *36. Alcorn Agricultural and Mechanical College | Alcorn | 1871 |

Missouri:
| 37. University of Missouri | Columbia | 1863 |
| *38. Lincoln University | Jefferson City | 1891 |

Montana:
| 39. Montana State College | Bozeman | 1889 |

Nebraska:
| 40. University of Nebraska | Lincoln | 1869 |

Table C-1 *(continued)*

Nevada:
41. University of Nevada   Reno   1866

New Hampshire:
42. University of New Hampshire   Durham   1866

New Jersey:
43. Rutgers, The State University   New Brunswick   1863

New Mexico:
44. New Mexico State University   University Park   1889

New York:
45. Cornell University   Ithaca   1863

North Carolina:
46. North Carolina State College   Raleigh   1866
*47. Agricultural and Technical
    College of North Carolina   Greensboro   1891

North Dakota:
48. North Dakota State University   Fargo   1889

Ohio:
49. Ohio State University   Columbus   1864

Oklahoma:
50. Oklahoma State University   Stillwater   1890
*51. Langston University   Langston   1897

Oregon:
52. Oregon State University   Corvallis   1868

Pennsylvania:
53. The Pennsylvania State
    University   University Park   1863

Puerto Rico:
54. University of Puerto Rico   Mayaguez   1908

Rhode Island:
55. University of Rhode Island   Kingston   1863

South Carolina:
56. Clemson Agricultural College   Clemson   1893
*57. South Carolina State College   Orangeburg   1896

South Dakota:
58. South Dakota State College   Brookings   1883

Tennessee:
59. The University of Tennessee   Knoxville   1868
*60. Tennessee Agricultural and
    Industrial State University   Nashville   1891

Texas:
61. Texas Agricultural and
    Mechanical University   College Station   1866
*62. Prairie View Agricultural
    and Mechanical College   Prairie View   1891

Table C-1 (continued)

Utah:		
63. Utah State University	Logan	1888
Vermont:		
64. University of Vermont	Burlington	1862
Virgin Islands:		
65. University of the Virgin Islands	St. John	1935
Virginia:		
66. Virginia Polytechnic Institute	Blacksburg	1870
67. Virginia State College	Petersburg	1872
Washington:		
68. Washington State University	Pullman	1889
West Virginia:		
69. West Virginia University	Morgantown	1867
Wisconsin:		
70. University of Wisconsin	Madison	1863
Wyoming:		
71. University of Wyoming	Laramie	1889

*Black Land-Grant Colleges created under the Morrill Act of 1890.

TABLE C-2. List of Predominantly Black Colleges, Based on Fall 1972 Undergraduate Enrollment.[1]

	Estimated Fall Enrollment
Chicago City Community Colleges	29,000
Kennedy-King	
The Loop Campus	
Malcolm X	
Olive-Harvey	
College of the Virgin Islands	1,698
Compton College	6,850
Detroit Institute of Technology	1,053
Durham Technical Institute	777[2]
Edgecomb County Technical Institute	3,416
Essex County Community College	4,540
Federal City College	7,144
Highland Park Community College	3,597
Malcolm-King	657
Martin Technical Institute	325
Medgar Evers College (part of C.U.N.Y)	1,184

Table C-2 *(continued)*

Mt. Providence Junior College	44[1]
Shaw College at Detroit	718
Wayne County Community College	1,680
Washington Technical Institute	4,664
Total Enrollment	67,347

SOURCE: Institute for Services to Education (1974). *Degrees Granted and Enrollment Trends In Historically Black Colleges: An Eight-Year Study*, pp. 11-12.

[1]Does not include historically Black colleges.
[2]Fall 1970 enrollment.

TABLE C-3. State Institutions in NASUL-G with Highest and Lowest Charges for Tuition and Required Fees, Fall 1972.

RESIDENT TUITION AND FEES

Highest		*Lowest*	
Cornell University	$1,350.00	City University of New York	$ 70.00
University of Vermont	1,087.50	Federal City College	117.00
Temple University	1,050.00	Prairie View A&M University[2]	197.50
University of Pittsburgh	1,012.00	University of Hawaii	227.00
University of New Hampshire	993.39	University of Guam	230.00
University of Michigan[1]	904.00	University of Houston	266.00
Pennsylvania State University	900.00	Alabama A&M University[2]	280.00
Kent State University	804.00	Southern University	284.00
Miami University (Ohio)	780.00	Texas A&M University	288.00
Colorado State University	778.00	Texas Tech University	292.00

NON-RESIDENT TUITION AND FEES

Highest		*Lowest*	
University of Michigan	$2,800.00	University of Guam	$400.00
University of Vermont	2,687.50	City University of New York	620.00
University of New Hampshire	2,233.30	Alabama A&M University[2]	630.00
University of California	2,144.00	Lincoln University[2]	640.00
Pennsylvania State University	2,100.00	University of Maryland Eastern Shore[2]	695.00
North Carolina A&T State University	2,074.50	Federal City College[2]	732.00
Colorado State University	2,069.00	University of Hawaii	733.00
North Carolina State University	2,033.50	College of the Virgin Islands	814.00
University of Wisconsin[3]	2,006.00	Langston University	832.00
Kent State University	2,004.00	Southern University[2]	914.00

SOURCE: National Association of State Universities and Land-Grant Colleges, *1973-74 Student Charges at State and Land-Grant Universities*. October 1973, p. 7.

[1]The amount paid by juniors and seniors. University of Michigan freshmen and sophomores pay $800 (Residential) and $2,600 (non-Residential).
[2]Over 75% Black undergraduate enrollment, Fall 1972.
[3]The amount paid by juniors and seniors. University of Wisconsin freshmen and sophomores pay $1,906.

AID TO DEVELOPING INSTITUTIONS, HEA TITLE III

Of the 2,700 institutions in higher education, approximately 1,000 qualified for the Aid to Developing Institutions Program under Title III of the Higher Education Act of 1965, according to the U.S. Office of Education. In Fiscal Year 1973, 470 institutions requested $220,000,000, in grant aid. But only 235 awards were made, totaling $51,850,000. One-half of all institutions requesting aid under Title III, then, did not receive it; and the dollars awarded were approximately one-fourth of the total amount requested.

Table C-4 summarizes the Fiscal Year 1973 funding for the Basic Grants Programs in Title III. Of the 235 institutions receiving grants in the Basic Institutional Development Program, 41% (or 98 grantees) were predominantly Black institutions, the remaining 58.3% (or 137 grantees) were predominantly white institutions. The predominantly Black institutions received $30,658,320, with an average grant of $312,840 to each institution, while predominantly white institutions received $21,191,680 with an average award of $154,683 to each institution. Although there were more predominantly white than Black institutions participating in the Basic Grants Program in FY 1973, the average Basic Grants to predominantly Black colleges were larger than those to their white counterparts.

Table C-5 provides similar data for the Advanced Institutional Development Program. Of the 28 grants awarded in Fiscal Year 1973, 13 went to predominantly Black colleges and 15 to predominantly white institutions. Both the average size of the grant and the total amount awarded to Black colleges were greater than that received at white institutions.

(In Fiscal Year 1973, the total amount disbursed under Title III was $87,350,000, of which $51,850,000 went to Basic Programs and $35,500,000 to the Advanced Programs).

TABLE C-4. Title III, Higher Education Act of 1965, Strengthening Developing Institutions, Basic Institutional Development Program.

| | AWARDS BY TYPE OF INSTITUTION, FISCAL YEAR 1973 | | | | | | |
	Number of Grantees	Percent of Grantees	Total Funds	Percent of Funds	Average Grant	No. of NTF's*	No. of PE's**
		%	$	%	$		
All Grantee Institutions	235	100	51,850,000	100	220,638	354	45
Four-Year	156	66.4	39,394,320	76.0	252,527	322	45
Two-Year	79	33.6	12,455,680	24.0	157,666	32	0
Public Institutions	116	49.4	25,269,220	48.8	217,838	126	13
Four-Year	54	23.0	15,429,540	29.8	285,732	102	13
Two-Year	62	26.4	9,839,680	19.0	158,704	24	0
Private Institutions	119	50.6	26,580,780	51.2	223,367	228	32
Four-Year	102	43.4	23,964,780	46.2	234,948	220	32
Two-Year	17	7.2	2,616,000	5.0	153,882	8	0

Table C-4 (continued)

	Number of Grantees	Percent of Grantees	Total Funds	Percent of Funds	Average Grant	No. of NTF's*	No. of PE's**
Predominantly		%	$	%	$		
Black Institutions	98	41.1	30,658,320	59.1	312,840	125	29
Four-Year	82	34.9	27,503,320	53.0	335,406	125	29
Two-Year	16	6.8	3,155,000	6.1	197,187	0	0
Predominantly							
White Institutions	137	58.3	21,191,680	40.9	154,683	229	16
Four-Year	74	31.5	11,891,000	23.0	160,689	197	16
Two-Year	63	26.8	9,300,680	17.9	147,629	32	0

SOURCE: U.S. Office of Education, *Strengthening Developing Institutions, Title XXI, of the Higher Education Act of 1969 Annual Report*, March 1974, p. 44.

*National Teaching Fellowships
**Professors Emeriti

TABLE C-5. Title III, Higher Education Act of 1965, Strengthening Developing Institutions, Advanced Institutional Development Program.

AWARDS BY TYPE OF INSTITUTION, FISCAL YEAR 1973

	Number of Grantees	Percent of Grantees	Total Funds	Percent of Funds	Average Grant
		%	$	%	$
All Grantee					
Institutions	28	100	35,500,000	100	1,267,857
Four-Year	17	60.7	26,980,000	76.0	1,587,639
Two-Year	11	39.3	8,520,000	24.0	744,545
Public					
Institutions	13	46.4	14,566,375	41.0	1,120,490
Four-Year	5	17.8	8,550,000	24.1	1,710,000
Two-Year	8	28.6	6,016,375	16.9	752,046
Private					
Institutions	15	53.6	20,933,625	59.0	1,395,575
Four-Year	12	42.9	18,430,000	51.9	1,535,833
Two-Year	3	10.7	2,503,625	7.1	834,541
Predominantly					
Black Institutions	13	46.4	23,380,000	65.9	1,798,461
Four-Year	13	46.4	23,380,000	65.9	1,798,461
Two-Year	0	0.0	0	0	0
Predominantly					
White Institutions	15	53.6	12,120,000	34.1	808,000
Four-Year	4	14.3	3,600,000	10.1	900,000
Two-Year	11	39.3	8,520,000	24.1	774,545

SOURCE: U.S. Office of Education, *Strengthening Developing Institutions Title III, of the Higher Education Act of 1965 Annual Report*, March 1974, p. 45.

TABLE C-6. Rank Order of Top Ten States by Public Two-Year College Enrollments, Fall 1973.

RANK	STATE	FALL 1973 ENROLLMENT	NO. OF INSTITUTIONS
1	California	847,759	98
2	New York	233,682	45
3	Illinois	214,400	48
4	Texas	156,632	56
5	Michigan	151,000	32
6	Florida	133,793	28
7	Washington	104,236	27
8	Wisconsin	94,624	28
9	Ohio	80,846	41
10	Pennsylvania	72,026	34
TOTAL		2,088,998	437
Percent of All Two-Year Public Colleges		64.3%	46.8%

SOURCE: American Association of Community and Junior Colleges, *Community and Junior College Directory 1974*, Table III.

TABLE C-7. Rank Order of Top Ten States by Private Two-Year College Enrollments, Fall 1973.

RANK	STATE	FALL 1973 ENROLLMENT	NO. OF INSTITUTIONS
1	Massachusetts	12,563	21
2	Pennsylvania	9,121	14
3	New York	7,221	14
4	Illinois	6,976	8
5	North Carolina	6,198	10
6	New Jersey	5,886	8
7	Texas	4,864	8
8	Idaho	4,750	2
9	Delaware	3,567	3
10	South Carolina	3,404	6
TOTAL		64,550	94
Percent of All Two-Year Private Colleges		49.4%	40.5%

SOURCE: American Association of Community and Junior Colleges, *Community and Junior College Directory 1974*, Table IV.

TABLE C-8. Private College Enrollment Ranked by State, Fall 1973.

Rank Order[1]	State	Private Enrollment	Total U.S. Enrollment	Percent Distribution of Total U.S.[2]	Private as Percent of Total[3]
1	New York	352,992	895,400	9.4	39.4
2	Massachusetts	191,652	329,693	3.4	58.1
3	Pennsylvania	178,808	440,321	4.6	40.6
4	California	146,696	1,467,355	15.3	10.0

Table C-8 *(continued)*

5	Illinois	132,991	494,859	5.2	26.8
6	Ohio	94,950	394,200	4.1	24.1
7	Texas	80,774	503,612	5.3	16.0
8	New Jersey	67,616	255,314	2.7	26.5
9	District of Columbia	65,686	80,326	.8	81.8
10	Missouri	54,069	191,749	2.0	28.2
11	Indiana	42,992	198,457	2.1	26.7
12	Connecticut	52,375	135,250	1.4	38.7
13	Michigan	51,675	426,126	4.4	12.1
14	North Carolina	49,438	204,080	2.1	24.2
15	Florida	46,541	281,394	2.9	16.5
16	Tennessee	37,257	154,410	1.6	24.1
17	Iowa	35,483	109,118	1.1	32.5
18	Minnesota	32,416	163,781	1.7	19.8
19	Maryland	32,305	177,166	1.8	18.2
20	Utah	30,478	80,465	.8	37.9
21	Wisconsin	29,985	221,256	2.3	13.6
22	Virginia	28,320	193,277	2.0	14.7
23	Georgia	27,129	146,356	1.5	18.5
24	Rhode Island	25,133	55,122	.6	45.6
25	South Carolina	22,856	94,699	1.0	24.1
26	Washington	22,707	199,478	2.1	11.4
27	Oklahoma	20,027	125,740	1.3	15.9
28	Louisiana	19,809	135,247	1.4	14.6
29	Kentucky	18,746	110,611	1.2	16.9
30	Alabama	16,314	125,076	1.3	13.0
31	Oregon	14,200	131,281	1.4	10.8
32	New Hampshire	14,135	32,924	.3	42.9
33	Colorado	14,016	131,189	1.4	10.7
34	Nebraska	13,355	65,788	.7	20.3
35	Kansas	12,419	107,986	1.1	11.5
36	Vermont	11,548	27,705	.3	41.7
37	West Virginia	10,125	68,074	.7	14.9
38	Mississippi	9,332	82,255	.9	11.3
39	Maine	8,825	36,122	.4	24.4
40	Arkansas	8,774	52,512	.5	16.7
41	Idaho	6,719	35,198	.4	19.1
42	South Dakota	6,035	26,530	.3	22.7
43	Arizona	4,684	138,241	1.4	3.4
44	New Mexico	4,238	48,636	.5	8.7
45	Delaware	4,057	28,841	.3	14.1
46	Hawaii	3,144	42,717	.4	7.4
47	Montana	2,641	29,189	.3	9.0
48	North Dakota	1,266	29,442	.3	4.3
49	Alaska	1,237	14,184	.1	8.7
50	Nevada	117	20,044	.2	.6
51	Wyoming	0	17,922	.2	.0
	Total	2,169,087	9,571,118	100.0	22.7

SOURCE: U.S. Office of Education, *Opening Fall Enrollment in Higher Education*, preliminary data, 1973. *Diversity Among the Fifty States in Higher Education*, American Council on Education, July 1974.

[1]Ranked by private enrollment.
[2]Percent of state enrollment in aggregate total. Percentages may not add to total due to rounding.
[3]Percent of private enrollment in state total.

TABLE C-9. Enrollment in 185 Two-Year Colleges by Sex and Type of Institution, Fall 1973.

			Type of Institution		
Sex	*Junior*	*Community*	*Tech*	*Tech/Voc*	*Total*
Male	16,245	72,973	32,275	13,210	134,703
Female	20,597	55,990	14,798	5,186	96,571
Total	36,842	128,963	47,073	18,396	231,274
			Percent Distribution/Sex		
Sex					
Male	44.1	56.5	68.5	71.8	58.2
Female	55.9	43.4	31.4	28.1	41.7
Total	100.0	100.0	100.0	100.0	100.0
			Percent Distribution/Institution		
Sex					
Male	12.1	54.2	23.9	9.8	100.0
Female	21.3	58.0	15.3	5.4	100.0
Total	15.9	55.8	20.4	7.9	100.0

SOURCE: ACT Special Report No. 11, *Career Education and Transfer Program Enrollment in Two-Year Colleges, 1973-74*, Table 5.

TABLE C-10. Percent Enrolled in Career Education and Transfer Programs in 158 Two-Year Colleges by Sex and Type of Institution, Fall 1973.

			Type of Institution (N=158)			
	Total Enrolled	*All Institutions*	*Junior*	*Community*	*Tech.*	*Tech/Voc.*
All Students						
Career Ed.	132,176	57.2	41.8	49.1	78.1	90.0
Transfer	99,098	42.8	58.1	50.8	21.8	9.9
Total	231,274	100.0	100.0	100.0	100.0	100.0
Males Only						
Career Ed.	80,012	59.4	32.4	50.3	80.3	91.3
Transfer	54,691	40.6	67.5	49.6	19.6	8.6
Total	134,703	100.0	100.0	100.0	100.0	100.0
Females Only						
Career Ed.	52,164	54.0	49.2	47.6	73.3	86.5
Transfer	44,407	46.0	50.7	52.3	26.6	13.4
Total	96,571	100.0	100.0	100.0	100.0	100.0

SOURCE: ACT Special Report No. 11, *Career Education and Transfer Program Enrollments in Two-Year Colleges*, 1973-74, Table 5.

Graduate and Professional School Enrollment

TABLE D-1. Proposed Graduate Majors of Black Graduate Availability Pool, Spring 1974.

Proposed Graduate Major	Male	Female	Total
HUMANITIES	(87)	(134)	(221)
English	21.8	18.6	19.9
Music, Fine Arts and Speech	32.1	33.5	33.0
Other	45.9	47.7	47.0
Total	100%	100%	100%
SOCIAL SCIENCES	(728)	(961)	(1,689)
Business	11.9	4.1	7.5
Education and Guidance			
Counseling	18.6	29.4	24.8
History and Political Sci.	9.3	5.3	7.0
Psychology and Sociology	14.1	18.5	16.6
Other	45.8	42.4	43.9
Total	100%	100%	100%
BIOLOGICAL SCIENCES	(94)	(133)	(227)
Biology	10.6	5.2	7.4
Home Economics and Nursing	5.3	9.0	7.4
Hospital Administr. and			
Public Health	31.9	27.0	29.0
Other	52.1	58.6	55.9
Total	100%	100%	100%
PHYSICAL SCIENCES	(71)	(28)	(99)
Chemistry	14.0	3.5	11.1
Engineering	28.1	0	20.2
Mathematics	9.8	32.1	16.1
Other	47.8	64.2	52.5
Total	100%	100%	100%

SOURCE: Educational Testing Service, Minority Graduate Student Locater Service, unpublished data (1975).

TABLE D-2. Undergraduate Majors of Black Graduate Availability Pool, Spring 1974.

Undergraduate Major	Male	Female	Total
HUMANITIES	(133)	(244)	(377)
English	32.3	44.6	40.3
Music, Fine Arts, and Speech	27.8	20.0	22.8
Other	39.8	35.2	36.8
Total	100%	100%	100%
SOCIAL SCIENCES	(696)	(878)	(1,574)
Business	11.3	3.4	6.9
Education	6.0	20.6	18.3
History and Political Sci.	25.2	12.8	35.9
Psychology and Sociology	30.3	40.3	35.9
Other	27.2	22.9	24.7
Total	100%	100%	100%
BIOLOGICAL SCIENCES	(66)	(101)	(167)
Biology	68.1	36.6	49.1
Home Economics and Nursing	0	35.6	21.5
Other	31.8	27.7	29.3
Total	100%	100%	100%

SOURCE: Educational Testing Service, Minority Graduate Student Locater Service, unpublished data (1975).

TABLE D-3. Characteristics of the ETS Black Graduate Availability Pool, Spring 1974.

	Male		Female		Total	
Characteristics	Number	Percent	Number	Percent	Number	Percent
Marital Status						
Single	699	70.5	1,043	81.4	1.742	76.6
Married	270	27.2	148	11.5	418	18.3
Other	22	2.2	90	7.0	112	4.9
Total	991	100%	1,281	100%	2,272	100%
Military Status						
Veterans	205	20.9	17	1.4	222	10.4
Non-veterans	772	79.0	1,140	98.5	1,912	89.5
Total	977	100%	1,157	100%	2,134	100%
Educational Status						
Enrolled	(717)	(72.5)	(972)	(75.9)	(1,689)	(74.5)
Junior Year	58	5.9	73	5.7	131	5.8
Senior Year	594	60.0	859	67.1	1,453	64.1
Grad School	65	6.6	40	3.1	105	4.6
Not enrolled	(258)	(26.1)	(293)	(22.9)	(551)	(24.3)
No Degree	0	0	2	0.15	2	.08
Bachelor	199	20.1	233	18.2	432	19.0

Table D-3 (continued)

Characteristics	Male		Female		Total	
	Number	Percent	Number	Percent	Number	Percent
Masters	59	6.0	58	4.5	117	5.2
Other	(14)	(1.4)	(14)	(1.1)	(28)	(1.2)
Total	989	100%	1279	100%	2268	100%
Overall GPA						
C or Lower	321	32.4	306	24.0	627	27.7
B or A	667	67.5	964	75.4	1631	72.2
Total	988	100%	1270	100%	2258	100%
Characteristics						
GPA In Major						
C or Lower	154	15.7	159	12.5	313	13.9
B or A	829	84.3	1,114	87.5	1,943	86.1
Total	983	100%	1,273	100%	2,256	100%
GPA Last Two Years of College						
C or Lower	131	13.5	172	13.7	303	13.6
B or A	840	86.5	1,086	86.3	1,926	86.4
Total	971	100%	1,258	100%	2,229	100%
Immediate Objective						
No Degree	5	0.50	10	0.78	15	0.66
Masters Degree	614	62.3	926	72.5	1,540	68.1
Doctorate Degree	366	37.2	341	26.7	707	31.2
Total	985	100%	1,277	100%	2,262	100%
Long Range Objective						
No Degree	0	0	0	0.23	3	0.13
Masters Degree	224	22.7	395	40.0	619	27.4
Doctorate Degree	761	77.3	878	68.8	1,639	72.5
Total	985	100%	1,276	100%	2,261	100%
Age						
Under 21	83	8.4	186	14.6	269	11.9
21 to 23	502	51.1	777	60.9	1,279	56.6
24 to 26	194	19.7	143	11.2	337	14.9
27 to 29	99	10.1	59	4.6	158	7.0
30 and Above	105	10.7	111	8.7	215	9.5
Total	983	100%	1,276	100%	2,258	100%
Regional Origin						
New England	69	7.0	98	7.7	167	7.4
Mid Atlantic	350	35.6	480	37.7	830	36.8
South	243	24.7	327	25.7	570	25.3
Midwest	177	18.0	213	16.7	390	17.3
Southwest	117	11.9	131	10.3	248	11.0
West and Territories	26	2.6	24	1.9	50	2.2
Total	982	100%	1,273	100%	2,255	100%

Table D-3 (continued)

Characteristics	Male Number	Male Percent	Female Number	Female Percent	Total Number	Total Percent
Regional Preferences						
New England	59	6.0	76	5.9	135	6.0
Mid Atlantic	207	21.0	346	27.1	553	24.4
South	71	7.2	122	9.5	193	8.5
Mid West	86	8.7	135	10.6	221	9.8
Southwest	104	10.5	106	8.3	210	9.3
West	19	1.9	20	1.6	39	1.7
No Preference	441	44.7	473	37.0	914	40.3
Total	987	100%	1,278	100%	2,265	100%

SOURCE: Educational Testing Service (1975). Minority Graduate Student Locater Service, unpublished data.

TABLE D-4. Doctorates earned, by field of study and race, Spring 1973.

Field of Study	(Citizens and Noncitizens) Total*	Black	White	Other
Physical Sciences	4,338	45	3,396	897
Engineering	2,738	27	1,902	809
Life Sciences	4,073	96	3,185	792
Social Sciences	4,796	87	4,069	640
Arts and Humanities	4,461	74	3,894	493
Professional Fields	1,151	24	994	133
Education	5,670	382	4,811	477
Total	27,227	735	22,251	4,241
	Percent Distribution (Within Race)			
Physical Sciences	15.9	6.1	15.3	21.2
Engineering	10.1	3.7	8.5	19.1
Life Sciences	15.0	13.1	14.3	18.7
Social Sciences	17.6	11.8	18.3	15.1
Arts and Humanities	16.4	10.1	17.5	11.6
Professional Fields	4.2	3.2	4.4	3.1
Education	20.8	52.0	21.6	11.2
Total	100	100	100	100
	Percent Distribution (Within Field of Study)			
Physical Sciences	100	1.0	78.3	20.7
Engineering	100	1.0	69.5	29.5
Life Sciences	100	2.4	78.2	19.4
Social Sciences	100	1.8	84.8	13.4
Arts and Humanities	100	1.7	87.3	11.0
Professional Fields	100	2.1	86.4	11.5
Education	100	6.7	84.9	8.4
Total	100	2.7	81.7	15.6

SOURCE: National Research Council (1974). *Summary Report 1973 Doctorate Recipients From United States Universities*, pp. 4 and 5.

*Equals 81% of the 33,727 doctorates awarded Spring 1973.

TABLE D-5. Doctorates Awarded Within Fields of Study to Native-Born U.S. Citizens, by Race (Equals 85% of the Doctorates Awarded), Spring 1973.

Field of Study	Total	Black	Mexican American/ Spanish	Puerto Rican	Ameri- can Indian	Orien- tal	White (Inc) Other)
Physical Sciences and Mathematics	3,051	32	12	3	10	18	2,976
	100%	1.0%	.4%	.1%	.3%	.6%	97.5%
Physics & Astronomy	876	9	—	—	3	2	862
	100%	1.0%	—	—	.3%	.2%	98.4%
Chemistry	1,122	18	7	1	3	7	1,086
	100%	1.6%	.6%	.1%	.3%	.6%	96.8%
Earth Sciences	334	—	1	2	3	3	325
	100%	—	.3%	.6%	.9%	.9%	97.3%
Mathematics	719	5	4	—	1	6	703
	100%	.7%	.6%	—	.1%	.8%	97.8%
Engineering	1,546	17	1	3	6	14	1,505
	100%	1.1%	.1%	.2%	.4%	.9%	97.3%
Life Sciences	2,923	51	15	6	17	44	2,790
	100%	1.7%	.5%	.2%	.6%	1.5%	95.4%
Basic Medical Sciences	1,144	27	5	6	5	22	1,079
	100%	2.3%	.4%	.5%	.4%	1.9%	94.3%
Other Biosciences	901	10	6	—	5	13	867
	100%	1.1%	.7%	—	.5%	1.4%	96.0%
Medical Sciences	304	8	2	—	2	6	286
	100%	2.6%	.7%	—	.7%	2.0%	94.1%
Agricultural Sciences	512	5	2	—	5	3	497
	100%	1.0%	.4%	—	1.0%	.6%	97.1%
Environmental Sciences	62	1	—	—	—	—	61
	100%	1.6%	—	—	—	—	98.4%
Social Sciences	3,745	59	16	8	21	22	3,619
	100%	1.6%	.4%	.2%	.6%	.6%	96.6%
Psychology	1,691	23	7	4	9	10	1,638
	100%	1.4%	.4%	.2%	.5%	.6%	96.6%
Economics	481	2	1	1	3	3	471
	100%	.4%	.2%	.2%	.6%	.6%	97.9%
Anthropology	587	19	2	2	6	5	553
	100%	3.2%	.3%	.3%	.5%	.8%	94.2%
Pol. Sci., Public Admin., & Internatl. Relations	547	6	3	1	2	3	532
	100%	1.0%	.5%	.2%	.4%	.5%	97.3%
Other Social Sciences	439	9	3	—	1	1	425
	100%	2.1%	.7%	—	.2%	.2%	96.8%

Table D-5 (continued)

Field of Study	Total*	Black	Mexican American/ Spanish	Puerto Rican	American Indian	Oriental	White (Inc.) Other)
Arts & Humanities	3,512	50	19	6	18	10	3,409
	100%	1.4%	.5%	.2%	.5%	.3%	97.1%
History	835	17	2	2	3	1	810
	100%	2.1%	.2%	.2%	.4%	.1%	97.0%
English & American Lang & Lit.	1,035	12	3	—	6	3	1,011
	100%	1.1%	.3%	—	.6%	.3%	97.7%
Foreign Lang & Lit.	513	6	11	4	1	2	489
	100%	1.2%	2.1%	.8%	.2%	.4%	95.3%
Other Arts & Humanities	1,129	15	3	—	8	4	1,099
	100%	1.3%	.3%	—	.7%	.4%	97.3%
Other Professional Fields	873	17	—	—	1	3	852
	100%	1.9%	—	—	.1%	.3%	97.6%
Education	4,991	346	30	10	34	12	4,559
	100%	6.9%	.6%	.2%	.7%	.2%	91.3%

SOURCE: National Board on Graduate Education (NRC National Academy of Sciences, Doctorate Records File), 1975.

TABLE D-6. Enrollment in Ph.D.-Granting Institutions in 1973, by Race and Control (n=154).

Type of Enrollment	Public (n = 93)	Private (n = 61)	Total (n = 154)
Graduate Enrollment	283,723	89,241	372,964
Black Enrollment	12,768	3,570	16,338
Average Black Enrollment	137.2	58.5	106.0
Percent Distribution			
Graduate Enrollment	76.07%	23.9%	100%
Black Enrollment	78.14%	21.8%	100%

SOURCE: El-Khawas, Elaine H. and Kinzer, Joan L., *Enrollment of Minority Graduate Students at Ph.D.-Granting Institutions.* Higher Education Panel Reports, No. 19, ACE (1974), Table 1.

TABLE D-7. Field of Study of College Students 14 to 34 Years Old by Race and Sex, October 1972 (In Thousands).[a]

Race and Sex	Total	Agriculture or Forestry	Biological Sciences	Business or Commerce	Education	Engineering	English or Journalism	Other Humanities
WHITE								
Total	7,458	95	234	1,048	904	331	270	410
Males	4,397	85	148	831	257	327	136	213
Females	3,061	11	89	216	649	3	134	197
BLACK								
Total	727	2	19	90	90	19	17	33
Males	384	2	17	48	20	19	3	21
Females	342	–	3	41	71	–	15	12

Race and Sex	Health or Medical Profession	Law	Mathematics or Statistics	Physical or Earth Sciences	Social Sciences	Other Fields	Don't Know or Not Reported
WHITE							
Total	617	207	216	140	837	1,392	755
Males	266	175	144	103	443	839	437
Females	352	33	73	38	395	533	317
BLACK							
Total	67	28	12	10	103	99	136
Males	28	21	7	7	51	58	81
Females	39	7	5	3	52	41	55

SOURCE: *Social and Economic Characteristics of Students, October 1972*, Population Characteristics, Series P-20 No. 260, February 1974, U.S. Department of Commerce, Bureau of the Census, Table 17.

[a]Weighted Totals.

TABLE D-8. Percent Distribution of Field of Study of College Students 14 to 34 Years Old by Sex and Race, October 1972 (In Thousands).

Race and Sex	Total	Agriculture or Forestry	Biological Sciences	Business or Commerce	Education	Engineering	English or Journalism	Other Humanities
WHITE								
Total	100	1.3	3.1	14.1	12.1	4.4	3.6	5.5
Males	100	1.9	3.3	18.9	5.8	7.4	3.1	4.8
Females	100	.4	2.9	7.1	21.2	.1	4.4	6.4
BLACK								
Total	100	.3	2.6	12.5	12.4	2.6	2.3	4.5
Males	100	0.5	4.4	12.5	5.2	4.9	.8	5.5
Females	100	–	.9	11.9	20.7	–	4.3	3.5

Race and Sex	Health or Medical Profession	Law	Mathematics or Statistics	Physical or Earth Sciences	Social Sciences	Other Fields	Don't Know or Not Reported
WHITE							
Total	8.3	2.8	2.9	1.9	11.2	18.7	10.1
Males	6.0	4.0	3.3	2.3	10.1	19.1	9.9
Females	11.5	1.1	2.4	1.2	12.9	18.1	10.3
BLACK							
Total	9.2	3.9	1.7	1.4	14.2	13.6	18.7
Males	7.3	5.5	1.8	1.8	13.3	15.1	21.1
Females	11.4	2.0	1.4	0.8	15.2	11.9	16.0

SOURCE: Table D-7.

TABLE D-9. Field of Study of College Students 14 to 34 Years Old by Region of Residence, Type of College, Whether Attending Full- or Part-Time, and Race, October 1972 (In Thousands).

Region, Type of College, and Full- or Part-Time Attendance	Total	Agriculture or Forestry	Biological Sciences	Business or Commerce	Education	Engineering	English or Journ.	Other Humanities
WHITE								
Region of Residence								
USA	7,458	95	234	1,048	904	331	271	410
Northeast	1,968	17	70	239	246	74	65	141
North Central	2,061	31	54	326	290	119	87	98
South	1,877	22	68	305	230	78	55	84
West	1,551	26	41	179	138	60	64	87
Type of College								
All Colleges[1]	7,458	95	234	1,048	904	331	271	410
Two-Year College	1,670	18	33	298	126	77	33	91
Four-Year College or University	4,396	66	167	644	566	201	183	250
1st and 2nd Year	2,088	43	67	291	239	82	71	131
3rd and 4th Year	2,308	23	100	353	327	119	111	119
Graduate School[2]	1,213	11	32	105	212	51	53	65
Full- or Part-Time Attendance								
All Students	7,458	95	234	1,048	904	331	271	410
Full-time	5,678	89	207	710	646	246	215	322
Part-time	1,779	6	27	337	259	84	55	89

Table D-9 (continued)

Region, Type of College, and Full- or Part-Time Attendance	Health or Medical Profession	Law	Mathematics or Statistics	Physical or Earth Sciences	Socal Sciences	Other Fields	Don't Know or Not Reported
WHITE							
Region of Residence							
USA	617	207	216	140	837	1,391	756
Northeast	154	50	58	27	289	349	191
North Central	168	51	53	31	199	383	171
South	174	54	63	42	190	314	197
West	121	52	41	40	160	345	197
Type of College							
All Colleges[1]	617	207	216	140	837	1,391	756
Two-Year College	144	29	41	23	124	439	192
Four-Year College or University	359	92	141	91	581	691	363
1st and 2nd Year	209	53	59	53	218	296	275
3rd and 4th Year	149	39	82	38	363	396	88
Graduate School[2]	109	86	31	26	126	258	47
Full- or Part-Time Attendance							
All Students	617	207	216	140	837	1,391	756
Full-Time	525	176	151	117	663	1,021	590
Part-Time	92	31	65	23	175	371	166

Region, Type of College, and Full- or Part-Time Attendance	Total	Agricultural or Forestry	Biological Sciences	Business or Commerce	Education	Engineering	English or Journ.	Other Humanities
BLACK								
Region of Residence								
USA	727	2	19	90	90	19	17	33
Northeast	138	—	5	8	26	5	2	5
North Central	183	—	3	34	21	5	5	11
South	301	2	8	36	37	5	8	9
West	105	—	2	13	6	4	1	7
Type of College								
All Colleges[1]	727	2	19	90	90	19	17	33
Two-Year College	200	—	11	37	9	9	4	12
Four-Year College or University	397	2	6	45	66	8	11	16
1st and 2nd Year	229	—	4	32	34	6	8	6
3rd and 4th Year	168	2	2	14	32	2	3	10
Graduate School[2]	87	—	2	8	15	2	2	5
Full- or Part-Time Attendance								
All Students	727	2	19	90	90	19	17	33
Full-Time	525	2	12	65	65	14	12	25
Part-Time	201	—	7	25	25	5	4	9

Table D-9 (continued)

Region, Type of College, and Full- or Part-Time Attendance	Health or Medical Profession	Law	Mathematics or Statistics	Physical or Earth Sciences	Social Sciences	Other Fields	Don't Know or Not Reported
BLACK							
Region of Residence							
USA	67	28	12	10	103	99	136
Northeast	16	5	—	4	13	20	29
North Central	18	9	1	2	20	19	34
South	15	13	10	3	51	51	53
West	18	1	1	2	19	10	20
Type of College							
All Colleges[1]	67	28	12	10	103	99	136
Two-Year College	21	8	5	5	17	32	30
Four-Year College or University	38	12	3	6	70	47	66
1st and 2nd Year	17	6	1	4	37	27	46
3rd and 4th Year	21	6	2	2	33	20	19
Graduate School[2]	8	8	5	—	14	18	1
Full- or Part-Time Attendance							
All Students	67	28	12	10	103	99	136
Full-Time	53	22	8	10	67	60	110
Part-Time	14	7	5	—	36	39	26

SOURCE: U.S. Census. *Social and Economic Characteristics of Students, October 1972.* Table 18.

[1]Includes persons who did not report on type of college attended, not shown separately.

[2]Comprised of persons enrolled in the fifth or higher year of college.

TABLE D-10. Enrollments in Health Professions by Race and Field of Study, Fall 1971 or 1972.

Field	Total	Black	Percent Black
Medicine (1972)	47,366	2,582	5.5
Osteopathic Medicine (1971)	2,303	27	1.2
Veterinary Medicine (1971)	5,205	96	1.8
Optometry (1971)	3,068	32	1.0
Pharmacy (1972)	17,909	659	3.7
Podiatry (1971)	1,267	27	2.1

SOURCE: DHEW, Public Health Service. *Minorities and Women in the Health Fields.*

Table D-11. Distribution of Health Aspirants, by Health Study and by Race, for 1972 (in Percentage).

Field	Black	Non-Black	Total
Biology	6.7	8.4	8.3
Biochemistry	1.4	2.2	2.2
Biophysics	.3	.2	.2
Botany	.1	.8	.7
Zoology	.6	2.4	2.3
Other Biological Sciences	2.0	6.0	5.7
Health Technology	13.6	14.4	14.3
Nursing	40.1	20.9	22.4
Pharmacy	3.7	4.4	4.3
Predentistry	2.6	4.2	4.1
Premedicine	17.8	19.6	19.5
Preveterinary Medicine	1.1	6.7	6.2
Therapy	10.0	9.8	9.8
Total	100.0	100.0	100.0
N	22,508	277,664	300,172

SOURCE: American Council on Education, *Trends and Career Changes of Students in the Health Fields,* p. 37.

**TABLE D-12. Enrollment in U.S. Dental Schools
By Race and Year in Training, Fall 1973.**

	1st	2nd	3rd	4th	Total
Black					
Number	273	232	233	134	872
Percent	5.0	4.4	5.2	3.1	4.5
Puerto Rican					
Number	5	1	4	2	12
Percent	.09	.01	.08	.04	.06
Mexican American					
Number	64	56	27	27	174
Percent	1.2	1.0	0.6	0.6	0.8
American Indian					
Number	12	6	6	4	28
Percent	2.2	0.1	0.1	.09	0.1
Asian American					
Number	141	158	93	98	490
Percent	2.5	3.0	2.0	2.3	2.5
Other Minority					
Number	34	26	14	6	80
Percent	0.6	0.5	0.3	0.1	0.4
Non-minorities					
Number	4,916	4,750	4,080	3,967	17,713
Percent	90.2	90.8	91.5	93.6	91.4
All Students					
Number	5,445	5,229	4,457	4,238	19,369
Percent	100	100	100	100	100

SOURCE: Annual Report, *Dental Education 1973/74.* American Dental Association, p. 4, Figures 2 and 3.

TABLE D-13. Total Dental Auxiliary Enrollment, by Race and Type of Program, Fall 1972.

	All Races	White	Black	Puerto Rican	Mexican American	American Indian	Oriental	Other	Unidentified*
Total Enrollment	18,812	15,616	642	139	309	77	252	48	1,729
Percentage	100%	83.0	3.4	0.8	1.6	0.4	1.3	0.3	9.2
Dental Hygiene-Bachelor's Program									
1st Year	100%	90.9	1.6	0.2	0.2	0.0	2.1	0.0	5.0
2nd Year	100%	94.2	1.7	0.3	0.1	0.1	1.2	0.0	2.4
Total	100%	92.4	1.7	0.2	0.1	0.1	1.7	0.0	3.8
Dental Hygiene-Certificate Program									
1st Year	100%	90.5	2.0	0.7	0.3	0.1	0.9	0.4	5.1
2nd Year	100%	89.0	1.4	0.6	0.3	0.2	0.8	0.3	7.4
Total	100%	89.8	1.7	0.7	0.3	0.1	0.9	0.3	6.2
Dental Assisting Program									
1st Year	100%	76.9	4.1	0.9	2.2	0.9	1.0	0.0	14.0
2nd Year	100%	78.0	3.7	0.5	5.6	0.2	2.1	0.2	9.7
Total	100%	77.1	4.1	0.7	2.8	0.8	1.2	0.2	13.1
Dental Laboratory Technology Program									
1st Year	100%	68.7	9.9	2.2	3.2	0.2	3.8	0.8	11.2
2nd Year	100%	76.4	9.0	0.8	4.8	0.2	4.7	0.2	3.9
Total	100%	71.5	9.5	1.7	4.0	0.2	4.0	0.6	8.5

SOURCE: Minority Enrollment 1972 Auxiliary Programs. Annual Report, *Dental Education Supplement 1972/1973*, American Dental Association, p. 1.

*Unidentified—school failed to give ethnic breakdown.

TABLE D-14. Enrollment in U.S. Medical Schools by Race for First-Year Classes and Total, Fall 1973.

	First-Year Class	Total Enrolled
Black		
Number	1,019	3,041
Percent	7.3	6.0
American Indian		
Number	44	96
Percent	0.3	0.2
Mexican American		
Number	174	496
Percent	1.2	1.0
Puerto Rican		
Number	55	122
Percent	0.4	0.2
Non-minorities (Including Foreign Students)		
Number	12,752	46,881
Percent	90.8	92.6
Total		
Number	14,044	50,636
Percent	100	100

SOURCE: "Information for Minority Group Students" (Reprint), *Medical School Admission Requirements, 1975-76, U.S.A. and Canada.* Association of American Medical Colleges, Tables 6-B and 6-C.

TABLE D-15. First-Year U.S. and Foreign Student Enrollments in U.S. Medical Schools by Race, 1968 through 1972.

Groups	1968-69 (99 schools) No.	%*	1969-70 (101 schools) No.	%*	1970-71 (102 schools) No.	%*	1971-72 (108 schools) No.	%*	1972-73 (114 schools) No.	%*	Incr. from 1971-72 to 1972-1973 No.	%*
Selected U.S. Minorities												
Black American	266	2.7	440	4.2	697	6.1	882	7.1	957	7.1	75	8.5
American Indian	3	†	7	.1	11	.1	23	.2	34	.3	11	47.8
Mexican American	20	.2	44	.4	73	.6	118	1.0	137	1.0	19	16.1
Puerto Rican—Mainland	3	†	10	.1	27	.2	40	.3	44	.3	4	10.0
Total	292	2.9	501	4.8	808	7.0	1,063	8.6	1,172	8.6	109	10.3
Other U.S. Minorities												
American Oriental	121	1.2	140	1.3	190	1.7	217	1.8	231	1.7	14	6.5
Other‡	—	—	—	—	—	—	—	—	34	.3	34	.3
Total	121	1.2	140	1.3	190	1.7	217	1.8	265	2.0	48	2.1
Foreign Students												
Non-U.S. Black	39	.4	48	.5	87	.8	57	.5	88	.7	31	54.4
Other	82	.8	122	1.2	143	1.2	182	1.5	153	1.1	−29	−15.9
Total	121	1.2	170	1.6	230	2.0	239	1.9	241	1.8	2	.8
Total Non-minorities	9,329	94.7	9,611	92.3	10,120	89.8	10,842	87.7	12,133	87.6	1,050	9.7
Total U.S. Minorities	413	4.1	641	6.1	998	8.7	1,280	10.4	1,437	10.6	157	12.3
All Students	9,863	100%	10,422	100%	11,348	100%	12,316	100%	13,570	100%	1,209	9.8%

SOURCE: "U.S. Medical Student Enrollments, 1968-1969 through 1972-1973," *Journal of Medical Education*, p. 294, Tables 1 and 2.

*Percentage of first year U.S. medical school enrollment.

†Less than 0.1 percent.

‡Includes U.S. citizens from the following backgrounds: Arab Republic (1), Dominican Republic (1), East India (1), Ecuador (1), Egypt (1), Guam (1), India (1), Iran (1), Latin or Spanish America (4), Philippines (9), Samoa (2), not stated (11).

TABLE D-16. Percent Minority Enrollment in U.S. Medical Schools by Region, 1969-1970 and 1972-1973.*

Region	Black		Mexican-American		Asian-American	
	1969-70	1972-73	1969-70	1972-73	1969-70	1972-73
New England	2.6	5.8	0.05	0.3	1.1	2.4
Mid. Atlantic	1.8	5.4	—	—	0.9	1.2
East N. Central	1.8	5.3	0.06	0.4	0.9	1.0
West N. Central	0.5	3.0	0.05	0.3	0.8	0.9
South Atlantic	5.3	7.9	0.02	0.1	0.6	0.9
	(1.4)†	(3.9)†	—	—	—	—
East S. Central	9.3	11.7	—	—	0.2	0.3
	(0.7)†	(1.8)†	—	—	—	—
West S. Central	0.7	1.8	1.0	2.0	0.5	0.9
Mountain	0.4	1.6	1.5	4.9	1.9	1.6
Pacific	2.6	4.3	1.0	3.5	6.4	7.1
Total	2.7	5.5	0.2	0.8	1.3	1.6
	(1.5)†	(4.8)†	—	—	—	—

SOURCE: "Medical Education in the U.S., 1972-1973," *Journal of the American Medical Association*, Vol. 226, November 19, 1973, p. 914, Table 23.

*Percentages for 1969-1970 are based on enrollment in 100 schools; percentages for 1972-1973 are based on enrollment in 111 schools.

†Excluding Howard and Meharry Medical Schools.

TABLE D-17. AACP* Undergraduate Enrollment in Pharmacy by Class and Race for Final Three Years of Training, Fall 1973.

	Black			Other Minority			Total Minority		
	Male	Female	Total	Male	Female	Total	Male	Female	Total
Last Year									
Predominantly Minority Colleges[b]	29	21	50	22	4	26	51	25	76
Predominantly Non-minority Colleges	57	20	77	327	279	606	384	299	683
TOTAL	86	41	127	349	283	632	435	324	759
2nd Last Year									
Predominantly Minority Colleges[b]	80	49	129	36	48	84	116	97	213
Predominantly Non-minority Colleges	65	32	97	400	266	666	465	298	763
TOTAL	145	81	226	436	314	750	581	395	976
3rd Last Year									
Predominantly Minority Colleges[b]	79	56	135	50	13	63	129	69	198
Predominantly Non-minority Colleges	76	55	131	500	365	865	576	420	996
TOTAL	155	111	266	550	378	928	705	489	1,194
All Years and Institutions	386	233	619	1,335	975	2,310	1,721	1,208	2,929

Table D-17 (continued)

	Non-minority[c]			All Students[c]		
	Male	*Female*	*Total*	*Male*	*Female*	*Total*
Last Year						
Predominantly[b] Minority Colleges	61	26	87	112	51	163
Predominantly Non-minority Colleges	3,784	1,158	4,942	4,168	1,457	5,625
TOTAL	3,845	1,184	5,029	4,280	1,508	5,788
2nd Last Year						
Predominantly[b] Minority Colleges	55	5	60	171	102	273
Predominantly Non-minority Colleges	4,752	1,413	5,865	4,917	1,711	6,628
TOTAL	4,507	1,418	5,925	5,088	1,813	6,901
3rd Last Year						
Predominantly[b] Minority Colleges	31	11	42	160	80	240
Predominantly Non-minority Colleges	5,049	1,858	6,907	5,625	2,278	7,903
TOTAL	5,080	1,869	6,949			
All Years and Institutions	13,411	4,499	17,901	15,123	5,707	20,830

SOURCE: *Report on Enrollment in Schools and Colleges of Pharmacy First Semester, Term or Quarter, 1973-1974*, AACP.

* American Association of Colleges of Pharmacy.

[a] Includes six-year candidates for Pharm. D. who do not hold baccalaureate degree in Pharmacy.

[b] Refers to Howard University, Florida A&M, Xavier University and Texas Southern University.

[c] Includes foreign students.

TABLE D-18. AACP Graduate Enrollment in Pharmacy by Degree Level, Fall 1973.

Race	Masters		Doctoral		Total	
	No.	%	No.	%	No.	%
Black	19	2.0	10	0.6	29	1.0
Asian-American	36	3.0	45	3.0	81	3.0
Spanish-Surnamed	15	1.0	10	0.6	25	0.8
Other Minority	9	0.7	8	0.4	17	0.5
Non-Minority	1,144	94.0	1,585	96.0	2,729	95.0
TOTAL	1,223	100.0	1,658	100.0	2,881	100.0

SOURCE: *Graduate Enrollment Data, October 1973, and Graduate Study in Member Colleges,* 1974-1975. American Association of Colleges of Pharmacy.

TABLE D-19. Black Engineering College Enrollments by Year in School, 1969 to 1973.

Year In School	1969	1970	1971	1972	1973
Full-Time Only					
Freshmen	977	1,424	1,289	1,477	1,684
Sophomores	704	811	926	965	950
Juniors	430	664	693	838	784
Seniors	397	575	588	661	671
Fifth Year	25	24	26	34	42
Total Full-Time	2,533	3,498	3,522	3,975	4,131
All Undergraduate	2,757	3,753	4,136	4,356	4,869
M.S. Full-Time	55	106	112	165	221
Part-Time	84	109	140	172	157
Total	139	215	252	337	378
Ph.D. Full-Time	22	44	44	49	38
Part-Time	4	8	13	9	15
Total	26	52	57	58	54
Grad. Full-Time	81	171	192	238	272
Part-Time	88	119	154	181	183
Total	169	290	346	419	455

SOURCE: *Minorities in Engineering.* Planning Commission for Expanding Minority Opportunities in Engineering, Table 3-17.

TABLE D-20. Total Minority Enrollments in Law Schools[1], by Race and Ethnic Group, 1971-72 to 1973-74[2].

Race and Ethnic Group	1971-72	1972-73	1973-74
Black Americans	3,744 (4.0%)	4,423 4.3%)	4,817 (4.5%)
Mexican Americans	883 (.9%)	1,072 (1.0%)	1,259 (1.2%)
Puerto Ricans	94 (.1%)	143 (.1%)	180 (.2%)
American Indians	140 (.2%)	173 (.2%)	222 (.2%)
Asian Americans	480 (.5%)	681 (.7%)	850 (.8%)
Other Hispanic Americans	179 (.2%)	231 (.2%)	242 (.2%)
Total Minority	5,520 (5.9%)	6,723 (6.6%)	7,570 (7.1%)
Total: All Students[3]	93,118	101,664	106,102

SOURCE: National Board on Graduate Education. *Minority Participation in Graduate Education* (forthcoming), Adapted from *Law Schools and Bar Admission Requirements. A Review of Legal Education in the United States-Fall 1973* (Chicago: American Bar Association, 1974), pp. 44, 47.

[1]Includes all but one of the 148 continental U.S. law schools approved by the American Bar Association and excludes the three ABA-approved law schools in Puerto Rico.

[2]These are lower limits of estimated percentages due to exclusion of enrollments from four schools in the numerator. Estimated error is approximately 2% of the percentage shown.

[3]Includes all ABA-approved law schools.

TABLE D-21. Percent Distribution of Black Enrollment in 148 ABA-Approved Law Schools by Year in School, 1973.

Type of Law School	Total	I Yr.	II Yr.	III Yr.	IV Yr.	Yr. Not Stated
		Percent Distribution Within Institution				
Other	100	39.8	29.8	25.3	1.5	—
Black Colleges	100	37.9	32.9	29.2	—	—
All Institutions	100	39.4	30.4	26.1	1.1	2.8
		Percent by Institution				
Other	79.4	80.1	77.7	76.9	100	—
Black Colleges	20.6	19.8	22.3	23.1	—	—
All Institutions	100	100	100	100	100	100

SOURCE: Ruud, Millard, *Minority Law Enrollments.*

TABLE D-22. Undergraduate Black Enrollment in 47 Schools of Business by Field of Study, 1972.

Field of Study	Number Enrolled
Total	10,496
Accounting	2,570
Economics	260
Finance	260
General Business	477
Management	2,106
Marketing	1,215
Quantitative Methods	84
Information Systems	82
Insurance	60
International Business	10
Personnel and Organizational Behavior	217
Private Policy and Administration	7
Production Management	10
Real Estate	50
Transportation	15
Business Education	649
Public Administration	30
Other Business Fields	679
No Major	1,718

SOURCE: American Assembly of Collegiate Schools of Business, *Minority Report*, October 1973.

TABLE D-23. Graduate Students in Business Currently Enrolled in Doctoral Programs, by Race (Based on Responses From 47 Graduate Schools of Business), Fall 1973.

Student Enrollment	Total	White	Black
Number	3,583	2,397	468
Percent	100	66.8	13.0

Student Enrollment	American Indians	Asian American	Foreign Students
Number	1	20	697
Percent	.03	.6	19.4

SOURCE: American Assembly of Collegiate Schools of Business, unpublished data.

TABLE D-24. Black Enrollment in Schools of Business, Masters Programs, Fall 1972 (52 Institutions Represented).

Type of Degree	Black Enrollment
MBA	1,380
MA	41
MS	89
Other	148
Total	1,658

SOURCE: American Assembly of Collegiate Schools of Business. *Minority Report*, 1973, p. 7.

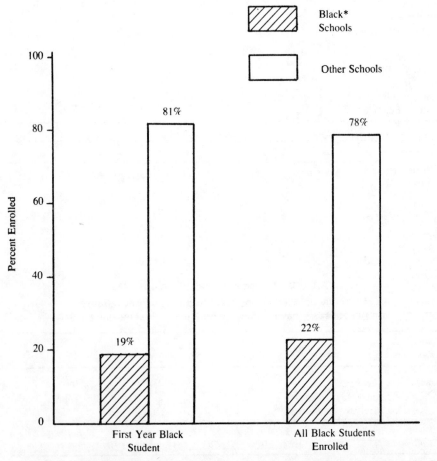

SOURCE: "Information for Minority Group Stuc nts," (Reprint) *Medical School Admission Requirements, 1975-76, U.S.A. and Canada.* Association of American Medical Colleges, Tables 6-B and 6-C.

(*Black Schools are Howard and Meharry Medical Schools.)

FIGURE D-1. Black Enrollment in U.S. Medical Schools that are Predominantly White or Black, Fall 1973.

**TABLE D-25. Percent Black Enrollments in Business
by Degree Level, Fall 1972.**

	Enrolled		
Degree Level	*Total*	*Black*	*Percent Black*
Bachelors	48,140	10,496	21.8
Masters	38,281	1,658	4.3
Total	86,421	12,154	14.0

SOURCE: Table D-21 and Table D-22.

Table D-26. Black Enrollment in Doctors of Religion by Field of Study, 1973

Field of Study	*Number Enrolled*
Social Ethics	12
Christian Ethics	5
Religion and Society	2
Systematic Theology	12
Applied Theology	1
Pastoral Theology	2
Theology and Culture	1
Theology and Personality	2
Theology and Religion	1
History of Religions	3
History of Christianity	1
Church History	3
Afro-American Religious History	3
Historical Studies	6
Old Testament	1
New Testament	4
Biblical Studies	3
Religion and Literature	2
Religion and Personality Sciences	0
Religion and Psychological Studies	3
Philosophy of Religion	3
Sociology of Religion	5
Pastoral Psychology	1
Church Administration	1
Religious Education	1
Professional Doctoral Program	30
Total	111

SOURCE: Grigsby, Marshall C. *Black American Graduate and Professional Doctors in Religion*, p. 289. American Association of Theological Schools.

**Table D-27. Minority Enrollment in Graduate Programs in Public Affairs
and Public Administration at NASPAA Institutions, Fall 1972.**

Race and Ethnic Group	Number	Percent
Blacks	995	75
Mexican Americans	176	13
American Indians	18	1
Asian Americans	53	4
Puerto Ricans	81	6
Total Minority	1,323	100%

SOURCE: National Association of Schools of Public Affairs and Administration, *Graduate School Programs in Public Affairs and Public Administration.* 1974, p. 2.

College Costs

TABLE E-1. Itemized Costs of Health Training by Type of Institution, 1973.

	Public Institutions			Private Institutions		
	Univ.	*4-Year*	*2-Year*	*Univ.*	*4-Year*	*2-Year*
Tuition & Required Fees	$ 520	$ 394	$ 242	$ 2,266	$ 1,881	$1,401
Board Rates	618	555	528	691	622	667
Dormitory Rooms	483	441	398	629	519	568
Total per Academic Year	1,621	1,390	1,168	3,584	3,022	2,636
4-Year Total	6,484	5,560	—	14,344	12,088	—
2-Year Total	—	—	2,336	—	—	5,272

SOURCE: Health Resources Administration, U.S. DHEW. *How To Pay For Your Health Career Education, A Guide for Minority Students*, (1974), pp. 2-3.

TABLE E-2. Average Annual Expenses of Students in Medical Schools, 1968.

	All Students	*Public Schools*	*Private Schools*
Total Expenses	$4,394	$3,982	$4,839
School Expenses	1,511	1,009	1,956
Lodging & Maintenance of Living Quarters	921	972	952
Board	809	825	853
All Other Expenses	1,153	1,182	1,076

SOURCE: Health Resources Administration, U.S. DHEW. *How to Pay For Your Health Career Education, A Guide for Minority Students*, (1974), p. 3.

TABLE E-3 Costs of Attending College in Health Fields, 1973.

	Annual Rate*	
Field	Public	Private
Dentistry	$1,211	$2,796
Pharmacy	$1,922 (Resident)	$3,107 (Resident)
	$2,707 (Non-Resident)	$3,151 (Non-Resident)
Veterinary Medicine (1972)	$2,000	$5,000
Nursing (1972		
Diploma	$1,445	
Associate Degree	$2,075	
Baccalaureate	$2,558	

SOURCE: Health Resources Administration. U.S. DHEW. *How To Pay For Your Health Career
       Education, A Guide for Minority Students,* (1974), pp. 4-5.
*Includes Tuition, Room and Board

A survey of public and private medical schools in Fall 1973 was done to estimate
the first-year expenses of U.S. medical schools in the 1975 school year AAMC,
1974. Table E-4 below summarizes the findings. In addition to books and supplies,
first-year medical students may have the costs for a microscope, which ranged from
$400 to $900 for monocular instruments, and $725 to $1,250 for binocular instruments. This expensive piece of equipment should be added to the other costs listed in
Table E-4.

**TABLE E-4. Estimated Minimum Expenses for First-Year Students
At U.S. Medical Schools (1975-76)*.**

	Private Schools			*Public Schools*		
First Year Expense Item	*Range*	*Median*	*Average*	*Range*	*Median*	*Average*
	$	$	$	$	$	$
Total Expenses		5,390	5,569	(R)	3,110	3,299
				(NR)	4,210	4,397
Tuition and Fees						
Resident	1,200-4,000	3,075	3,139	300-3,500	960	1,031
Non-Resident				570-4,500	2,060	2,129
Room and Board						
(Minimum)	1,080-3,500	2,000	2,086	940-4,000	1,800	1,898
Books and Supplies						
(Not including						
microscope)	180-700	315	344	150-1,100	350	370

SOURCE: *Medical School Admission Requirements, 1975-76, U.S.A. and Canada.* Reprint.
　　　　Chapter 4, p. 33, (1974).

*Figures based on data provided Fall 1973 by 45 private schools and 69 public schools. Four private
schools—Baylor, Mayo, Pittsburgh and Rush—report lower tuition for residents than for nonresi-
dents. The higher fees for these schools are used in the table.

TABLE E-5. Admissions Policies and Practices of Public and Private Colleges and Universities, Spring 1973.

Item	Two-Year Colleges			Four-Year Colleges			Universities			Total, All Institutions		
	Public	Private	Total	Public	Private	Total	Public	Private	Total	Public	Private	Total
Stated minimum admissions requirements for all first-year, nontransfer students	63.4	72.6	65.5	87.6	64.8	71.1	81.4	61.2	74.1	71.9	66.0	69.0
Special selection standards to control the proportion of women students	—	2.6	0.6	4.8	2.1	2.8	2.5	4.5	3.2	1.6	2.3	1.9
Special selection standards to control the proportion of Black Students	—	—	—	3.2	4.1	3.9	5.1	20.9	10.9	1.5	4.3	2.9
Special selection standards to control the proportion of students from other ethnic groups	—	—	—	3.8	3.3	3.4	8.5	16.2	11.3	1.8	3.4	2.6
Special admissions policies to control the proportion of students by geographic origin	9.7	2.6	8.1	19.6	1.8	6.7	28.0	10.4	21.6	14.2	2.4	8.4
Special efforts to recruit students from specific ethnic groups	44.5	35.9	45.2	64.2	56.3	58.5	77.1	83.8	79.6	53.1	54.0	53.5

Preferential admissions to spouses of matriculated students	0.9	4.7	1.7	—	8.2	5.9	5.9	11.8	8.1	1.1	7.7	4.4
Preferential admissions to veterans	37.2	18.4	33.0	41.1	34.1	36.1	41.5	29.9	37.3	38.8	31.0	35.0
Enrollment in some under-graduate courses by high school students (exclude extension, correspondence, or adult education)	78.6	68.8	76.4	74.7	67.3	69.3	81.4	65.7	75.7	77.7	67.4	72.7
Highly individualized admissions decisions based on appraisal of total applicant dossier	18.7	46.6	25.0	43.0	70.3	62.7	36.4	83.8	53.8	27.3	66.7	46.7
Open admissions by lottery	0.7	0.0	0.6	0.0	0.3	0.2	0.0	0.0	0.0	0.5	0.2	0.4
Open admissions on a first-come, first-served basis	38.9	12.4	33.0	7.5	5.8	6.3	4.2	0.0	2.7	26.8	6.8	17.0
Open admissions to any high school graduate	64.3	37.2	58.2	18.8	7.3	10.5	13.7	1.5	9.2	46.8	12.5	29.9
Open admissions, other	35.4	10.7	29.9	14.8	8.3	10.1	6.8	4.4	5.9	27.0	8.6	17.9

SOURCE: Creager, John A. *Selected Policies and Practices in Higher Education.* American Council on Education, Vol. 8, No. 4, (1973), Table 2.

**TABLE E-6. Graduate and Professional Schools Requiring One or More
Entrance Exams by Field, 1973-74 Academic Year.**

Fields	Total Number of Institutions	Requiring One or More Entrance Exams	
		Number	% of all institutions
Business	126	124	98.4
Law	122	122	100
Medical	76	75	98.7
Dental	27	27	100
Optometry	9	8	88.9
Graduate	282	244	86.5
Agriculture & Related	41	18	43.9
Anatomy	5	2	40.0
Animal Science	6	3	50.0
Anthropology	9	7	77.8
Architecture	13	11	84.6
Area Studies	7	5	71.4
Art	19	15	78.9
Atmospheric Sciences	3	2	66.7
Biochemistry & Biophysics	13	10	76.9
Biology	29	26	89.7
Botany	13	6	46.2
Business & Management	9	9	100
Chemistry	31	24	77.4
Child Development	6	5	83.3
Classics	6	4	66.7
Communications	15	13	86.7
Community Services	3	2	66.7
Comparative Literature	8	5	62.5
Computer Sciences	9	6	66.7
Dance	1	1	100
Earth Sciences	6	4	66.7
Economics	22	20	90.9
Education	74	58	78.4
Educ. Admin. & Superv.	12	11	91.7
Engineering	107	64	59.8
English	28	23	82.1
Epidemiology	2	2	100
Family Planning	2	0	——
Genetics	4	4	100
Geography	13	11	84.6
Geology	17	14	82.3
History	30	24	80.0
History & Philosophy of Education	1	1	100
Home Econ. & Related	31	18	58.1
Hospital & Health Care Admin.	2	2	100
Humanities	3	3	100
Laboratory Medicine	2	0	——

Table E-6 (continued)

Fields	Total Number of Institutions	Requiring One or More Entrance Exams	
		NUMBER	% of all institutions
Languages	45	26	57.8
Library & Information Sciences	12	11	91.7
Linguistics	7	6	85.7
Marine Sciences	3	3	100
Material Sciences & Rel.	8	3	37.5
Mathematics	33	20	60.6
Medical & Dental Specialties	15	2	13.3
Medical Sciences	3	2	66.7
Medical Technology	1	0	——
Microbiology & Immunology	12	10	83.3
Music	18	11	61.1
Nursing	6	6	100
Occupational Therapy	1	0	——
Pathology	6	4	66.7
Pharmacology	10	9	90.0
Pharmacy	7	3	42.9
Philosophy	18	14	77.8
Physical Education	26	18	69.2
Physical Therapy & Rehabilitation	6	4	66.7
Physics	36	28	77.8
Physiology	9	6	66.7
Political Science	32	28	87.5
Psychology	24	23	95.8
Public Admin.	8	6	75.0
Public Health	7	4	57.1
Religion	10	8	80.0
Social Work	8	5	62.5
Sociology	21	20	95.2
Special Education	7	5	71.4
Speech	4	1	25.0
Speech Communication	4	2	50.0
Speech Path. & Audiology	8	6	75.0
Speech & Theatre	10	6	60.0
Statistics	10	7	70.0
Student Personnel	10	8	80.0
Urban & Regional Planning	5	5	100
Urban Studies	1	1	100
Veterinary Med. Specialties	13	3	23.1
Zoology & Entomology	13	10	76.9
Total	1,718	1,367	79.6

SOURCE: Educational Testing Service, *Graduate and Professional School Opportunities for Minority Students*. Fifth Edition, 1973-74. (1974), pp. 14-209.

TABLE E-7. Financial Assistance Pattern of Black Full-Time Freshmen Attending Public Four-Year Colleges and Universities By Family Income, Fall 1973 (unweighted).

Family Income[1]	TYPE OF AID						
	Part-time or Summer Work	Full-Time Work	Savings	Spouse	Parents	Parents' Military Benefits	
$5,999 or less							
%Receiving Aid	39.8%	8.9%	18.6%	1.9%	41.0%	3.9%	
Average Aid Received	$387	$617	$392	$617	$454	$725	
$6,000 to $9,999							
% Receiving Aid	47.5%	8.8%	24.1%	2.3%	58.6%	4.4%	
Average Aid Received	$375	$806	$380	$692	$618	$925	
$10,000 to $14,999							
% Receiving Aid	48.3%	9.0%	30.0%	2.0%	71.5%	3.9%	
Average Aid Received	$375	$820	$452	$1,655	$999	$1,437	
$15,000 and Above							
%Receiving Aid	44.6%	8.1%	31.1%	2.5%	76.3%	3.6%	
Average Aid Received	$423	$848	$492	$1,582	$1,683	$1,167	

TYPE OF AID

	Parents Social Security	G.I. Benefits	Scholarship or Grant	Fed.-Insured Loans	Other Repayable Loans	Other Aid
$5,999 or less						
% Receiving Aid	14.6%	1.4%	54.2%	31.9%	9.5%	5.8%
Average Aid Received	$468	$1,261	$903	$839	986	$720
$6,000 to $9,999						
% Receiving Aid	7.4%	1.6%	51.0%	31.4%	10.9%	4.9%
Average Aid Received	$611	$1,274	$990	$875	$1,017	$1,004
$10,000 to $14,999						
% Receiving Aid	5.5%	1.5%	42.0%	22.0%	9.3%	5.4%
Average Aid Received	$669	$1,247	$954	$1,037	$1,181	$880
$15,000 and Above						
% Receiving Aid	4.6%	1.0%	27.9%	14.0%	7.5%	4.6%
Average Aid Received	$954	$1,440	$949	$1,342	$1,394	$1,216

SOURCE: American Council on Education, CIRP Freshmen Norms (1973), unpublished data.

[1]Gross family income.

Table E-8. Financial assistance pattern of white full-time freshmen attending public four-year colleges and universities by family income, Fall 1973 (unweighted).

Family Income[1]	Part-time or Summer work	Full Time Work	Savings	Spouse	Parents	Parents' Military Benefits
$5,999 or less						
% Receiving Aid	67.7%	6.3%	47.0%	1.2%	57.5%	9.0%
Average Aid Received	$411	$653	$318	$1,303	$788	$660
$6,000 to $9,999						
% Receiving Aid	72.1%	6.6%	51.4%	1.2%	70.8%	5.1%
Average Aid Received	$435	$728	$507	$1,196	$920	$868
$10,000 to $14,999						
% Receiving Aid	73.8%	6.6%	53.0%	1.2%	78.8%	2.8%
Average Aid Received	$483	$766	$530	$1,631	$867	$958
$15,000 and Above						
% Receiving Aid	65.7%	5.5%	45.9%	1.3%	86.4%	1.7%
Average Aid Received	$506	$780	$571	$2,080	$2,030	$1,014

TYPE OF AID

	TYPE OF AID					
	Parents Social Security	G.I. Benefits	Scholarship or Grant	Fed. Insured Loans	Other Repayable Loans	Other Aid
$5,999 or less						
% Receiving Aid	23.5%	0.6%	59.6%	28.9%	7.3%	6.4%
Average Aid Received	$636	$1,566	$844	$829	$789	$856
$6,000 to $9,999						
% Receiving Aid	10.5%	0.5%	51.6%	24.3%	7.7%	4.5%
Average Aid Received	$668	$1,407	$742	$875	$816	$939
$10,000 to $14,999						
% Receiving Aid	4.1%	0.4%	37.1%	17.0%	6.7%	3.6%
Average Aid Received	$821	$1,713	$658	$978	$935	$1,173
$15,000 and Above						
% Receiving Aid	2.0%	0.3%	18.4%	7.0%	3.6%	2.6%
Average Aid Received	$847	$2,161	$734	$1,164	$1,170	$1,498

SOURCE: American Council on Education, CIRP Freshmen Norms (1973), unpublished data.

¹Gross Family Income.

Table E-9. Financial assistance pattern of Black full-time freshmen attending private four-year colleges and universities by family income, Fall 1973 (unweighted).

	TYPE OF AID					
Family Income[1]	Part Time or Summer Work	Full Time Work	Savings	Spouse	Parents	Parents' Military Benefits
$5,999 or less						
% Receiving Aid	43.5%	10.5%	17.6%	2.2%	38.4%	4.8%
Average Aid Received	$190	$848	$339	$961	$469	$651
$6,000 to $9,999						
% Receiving Aid	50.4%	9.4%	23.9%	1.3%	60.1%	4.4%
Average Aid Received	$384	$1,866	$362	$450	$643	$740
$10,000 to $14,999						
% Receiving Aid	54.9%	9.5%	32.6%	3.2%	73.7%	4.9%
Average Aid Received	$408	$829	$399	$1,079	$1,184	$1,039
$15,000 and Above						
% Receiving Aid	52.7%	6.6%	34.0%	3.4%	82.1%	4.6%
Average Aid Received	$453	$1,016	$501	$2,243	$1,483	$909

	TYPE OF AID					
	Parents Social Security	G.I. Benefits	Scholarship or Grant	Fed. Insured Loans	Other Repayable Loans	Other Aid
$5,999 or less						
% Receiving Aid	13.8%	2.7%	75.4%	45.5%	10.3%	6.6%
Average Aid Received	$494	$1,354	$1,839	$1,050	$1,045	$882
$6,000 to $9,999						
% Receiving Aid	7.0%	1.1%	77.9%	50.9%	11.4%	5.9%
Average Aid Received	$580	$408	$1,902	$1,052	$949	$892
$10,000 to $14,999						
% Receiving Aid	5.9%	1.1%	68.0%	48.8%	15.0%	7.0%
Average Aid Received	$642	$2,036	$1,692	$1,084	$1,337	$929
$15,000 and Above						
% Receiving Aid	5.0%	2.7%	45.0%	29.8%	12.3%	6.2%
Average Aid Received	$956	$2,355	$1,584	$1,285	$1,610	$1,450

SOURCE: American Council on Education, CIRP Freshmen Norms (1973), unpublished data.

[1]Gross Family Income.

Table E-10. Financial assistance pattern of white full-time freshmen attending private four-year colleges and universities by family income, Fall 1973 (unweighted).

Family Income[1]	Part-time or Summer Work	Full Time Work	Savings	Spouse	Parents	Parents' Military Benefits
$5,999 or less						
% Receiving Aid	71.7%	5.9%	46.9%	0.8%	62.1%	7.8%
Average Aid Received	$433	$725	$572	$1,303	$1,031	$763
$6,000 to $9,999						
% Receiving Aid	76.6%	5.4%	52.4%	0.8%	74.2%	5.7%
Average Aid Received	$464%	$742	$547	$1,573	$1,132	$856
$10,000 to $14,999						
% Receiving Aid	78.0%	6.3%	55.0%	0.9%	81.8%	2.8%
Average Aid Received	$525	842	$738	$1,753	$1,540	$904
$15,000 and Above						
% Receiving Aid	64.3%	4.4%	44.3%	1%	89.7%	1.2%
Average Aid Received	$543	$973	$672	$2,709	$3,056	$1,211

TYPE OF AID

TYPE OF AID

	Parents Social Security	G.I. Benefits	Scholarship or Grant	Fed. Insured Loans	Other Repayable Loans	Other Aid
$5,999 or less						
% Receiving Aid	23.6%	0.2%	76.4%	43.7%	8.8%	6.5%
Average Aid Received	$726	$1,644	$1,685	$1,077	$1,049	$1,025
$6,000 to $9,999						
% Receiving Aid	11.4%	0.5%	75.1%	45.1%	10.2%	5.9%
Average Aid Received	$790	$1,298	$1,552	$1,076	$997	$955
$10000 to $14,999						
% Receiving Aid	4.4%	0.2%	64.1%	37.3%	9.9%	4.5%
Average Aid Received	$817	$1,827	$1,386	$1,131	$1,134	$1,045
$15,000 and Above						
% Receiving Aid	0.2%	0.1%	27.8%	13.2%	5.1%	2.9%
Average Aid Received	$1,024	$1,719	$1,099	$1,368	$1,564	$1,559

SOURCE: American Council on Education, CIRP Freshmen Norms (1973), unpublished data.
¹Gross Family Income.

TABLE E-11. Total number of awards by sources of income for Black and all post-secondary students 16 years old and over, Fall 1973.

Source of Income	All Students (In Thousands)	Percent Black of All Students
Total Students	9,673	8%
Personal Sources:		
Personal Savings	3,254	5
Personal Loan	370	12
Earnings while taking courses	4,855	7
Spouses earnings or savings	1,809	7
Parents	3,924	5
Federal Sources:		
College Work-Study Program	441	21
National Direct Student Loan	524	15
Supplemental Educational Opportunity Grant	323	27
Federal Guaranteed Student Loan Program	513	10
Basic Educational Opportunity Grant	105	18
Veterans Administration Benefits	1,146	8
Social Security Benefits	395	15
State and Other Sources:		
State Scholarship or Grant	775	10
Local Scholarship or Grant	699	9
Public Assistance	104	24
Educational expenses from employer	488	5
Other Sources	811	10
Not Reported	246	13

SOURCE: U.S. Census (1975). *Social and Economic Characteristics of the Black Population in the United States 1974*, Table 71.

TABLE E-12. Distribution of federal loans to low-income students ($5,999 or less)[1] in public and private 4-year colleges and universities by race, Fall 1973.

Amount of Loan	Percents (Unweighted numbers)			
	Black	White	Other	Total
Public Institutions				
None	57.0	63.7	73.8	61.5
$1 - 499	16.0	13.7	13.2	14.6
$500 - 999	16.9	12.2	6.9	13.8
$1,000 - 1,999	7.8	8.9	4.8	8.3
$2,000 - 4,000	1.3	0.8	9.3	1.0
Ove. $4,000	0.7	0.3	0.6	0.5
Total	100.0	100.0	100.0	100.0
	(2,513)	(3,595)	(287)	(6,395)

Table E-12 *(continued)*

Amount of Loan	Percents (Unweighted numbers)			
	Black	White	Other	Total
Private Institutions				
None	39.5	47.8	40.0	44.6
$1 - 499	13.0	9.3	11.1	10.6
$500 - 999	24.2	19.7	28.8	21.7
$1,000 - 1,999	18.6	19.8	16.1	19.2
$2,000 - 4,000	3.7	2.8	3.8	3.2
Over $4,000	0.7	0.3	0.0	0.4
Total	100.0	100.0	100.0	100.0
	(1,514)	(2,826)	(260)	(4,600)

SOURCE: American Council on Education. CIRP Freshmen Norms (1973). unpublished data.

[1]Gross family income.

TABLE E-13. Distribution of federal loans to moderate income students ($6,000 to $9,999)[1] in public and private 4-year colleges and universities by race, Fall 1973.

Amount of Loan	Percents (Unweighted numbers)			
	Black	White	Other	Total
Public Institutions				
None	57.6	69.2	73.0	67.7
$1 - 499	15.0	10.7	13.6	11.4
$500 - 999	14.5	10.2	7.8	10.8
$1,000 - 1,999	10.5	8.4	4.2	8.5
$2,000 - 4,000	1.7	0.8	0.6	1.0
Over $4,000	0.3	0.3	0.6	0.3
Total	100.0	100.0	100.0	100.0
	(1,413)	(8,225)	(330)	(9,968)
Private Institutions				
None	35.7	47.3	36.5	45.1
$1 - 499	13.8	9.2	12.6	10.0
$500 - 999	26.5	19.1	27.7	20.6
$1,000 - 1,999	18.8	21.4	19.7	21.0
$2,000 - 4,000	4.2	2.4	2.9	2.7
Over $4,000	0.8	0.3	0.2	0.3
Total	100.0	100.0	100.0	100.0
	(1,180)	(6,461)	(339)	(7,980)

SOURCE: American Council on Education, CIRP Freshmen Norms, unpublished data, 1973.

[1]Gross family income.

**TABLE E-14. Distribution of federal loans to middle income students
($10,000 to $14,999)[1] in public and private 4-year colleges
and universities by race, Fall 1973.**

Amount of Loan	Black	White	Other	Total
		Percents (Unweighted numbers)		
		White	Other	Total
Public Institutions				
None	69.9	78.3	79.1	78.0
$1 - 499	9.0	6.1	7.6	6.3
$500 - 999	9.3	7.1	6.4	7.2
$1,000 - 1,999	9.8	7.2	5.8	7.3
$2,000 - 4,000	0.7	0.7	0.6	0.7
Over $4,000	1.1	0.2	0.2	0.3
Total	100.0	100.0	100.0	100.0
	(995)	(20,731)	(495)	(22,221)
Private Institutions				
None	38.8	55.0	47.8	53.9
$1 - 499	10.3	6.9	9.0	7.2
$500 - 999	25.5	15.9	19.9	16.6
$1,000 - 1,999	20.7	19.1	19.9	19.2
$2,000 - 4,000	3.9	2.5	2.9	2.6
Over $4,000	0.4	0.3	0.2	0.3
Total	100.0	100.0	100.0	100.0
	(1,026)	(16,066)	(476)	(17,568)

SOURCE: American Council on Education, CIRP Freshmen Norms, (1973), unpublished data.
[1]Gross family income.

**TABLE E-15. Distribution of federal loans to upper income students
($15,000 and above)[1] in public and private 4-year colleges
and universities by race, Fall 1973.**

Amount of Loan	Black	White	Other	Total
		Percents (Unweighted numbers)		
		White	Other	Total
Public Institutions				
None	81.2	90.7	87.6	90.4
$1 - 499	4.1	1.8	3.6	1.9
$500 - 999	4.9	2.4	2.4	2.5
$1,000 - 1,999	7.2	4.1	4.5	4.1
$2,000 - 4,000	1.1	0.5	1.2	0.5
Over $4,000	1.2	0.2	0.4	0.2
Total	100.0	100.0	100.0	100.0
	(772)	(35,034)	(658)	(36,464)
Private Institutions				
None	62.3	82.6	70.9	81.9
$1 - 499	6.1	2.0	4.1	2.1
$500 - 999	11.5	4.5	9.1	4.8
$1,000 - 1,999	15.5	8.5	12.4	8.7
$2,000 - 4,000	3.4	1.8	2.7	1.8
Over $4,000	1.1	0.4	0.5	0.4
Total	100.0	100.0	100.0	100.0
	(999)	(38,969)	(724)	(40,692)

SOURCE: American Council on Education, CIRP Freshmen Norms, (1973), unpublished data.
[1]Gross family income.

Income Redistribution

TABLE F-1. Income Redistribution of Blacks with College Experience to Equal Incomes of Whites with College Experience, Fall 1973.

Family Income	Distribution of Whites with college experience	Distribution of Black with college experience	Adjusted distribution of Blacks to equal Whites
Under $3,000	2.85	7.88	0.79
$3,000 to $4,999	5.19	12.83	1.53
$5,000 to $7,499	9.94	19.65	3.73
$7,500 to $9,999	10.71	12.83	4.14
$10,000 to $14,999	26.95	21.25	11.48
$15,000 and Above	35.31	16.57	15.98
Not Reported	9.00	7.75	3.83
Total	100	100	41.53

SOURCE: U.S. Census, *Social and Economic Characteristics of Students: October 1973*, Table 13.

TABLE F-2. Income Redistribution of Blacks in Availability Pool to Equal White Distribution by Income Level, Fall 1973.

Family Income	(In Thousands) Number of Blacks Distributed as Whites by family Income	Percent w/ College
Under $3,000	86	68.6
$3,000 to $4,000	129	74.4
$5,000 to $7,499	140	105.0
$7,500 to $9,999	118	81.3
$10,000 to $14,999	256	62.1
$15,000 and Above	143	40.5
Not Reported	80	72.5
Total	957	78.1

SOURCE: U.S. Census (1974), *Social and Economic Characteristics of Students: October 1973*, Table 13.

REFERENCES

Abramowitz, Elizabeth A. Access Test Battery Survey. Washington, D.C.: College Entrance Examination Board, 1972.

—————————. *Final Report Project Access–D.C.* Washington, D.C.: College Entrance Examination Board, 1972.

Abramowitz, Elizabeth A. and Michael E. *Sex Is Not Enough: Status of Women in Higher Education.* Washington, D.C.: 1976 (Forthcoming).

—————————. *Racism, Research and Reform.* Presented at American College Personnel Association Annual Meeting, 1973.

Abramson, Schwartz. *Admission of High Risk Students at Michigan State University.* East Lansing, Mich.: Michigan State University, 1968.

Abt Associates, Inc. *A Study of the Education Professions Development Act Training Programs For Higher Education Personnel.* Volume I. Boston, Massachusetts: 1973.

American Association of Colleges of Pharmacy. *Recruiting Minorities for Pharmacy: A Guide.* Silver Spring, Md.: 1973.

American Association of Community and Junior Colleges. *1974 Community and Junior College Directory.* Washington, D.C.: 1974.

American Council on Education. *Federal Programs In Postsecondary Education: An Agenda for 1975.* Washington, D.C.: 1974.

—————————. *Impact of Office of Education Student Assistance Programs. Fall 1973.* Washington, D.C.: 1974.

Association of American Medical Colleges. *Report of the Association of American Medical Colleges Task Force to the Inter-Association Committee on Expanding Educational Opportunities in Medicine for Blacks and Other Minority Students.* Washington, D.C.: 1970.

—————————. "Information for Minority Group Students." Chapter 6, reprinted from *Medical School Admissions Requirements 1975-76, U.S.A. and Canada,* pp. 52-64. Washington, D.C.: 1974.

—————————. "Financial Information for Undergraduate and Medical Students." Chapter 4, reprinted from *Medical School Admissions Requirements 1975-76, U.S.A. and Canada,* pp. 31-42. Washington, D.C.: 1974.

Association Transfer Group. *College Transfer Working Papers and Recommendations from the Airlie House Conference* 2-4 December 1973. Washington, D.C.: 1974.

Bayer, Alan E. *The Black College Freshman: Characteristics and Recent Trends.* Vol. 7, No. 3. Washington, D.C.: American Council on Education, October 1972.

Becker, Gary S. *Human Capital.* New York: Columbia University Press, 1964.

—————————. *The Economics of Discrimination.* 2nd Edition. Illinois: University of Chicago Press, 1971.

Blaug, M. (Ed.) *Economics of Education I and II.* New York: Penguin Books, 1969.

Blewett, William E. "Minority Students' Special Needs and Recruitment," *Journal of Allied Health.* Winter 1974, pp. 22-25.

Borgen, Fred H. *Able Black Americans in College: Entry and Freshman Experiences.* Evanston, Ill.: National Merit Scholarship Corporation, 1970.

—————————. *Differential Expectations? Predicting Grades for Black Students in Five Types of Colleges.* Evanston, Ill.: National Merit Scholarship Corporation, 1971.

Breland, Hunter M. *Defunis Revisited: A Psychometric View.* Princeton, N.J.: Educational Testing Service, August 1974.

Carlisle, Donald. *The Disadvantaged Student in Graduate School Master's and Doctoral Degree Programs in Predominantly Non-Negro Universities.* Los Angeles, Calif.: UCLA, 1968.

Carnegie Council on Policy Studies in Higher Education. *The Federal Role In Postsecondary Education, Unfinished Business 1975-1980.* San Francisco: Jossey-Bass, 1975.

_____. *Higher Education: Who Pays? Who Benefits? Who Should Pay?* New York: McGraw-Hill, 1973.

Centra, John A. *Black Students at Predominantly White Colleges: A Research Description.* Princeton, N.J.: Educational Testing Service, 1970.

Cheit, Earl F. *The New Depression in Higher Education.* Carnegie Commission on Higher Education. New York: McGraw-Hill, 1971.

_____. *The New Depression in Higher Education–Two Years Later.* New York: Carnegie Commission on Higher Education, 1973.

Cobb, Jewel P. and McDew, Carolyn (Eds.). *The Morning After: A Retrospective View of a Selected Number of Colleges and Universities with Increased Black Student Enrollment in the Past Five Years.* Connecticut: Racine Printing, Inc. 1974.

College Entrance Examination Board. *Financing Equal Opportunity in Higher Education.* NY, New York: 1969.

_____. *Admission of Minority Students in Midwestern Colleges. Higher Education Survey.* Evanston, Ill.: 1970.

_____. *College Guide to the ATP Summary Reports on 1972-73 College-Bound Seniors.* NY, New York: CEEB, 1973.

_____. *College-Bound Seniors*, 1973-74. NY, New York: CEEB, 1974.

Committee on Graduate Education of Ethnic Minority Students. *Graduate Education and Ethnic Minorities.* Colorado: Western Association of Graduate Schools and Western Interstate Commission for Higher Education, 1970.

Congressional Quarterly Almanac. 93rd Congress, 1st Session, 1973. Vol. XXIX. Washington, D.C.: 1974.

Cooke, W.D. *Recruiting Black Graduate Students.* Ithaca, N.Y.: Cornell University, 1970.

_____. *A Study of the Number of Black Graduate Student Applications for Fall 1970.* Ithaca, N.Y.: Cornell University, 1970.

Creager, John A. *Selected Policies and Practices in Higher Education.* Washington, D.C.: American Council on Education. Vol. 8, No. 4, 1973.

Crossland, Fred E. *Graduate Education and Black Americans.* New York: Ford Foundation, 1968.

Davis, James A. *The Validity of Tests and Achievement in High School for Predicting Initial Performance in the Public University of North Carolina with Special Attention to Black Students.* Princeton, N.J.: Educational Testing Service, 1971.

_____. *Black Students in Predominantly White North Carolina Colleges and Universities.* New York: College Entrance Examination Board, 1973.

DiCesare, Anthony C.; Sedlacek, William E.; and Brooks, Glenwood C., Jr. *Non-Intellectual Correlates of Black Student Attrition.* College Park, Md.: University of Maryland, 1970.

Doeringer, Peter and Piore, Michael. *International Markets and Manpower Analysis.* Lexington, Mass.: Lexington Books, 1971.

Eckaus, P.S. et. al. "An Appraisal of the Calculations of Rates of Return to Higher Education" in *Higher Education and the Labor Market.* New York: McGraw-Hill, 1974.

Freeman, Richard. "The Implications of Changing Labor Markets for Members of Minority Groups" in *Higher Education and the Labor Market.* Margaret Gordon (Ed.). New York: McGraw-Hill, 1974.

_____, and Holloman, Herbert. "The Declining Value of College Going" in *Change*, September, 1975.

Godard, James M. *Recruitment and Support of Culturally Distinct Students. Ethical and Educational Implications.* Washington, D.C.: American Association for Higher Education, 1969.

_____. *Suggestions for Achieving Unitary State Systems of Higher Education. A Staff Paper.* Atlanta, Ga.: Southern Regional Education Board. October, 1973.

Gordon, Margaret S. (Ed.). *Higher Education and the Labor Market.* New York: McGraw-Hill, 1974.

Greene, Carolyn and Kester, Donald L. *Black Community College Students Have Special Problems.*

What Are These Special Problems? Educational Research Information Center in Higher Education. Washington, D.C.

Hamilton, I. Bruce. *Graduate School Programs for Minority/Disadvantaged Students. Report on an Initial Survey.* Graduate Record Examinations Board, Council of Graduate Schools in the U.S., Educational Testing Service, Princeton, N.J.: 1973.

Haworth, J.G., Gwartney, J., and Haworth, C. "Earnings, Productivity, and Changes in Employment Discrimination During the 1960's" in *American Economic Review.* March, 1975.

Health Resources Administration. *How Health Professions Students Finance Their Education.* Washington, D.C.: October, 1973 (HRA, 74-13).

——————————. *How to Pay for Your Health Career Education. A Guide for Minority Students.* Washington, D.C.: U.S. Dept. of Health, Education and Welfare, Public Health Service, 1974. (HRA, 74-8).

Hedegard, James M. "Experiences of Black College Students at Predominantly White Institutions" in *Black Students in White Schools.* Edgar A. Epps (Ed.). Worthington, Ohio: Charles A. Jones Publishing Co., 1972, pp. 43-59.

Heyns, Roger. *Higher Education and Inflation.* Presented at White House Conference on Inflation, September 19, 1974. Washington, D.C.: American Council on Education, 1974.

Higher Education Daily Supplement. "Final Recommendation National Task Force on Student Aid Problems," May 30, 1975.

Holmstrom, Engin I. and Smith, Patricia. "Who Are the Users of Federally Insured College Loan Programs?" *Policy Briefs* (ACE). Vol. 1, Nov. 2, 1974.

Horowitz, Joseph L. *Correlates of Black and White University Student Grades Beyond the Freshman Year.* College Park, Md.: Cultural Study Center, University of Maryland, 1972.

Howard, Lawrence C. *Graduate Education for the Disadvantaged and Black-Oriented University Graduates.* Washington, D.C.: Council of Graduate Schools in the U.S., 1968.

Hull, W. Frank IV. *Higher Education in Black Atypical Students.* University Park, Pa.: Penn State University, 1970.

Institute for Higher Educational Opportunity. *New Challenges To The Junior Colleges. Their Role in Expanding Opportunity for Negroes. A Progress Report.* Atlanta, Ga.: Southern Regional Education Board, April 1970.

——————————. *The White Student Enrolled In The Traditionally Public Black College and University.* Atlanta, Ga.: Southern Regional Education Board, September 1973.

Jellema, William W. *Higher Education Finance. A Comparative Study of Matched Samples of Black and White Private Institutions.* Atlanta, Ga.: Southern Regional Education Board, 1972.

Jones, J. Charles et al. *Differences in Perceived Sources Of Academic Difficulties: Blacks in Predominantly Black and Predominantly White Colleges,* 1970.

Kaun, David E. "The College Dropout and Occupational Choice." in *Higher Education and the Labor Market.* Margaret Gordon (Ed.). New York: McGraw-Hill, 1974.

Kendrik, S.A. *Verbal Ability: An Obsolete Measure.* New York: CEEB, 1968.

——————————. *Extending Educational Opportunity–Problems of Recruitment and Admission, High Risk Students, Cultural Deprivation, Etc.* Washington, D.C.: Association of American Colleges, 1969.

Kerner, Otto (Chairman). *Report of the National Advisory Commission on the Cause of Civil Disorders.* Washington, D.C. March 1, 1968.

National Advisory Council on Education Professions Development. *Teacher Corps: Past or Prologue? A Report with Recommendations.* Washington, D.C.: 1975.

National Advisory Council on Extension and Continuing Education. *A Measure of Success, Federal Support for Continuing Education. 7th Annual Report and Recommendations.* Washington, D.C.: 1973.

National Association of State Universities and Land-Grant Colleges. *Investment in Opportunity. The Importance of Voluntary Support to Predominantly Negro Public Colleges.* Washington, D.C. 1967.

——————————. *Circular Letter,* No. 11, June 12, 1972

——————————. *1973-74 Student Charges at State and Land-Grant Universities (Tuition, Required Fees, Room and Board).* Washington, D.C.: October, 1973.

National Board on Graduate Education. *Federal Policy Alternatives Toward Graduate Education.* Washington, D.C.: National Academy of Science, 1975.

National Scholarship Service and Fund for Negro Students. *Minority Youth: The Classes of 1972 and 1973.* New York: NSSFNS. Vol. 2, No. 1, April, 1974.

National Task Force on Student Aid Problems. *Draft Final Report.* California: March 24, 1972.

Nelson, Bernard W. *Report of the Association of American Medical Colleges Task Force to the Inter-Association Committee on Expanding Educational Opportunities in Medicine for Black and Other Minority Students.* Stanford, California: 1970.

Office of Federal Register. "Basic Educational Opportunity Program." *Federal Register,* Vol. 38, No. 134, July 13, 1973.

_____. *Code of Federal Regulations 45. Public Welfare Parts 1 to 99 and 100 to 199.* Washington, D.C.: National Archives of the United States, April, 1974.

O'Neil, Robert M. *Beyond the Threshold: Changing Patterns of Access to Higher Education.* Washington, D.C.: American Council on Education, 1970.

O'Toole, James. "The Reserve Army of the Unemployed: In the World of Work," *Change,* May/June, 1975.

Palola, Ernest G. *Changing Centers of Power in Higher Education: A Challenge to Institutional Leadership.* Berkeley, California: Junior College Presidents Seminar, 1968.

Parker, Garland G. *Career Education and Transfer Program Enrollments in 2-year Colleges, 1973-74.* ACT Special, No. 11, Iowa: ACT Publications, 1974.

Pincus, Fred L. *Tracking in the Community Colleges.* Maryland: Research Group One, 1973.

Piore, Peter. "Dual Labor Markets." In *Problems in Political Economy.* David M. Gordon (Ed.). Mass.: Heath, 1971.

Prieto, Dario O., Tarnoff, Stephen L., and Hedgepeth, Connie, *Report of the Association of American Medical Colleges Office of Minority Affairs to the Grant Foundation on the Presentation of Regional Workshops to Assist in the Development of Minority Student Programs in U.S. Medical Schools.* Washington, D.C.: Association of American Medical Colleges, 1974.

Rempson, Jane L. *Minority Access to Higher Education in New York.* New York: New School for Social Research, 1972.

Rice, Lois D. *Comments on the Report of the National Commission on Financing Postsecondary Education.* Prepared at request of John Brademas and John Dellenback, April 30, 1974.

Sample, David R. *Predictions of Academic Success of Black Students: A Dilemma.* Des Moines, Iowa: Drake University, 1969.

Saunders, Charles B., Jr. *The Changing Federal Role in Higher Education.* Denver, Colorado: Annual Convention of National Association of College and University Business Officers, 1972.

Sedlacek, William E. and Pfeifer, Michael C., Jr. *Non-Intellectual Correlates of Black and White Student Grades at the University of Maryland.* College Park, Md.: Cultural Study Center, University of Maryland, 1970.

_____. *Black and Other Minority Admissions to Large Universities: A Four Year National Survey of Policies and Outcomes.* College Park, Md.: University of Maryland, 1973.

_____. Strader, Mary A.; and Brooks, Glenwood C., Jr. *A National Comparison of Universities Successful and Unsuccessful in Enrolling Blacks Over a Five Year Period.* College Park, Md.: Cultural Study Center, University of Maryland. Research Report; No. 3-74, 1974.

Selby, James E. *Relationship Existing Among Race, Persistence and Student Aids.* Columbia, Mo.: University of Missouri, 1970.

Shea, Brent. "Two-Year Colleges: A Review of the Literature." *The Generator,* Vol. 5, No. 1, Fall 1974.

Skypek, Dora Helen and Lee, Eugene C. *Progress Report #1 on Factors Which Influence Women in Science Career Choices and Stability.* Atlanta, Ga.: Division of Educational Studies, Emory University, January 1975.

Smith, Vernon C., Jr. *The Study of Recruitment and Progress of Minority Group Medical Students.* Washington, D.C.: Student National Medical Association, Inc., 1974.

Spurlock, Langley A. *Minorities in White Colleges. A Survey of Opinion from Students, Faculty, and Administrators.* Washington, D.C.: American Council on Education, April 1974.

Swinton, David and Ellison, Julian. *Aggregate Personal Income and the Black Population in the U.S.A. 1947-1980*. New York: Black Economic Research Center, 1973.

Swinton, David H. *The Logic of Discrimination in Noncompetitive Labor Markets*. Unpublished Ph.D. Dissertation. Harvard University, 1974.

Tarbert, Jeffrey J. *Federal Trends in Higher Education, 1958-1971: The Congress Turns to the Junior Community College*. Washington, D.C.: George Washington, University, 1971.

Thurow, Lester C. *Poverty and Discrimination*. The Brookings Institution. Washington, D.C. 1969.
_____. "Measuring the Economic Benefits of Education." in *Higher Education and the Labor Market*. Margaret Gordon (Ed.). McGraw-Hill, 1974.

Tucker, Samuel J. *Multiple Predictors of Academic Success of the Black Male College Student*. Gainesville: University of Florida, 1973.

Turner, Joseph. *Toward More Active Learning*. Washington, D.C.: Institute for Services to Education, February 1972.

U.S. Census, *College Plans of High School Seniors: October 1972*. Current Population Reports. Series P-20, No. 252, August 1973.
_____. *Detailed Characteristics of the Population*. U.S. Summary PCCD-D1. Washinglon, D.C., 1973.
_____. *Earnings by Occupation and Education*. PC (2)-8B. Washington, D.C.: 1973.
_____. *Educational Attainment*. PC(2)-5B. Washington, D.C.: 1973.
_____. *Social and Economic Characteristics of Students, October 1972*. Series P-20, No. 260, 1974.
_____. *Social and Economic Characteristics of Students: October 1973*. Series P-20, No. 272. Washington, D.C.: 1974.
_____. *Social and Economic Status of the Black Population in the United States, 1973*. Series P-23, No. 48. Washington, D.C.: 1974.
_____. *Social and Economic Status of the Black Population in the United States, 1974*. Series P-23, No. 54. Washington, D.C.: 1975.

U.S. Commission on Civil Rights. *The Federal Civil Rights Enforcement Effort–1974*. Volume III "To Ensure Equal Educational Opportunity." Washington, D.C.: January 1975.

U.S. Congress. *Problems of the Upward Bound Program in Preparing Disadvantaged Students for a Postsecondary Education*. Washington, D.C.: General Accounting Office, 1974.
_____. *Education Amendments of 1974 (Public Law 93-380)*. Washington, D.C.: 1974

U.S. Department of Labor. *Employment of High School Graduates and Dropouts. October 1973*. Washington, D.C. 1974.

U.S. Office for Civil Rights. *Racial and Ethnic Enrollment Data from Institutions of Higher Education Fall 1972*. Washington, D.C.: DHEW. 1975.

U.S. Office of Education. *Fact Sheet*. Washington, D.C.: DHEW, 1973.
_____. *Important Basic Grants Material*. Washington, D.C.: 1974.
_____. *GSLP Loan Estimation Model Borrower, Lender, and Institutional Characteristics*. Vol. II. Office of Planning, Budgeting, and Evaluation. September 1974.
_____. *Guaranteed Student Loan Program*. Washington, D.C.: 1974.
_____. *Federal Register*. Vol. 39, No. 104. May 29, 1974. pp. 18649-18655.
_____. *Institutional Fiscal Operations Report for Federal Student Financial Aid Programs*, 1968, 1969, 1970.
_____. *Strengthening Developing Institutions, Title III of the Higher Education Act of 1965 Annual Report*, March 1974.

U.S. Senate. *Report on the Education Amendments of 1974*. Washington, D.C.: Senate Committee on Labor and Public Welfare, 1974.

Valien, Preston, *Undergraduate Educational Opportunity Programs*. San Francisco, Calif.: 8th Annual Meeting of the Council of Graduate Schools, 1968.

Watley, Donovan J. *Black and Non-black Youth: Does Marriage Hinder College Attendance?* Evanston, Ill.: National Merit Scholarship Corporation, 1971.
_____. *Bright Black Youth: Their Educational Plans and Career Aspirations*. Evanston, Ill.: National Merit Scholarship Corporation, 1971.

Weiss, R. "The Effect of Education on the Earnings of Blacks and Whites." *Economic Statistics Review*, May, 1970.

Welch, Finis, "Black-White Differences in Return to Schooling." *American Economic Review*, December, 1973.

Wilburn, Adolph Y. "Careers in Science and Engineering for Black Americans." *Science*, Vol. 184, pp. 1148-1154.

Williams, Donald T., Jr. *Black Higher Education: Whence and Whither?* Minneapolis, Minn.: American Education Research Association, 1970.

Willingham, Warren W. *The No. 2 Access Problem: Transfer to the Upper Division*. ERIC Clearinghouse on Higher Education. Washington, D.C.: American Association for Higher Education, 1972.

Winkler, Karen J. "States Raise Aid to Students 25 Pct." *The Chronicle of Higher Education*. Vol. IX, No. 9.

Wohsbetter and Coleman. *Race Differences in Income: A Report Prepared for Office of Economic Opportunity*. Santa Monica, California: Rand Corp. R-578-OEO.

Wolanin, Thomas and Gladieux, Lawrence. "A Charter for Federal Policy Toward Postsecondary Education: The Education Amendments of 1972." *Journal of Law Education* (Reprint) Vol. 14, No. 2, April, 1975.

Wynn, Richard G. *At the Crossroads. A Report on the Financial Condition of the Forty-Eight Liberal Arts Colleges Previously Studied in "The Golden Year, The Turning Point."* Michigan: Center of the Study of Higher Education. April 1974.

NOTES

NOTES